Rabble Rousers

Clive Webb

Rabble Rousers

The American Far Right in the Civil Rights Era

The University of Georgia Press   Athens and London

© 2010 by the University of Georgia Press
Athens, Georgia 30602
www.ugapress.org

All rights reserved

Set in 10.5/13.5 Adobe Caslon
  by Graphic Composition, Inc. Bogart, Georgia

Printed digitally in the United States of America

Library of Congress Cataloging-in-Publication Data

Webb, Clive, 1970–
Rabble rousers : the American far right in the
civil rights era / Clive Webb.
    p. cm. — (Politics and culture in the
twentieth-century South)
Includes bibliographical references and index.
ISBN-13: 978-0-8203-2764-8 (hardcover : alk. paper)
ISBN-10: 0-8203-2764-6 (hardcover : alk. paper)
ISBN-13: 978-0-8203-3577-3 (pbk. : alk. paper)
ISBN-10: 0-8203-3577-0 (pbk. : alk. paper)
1. Right-wing extremists—United States—History—
20th century. 2. Segregation—United States—History—
20th century. 3. Civil rights movements—United States—
History—20th century. 4. African Americans—
Civil rights—History—20th century. 5. Racism—
United States—History—20th century.
6. Bowles, Bryant William, 1920–1997.
7. Kasper, John, 1929–1998.
8. Crommelin, John G.
9. Walker, Edwin A. (Edwin Anderson), 1909–1993.
10. Stoner, Jesse Benjamin, 1924–2005 I. Title.
  E185.61.W343 2010
  323.1196'073—dc22   2009039082

British Library Cataloging-in-Publication Data available

For Kathy

Contents

Contents

Acknowledgments

A few years ago, I interviewed for a position at a prestigious university. One member of the appointing committee questioned the significance of studying what he described as a bunch of losers who had made little political impact. I offered what I thought was a robust intellectual defense, challenging the premise of this argument with a protracted explanation of their importance to our understanding of modern race relations.

Needless to say, I did not get the job.

Some years later, and with the help of many people who have refined my analysis, I hope that readers will find the interpretation of racial militants offered in these pages more persuasive than did that interview panel.

I have accumulated many debts in the process of researching and writing this book. Many scholars shared their thoughts on specific issues that I raised with them. I am especially grateful in this regard to W. Fitzhugh Brundage, David L. Chappell, Adam Fairclough, and Eric L. Goldstein. My initial intention was only to write an article on this subject for a collection edited by Paul A. Cimbala and Barton C. Shaw, both of whom provided very important suggestions that shaped not only that piece but also the larger manuscript. My close friend and colleague William Carrigan helped me formulate my ideas while the project was still in its infancy and assisted me in my initial search for FBI files. I must also thank my mentor William Dusinberre for encouraging me to produce a book-length study of white supremacists.

Over the past several years, I have presented my research at numerous conferences and seminars. These occasions have provided me with an excellent opportunity to sharpen my ideas. I am very grateful to those friends and colleagues who invited me to speak at their institutions, particularly

Stephen Tuck at Oxford and Brian Ward at Manchester. My thanks also to those historians who served as commentators on my conference papers, including Mark K. Bauman, Jane Dailey, and Frederic Jaher.

Many scholars took the time to read and comment on substantial parts of the manuscript. All of them offered invaluable advice on how to improve my arguments, although none bears responsibility for any remaining errors of interpretation. I owe thanks for their critical advice and support to Dan T. Carter, Joseph Crespino, David J. Garrow, Kevin M. Kruse, and Stephen J. Whitfield. My colleague Richard Follett made some decisive interventions at a late stage in the project, helping me to turn my meandering prose into a more coherent line of argument. I am thankful also to George Lewis for reassuring me of the significance of the project and to Jonathan Bell for providing me with a sharper understanding of race and conservatism in California.

Two scholars read the entire manuscript and provided extensive feedback that substantially improved my analysis. Both encouraged me to push on with the manuscript when I despaired of completing it and responded swiftly to my often unreasonable demands on their time. David Brown yelled me on like a trackside coach when I felt like the weariest and most flat-footed of athletes, pushing me to interrogate my sources more thoroughly. Robert Cook provided helpful corrections on specific aspects of detail as well as broader conceptual critiques of the manuscript. It has been a great pleasure to have my former tutor become one of my colleagues at the University of Sussex.

Many librarians and archivists have provided gracious assistance in locating research materials. I am particularly appreciative of the help offered by Toni Bressler at the Spencer Research Library at the University of Kansas, Tara Craig of the Rare Book and Manuscript Library at Columbia University, David M. Hardy of the FBI, and Kevin Proffitt of the American Jewish Archives in Cincinnati. Mark I. Greenberg, director of the Special Collections Department and Florida Studies Center at the University of South Florida, enthusiastically championed the project and tracked down some elusive research materials.

I am very grateful to several members of the team at the University of Georgia Press. Derek Krisoff commissioned the book and offered enthusiastic support. Nancy Grayson provided invaluable encouragement and demonstrated remarkable patience as I continued to fall farther behind schedule. I hope that the manuscript in some way repays the wait.

It would have been even more difficult to finish the manuscript with-

Acknowledgments

out research leave from the University of Sussex, a period extended by the award of a grant from the Arts and Humanities Research Council.

My family has offered support and interest throughout the long gestation of the book. Love and thanks to my parents, Brian and Marjorie, and my brothers, Paul and Neil. Boo and Grover also provided important companionship during the long and otherwise lonely hours hunched over a computer keyboard. My greatest intellectual and emotional debt is to my wife, Kathy Kendall, who endured my endless expressions of doubt about ever completing the manuscript and offered crucial ideas and feedback. Dedicating a book about white supremacists to one's wife may not be everyone's idea of a perfect gift, but it is an entirely heartfelt one.

Rabble Rousers

Introduction

In 1936, the United States became a fascist dictatorship. Popular discontent with the failure of the New Deal to alleviate the
impact of the Great Depression led the Democrats to dump
Franklin D. Roosevelt and to nominate as their presidential
candidate midwestern Senator Berzelius Windrip. The November election saw Windrip comfortably defeat his Republican opponent Walt Trowbridge. Once installed in the White
House, President Windrip proclaimed that it was "Zero Hour,"
the time to launch a new direction in the history of the nation.
Windrip used the pretext of the economic crisis to impose martial law on the country. He suspended Congress, stripped the
Supreme Court of its power to overrule federal legislation, and
deployed his private militia to arrest, incarcerate, and execute
political dissidents. The new regime also restricted the rights of
minorities, curtailing the autonomy of women, African Americans, and Jews.

This is not, of course, a factual account of American history.
The rise to power of a totalitarian regime forms the opening
narrative of Sinclair Lewis's 1935 novel *It Can't Happen Here*.
Although a work of fiction, the book's dystopian setting articulated a deep-rooted concern at the upsurge of political extremism occasioned by the unprecedented economic emergency that
beset the nation.[1] Historians estimate that there were as many as
120 fascist organizations in the United States during the 1930s.[2]
Among the many political demagogues who rose to political
prominence were Fritz Kuhn of the German-American Bund,

Gerald Winrod of the Defenders of the Christian Faith, William Dudley Pelley of the Silver Legion, and the influential Catholic radio priest Father Charles Coughlin. These insurgents shared not only the conviction that a cabal of communist Jews had conspired to destroy the American government from within, but also that a violent revolution might be the only means to save the United States from this insidious enemy.

Despite the proliferation of paramilitary organizations in the 1930s, they proved only a passing threat to the democratic process. None possessed a leader with the charisma to unite the disparate forces of the American far right. Nor could they withstand the wartime arrest and incarceration of their members for sedition. Public exposure of the horrors of the Holocaust further undermined popular support for the racial supremacist doctrines of right-wing extremists.[3]

The far right never recovered the influence that it had commanded during the Depression. This, however, did not forestall the efforts of a new generation of activists to lead its resurgence. These radicals had their own opportunity to make political capital out of a national crisis during the black freedom struggle that followed World War II. Gunnar Myrdal, author of the seminal study *An American Dilemma*, observed that there was a small but dedicated band of racial fanatics who "hoped to build a full-scale fascist movement out of the Southern resistance to desegregation."[4]

Despite the recent resurgence of interest in massive resistance, the organized white southern opposition to the Supreme Court's May 1954 ruling in *Brown v. Board of Education* outlawing school segregation, the racial militants whose aggravation of racial violence provoked Myrdal's warning have all but disappeared from the historical record.[5] After the barren years that immediately followed World War II, the far right found newly fertile political ground in the southern states during the desegregation crisis. This book assesses the causes, characteristics, and consequences of far-right activism in the South from the 1950s to the 1970s. It uses a series of case studies of the white militants who assumed most public prominence and had the most direct political impact on the civil rights struggle, situating them within the broader context of massive resistance to racial reform. The study therefore attempts not only to analyze how the far right responded to the black freedom movement, but how this affected the broader political dynamics of white southern opposition.

Part One focuses on two agitators who mobilized some of the earliest grassroots insurgencies against school desegregation. Bryant Bowles of the

National Association for the Advancement of White People (NAAWP) led opposition to school desegregation in Milford, Delaware. Although personal troubles led to Bowles rapidly disappearing from the political scene, the success of his campaign provided a blueprint for other racial militants. John Kasper, leader of the Seaboard White Citizens' Council, precipitated a series of disorders in Virginia, Tennessee, and Florida. The strong similarities between the two activists raise broader issues about the political conditions in the Upper and Peripheral South that facilitated the activism of lone extremists.

One of the most important influences on Kasper was Rear Admiral John Crommelin, who is the principal subject of Part Two. A decorated hero of World War II, Crommelin was forced into retirement because of outspoken attacks on his superiors that he made during a controversy over unification of the armed forces in 1949. For the next two decades, Crommelin campaigned relentlessly for public office in his home state of Alabama. Although he failed to win election, the rear admiral had a crucial effect on state politics, forcing moderate politicians to take a more conservative stand on civil rights issues. Through his tireless networking he also did more than any other activist of his time to try to unify the fractious far right. Far from being a maverick political figure, Crommelin was one of many former senior military officials who were active in militant racist circles, a dangerous band of self-professed patriots who paradoxically conspired to overthrow their own democratically elected government. Part Two concludes with an assessment of the most infamous of these retired officers, Major General Edwin Walker. Having helped enforce the desegregation of Little Rock Central High School in 1957, five years later Walker led white resistance to the admission of black student James Meredith to the University of Mississippi.

By the early 1970s, these far-right activists had faded into obscurity. Yet one of their closest associates, decades after most white southerners had come to terms with racial reform, continued to wage a vicious hate campaign against racial and religious minorities. Part Three assesses J. B. Stoner, whose role in the far right not only spanned six decades, but also earned him a reputation as perhaps the most dangerous hate peddler in the United States. The seemingly inexorable advance of the civil rights movement induced a desperate counterattack by diehard segregationists. Stoner capitalized on this conflict, roaming from one racial trouble spot to another. He became embroiled in violent confrontations between segregationists and civil rights activists first in Birmingham, Alabama, then in St. Augustine, Florida, and finally in Bogalusa, Louisiana.

These case studies contribute to our understanding of white opposition to racial integration in a number of respects. Analysis of white racial extremists reveals in sharper detail the scale, diversity, and direction of massive resistance.

The classic interpretative model of massive resistance by Numan Bartley is of a counterrevolutionary movement led by neo-bourbon elites in the Black Belt areas of the South.[6] White extremists complicate this analysis in numerous ways. Outside of the Black Belt, political and economic leaders did not always direct rebellion. On the contrary, ordinary whites mobilized in grassroots insurgencies against desegregation. What they lacked was leadership. The power vacuum created by the apparent passivity of local and state elites provided an opportunity for extremists to take control. In those parts of the South where they assumed political influence, white resistance operated on a bottom-up, rather than top-down, basis. The contrasting dynamics of segregationist resistance demonstrate the heterogeneous nature of the white South. Massive resistance was not a monolith, but a more complicated and diverse phenomenon shaped by intraregional forces.

The extremists were also important because they gave greater meaning to the concept of massive resistance. Historian David Chappell attributes the failure of southern whites to withstand racial reform in part to the circumspection of their political leaders. Racism, he argues, did not possess the same cultural and intellectual credibility after World War II as it had only a generation earlier. Many segregationists therefore refrained from crude race-baiting rhetoric. While such tactics would appeal to many ordinary whites, they ran the risk of alienating white northerners whose hearts and minds segregationists also needed to win if they were to stem federal intrusion on the race issue. According to Chappell, segregationist leaders could not resolve this dilemma. The tone of their rhetoric remained cautious and indecisive. Their inability to "harness the resentments and energies of the lower classes" restricted the scale of white opposition to the civil rights movement. Massive resistance was, in short, not really all that massive.[7] Many southern politicians were also willing to compromise on the race issue, believing as historian Kevin Finley argues that at best they could achieve the "strategic delay" of desegregation.[8]

In contrast, white racial militants succeeded in energizing the grassroots. They mobilized large numbers of lower-class whites who had otherwise been excluded from organized opposition to civil rights reform, imbuing them with a belief that it was possible not only to postpone, but actually to prevent, integration. Moreover, they often did this in places where there was little expectation of a fight over racial change. In the wake of the *Brown* decision, most commentators assumed that the fiercest racial confrontation would occur in the Deep South, where the concentration of the African American population constituted the most serious threat to white hegemony. White extremists redrew and enlarged the battle lines by starting unanticipated trouble in the states of the Upper and Peripheral South, like Delaware and Tennessee. Racial militants not only helped to turn massive resistance into a potent political phenomenon, but also sustained grassroots opposition even after many southern white leaders had accepted the need for compromise on the race issue.

The question remains why racial militants succeeded in mobilizing white opposition. Of particular importance is the focus on racial populism in the rhetoric of the far right. Militant segregationists placed their principal intellectual emphasis on the supposedly innate biological and cultural differences between the races. Intertwined with their racial arguments was an emphasis on class politics, specifically the supposed treachery of civic and economic elites willing to capitulate to federal reform. According to militants, the wealth and status of these elites offered them some immunity from the effects of racial integration, in contrast to lower-class whites who would have to absorb its full impact. The populist tone of the far right was in some respects ironic. Their emphasis was on the right to local autonomy in racial matters even though they were themselves not members of the communities they led in revolt. Clearly white southerners' condemnation of "outside agitators," whom they blamed for racial disorder, extended only to black activists who opposed segregation and not to white militants who fought to preserve it. Moreover, although they proclaimed themselves champions of the white working class, most leaders of the far right were actually members of the middle or upper-middle class.

This study also emphasizes the importance of evangelical churches in providing intellectual and institutional support to segregationist resistance. Historians have not reached consensus on the role of religion in sustaining white opposition to racial reform. The reason for this is perhaps that white churches did not forge a common ecumenical front on the race issue. In communities such as Milford, Delaware, and Nashville, Tennessee, mainstream churches either supported desegregation or retained a position of neutrality. Yet the mobs that rallied in opposition to reform acted in the conviction that the separation of the races was divinely ordained. This tension further underlines the disparity between elites and the grassroots.

The heterogeneity of massive resistance was a source of both strength and weakness. In contrast to the fatalistic attitude of politicians who believed they could postpone but not prevent desegregation, militants were convinced that victory was theirs provided they used whatever means were necessary. The different tactical approaches of the extremists created opportunities for ordinary people excluded by political elites to become involved in acts of resistance.

Yet extremists' resort to racial demagoguery and terrorist tactics also undermined the efforts of a segregationist leadership desperate to present itself as a lawful and respectable political force. In the aftermath of World War II, societal changes had rendered the defense of Jim Crow increasingly difficult. For a white South that was already on the defensive, the internal divisions between elite and grassroots forces rendered resistance to reform all the more difficult.

A number of factors pushed white racial militants beyond the pale of political respectability. First, their advocacy of violence made them anathema to segregationist leaders intent on maintaining a public image of propriety. The foremost instrument of segregationist resistance was the Citizens' Council, founded in Mississippi in the summer of 1954 and spreading across the southern states in the months that followed. Despite their shared determination to safeguard segregation, the leaders of the Citizens' Councils were at pains to promote a public image of respectability by dissociating themselves from the lawless elements within their midst. "This is no Klan revival," affirmed one Citizens' Council publication. "The organizations are determined not to be taken by lunatics of the far right, either by American fascists and fanatics who always try to horn in on States' Rights Southerners."[9] This fear that the anarchic tactics of extremists could fatally compromise the legitimate protest of more responsible segregationists was forcefully articulated by South Carolina journalist William D. Workman. According to him, there were four enemies that most endangered the southern social order. The first three, predictably, were the Supreme Court, the National Association for the Advancement of Colored People (NAACP), and northern liberals. The fourth—the Ku Klux Klan and other "fringe elements which dabble in violence and vituperation"—was not an external but an internal threat. Workman used these militants as a foil to the Citizens' Council. "For every hate-mongering crackpot or bully-boy who hits the headlines with an act of brutality or of utter stupidity," he asserted, "there are literally thousands of solid, substantial citizens whose opposition to enforced integration is as constant and steadfast as it is peaceable."[10]

A second factor that rendered militants anathema to mainstream segregationists was their association with fascism. During World War II, African Americans protested the hypocrisy of whites who condemned the persecution of Jews in Nazi-occupied Europe but condoned Jim Crow practices in their own country. White southerners nonetheless resisted any comparison between the Nazi racial system and their own segregated society. This was especially so after Allied forces liberated the Nazi concentration camps. Public awareness that Nazi racial policies had resulted in the systematic extermination of millions of people forced segregationists on the defensive. They disavowed overt white supremacist rhetoric and instead emphasized legalistic justifications for Jim Crow. Southern authorities also cracked down on political organizations whose ideology and tactics bore the taint of fascism. The determination of southern segregationists to emphasize that their support of Jim Crow was consistent with American values led them to disown the far-right militants within their midst. This included the infiltration and arrest of white supremacists such as the Columbians and the Ku Klux Klan.[11]

One specific aspect of fascism with which segregationists wanted to avoid association was anti-Semitism. Militants who accused Jewish Communists of secretly masterminding the civil rights movement threatened the intellectual and political respectability of massive resistance leaders. There was a residual prejudice toward Jews in the South, which surfaced in times of tension such as the Civil War and the agricultural depression of the late nineteenth century. The small and acculturated Jewish population nonetheless posed an insufficient threat to provoke pervasive discrimination. Public exposure of the Holocaust also led in the South as well as the North to what historian Peter Novick describes as the "repudiation of anti-Semitic discourse and its virtual disappearance from the public realm."[12]

A study of white racial militants is therefore important because it places the actions of more mainstream segregationists in sharper perspective. Through an understanding of why most white southerners refused to support the tactics of extremists we can see more clearly what segregationists were, and were not, prepared to do to sustain the racialized order of their region.

Malcolm X maintained that his militant criticism of the civil rights movement paradoxically buttressed support for racial reform because he forced the federal government to recognize what it would have to deal with if it failed to collaborate with the likes of Martin Luther King, Jr. As Malcolm informed Coretta Scott King, "he wanted to present an alternative; that it might be easier for whites to accept Martin's proposals after hearing him."[13] In a way, white extremists had a similar, although unintentional, influence on mainstream segregationists. Their actions forced fellow white southerners to calculate the cost of uncompromising resistance to civil rights reform.

The most important factor that undermined tolerance of white racial extremism was the rise of what historian Matthew Lassiter refers to as "the pragmatic South."[14] In a process that started with the New Deal and then accelerated during and after World War II, federal recovery and investment programs started to transform the underdeveloped southern economy. Business and civic leaders in new and expanding metropolitan centers recognized that an outbreak of racial violence would blemish the reputation of their community and discourage northern capital investment.[15] Confronted by a choice between at least token integration and the social and economic chaos created by violent resistance to the civil rights movement, southern whites increasingly came to realize the limitations of Jim Crow. The irony of white extremists is that although they gave massive resistance much of its impetus, they also planted the seeds of its destruction.

Before telling the stories of these racial extremists, it is appropriate to raise a few points about the scope and content of the book. One of my purposes is to show that members of the American far right were more complicated than the caricatures that normally suffice for analysis of their political careers. Since the 1950s, the predominant interpretation of the far right is that its supporters suffer from not only social and economic marginalization, but also some form of psychopathology. This explanative model is associated with such scholars as Daniel Bell, Earl Raab, and Seymour Martin Lipset.[16] Their argument is that the far right comprises some of the dispossessed elements of society, women and especially men influenced by a sense of failure and frustration in their lives. These people attempt to compensate for their own deficiencies by projecting the blame onto others, particularly racial and religious minorities. Some also see involvement in far-right politics as a means to attain the public attention otherwise denied them. Their activism is therefore motivated less by a sincere conviction in their cause than by a desire for fame and fortune. Sociologist James W. Vander Zanden asserts that white racial militants were "frustrated and disgruntled individuals whose basic motivations were not necessarily directly related to race."[17] Criminologist Stephen Schafer similarly describes as "pseudoconvictional" persons who use the claim of a political cause as cover for their self-aggrandizing behavior, which he attributes to a form of "psychological deviation."[18] As psychologist Gordon Allport more succinctly states in his seminal study *The Nature of Prejudice,* demagoguery is a "lucrative racket."[19] Much of the contemporary literature on the far right continues to dismiss its members as lunatics entirely at odds with mainstream American values.[20]

Some scholars have nonetheless reevaluated the traditional pathological interpretation of the far right. Revisionist studies such as those by Scott Berkman, Sara Diamond, and Leo Ribuffo force us to reassess our assumptions about the motivations and beliefs of political extremists.[21] First, the emphasis on the social and economic marginality of the far right is too deterministic. Other people endure similar circumstances in life but do not become political fanatics. Second, it is inaccurate to represent the far right as comprising only people drawn from the fringes of society. On the contrary, the far right consists of not only poor and alienated persons who benefit from their inclusion within its ranks, but also, as sociologist Kathleen Blee observes, "intelligent, educated people, those with resources and social connections, those with something to lose."[22] Second, scholars who attribute far-right radicalism to a form of individual pathology minimize the influence of broader societal forces. The political ideology of the far right—racial and religious chauvinism, social and cultural traditionalism, antistatism—is not formed in isolation but rather draws on ideas and values held by the society around its adherents. Third, dismissing the far right as paranoid megalomaniacs underestimates the seriousness of the threat they pose to society. As Michael Kazin comments, right-wing militants "are dangerous not because they are crazy irrational zealots—but because they are not."[23] Between 1956 and 1963, white terrorists bombed at least 130 homes and institutions in the South. Those responsible calibrated their tactics to cause maximum effect in terms of publicity and political intimidation.[24]

A further matter relates to structure. Although most of the protagonists of this study were all members of the National States' Rights Party—the most important far-right organization of its time, founded in 1958—their stories are too complex to analyze within a straightforward history of that organization. The far right was a loose confederation of small political groups, often with overlapping memberships, who enhanced their collective strength by sharing resources and conferring on strategy. This permeability allowed for members of the same organization to collaborate with completely different partners. Kasper, Crommelin, and Stoner were uncompromising individualists unwilling to accept the restrictions imposed by loyalty to one political association. Instead, they formed alliances with whoever most facilitated their ambitions. Kasper, for instance, was associated with not only the National States' Rights Party, but also the Seaboard White Citizens' Council, the Citizens' Council of Kentucky, and the Ku Klux Klan. A biographical approach allows us not only to reconstruct the convoluted narratives of militant segregationists but also to illuminate the intricate dynamics of political organization on the far right.

My focus on individual life histories nonetheless raises a potential methodological problem. Concentration on the leaders of the far right can create the false impression of a compliant group of followers who uncritically accepted their political strategy and philosophy. The way that grassroots supporters interpreted the rhetoric of militant leaders is therefore as significant as the rhetoric itself. Where possible, I have included the unmediated voices of these followers.

One further issue concerns taxonomy. There is no term that categorizes with complete accuracy the militant arm of massive resistance. The labels applied by scholars—*radical right*, *racist right*, *far right*, and *fascist*—are all problematic. *Radical right* is commonly, but not completely, used to describe anticommunist organizations such as the Christian Crusade and John Birch Society, which espoused an ideological militancy but still maneuvered within the confines of the law. *Racist right* implies that reactionary prejudice was an attribute only of militants rather than the political mainstream, a far cry from the white South of the 1950s and 1960s. While some militants, including J. B. Stoner and to a lesser extent John Kasper, explicitly identified themselves as fascists, others did not. Bryant Bowles, John Crommelin, and Edwin Walker were ex-soldiers who never disputed that their country had fought on the right side in World War II. The inappropriateness of these terms has led me, to some extent by default, to use the term *far right* to describe militant white supremacists. Although this is the label most broadly used by scholars, it is not without its own difficulties. The term suggests a large gulf between militants and the mainstream but the sobering reality is that there was often little to separate them. Racial militants certainly defined themselves in opposition to elected officials they claimed did not represent the opinions of ordinary people. However, the center ground in southern politics shifted significantly to the right in reaction to the threat of racial integration. The space between the mainstream and the margins narrowed to the point, in some instances, where the two intersected.

Ultimately, the prevailing of political realism over uncompromising resistance on the part of white southerners provides one explanation for the relatively peaceful enforcement of federal civil and voting laws in the 1960s. Although extremists continued to stir violent dissent, as evidenced by the intervention of J. B. Stoner in Bogalusa, Louisiana, shortly after enactment of the Voting Rights Act in 1965, the enforcement of federal reform occurred without the South descending into racial warfare.

PART ONE

Outside Agitators

Bryant Bowles and John Kasper

1. A Blueprint for Rebellion

Bryant Bowles and the Milford School Crisis

Only four months after the U.S. Supreme Court handed down its landmark decision in *Brown v. Board of Education*, the desegregation process faced its first serious challenge. That challenge was to end in defeat for the forces of racial reform.

In September 1954, a stranger appeared in a small town. Although the community had no historical record of racial conflict, the intruder adroitly manipulated popular unease at the admission of African American students to a white school. The town hit international headlines as angry whites organized picket lines outside the schools and through acts of harassment and intimidation induced officials to withdraw the black children. The stranger was Bryant W. Bowles, Jr., and the community in which he launched his counteroffensive against school desegregation was Milford, Delaware.

The drama enacted on the streets of Milford was of considerable historical consequence. It constituted—along with simultaneous demonstrations in Greenbrier County, West Virginia—the first mobilization of mass opposition to the *Brown* decision. The outcome was a victory for the forces of white resistance. Segregationists were not the only ones who gained political capital from the forced removal of the black students. The protests, for instance, exposed the damage that domestic racial problems inflicted on the international reputation of the United States. White resistance in Milford armed the Soviet Union with ammunition in the propaganda battle with its cold war adversary; Radio Moscow used the incident to demonstrate how race relations exposed the hypocrisy of American claims to represent freedom and democracy.[1]

The Milford crisis forces us to reconsider conventional interpretations of massive resistance as having been orchestrated by a neo-bourbon elite in the Deep South. On the contrary, it was a spontaneous grassroots insurgency whose supporters defined themselves as opposing a local civic and business establishment they accused of weakness and betrayal on the race issue. The efforts of local leaders to enforce desegregation led to accusations that they had disenfranchised ordinary whites. By contrast, Bowles used populist appeals to cultivate this alienated white working-class constituency and claim a mandate in opposition to reform.

That he succeeded in doing so in a town like Milford is significant. Political observers had anticipated that white resistance to desegregation would be most entrenched in the Deep South. Yet Bowles stirred violent dissent on the streets of a community in the Peripheral South with no history of racial unrest. In the process, he demonstrated that segregationist resistance was deeper and more pervasive than many commentators had anticipated. The success of the protests on the margins of the Jim Crow South inspired segregationists in more central parts of the region. If whites in such an outpost could resist racial reform, they reasoned, then segregation's real strongholds would surely withstand assault.

Delaware was the source of one of the five cases consolidated by the Supreme Court under the title *Brown v. Board of Education*. African Americans had gained admission both to the University of Delaware and to Catholic schools in Wilmington as early as 1950. The following year, the National Association for the Advancement of Colored People (NAACP) filed two suits in the Delaware Court of Chancery seeking the desegregation of schools in Claymont and Hockessin. On April 1, 1952, the court upheld the claims of the plaintiffs and ordered the local education authorities to admit black students to white institutions until they equalized facilities throughout their school districts. State authorities appealed the decision but consented to the enrollment of black students at the schools involved in the NAACP lawsuits. Although the state supreme court turned down their appeal, Delaware authorities were undaunted. They appealed to the U.S. Supreme Court, which heard the case as one of those combined in *Brown*.[2]

In spite of the initial resistance of state authorities, once the Supreme Court issued its ruling there appeared to be a strong prospect of a swift and orderly process of desegregation throughout the Delaware public school system. Governor J. Caleb Boggs promptly asked the state board of education to devise a strategy for the admission of African American students to formerly all-white schools. The board issued a statement on June 11, 1954, that established its broad commitment "to carry out the mandates of the United States Supreme Court decision as expeditiously as possible."[3]

However, although the board insisted that all local school authorities must submit a desegregation plan by October 1, it allowed each district to determine its own pace of reform. The lack of a properly coordinated plan led to complete inconsistency. For instance, while Wilmington education authorities intended in the first instance only to desegregate at the elementary level, their counterparts in Newark proposed restricting the admission of African Americans to previously white-only high schools.

Moreover, the policy of local autonomy exposed the sharp political and cultural divisions within the state. All but two of the thirteen school districts that implemented a desegregation plan at the start of the 1954–55 academic year were located in the more liberal industrial and urban centers of northern Delaware. South of the Chesapeake River and Delaware Canal, a location described as the state's Mason-Dixon Line, school authorities responded to white public opinion by delaying desegregation until the Supreme Court issued an implementation decree.[4] An opinion poll conducted more than two years after the *Brown* decision underlined the persistent disparity between white opinion on the race issue in northern New Castle County and in the more southerly Kent and Sussex counties. White respondents in New Castle County divided more or less evenly between the 43 percent who supported school desegregation and the 42 percent who disagreed with it. In Kent and especially Sussex County, the balance of opinion tilted far more toward opponents of reform. While 33 percent of whites in Kent County approved of the court ruling, 59 percent disapproved; in Sussex County, only 22 percent were in favor and an overwhelming 75 percent were against.[5]

The small town of Milford sits on the border between Kent and Sussex counties. A television documentary made during the disturbances over school desegregation described it as an otherwise "lovely little residential town" in which horse-drawn carts could be seen slowly winding their way along a leafy street.[6] According to the 1950 census, there were 5,179 townspeople, 865 of whom were African American. Although custom and law imposed the separation of the races in public life, there was no history of conflict between local blacks and whites.

The local school system served the needs of students not only from Milford but also from the small towns and farming communities that surrounded it. Its provision of education for blacks and whites was both separate and unequal. While the Lakeview Avenue School offered white students classes from the elementary to the secondary level, the William Banneker School educated African American children only from the first to the ninth grade. Black pupils who wanted to pursue their education had to travel nineteen miles by bus to the William Henry School in Dover.

Three months after the *Brown* decision, the Milford board of education announced that it would entrust responsibility for formulating a desegregation plan to a newly formed citizens' advisory committee. Faced, however, with the prospect of legal action by the Sussex County NAACP, the board decided to abandon the consultation process and implement a phased desegregation program that provided for the admission of black students to the tenth grade at Lakeview Avenue.[7]

There was no initial indication of trouble. On the morning of Wednesday, September 8, eleven black students enrolled for classes at Lakeview Avenue. Twenty other pupils eligible for admission to the tenth grade chose instead to register at the William Henry School. Despite the limited number of African American students admitted to the Lakeview Avenue School, desegregation appeared to be a fait accompli. Some of the black male students tried out for the school football team with the support of the coach and many of the players; classes proceeded without incident.

The calm did not last, however. The abandonment of the citizens' advisory committee had alienated many local whites, who resented what they perceived as their lack of a participatory voice on an important public issue. What compounded their bitter sense of betrayal was the decision of the board not to make a public announcement of its decision. Many local whites had initially been too stunned to react to the surprise presence of black students at the school. Once the situation had fully permeated their consciousness, however, they reacted with fury. A school dance scheduled for Saturday, September 18, aroused fears that the black male students would try to date white females from their class. As the days passed, the rumors became more alarmist. On Friday, September 17, an estimated 1,500 people packed the local American Legion Hall in a public protest against the admission of the African American students. A petition circulated at the meeting was presented to the school board the following Monday. By then, the board had, in agreement with Mayor Edward C. Evans, already decided to close all schools within the district in order to hold a public meeting at the Lakeview Avenue School. The meeting did nothing to abate white anger. Although the board secured an agreement from black community leaders for the temporary withdrawal of the African American students, the persistent threat of violence led it to order the indefinite closure of the school.[8]

On Wednesday, September 22, the school board met with Delaware Attorney General H. Albert Young. Young advised the board that its decision to admit the black students was not in breach of federal or state law, but that it would be acting illegally if it failed to readmit them. The following day, the Milford school authorities also met with the state board of education and Governor Boggs. The board resolved that the Milford authorities should permit the black students to return to the reopened school on Monday, September 27. However, it also censured local officials for attempting to implement a plan it had not approved. In protest at the lack of emphatic support they had received from the state authorities, the members of the local board of education tendered their resignations. As a result, the state board of education assumed temporary responsibility for overseeing the reopening of the school.[9]

Events then took another unanticipated turn. On the morning of Sunday, September 26, the citizens of Milford awoke to an unusual sight in the skies above the town. Four planes furnished with loudspeaker systems flew overhead advertising a public meeting to discuss the school issue. More than three thousand people attended the rally at the Harrington Air Field, eight miles west of Milford. While most of the crowd were locals, some had traveled from other states, including Maryland and Virginia. The principal speaker was Bryant W. Bowles, Jr., who identified himself as founder and president of an organization named the National Association for the Advancement of White People (NAAWP). Bowles encouraged parents to protest the admission of black students to the Lakeview Avenue School by withdrawing their own children. To those members of the crowd who hesitated at the prospect of violating state truancy laws, he insisted the NAAWP would provide a legal defense against prosecution. Then, in a moment of sheer melodrama, he demonstrated his solidarity with local whites by holding up his three-year-old daughter and hollering, "Do you think this little girl will attend school with Negroes? Not while there's a breath in my body or gunpowder burns!" The speech over, the first recruits stepped forward to sign up as members of the NAAWP. More people added their names to its membership roll at a second rally held south of Milford later that night.[10]

The following morning, only 456 of a total 1,562 students turned up at the reopened Lakeview Avenue School. State troopers escorted ten of the eleven African American students through the crowd that had gathered outside the school, although once inside they were able to attend classes without incident. The parents of the other black pupil had decided, in the face of mounting white opposition, to enroll their child at the William Henry School in Dover.[11]

In the ensuing days, the boycott not only increased in intensity, but also spread to surrounding towns. The NAAWP circulated a petition demanding the resignation of local school officials, including Lakeview Avenue principal Alex Glasmire. Glasmire received numerous threats from anonymous telephone callers, as did white parents who continued to send their children to school.[12] Bowles intensified the pressure by promoting a consumer boycott of businesses owned by white parents who defied the NAAWP. In the unlikely event that someone still did not get the segregationist message, a wooden cross was set on fire outside the school. Segregationists also staged a motorcade through the black section of town in an effort to intimidate African Americans. Local authorities feared that the violence would escalate out of their control. According to the chief of police, the people of Milford were "sitting on a powder keg of dynamite."[13]

Nor was the situation confined to Milford. Acting in response to an appeal from Bowles, whites in the nearby communities also organized "sympathy strikes." Parents withdrew their children from schools in Dagsboro, Ellendale, Gumboro, Lincoln, Millsboro, and Ocean View.[14]

A series of meetings between local and state representatives that took place in the meantime led to the establishment, on Thursday, September 30, of a new Milford school board. The first decision taken by the newly reconstituted board was to order the removal of the black students from Lakeview Avenue, which, it claimed, was "in the interest of the welfare of the children and the community as a whole." Bowles, who had a hand in selecting the members of the new board, jubilantly announced, "The only thing black in the schools tomorrow will be the blackboards." With the black students withdrawn from the school, whites in Milford and other communities called off the boycott. Although Governor Boggs took the cautionary measure of redeploying state troopers to Milford, there was no further unrest.[15]

The situation was nonetheless still unresolved. On October 2, the NAACP filed suit in the Delaware Court of Chancery seeking an injunction against the school board's decision to remove the black students. Twelve days later, Vice Chancellor William Marvel ruled that the students had a "clear legal right" to return to the school. However, the state supreme court agreed to stay the order pending an appeal from the school board. The appeal led to a ruling in December that while the *Brown* decision nullified state segregation laws, school authorities were under no obligation to comply until the U.S. Supreme Court issued an implementation decree.[16]

Mounting frustration in the wake of *Brown II* led black parents to file a further class action lawsuit in 1956. A federal district court upheld the complaint of the plaintiffs in July 1957 and ordered the state board of education to produce a plan for desegregation of the entire Delaware public school system. Further appeals delayed the presentation of a plan until 1959, when the board of education announced its intention to desegregate schools one grade a year over the course of twelve years.[17] Even then, there was little cause for optimism about the future state of race relations in the community. "This is a closed town," black minister Dave DeBerry affirmed: "You have an authoritarian situation. The white people are dominant, they are ruling." Bryant Bowles appeared to have won.[18]

When state and local authorities resolved to implement school desegregation in Milford, they had not anticipated trouble. Yet within weeks they had essentially lost control of the community to an interloper operating outside the structures of municipal governance. To determine how Bryant Bowles stirred a small and seemingly peaceable community into violent revolt it is important to assess the intellectual and institutional forces that fueled his counterrevolutionary campaign. At the core of his appeal to white townsfolk was a demagogic pandering to racial prejudice, particularly fear of miscegenation. There were, however, other polemical strands woven into his white supremacist rhetoric, including his manipulation of class resentment and an emphasis on the preservation of local political autonomy that translated into an assault on the supposed intervention of Jewish conspirators in the race issue.

Bryant William Bowles, Jr., was born on March 4, 1920, in Alford, a small town in the Florida Panhandle with a population at the time of around two hundred. The location of his birthplace had an important bearing on his racial politics, situated as it is in rural Jackson County, which culturally had more in common with southern Alabama than with other parts of the state.[19] Bowles's father, Bryant, Sr., worked as a contractor in the timber business; his mother, Nellie, focused on raising her five children.[20] At the age of nineteen, he enlisted in the Marine Corps, reaching the rank of staff sergeant before his discharge at the end of World War II.[21] Within two years of returning to civilian life, he had married and divorced, becoming a father in the short interval between. In 1949, he wed his second wife, Eloise Williford, who as a nurse had tended to the injuries he sustained in a dynamite blast while working for an oil company in Beaumont, Texas. Bowles returned to the marines during the Korean War. Released from active duty in December 1951, he moved to Baltimore and set up his own construction company.[22]

Despite the fact that he had no prior history of political activism, in December 1953 Bowles invested $6,000 of his own money in establishing the National Association for the Advancement of White People.[23] While there is no explicit explanation for his actions, it is possible that the timing owed in part to the mounting expectation that the U.S. Supreme Court would soon issue a ruling outlawing segregation in public schools. How Bowles came to name his organization is also open to speculation. According to the minister and civil rights activist Ralph Lord Roy, representatives of numerous far-right groups had founded an umbrella association with the same title eighteen months earlier in Chicago. Information about this earlier incarnation of the NAAWP is almost impossible to locate and there is no means to determine whether Bowles was aware of its existence when he established his own organization.[24]

Writers who at the time searched for an answer to the apparently sudden politicization of Bowles drew skeptical conclusions. Many political commentators dismissed him as an opportunist who sought to compensate for the failure of his personal life by attaining momentary public fame. As Benjamin Muse observed, the desegregation crisis "provided a means by which a previously unimportant and little-known person could quickly attract a large following, get into the limelight, and enjoy a sense of power."[25]

While there is some substance to this interpretation of Bowles, it betrays a liberal bias that obscures a more compelling motivation for political extremism. Muse did not doubt the sincerity of African Americans who emerged from obscurity to claim prominent positions within the ranks of the civil rights movement, but appeared incapable of accepting that what inspired Bowles was also an earnest conviction in his cause. The misrepresentation of Bowles made it impossible for contemporary commentators to understand what drew people toward him. It also led them to underestimate the political threat that racial demagogues posed to the desegregation process. The propensity of liberal journalists to caricature militant segregationists as socially marginal people touched by madness stretched to physical descriptions of Bowles. According to James Rorty, the NAAWP leader was "of medium height and slightly built, with a ravaged face and troubled eyes."

Photographs of Bowles actually show a handsome and smartly dressed man, one possible source of his appeal. As a more candid correspondent conceded, what made Bowles such a threat was the fact that he could not be dismissed as some rube who had wandered out of the backwoods of Florida. On the contrary, he was "good-looking, well dressed, and clearly several steps removed from the red-necked, foulmouthed race agitator of Northern imagination."[26]

Bowles was also more than a hustler on the make. He had been drawn into far-right politics under the influence of one of its principal propagandists, Conde J. McGinley. The historical record does not reveal when or where Bowles first met McGinley, but the New Jersey agitator was a recurring presence at NAAWP rallies in Milford and his propaganda material circulated widely throughout the town and surrounding area.[27] Born in Norman, Oklahoma, on October 13, 1890, McGinley was of Irish immigrant stock. Having spent some time in Texas, he moved to New Jersey in 1929, opening a chain of restaurants along the state shoreline. In 1946, he started to publish a weekly paper titled *Think*. When McGinley relocated from Trenton to Union City the following year, the paper metamorphosed into the semimonthly magazine *Common Sense*.

The influence that McGinley wielded over Bowles is apparent in a number of ways. While his southern background instilled in Bowles a racial animosity toward African Americans, his conviction that the civil rights movement was a Jewish conspiracy owed to the inspiration of the New Jersey agitator. A virulent anti-Semitism coursed through every page of *Common Sense*. According to McGinley, communism was nothing more than "a false face for Judaism" and the civil rights movement part of a "plan for enslavement" of white Americans by a "Zionist Invisible Government." Shortly before the U.S. Supreme Court handed down the *Brown* decision, McGinley published a booklet warning readers that desegregation was part of *The Coming Red Dictatorship*. The resonance of these accusations is perceptible in the tone and content of the speeches made by Bowles during the Milford school crisis.[28]

McGinley also encouraged Bowles to see himself as an heir to the heroes of the American Revolution. Given its content, *Common Sense* may seem to have been one of the most inappropriately named publications in American history. Yet in evoking the spirit of Tom Paine, it showed how white supremacists attempted to claim the high moral ground for their cause by maintaining that they were acting in the interest of protecting individual liberty against a despotic government.

Although the public addresses delivered by Bowles bore the obvious imprimatur of McGinley, it would be wrong to see the NAAWP leader as having been nothing more than a marionette. It was Bowles, not McGinley, who spearheaded the rebellion in Milford. Segregationist resistance was already underway by the time Bowles turned up in the town. There was, however, no local person who possessed the charismatic authority to assume leadership of the movement. The willingness of white citizens to cede control of the protests to an outsider owed in part to the fact that he was a compelling public speaker whose addresses combined passion, authority, and wit. His interaction with audiences is illustrated by a sound recording of one NAAWP rally. A vote is being taken on a motion that parents withdraw their children from school. "All in favor, say 'Aye,'" announces Bowles. "Aye" yells the crowd, as though speaking with one voice. "All opposed," continues Bowles, "say no—and run!" The meeting collapses into laughter.[29]

The existence of this and other sound recordings of Bowles demonstrates the importance of radio as a medium through which white supremacists mobilized support. Although historian Brian Ward has admirably documented the role of radio in facilitating the black freedom struggle, scholars have paid less attention to how segregationists used the airwaves to defend Jim Crow.[30] Radio was especially advantageous to politically marginal campaigners like Bowles. With no personal or political ties to Milford, he had no immediate entrée to the local social networks that were essential to the mobilization and recruitment of NAAWP members. While Bowles attempted to enroll local whites through churches and union halls, radio afforded free and immediate access to the ears, hearts, and minds of local townspeople. Bowles appeared regularly on radio shows during the Milford school crisis. Local station WKSB broadcast numerous NAAWP rallies. Bowles also won plaudits when he went head to head with confrontational talk show host Joe Pyne on Wilmington station WILM. Bowles flustered the normally unflappable presenter by accusing him of hiding a secret from the audience. "Joe, why are you ashamed of your Negro blood?" Although it was a complete fabrication, the force with which Bowles delivered the accusation impressed many listeners. Suspicion of Pyne led shortly thereafter to some segregationists planting bombs both in his car and on his front lawn, although neither detonated.[31]

The rhetoric of Bowles also resonated with ordinary whites because he placed his emphasis less on intellectual abstractions such as states' rights than on emotional appeals to racial prejudice. Bowles paradoxically sought to protect white privilege by portraying his supporters as the victims of oppression. His misappropriation of the name of the NAACP is a clear illustration of this rhetorical strategy. Implicit in this choice was the notion that whites, more than blacks, had claim to an organization that would protect and promote their endangered rights. As Bowles wrote in one of his recruiting pamphlets, the purpose of the NAAWP was "to re-establish the rightful status" of whites, "whose design for living teeters on the brink of disaster" because of the relentless pressure of civil rights reformers.[32]

The racial demagoguery of Bowles placed particular emphasis on the physical threat that desegregation posed to whites. White women were at risk of being violated by predatory black males, whose inherent foulness, he claimed, made them transmitters of dangerous sexual diseases. The *National Forum*, a newsletter published by the NAAWP, reinforced this message by reproducing images such as the black king and white queen of a university prom in Iowa. Bowles also published photographs depicting celebrities in intimately interracial situations—Marlene Dietrich kissing the black singer Billy Daniels, musicians Peggy Lee and Louis Armstrong in a tight embrace—as a means to condemn a liberal secular culture he believed had eroded traditional American values.[33]

Bowles claimed biblical sanction for his belief in the separation of the races. Scholars have long recognized the important role of black churches as centers for the mobilization of civil rights protest.[34] However, only recently have they paid attention to the part that white churches played in mobilizing opposition to racial reform. The new wave of scholarship on massive resistance has stimulated debate about the role of religion in the ideological defense of Jim Crow. On one side of the discussion is David Chappell, who claims that white southern church leaders failed to provide the massive resistance movement with intellectual and institutional support. Chappell contrasts this situation with the pivotal role that black clergymen performed in inspiring ordinary African Americans to believe that the civil rights struggle was an expression of divine purpose.[35] On the other side of the argument is Jane Dailey, who contends that many ordinary white southerners drew on religious doctrine to legitimize their animosity toward racial integration.[36]

The Milford school crisis demonstrates the merits of both interpretations. Mainstream church leaders proffered no support for the school boycott. Both the Milford Ministerial Association and the local Catholic priest promoted public acceptance of racial reform. As Bowles observed in a *National Forum* editorial, "some Christian ministers have been duped by the enemy."[37]

There was, however, considerable tension between clergymen and their congregations. Although massive resistance is usually characterized as an elite phenomenon, the use by ordinary laypersons of religious doctrine to support their opposition to integration demonstrates the grassroots strength of white racism. The protesters who stood on picket lines outside the schools bore placards that proclaimed segregation represented God's will. They saw themselves as soldiers of Christ fighting a holy crusade against the evil forces of racial integration. Declaring their support for segregation was an act of religious witnessing. As NAAWP activist Mildred Sharp proudly declaimed at its first organizational meeting, "I am a servant of God."[38]

Bowles used the religiosity of local whites to his political advantage. It was through his association with neighborhood evangelical churches that Bowles attained the financial, social, and cultural capital essential to his securing leadership of segregationist resistance in Milford. His status as an outsider to the community complicated his ability to lead a local protest movement, forcing him to deflect criticism from town authorities who accused him of being an interloper. In his speeches he stressed that he and his organization were not intruders but rather had come to Milford at the invitation of Joseph Danes, a local employee of the Department of the Navy. "We are not outsiders," he insisted. "We are legally incorporated under the state laws of Delaware."[39]

Bowles also enhanced his legitimacy by enlisting the support of fundamentalist preachers. One of the first actions he took on arriving in Milford was to appoint a local evangelist named Manaen Warrington as a director of the NAAWP. He also recruited a number of other fundamentalist preachers, including Reverends Claude Lynch and Fred Whitman, who blessed the segregationist cause in their opening prayers at NAAWP meetings.[40]

The churches of these clergymen provided immediate access to established social networks that were otherwise inaccessible to an interloper like Bowles. These relations and contacts afforded the NAAWP with the surest means to secure the rapid mobilization of white opposition to school desegregation. The NAAWP served as what social scientists term a parachurch organization, building connections between numerous clergymen and their congregations to create an ecumenical movement against integration. Bowles enhanced his political power by uniting the social networks within individual churches into a larger and more elaborate set of ties that cut across denominational lines. This also facilitated the efforts of the underfunded NAAWP to secure financial donations.[41]

Evangelical churches also provided Bowles and his supporters with important cultural capital that buttressed their belief in the innate racial superiority of whites. The preachers recruited to the ranks of the NAAWP attempted to reinforce the moral righteousness of white protest by asserting that there was scriptural support for racial segregation. Such was the position of another clerical recruit to the NAAWP, J. G. Rimmer of the Pilgrim Holiness Church in Gumboro. Rimmer stated unequivocally that segregation represented part of the divine plan for mankind. As he informed one NAAWP meeting, "God has a place for the white race to fill—and a place for the colored race to fill. I feel that a spirit which is foreign to God is working to unite the races."[42] Through such rhetoric, Rimmer and his fellow clergymen bestowed on the NAAWP the cultural status and legitimacy needed to lure local whites to its ranks. They claimed that Bowles acted on biblical authority in attempting to preserve the integrity of the white race. Whitman, for instance, introduced Bowles at one NAAWP rally by citing Psalm 94:16: "Who will rise up for me against the evildoers? Or who will stand up for me against the workers of iniquity?" Enter Bowles, to rapturous applause.[43] The NAAWP leader in turn endorsed the religious beliefs of the men and women who attended his rallies, claiming that biblical doctrine supported racial separation. "If the Negro would look up to the Lord," he asserted at one meeting, "he would say, 'Don't agitate—the white race gave you the opportunity to be an American—to be free of slavery . . . to be a worthwhile citizen and not an inhabitant of the jungle.'"[44]

While Bowles placed his principal emphasis on the preservation of white supremacy, he manipulated the vulnerabilities of his followers in a number of other ways. In particular, he promoted the victim status of his supporters in class as well as racial terms. According to one newspaper report, the protesters who formed the picket line outside Lakeview Avenue were "mostly farmers in working clothes."[45] Bowles channeled the resentment that many ordinary whites felt toward local and state authorities who, they believed, had advanced the interests of African Americans at their expense. "When I got out of the service I spent two years looking for a big shot to start this organization," the NAAWP leader informed one audience. "But the big shots aren't too concerned apparently. They can send their children to private schools and don't have to worry about Negroes attending the classes."[46] While it is not possible to corroborate the claim that Bowles searched for a more established political authority to lead white resistance, taken at face value it is further evidence that self-publicity was not his principal motivation.

Bowles subscribed to a simple majoritarian philosophy. The role of governmental institutions was to serve as instruments of the popular will. Since most Americans, black as well as white, were in his opinion opposed to racial integration, state and federal officials had no authority to enforce reform. Ordinary citizens therefore had a legitimate right to defy the admission of black students to the white high school. In a manner that expressed the political influence of Conde McGinley, Bowles attempted to strengthen his argument by channeling the spirit of 1776, when an earlier generation of Americans chose to resist the tyranny of government and to "fight for our homes and families and live as free men."[47]

In contrast to a local and state leadership that he claimed had willfully excluded them, Bowles provided ordinary men and women who otherwise felt alienated and powerless with a participatory voice in the political process. Bowles presented the NAAWP as an egalitarian alternative to the civic and political elite that had "controlled your town, your schools, and some of your churches for years."[48] He announced to the crowd who came to his first rally at the Harrington Air Field that his intention in establishing a Milford chapter of the NAAWP was to ensure "local control over local affairs." In contrast to the public officials who had failed to consult with townspeople before admitting the black students to Lakeview Avenue, Bowles assumed a more inclusive and democratic position. He invited persons interested in becoming members of the NAAWP board of directors to step forward and then asked the rest of his audience to endorse them, emphasizing that "They're only as strong as the people with them." This attempt to secure representative grassroots support led significantly to the election not only of two men, Charles West and Manaen Warrington, but also of a woman, Mildred Sharp.[49] Bowles also sought to consolidate the trust of local whites by making himself more accountable than public officials. "Everyone who has joined the organization is my boss," he declared at a later NAAWP rally. "I can be voted out in fifteen minutes. The people are the boss, I work for them."[50]

Although Bowles directed much of his animus toward the political elite, it is important to emphasize that class divisions over school desegregation were not clear-cut. The NAAWP leader commanded the support not only of working people, but also of prosperous farmers and businessmen.[51] These men maintained a public distance from Bowles in order to protect their social respectability; careful not to endorse the methods of the mob openly, they were nonetheless privately satisfied with the results. Their position was comparable to that of some of the white patricians who later watched with silent approval the hordes that obstructed black students from entering the Central High School in Little Rock. As newspaper publisher Hugh Patterson observed, the mob in the Arkansas state capital was "tolerated by people who have found them to be disreputable and sort of unclean before" but who nonetheless "don't themselves want to expose a profile for attack."[52]

In admonishing the political establishment, Bowles claimed that its members were acting, wittingly or unwittingly, in the interests of "an invisible clique of unscrupulous haters of the white race."[53] While some of his supporters may have struggled to interpret this oblique language, it soon became clear that Bowles was alluding to Jews. The imprint of Conde McGinley is evident in the shrilly anti-Semitic tone of the *National Forum*, which disputed the racial status of Jews, claiming that they were not only "alien to the white race," but also "most influential and instrumental in the spoiling, looting, and defilement of it."[54] The *Forum* accused Jews of manipulating African Americans into questioning what it claimed was their naturally subordinate status within the social hierarchy, creating discord in the otherwise harmonious relationship between the races. Having precipitated the collapse of the democratic social order, the Jewish conspirators would then construct in its place "an atheistic Anti-Christian Communist dictatorship."[55]

In an attempt to prove the existence of this conspiracy, Bowles accused public officials who supported desegregation of secretly being Jewish. He told his supporters, for instance, that the real name of State Attorney General H. Albert Young, who had aroused his ire by attempting to revoke the NAAWP charter, was Hyman Yanowitz.[56] Bowles also acted as a conduit through whom anti-Semites from across the country channeled their message. The NAAWP helped in particular to flood Milford with thousands of copies of Conde McGinley's *Common Sense*, which claimed "communist Jews" had precipitated the school situation.[57]

How receptive local whites were to these accusations is unclear. While the signs displayed by demonstrators outside the schools indicate the power of racial prejudice in the collective consciousness of local whites, none of the placards transcribed by reporters on the scene contained anti-Semitic statements. The slurs and stereotypes employed by Bowles nonetheless seem to have held some currency with local whites, not least because there were no Jews living in the town who could dispel them. Manaen Warrington, for instance, included in his address at one NAAWP rally a statement that Jews were Christ-killers.[58]

While Bowles made it clear who he believed was responsible for attempting to enforce desegregation, he was often less direct in articulating how local whites could withstand reform. Bowles continually stressed that his organization acted within the strict confines of the law. The NAAWP, he asserted, "does not wear any white sheets or burn any crosses, and it never will." Instead, Bowles insisted that his supporters must use other means to obstruct the admission of black students to white schools. "If you want people to maintain separate schools," he informed one audience, "you will not win in the end through violence. There is another way." That way was a boycott of schools that admitted African American students through their doors.[59]

Although the NAAWP leader claimed not to advocate violence as a means to resist school desegregation, he was being disingenuous. Despite his care not to issue his supporters with an explicit call to arms, Bowles still communicated his belief in violence as a legitimate political tool. His public addresses contained numerous allusions that allowed his audiences to infer that he deemed bloodshed not only inevitable but also desirable. It is not difficult to decipher the coded message in a speech Bowles gave on the evening before Lakeview Avenue School reopened on a desegregated basis. "You certainly have the right to protect your child if you anticipate any violence by keeping it in your home," he informed his audience. "If I thought my child would be harmed in school tomorrow, I would bar the door before it got out of my home, not after it left to go to that school."[60] Bowles began a later speech by congratulating members on their orderly conduct during the school boycott. However, he then drew their attention to the fate of Harry T. Moore, the Florida NAACP leader murdered by white terrorists on Christmas Day 1951. While he claimed not to approve of political assassination, Bowles also noted with satisfaction that no African American had stepped forward to succeed Moore. For those who still did not deduce his meaning, Bowles later invited Sheriff Willis McCall—a man whom Moore campaigned to indict for murder following his shooting of two black criminal suspects—to speak at a NAAWP rally in Milford.[61]

Consistent with his claim that whites were the real victims of racial conflict, Bowles insisted that segregationists would only take up arms if necessary to defend themselves from black aggression. However, he infused his rhetoric with images of racial warfare intended to stir the hearts of his supporters. Bowles encouraged his audiences to emulate southern segregationists such as the Klan, who "courageously threaten to spill their blood before it [desegregation] will happen in Dixie." One of the most devious aspects of his speeches was his ability to portray his preferred course of action as a last desperate resort. As he put it in a characteristic phrase that combined incitement with regret, "no matter if this means bloodshed we will see it through." Having roused whites into a state of unrest, Bowles disclaimed responsibility for the resultant disorder.[62]

Despite his talent for circumlocution, Bowles was the obvious source of racial turmoil. "Without the destructive influence of this rabble-rouser," Governor Caleb Boggs affirmed, "mob rule and mass hysteria would never have come to Milford."[63] Nonetheless, Bowles would not have been able to act with such latitude without a supportive political environment. It was politically expedient for local and state authorities to blame the racial turmoil in the town on the unwelcome intrusion of an outsider. It was, however, the hesitancy and equivocation of the authorities that provided an opportunity for an extremist to mobilize opposition to school desegregation. When NAACP representatives attended a meeting called by the governor to discuss the school situation, they discovered to their dismay that white resistance leaders had also accepted an invitation to attend. Moreover, Boggs gave greater weight to the segregationists. He tried to persuade the NAACP activists to accept the removal of the African American students until racial tensions had receded. As the black spokespersons pointed out, this "compromise" was nothing of the kind; the official recognition granted to white resisters only strengthened their determination to secure the permanent withdrawal of the black schoolchildren. The failure of the state board of education to support local school officials also led to the resignation of the latter and their replacement by segregationists who ordered the removal of the black students.[64] In a damning evaluation of the governor, Professor Kenneth B. Clark, who observed events at close hand, concluded: "Rather than using the prestige and power inherent in his office in support of lawful and stable government, he vacillated, negotiated and eventually surrendered to those who preached the gospel of hate and lawless defiance of constitutional government."[65]

The Milford crisis demonstrates that a lone agitator with limited resources could still mount a successful resistance of school desegregation. The same tactics that worked so well in a small town did not, however, translate when applied to a larger metropolitan environment. While he continued to lead white opposition to racial reform in Milford, Bowles also campaigned for the maintenance of segregation in the public school systems of Baltimore and Washington, D.C. In Milford, protest focused on one school and the authorities possessed limited manpower. By contrast, the larger scale of desegregation in cities with multiple educational establishments stretched Bowles beyond his political means. Alerted by the earlier disorders that the

NAAWP leader had created, city authorities also took swift measures to avoid similar disruption to school desegregation.

The Baltimore city school board implemented a plan to admit black students to 52 of the 186 institutions within its jurisdiction from the start of the new academic year on Tuesday, September 7, 1954. For the first few weeks, the plan appeared to have succeeded. However, when word of the resistance movement in Milford reached the city, it encouraged whites to campaign for the removal of black students from desegregated schools. Trouble flared with particular intensity in south Baltimore, an area densely populated with white industrial workers, many of whom were recent migrants from rural communities. Whites opposed to school desegregation established the Maryland Petition Committee, an affiliate of the NAAWP. On Thursday, September 30, they launched a picket of the Charles Carroll School, which had admitted twelve black students to its kindergarten. The arrival of Bowles resulted in the spread of white protest. Public unrest focused on the Southern High School, where police, teachers, and ministers had to escort black students through an angry mob. By Monday, October 4, segregationist demonstrations disrupted classes at more than twenty schools. The NAAWP filed suit against the school board, claiming it had acted illegally by desegregating schools before the Supreme Court had issued its implementation decree.[66]

However, the flames of white fury Bowles ignited did not burn for long. Baltimore learned from the Milford experience not to surrender the political initiative to Bowles. Political commentators concurred that much of the responsibility for the Milford crisis rested with what the NAACP described as "dillydallying, compromising public officials." The equivocation of state authorities undermined the legitimacy of the local school board and allowed mob rule to reign.[67] By contrast, civic groups and school officials in Baltimore issued public statements condemning the demonstrations as a threat to community order and educational standards. Following a speech by Bowles on October 4 that warned of violent resistance to school desegregation, Police Commissioner Beverly Ober broadcast a statement on local radio and television stations warning white protesters they risked arrest for violation of state laws prohibiting interference with public schools. The following morning, police dispersed the small number of picketers who had not heeded the exhortation of Commissioner Ober. Later that day, state Judge James K. Cullen dismissed the NAAWP lawsuit. Within days, school attendance had returned to normal.[68]

City officials in Washington, D.C., similarly frustrated the efforts of

Bowles to precipitate public disorder over school desegregation. On Monday, October 4, white students walked out of the Anacostia and McKinley high schools in protest at the admission of African Americans. The following day, students boycotted seven other schools. Bowles turned up at the Anacostia School with an offer to "counsel" the striking students. However, the police threatened him and the picketers with arrest unless they cleared the streets. School Superintendent Hobart M. Corning then issued a statement warning student protesters they would forfeit all honors and be reported to truant officers unless they returned to classes. The picket collapsed after only four days. Observing the success with which the authorities in Baltimore and Washington had eliminated the NAAWP threat, city officials in Philadelphia announced they would arrest Bowles if he attempted to interfere with local school desegregation. He did not.[69]

The failure of Bowles to replicate the success of a small town campaign in a larger metropolitan environment exposed the limitations of his rabble-rousing tactics and contributed to the precipitate demise of his political career. Other problems of his own making also denied him the opportunity to perform a longer-term leadership role in the massive resistance movement.

The sudden arrival of Bowles on the political scene aroused the curiosity of reporters, who started to probe into his past. What they discovered made for unsavory reading. In June 1953, a Baltimore court convicted Bowles on five counts of failing to pay his employees and passing bad checks. That same month, police arrested him for larceny after he allegedly misused funds entrusted to his construction company. Although a court later found him not guilty, his dubious financial practices soon found him again in trouble with the law. In July 1954, Bowles received a suspended sentence of one year's imprisonment at the Maryland House of Correction following a further conviction for acting on false pretenses. When the NAAWP started to create political trouble, the authorities searched through Bowles's financial records for additional misdeeds they could use to incarcerate or at least discredit him. Delaware police discovered that law enforcement officers in Tampa were pursuing Bowles for passing bad checks. The Internal Revenue Service in Baltimore also ordered him to account for $2,000 in taxes and social security deductions withheld from the wages of his employees.[70]

Local and state authorities used public disclosure of these past misdeeds to cast suspicion on the motivations of Bowles in leading resistance to school desegregation. There is no evidence that the prospect of pecuniary advantage inspired Bowles. Nonetheless, the exposure of his criminal past led some segregationists to dub him the "$5 man" because they suspected his sole interest was in pocketing the membership dues paid to the NAAWP.[71]

State officials took further action to remove the threat that Bowles still posed to public order. On October 8, 1954, State Attorney General Albert H. Young announced his intention to revoke the NAAWP charter, issuing Bowles a subpoena that demanded the public disclosure of his organization's membership and finances. Young accused the NAAWP of attempting "by means of mass hysteria, mob rule, boycott and dissemination of race prejudice," not only to intimidate black families and school officials, but also to encourage white parents to violate school attendance laws.[72] The following day, Governor Boggs ordered the arrest of Bowles on charges of violating compulsory school attendance laws and inciting to riot. Police took the NAAWP leader into custody on October 10 and had him arraigned before both the Kent and Sussex county courts. Released on a combined bond of $6,000, he flamboyantly flew to the Harrington Air Field for a sundown rally at which he announced, to the cheers of five thousand supporters, the death of Supreme Court Justice Robert H. Jackson.[73]

Bowles continued to stir unrest in Milford for the next six months. In December, his landlord forced him to vacate his office in Washington, D.C., and he relocated to the small Delaware town. The following month, he became a member of the local Parent-Teacher Association. Bowles used his position to push for the resignation of school officials. In March, he claimed his only scalp when School Superintendent Raymond C. Cobbs succumbed to a campaign of intimidation.[74] Bowles brought greater influence to bear on the school board election that took place on May 14, 1955, campaigning on behalf of four segregationist candidates who won a clean sweep against their moderate opponents.[75]

The political momentum of the NAAWP soon faltered, however. After much postponement of the trial, Bowles eventually came before the Court of Common Pleas in late March and early April 1955. The court found him guilty of violating state school attendance laws and fined him $300.[76] Moreover, Bowles became a victim of his own success. With the black students removed from Lakeview Avenue, there was no need for his rabble-rousing leadership. In July 1955, Bowles announced his resignation as NAAWP president, citing a lack of public interest. "I don't feel like helping people who won't help themselves," he complained to reporters.[77]

The few occasions thereafter when his name reappeared in the press marked his rapid decline and disgrace. In October, an altercation with a black mailman led to another court appearance.[78] Nothing more was heard of Bowles until August 1957. By that time, he had relocated to Beaumont, Texas. It was there that he participated in a series of segregationist protests. This included a demonstration outside a local theater that was screening *Island in the Sun*, a movie about interracial romance starring Harry Belafonte and Joan Fontaine. Police also arrested Bowles when he attempted to obstruct a dinner hosted by the Beaumont chapter of the NAACP.[79]

Despite these efforts to resuscitate his political career, time was running out for Bowles. In August 1958, he hit the headlines after responding to an assault on his wife by shooting dead his brother-in-law. A court in Hardin County, Texas, found him guilty of murder and sentenced him to life imprisonment.[80] He died in obscurity on April 13, 1997.[81] Bowles did bequeath a legacy of sorts. In the early 1960s, a white supremacist in Cincinnati named William Miller briefly appropriated the name of the NAAWP. It was resurrected a second time in 1980 by former Klansman David Duke.[82]

Bryant Bowles bequeathed a complicated legacy to the burgeoning massive resistance movement. On the one hand, the anarchic insurrection that he led in Milford constituted a threat to those segregationists who sought to represent their opposition to racial reform as both rational and lawful. Yet, on the other hand, the tactics used by the NAAWP leader had succeeded in accomplishing what those same segregationists desired, the maintenance of a dual public school system. The reaction of white southerners to Bowles demonstrated their difficulty in reconciling these conflicting factors.

The racial demagoguery of Bowles certainly threatened the efforts of massive resisters to stake out the high moral ground in the civil rights struggle. Segregationists avowed that they, rather than African Americans, were the real victims of the racial crisis. A tyrannical federal government determined to impose desegregation against their will was abusing the constitutional rights of law-abiding white citizens. Massive resisters maintained that they therefore had both moral and legal right on their side in resisting the *Brown* decision. The extremism of Bowles, however, undermined the credibility of this claim. According to one newspaper, most southern segregationists regarded the NAAWP as a "reckless hate group."[83] "A man cannot condemn another for thinking the court's mandate is wrong, and for trying to change that mandate through legal adventures," asserted Florida journalist Bill Bags. "But the appeal to hate and to prejudice and to ignorance, and the subsequent, natural rising of violence, is an entirely different matter. It runs hard against the grain of everything which is good in this country."[84]

Bowles endured similar criticism from otherwise staunchly segregationist elements of the southern press. One South Carolina newspaper responded to the formation of a local NAAWP chapter, for instance, by stating: "It is at least as undesirable as the organization it proposes to combat— the National Association for the Advancement of Colored People."[85] The paper contended that the integration issue should be resolved locally and that the NAAWP was no more welcome in the community than the federal government. It condemned the NAAWP for using the civil rights crisis as a means to promote anti-Semitism. Furthermore, it expressed a fear that the organization would precipitate widespread disorder that would damage the local economy and impair the reputation of the townspeople.[86] Responding to an allegation that Bowles was using NAAWP funds to purchase ammunition, the paper concluded that if it was necessary to use weapons to protect segregation, "it is debatable whether or not our society merits 'saving.'"[87]

When Bowles attempted to recruit supporters farther south, he met with significant resistance from segregationists who feared he would discredit their movement. As Harold Fleming of the Southern Regional Council concluded, Bowles's radicalism "forfeited the possibility of securing influential community backing."[88] The very name of the NAAWP was a disincentive to segregationists who sought to promote the respectability of their cause by defending Jim Crow in the supposedly racially neutral terms of state autonomy from federal interference. A South Carolina chapter of the NAAWP admitted altering their title to the Florence States Rights League because the more explicit emphasis on race "worked to the disadvantage of the organization."[89]

The moral condescension toward Bowles and the NAAWP nonetheless contained more than an element of hypocrisy. When Bowles traveled to Charlotte, North Carolina, in the hope of founding a local NAAWP chapter, local whites shunned him as a reckless extremist who endangered the credibility of the segregationist cause. Yet the same whites who disavowed his tactics then launched a campaign of intimidation that drove black student Dorothy Counts from the Harding High School.[90]

Although some southern newspapers adopted a defensively disdainful attitude toward Bowles, others were more nuanced in their appraisal of the NAAWP leader. While not expressing sympathy with Bowles per se, some segregationists saw in the efforts of state authorities and civil rights organizations to silence him implications for their own battle against desegregation.

Segregationists believed that the national news media was blatantly biased toward northern liberal opinion. White southerners, they insisted, were denied a representative voice in public discourses on the race issue. The press refused to accept that they had legitimate concerns about the usurpation of constitutional power by the federal government, instead portraying them as irrational bigots. A cartoon published by the Citizens' Council depicted a man who represented the "Mass Communications Media" being crushed in a giant vice to make him scream, "Awk! Integration is Great!" Another showed a set of scales tipped away from "Honest Northern Opinion" and toward "Biased Metropolitan Press."[91]

This defensiveness encouraged segregationists who otherwise condemned Bowles to close ranks with him over the issue of his constitutional rights to freedom of speech and assembly. The efforts of the authorities to suppress the NAAWP in their opinion established a potentially dangerous precedent that could be used to silence all protest against the *Brown* decision. One southern newspaper interpreted the arrest of Bowles for violating Delaware state laws as evidence of northern double standards. According to the paper, the incident demonstrated the hypocrisy of northerners who criticized the South for restrictions on freedom of speech about the race issue. Provided he did not advocate violence, Bowles had as much right to express his public opposition to desegregation as civil rights activists had to promote it. "Well, we don't know too much about the laws of Delaware; but, from this distance, it looks as if we have finally reached that incongruous situation in which the majority is being pushed around in a state which has been all too prone in the past to charge the south with oppressing the minority."[92] South Carolina reporter William D. Workman, Jr., similarly criticized NAACP national board chairman Channing H. Tobias for his decision to suspend a meeting of the New York State Conference when he learned Bowles was one of the invited speakers. While Workman condemned "fringe elements which dabble in violence and vituperation," he defended their right to freedom of speech. The attempt to gag Bowles demonstrated the hypocrisy of northern critics who accused the South of silencing public dissent.[93]

While many southern segregationists disputed the means by which Bowles led white resistance in Milford they also had to concede one crucial point: it worked. At a time when the massive resistance movement was still in a nascent phase of development—only two months after the formation of the first Citizens' Councils and sixteen months before the release of the Southern Manifesto—Bowles had effectively obstructed the admission of African American students to white schools. A number of scholars have noted that massive resistance leaders lacked a fundamental conviction that their cause could succeed; the mobilization of segregationist opposition could only retard, not reverse, racial reform. In contrast to the diffidence and indecisiveness of many white southern political leaders, the actions of ordinary whites in Milford offered an inspirational example of how mass mobilization could thwart school desegregation.[94]

According to a report by the Southern Regional Council, Bowles "undoubtedly gave impetus to the resistance movement in the deep South."[95] His success showed southern segregationists that it was possible to prevent desegregation.

Some civil rights leaders, including Walter White of the NAACP, insinuated that southern segregationists had secretly underwritten the Milford demonstrations as a means to demonstrate that whites outside the former Confederacy also opposed racial reform. This situation would, in turn, intimidate the Supreme Court into retreating from a timetable for implementation of the *Brown* decision.[96]

Although there is no evidence to support this conspiracy theory, Bowles's success did lead some segregationists to encourage him to come south in order to lead their own resistance struggles. Bowles claimed to have established chapters of the NAAWP in numerous southern cities, including Atlanta and Richmond. A speaking tour of his native state of Florida also led to his recruitment of an estimated two thousand members, most of them from in and around Jacksonville.[97] Bowles found further favor among militant segregationist organizations such as the North Carolina Knights of the Ku Klux Klan, which made him an honorary member.[98]

Whether Bowles could have used these new connections to mount a resistance campaign farther south is open to speculation. His arrest and conviction for murder in any case precluded his building on the momentum of the Milford protests. Yet in leading the first successful grassroots resistance of the *Brown* decision, he established an inspiring precedent for others willing to emulate his direct action tactics. No sooner had Bowles receded from the political arena then there rose to prominence another radical segregationist whose counterrevolutionary campaigns tactically and rhetorically emulated the NAAWP leader. His name was John Kasper.

2. A Collapse of Law and Order

John Kasper and Segregationist Resistance in Clinton

In Roger Corman's 1961 film *The Intruder*, a mysterious stranger suddenly arrives in the small southern town of Caxton. Claiming to be a "social reformer," the stranger—played by a young William Shatner—has come to rouse public opposition to the racial integration of the local high school. He succeeds in stirring the community into a state of chaos. African Americans are mobbed in the streets, their homes and churches targeted for terrorist attacks. White liberals who attempt to restore order are beaten in broad daylight. Despite this graphic depiction of racial unrest, the film tells us little of the principal protagonist, other than that his name is Adam Cramer and that he claims to represent an organization known as the Patrick Henry Society.[1]

This omission may not be important in a work of cinematic fiction, but *The Intruder* is based on historical fact. Adam Cramer is modeled on a militant segregationist named John Kasper who during the 1950s attracted international notoriety because of his brutal resistance to black civil rights. Kasper pursued a peripatetic career, traveling to numerous communities where he encouraged aggrieved whites to resist school desegregation. He first hit the headlines in August 1956, when he precipitated violent unrest over the desegregation of a high school in Clinton, Tennessee. His activities spread not only to other parts of the state, but also to Florida, Kentucky, North Carolina, and Virginia.

Despite the enormous publicity he attracted at the time, historians have almost entirely ignored Kasper. His story is nonetheless of considerable importance to our understanding of white resistance to racial change in the postwar era. Kasper's impact on massive resistance was complicated, both advancing and undermining its cause.

By turning a town where trouble had not been anticipated into a place where open revolt over racial integration erupted, Kasper transformed segregationist resistance, albeit briefly, into a formidable political force. Tennessee state authorities opposed the admission of black students to white schools on principle, but in practice were unwilling to challenge the constitutional authority of the Supreme Court. Organized resistance remained weak because of the reluctance of segregationist leaders to recruit lower-class whites to their cause. Defenders of Jim Crow understood that the success of their cause rested on their ability to sway northern public opinion on the race issue through rational intellectual argument. This necessitated their exclusion of lower-class whites, whose emotionally visceral reaction to integration, they feared, would translate into violence. Kasper in contrast drew on the power of white working-class fear and resentment to mount a grassroots insurgency against desegregation. Although his efforts ended in failure, his intervention made the integration process far more fraught than civil rights activists or local and state officials had foreseen.

While the arrest and incarceration of Kasper was a personal setback, it worked to the broader political advantage of segregationists. Kasper was the perfect foil for massive resistance leaders endeavoring to establish the political legitimacy of their cause. That a white southern jury should convict Kasper, they asserted, demonstrated that ordinary citizens within the region refused to tolerate lawless extremism on the race issue. Segregationists used this episode to show that white southerners were willing and able to root out the fanatics within their midst without federal intervention, an argument that helped them defeat a central component of a new civil rights bill.

The outcome of the school crisis may have strengthened the defense of Jim Crow at a national level, but it more seriously weakened it at the grassroots level. Many of the townspeople who at first rebelled against federal authority reevaluated the validity of massive resistance when forced to confront the consequences of their actions. Kasper unintentionally encouraged the white citizens of Clinton to acknowledge that the cost of uncompromising resistance to racial reform—school closures, economic instability, and the collapse of law and order—was not worth paying. It was for this reason that Clinton made history as the first southern community in which a black student graduated from a formerly all-white high school.

On a broader scale the Clinton crisis was also a portent of the ensuing decade of civil rights struggle. Historians cite the later confrontation over school integration in Little Rock as a watershed. David Garrow, for instance, notes that Little Rock attracted unprecedented attention from television and print media reporters, whose coverage of events contrasted the dignity of young black civil rights pioneers with the ugly prejudice of white mobs. National and international media attention created a groundswell of public support for desegregation that compelled the enforcement of federal authority.[2]

The scale of the emergency in Little Rock undoubtedly raised public consciousness of southern racism to a new level. While the Clinton disorder was more immediately contained, it nonetheless presaged later events in the Arkansas state capital. A number of renowned journalists, including David Halberstam, cut their teeth on the story. Sloan Wilson, author of the bestselling novel *The Man in the Gray Flannel Suit*, wrote a number of internationally syndicated stories on Clinton.[3] Edward R. Murrow also fronted a nationally broadcast documentary on the disorder. The unrest also made international news headlines. Newspapers not only in Europe but also in decolonizing nations in Asia and Africa ran photographs of the armed guardsmen escorting the black students through angry white picket crowds. Clinton therefore anticipated the media trend of exposing the disparities between the principles of freedom and democracy espoused by the United States and the persistence of racial prejudice. As one domestic black newspaper concluded, the unrest Kasper precipitated provided the Kremlin "twisted and dangerous propaganda fuel to feed the rest of the world."[4]

"Welcome to Clinton," read the roadside hoarding that greeted drivers as they reached the town, "A Wonderful Place to Live."[5] Before the fall of 1956, the community was a place that motorists passed through en route to another destination. Yet within the space of a few weeks, this small mill town had captured the attention of the world media.

Clinton is situated in Anderson County, close to the mining communities of the Cumberland Mountains and fifteen miles northwest of Knoxville. According to the 1950 census, the town had a population of less than four thousand. The small black community lived and labored on the social and economic margins of the town, specifically the segregated neighborhood of Foley Hill. Despite the strict observation of Jim Crow, race relations were relatively harmonious.[6]

The most serious issue of concern was the absence of a black high school. For years, African American students had to take a bus twenty-four miles north from Clinton to the black high school in La Follette. In December 1950, the National Association for the Advancement of Colored People (NAACP) filed suit on behalf of Joheather McSwain and five other black students to integrate the Clinton high school.[7] School authorities sought to anticipate the court decision by transferring African American students from the Grade D La Follette High School to the Grade A, but still segregated, Austin High School in Knoxville.

The efforts of the school board to provide a separate but equal education for black and white students at first appeared to have forestalled desegregation. On April 26, 1952, District Court Judge Robert L. Taylor ruled against the black plaintiffs. However, when the U.S. Supreme Court ruled two years later that school segregation was unconstitutional, the decision was overturned and the Anderson County school board was ordered to integrate the high school by the fall of 1956.[8]

The political omens appeared to indicate that there would be little resistance to the court order. Reaction to the *Brown* decision in Tennessee was more moderate than in other southern states. African Americans had been admitted to institutions of higher education since 1952, when the first black students registered at the University of Tennessee at Knoxville. Three years later, forty-five black students enrolled with little incident at the Robertson Junior High School in Oak Ridge. Incorporated in 1942, Oak Ridge was the location of an atomic energy center integral to the development of the Manhattan Project. Since its schools were outside the jurisdiction of the state public education system, the admission of the black pupils did not establish an immediate precedent for other schools. The peaceable implementation of desegregation nonetheless provided a practical example to state officials confronted by the Supreme Court mandate.[9]

There was indeed much hope that Tennessee authorities would promote a policy of compliance with the court ruling. Although legislators reaffirmed their commitment to segregated schools when they amended the state constitution in 1954, editorial reaction to *Brown* was unusually restrained. In a characteristic leader, the *Memphis Commercial Appeal* encouraged its readers to "approach this issue with calmness, reason, and a genuine spirit of cooperation."[10] Political restraint also prevailed in the 1954 gubernatorial race when racial moderate Frank Clement emphatically defeated his reactionary opponent. Clement established the progressive tone of his administration by vetoing four bills intended to remove state funds from integrated schools.[11] Further affirmation of the political restraint of state leaders came in 1956, when Senators Albert Gore and Estes Kefauver and Congressman Percy Priest refused to sign the Southern Manifesto, a declaration of resistance by southern legislators to the Supreme Court decision.[12]

Opponents of school desegregation were, by contrast, poorly organized. Politically, Tennessee was divided into three distinct sections: West, Middle, and East. Only in West Tennessee, which had more in common with Mississippi than with other parts of the state, was there a substantial mobilization of segregationist resistance. Even there, the forces of white resistance were too fractious to mount a united movement. Segregationists established so many competing organizations—the Tennessee Federation for Constitutional Government, the Tennessee Society to Maintain Segregation, the States' Rights Council of Tennessee—that none could command a strong support base. One newspaper cartoon captured the sense of helplessness among segregationists at their inability to withstand the *Brown* ruling. It depicted a man in a boat without a paddle forced by rapids with the words "integration flow" toward a precipitous waterfall.[13]

In his state address of January 1956, Governor Clement declared, "Tennessee is fortunate, and our people are to be commended, for the fact that there has been no physical violence and the good name of the State has not been blighted by an individual incident."[14] That note of optimism was about to be drowned out by the violent discord in Clinton.

As the first day of desegregated classes approached, the white citizens of Clinton appeared to have accepted the need for peaceful and orderly compliance. School authorities made a concerted attempt to calm the unease of white parents at the prospect of their sons and especially daughters sitting alongside African American students. Principal David Brittain arranged a series of meetings with both sections of the community during the summer months. His efforts seemed to have succeeded. On Monday, August 20, fifteen African Americans registered for school without incident.[15] The school was then closed for a week to allow teachers to attend a series of strategic planning sessions. "We have never heard anyone in Clinton say he wanted integration of students in the schools," asserted the editor of the local newspaper, "but we have heard a great many of the people say: 'We believe in the law. We will obey the ruling of the Court. We have no other lawful choice.'"[16]

However, the publicly compliant tone of city leaders could not entirely conceal the private misgivings of many white citizens. The townspeople were a potential army awaiting recruitment; all they needed was a commanding officer. He came to them in the form of the twenty-six-year-old John Kasper.

Kasper arrived in town late in the evening of Friday, August 24. Using the payphone at the Hoskins drug store on Main Street, he made a series of anonymous calls to local residents, encouraging them to attend an anti-integration meeting the following day. By Saturday morning, he had begun to stop people on the streets or call in person at their homes to publicize his cause. When word reached town elders, they sent a delegation to warn him not to obstruct the court order. A defiant Kasper held a small downtown rally on Sunday evening. Police arrested him on charges of vagrancy and attempting to incite a riot, before releasing him on bail.[17]

Classes at Clinton High School started as scheduled on Monday, August 27. The black students met with little resistance as they arrived at the school. A small number of white parents registered their protest by keeping their children out of classes. Some of the white students also organized a picket line, although most put down their placards and followed the black students into the school building when the bell sounded. The rest of the day passed without incident.[18]

The following morning, Kasper was cleared for lack of evidence of the charges against him. He wasted no time after his acquittal in confronting Principal Brittain, demanding that he "run the Negroes off or resign." Brittain stood his ground, reasserting his intention to implement the court order. In a climate of escalating tension, Kasper then organized a rally attended by several hundred townsfolk.[19]

Kasper had succeeded in igniting the flames of anger among the white citizens of Clinton, flames that soon fanned out of control. On the morning of Wednesday, August 29, he assembled a large crowd of angry protesters outside the high school. When the black students arrived, they were immediately set upon. One of them, Bobby Cain, attempted to protect himself with a pocketknife and was taken into police custody. The authorities took similar action to protect Eugene Gibson, a black teenager who had not enrolled at the high school but found himself in the wrong place at the wrong time and forced to flee from a gang of whites. The black students still in school had to be rescued from the mob by the campus football team, and then taken home under police escort.[20]

In an attempt to stem the violence, local officials later that day secured a temporary injunction restraining Kasper from further acts of public protest. U.S. marshals interrupted a rally in the courthouse square to read Kasper the restraining order and summon him to Knoxville to attend a hearing on a permanent injunction. To the cheers of his supporters, Kasper seized the papers and tore them to shreds, proclaiming as he did so that "no amount of injunctions, not even 10,000 of them, can stop something the people do not want and never will have." He was back on the picket line the following morning.[21]

The district court hearing took place over two days. Kasper denied he had advocated violence and defended his constitutional rights to freedom of speech and assembly. Nonetheless, on August 31, the court convicted him of contempt and sentenced him to one year in prison. A permanent injunction against interference with the desegregation of the high school was issued seven days later.[22]

On the night that followed Kasper's conviction, more than one thousand citizens assembled in the Clinton courthouse square. In the absence of Kasper, his political associate Asa Carter delivered a provocative address. "It's your duty as a Christian, Anglo-Saxon citizen to protect what your grandfathers gave you," exclaimed Carter. "The reason we don't have banana colored skin, kinky hair and thick lips is because of [Ku Klux Klan Grand Wizard] Nathan Bedford Forrest."[23] Inflamed by the speech, the crowd started to attack African American motorists passing through the town. As it marched through the streets, the mob shouted, "We want Kasper." The police proved powerless to dispel the rioters. Anderson County Sheriff Joe Owen was due to step down at midnight to make way for his newly elected successor, Glad Woodward. As a result, most of his deputies had not even bothered to report for duty.[24]

The unrest on Friday night was only a prelude to a weekend of violent disorder. On Saturday morning, the board of aldermen declared a state of emergency and issued a request to Governor Clement to restore order to the town or risk "bloodshed before the night is over." Clinton authorities also called up an auxiliary police force to control further disturbances in the event state aid failed to arrive.[25]

That evening an estimated two thousand citizens crowded into the courthouse square. When the mob attempted to storm the courthouse, the auxiliary police responded with a fusillade of tear gas grenades. The small band of special deputies could not withstand such assaults indefinitely; fortunately, they did not have to. As the crowd started to reassemble for a further attack, the Highway Patrol arrived on the scene and surrounded the square.

At noon the next day the National Guard assumed control of law and order in Clinton. Governor Clement sanctioned a massive demonstration of state military power: "Operation Law and Order" involved the use of seven tanks, three armed personnel carriers, and more than six hundred soldiers. Yet the crowd in the courthouse square that evening was actually larger than ever, up to three thousand according to one estimate. Violence once more erupted as members of the crowd started to throw firecrackers at passing cars and burned a cross on the schoolhouse lawn. National Guardsmen had to rescue an African American from the clutches of the mob.[26]

By the morning of Monday, September 3, an uneasy calm had settled over Clinton. National Guard Commander Joe Henry prevented further crowd trouble through the imposition of an evening curfew around the courthouse. Trouble continued to flare: cross burnings occurred both on the school campus and in the black section of town. Rioting also spread to the nearby community of Oliver Springs amid unfounded rumors that the local school there was also to be integrated. Nonetheless, as the week progressed the disturbances became more sporadic. School attendance rose steadily, from 324 students to 590. On September 11, the National Guard was withdrawn. Sheriff Woodward recruited a special force of two hundred citizens to maintain the renewed peace.[27]

The authorities had released Kasper on bond while Clinton was still in a state of siege. His attempts to launch a further counterattack on school desegregation proved unsuccessful because town officials denied him permission to hold further public rallies. Mounting frustration at his failure to rebuild his political momentum may have led him to take dramatic action. On September 26, a bomb exploded near the home of African American resident Ronald Hayden; no one was injured. Although it is uncertain whether Kasper was responsible for the attack, the renewal of terrorist violence shortly after his release from prison does not seem coincidental.[28]

The setbacks Kasper suffered in Clinton only encouraged him to open up new fronts in his counteroffensive against desegregation. He collaborated "very closely" with whites who resisted the admission of two black children to an elementary school in Clay, a small Kentucky mining town. The resultant disorder forced Governor A. B. Chandler to deploy more than two hundred National Guardsmen to enforce school integration.[29]

Kasper also attempted to stir dissent in Oak Ridge. His efforts to replicate the disorder in Clinton failed because most of the townspeople, black as well as white, were employees of the Atomic Energy Commission. Not only did this mean that local whites were more respectful of federal authority, but also it protected black parents who sent their children to desegregated schools from the sanctions often used by private employers. Local authorities moreover moved swiftly to neutralize Kasper. The police arrested him on September 24 on charges of sedition and incitement to riot, but only after a struggle in which Kasper repeatedly punched one of the arresting officers in the face before surrendering.[30]

Kasper stood trial in the Anderson County Criminal Court on Monday, November 5. Support for the segregationist leader remained strong among white Clintonians: a group of citizens seized the occasion of the trial to announce the start of John Kasper Week. The segregationist rose to the occasion, turning the courtroom into a stage on which he performed for his cheering followers. Throughout the trial, Kasper ignored the admonitions of the judge, interrupted his own counsel, and advised the district attorney how to prosecute his case. On November 20, after less than an hour of deliberation, the jury returned a verdict of not guilty on both counts. Kasper leaned back in his chair and smiled as the courtroom erupted in applause. Outside the courthouse, he told reporters he would step up his opposition to integration.[31]

The acquittal of Kasper coincided with renewed unrest at the high school. The black students suffered constant harassment; ink was spilled in their books, feet tripped them in corridors. Their assailants were members of the Tennessee White Citizens' Youth Council, chartered by Kasper after the conclusion of his trial. Black parents withdrew their children when the school refused to promise their protection. They also angrily rebuffed an offer to pay the tuition and transportation costs of any black student willing to return to Austin High.[32]

Confronted with a deteriorating situation, school officials contacted the U.S. Justice Department on December 3. Attorney General Herbert Brownell offered that the FBI would arrest and prosecute anyone who attempted to obstruct integration.[33] The announcement came too late to prevent a vicious assault on a white clergyman who had persuaded the black students to return to school. In an emotional sermon on Sunday, December 2, Baptist minister Paul W. Turner declared to his congregation that the black students had "the legal and the moral right to attend [school] without heckling or obstruction." Two days later, Turner escorted the children from Foley Hill. As soon as the students were inside the school, a mob brutally assaulted Turner. When the wife of Principal Brittain was hurt in a separate attack, he announced the closure of the school.[34]

Ironically, this desperate state of affairs promoted a stronger consensus in support of desegregation. The beating of Reverend Turner occurred on the same day as a local election. A segregationist organization known as the Clinton Committee for Honest, Forthright Government had run strong races for both mayor and the board of aldermen. Public shame over the assault of a clergyman helped sway the election away from hard-line opinion. Moderate mayoral candidate T. Lawrence Seeber secured almost four times the vote of his segregationist rival James Meredith. "He was a symbol," one citizen observed of Turner. "What happened, happened to us all—and it waked us up."[35]

The school crisis had reached a decisive turning point. The morning after the election, U.S. marshals arrested fifteen people for failure to comply with the injunction against anti-integrationist protests. Five days later, on December 10, the high school reopened. However, one of the black students was not in class. The family of Jo Ann Allen had faced too many threats from white racists and had decided to leave Clinton for a fresh start in Los Angeles.[36] White students continued to threaten and intimidate their remaining black classmates. The most dramatic incident occurred on February 14, 1957, when a dynamite blast on Foley Hill injured an African American woman and her infant.[37]

Days later, another terrorist incident that apparently bore Kasper's imprint underlined his determination to continue his crusade. On February 19, 1957, jazz musician Louis Armstrong appeared in concert at Chilhowee Park in Knoxville. Afraid of compromising his commercial status, Armstrong had assumed a publicly apolitical position on the race issue, a decision that led civil rights organizations to call for a boycott of his concert tour. The presence of two white musicians in his band nonetheless imparted an implicit message of interracial fellowship. The band was in full swing when dynamite hurled from a passing car exploded near the stage. "That's all right, folks," Armstrong calmed the unsettled crowd. "It's just the phone." Suspicion focused on Kasper, who had spent the past several weeks publicly protesting the decision of Knoxville's mayor, the aptly named Jack Dance, to permit mixed-race performances. Although there was insufficient evidence for authorities to arrest him, the timing of the incident seems more than happenstance. Kasper may have been imitating his associate Asa Carter, who a year earlier orchestrated an assault on another black musician, crooner Nat "King" Cole, in Birmingham, Alabama.[38]

It was a last defiant gesture. On February 26, District Court Judge Robert L. Taylor ordered the arrest of Kasper for continued obstruction of school integration. For the rest of the academic year the high school kept its doors open and the students stayed in class. On May 17, 1957, Bobby Cain became the first black student to graduate from a formerly all-white public high school in the South. That fall, two other African American students, Jo Ann White and Nevie Barton, registered as freshmen.[39]

The torrents of racial unrest had receded, but why had they swept so intensely through this small southern town? Who was John Kasper, the stranger who suddenly appeared on the eve of school desegregation and assumed control of public opposition?

Frederick John Kasper, Jr., was born on October 21, 1929, in Merchantville, New Jersey. His father, Frederick, was a graduate of the Massachusetts Institute of Technology who worked as a combustion engineer; his mother, Rose, was a housewife. A rebellious child, Kasper passed through a succession of educational establishments before serving briefly in the merchant marines. At age nineteen, he registered for the draft, but was classified physically and mentally unfit for service.[40]

Kasper found a more focused sense of purpose in September 1949, when he started pursuing a degree in English and philosophy at Columbia University. There, he developed an obsession with the disgraced poet Ezra Pound, whom authorities had convicted of treason for delivering a series of pro-fascist broadcasts during World War II and detained at the St. Elizabeths Hospital in Washington, D.C. Kasper started first to correspond with Pound, then to visit him in person. The journey from New York to Washington assumed the characteristics of a pilgrimage: when he reached his destination, Kasper would sit for hours at the feet of his political and spiritual mentor. In his correspondence, Kasper occasionally addressed Pound affectionately as "Grandpaw"; more commonly, he called him "Master." A letter written by Kasper to Pound on the poet's sixtieth birthday illustrates the intensity of this infatuation. "You are the mighty. You are god and the greatest of all men. You are MASTER, SAGE, WISDOM, POWER. You move all men to deed, deeds that are wise and virtuous. I praise you, I praise you, I praise you. I worship you. I love you."[41] The letter seems to contain homoerotic overtones, and it is indeed a possibility that Kasper was sexually drawn to Pound. In 1946, he had been briefly hospitalized at a psychiatric unit in Philadelphia, where doctors diagnosed him as suffering from "early homosexuality" and "general neurotic behavior."[42]

Kasper was initially inspired to research and write a doctoral thesis on Pound. However, he had no intention of producing the impartial critical analysis needed to meet the standards of the academy. On the contrary, he invited the poet to decide on the focus and approach of the proposed thesis to an extent that would reduce him to little more than a ghostwriter. "I would like you to choose a study which you think might serve to clarify or elaborate some phase of your work which has not received the attention it deserves," Kasper wrote Pound. Caught up in the excitement of becoming the literary emissary of the poet, he continued with a declaration that "I am willing to learn as many languages as you demand. To study history thoroughly, to learn calculus or how to make atomic bombs, if necessary."[43]

While Kasper was clearly prepared to do more than meet the standard entry requirements for most graduate schools, he soon abandoned his academic ambitions. "I doubt if I'll go on for the stinkin' Ph.D.," he confessed to Pound, "and will, instead, try to get my hooks into everyone of any importance and a little later, possibly find some effective method of communication."[44] Kasper soon settled on the world of publishing as the most appropriate means to propagate the political philosophy of his mentor. In 1952, a year after he graduated from Columbia, Kasper became proprietor of the Make-It-New Bookshop in Greenwich Village. The titles lining its shelves, including *Mein Kampf* and the *Protocols of the Learned Elders of Zion*, bore the explicit influence of Pound. In collaboration with David Horton, Kasper also established the Square Dollar Series, cheap paperback editions of titles written or recommended by Pound.[45]

Kasper also started to participate in direct action politics. In 1951, a U.S. district court had found Julius and Ethel Rosenberg guilty of atomic espionage and sentenced them to death. Supporters mounted an appeal for executive clemency. Shots taken by Magnum photographer Elliott Erwitt in 1953 show Kasper among a small band of counter-protesters standing outside the White House. In one of these images, Kasper smiles with characteristic insouciance as he holds a placard proclaiming "Burn All Reds." The arrest and conviction of two Jewish Communists for passing state secrets no doubt proved to Kasper the substance of Pound's anti-Semitic conspiracy theories.[46]

By 1956, Kasper had moved his business interests to Washington in order to be closer to his mentor. The ties between the two men strengthened further because of two incidents that occurred that same year.

First, Kasper attempted to secure the release of Pound from detention. In March 1956, he appeared as a witness at hearings held by a Senate Committee on the Alaska Mental Health Enabling Bill, which proposed the improved provision of psychiatric treatment facilities in America's northernmost state. Far-right organizations feared that the bill was an insidious attempt to establish concentration camps where the federal government would incarcerate political dissidents. Alaska, they claimed, would become to the United States what Siberia was to the Soviet Union. Kasper used the example of Pound to demonstrate how the authorities already used what he claimed was a false diagnosis of insanity to imprison political nonconformists. "There have been many people who have objected in history to current practices, current ideologies, and so on, and were called insane at the time, and of course, history vindicated them." While the incarceration of Pound provided the immediate context for this tirade against psychiatry, Kasper's own unhappy experience as a mental patient must also have influenced his outspoken opinions.[47]

Second, Kasper started to mount his resistance to the racial integration of public schools. There is no consensus among those who have studied the relationship between Pound and Kasper as to whether the younger man acted as the proxy of the incarcerated poet in resisting racial integration. Opinions range from those authors who absolve Pound of all responsibility to those who claim Kasper was little more than an automaton whose conduct the poet directed by remote control from his hospital room.

Those least inclined to hold the poet accountable are usually motivated by a desire to draw a distinct line between Pound as a man and Pound as an artist, protecting the reputation of his work by deemphasizing his racial and ethnic prejudices. Humphrey Carpenter, for instance, cites a letter written by Pound in which he stated that he was "vurry sceptic re/K's dislike of Afroamericans."[48]

Other authors take the position that Kasper was a young and impressionable person whom Pound willfully manipulated. Journalist Drew Pearson asserted that Kasper was a "confused young man" susceptible to the influence of the poet, a position later supported by Noel Stock, who deemed the young agitator "a poor waif who'd been exploited by Pound."[49] Contemporaries of Kasper also portrayed the poet as a Svengali who bent Kasper to his will. George Lincoln Rockwell, leader of the American Nazi Party, claimed Kasper received "almost daily letters of instruction" from Pound.[50] The FBI also suspected the poet. J. Edgar Hoover cited the racial disorder in Clinton as evidence of the threat Pound posed if the authorities released him from St. Elizabeths.[51]

It is difficult to determine the relative merits of the arguments about the relationship between Pound and Kasper because the evidence is both contradictory and elusive. Whether Kasper acted on the precise instructions of Pound is unclear since the communications between the two men during the late 1950s cannot be traced. Letters written by the poet to other correspondents at the time of the Clinton incident are also too ambiguous to offer precise answers. A letter of December 1956 suggests that Pound was strategically opposed to Kasper's participation in the crisis, believing there were better means to serve his economic agenda against Jews. "Kasper defeated, same as South was in 1864, cause mind diverted from money and taxes, customs, onto local issue having no broad and defensible theoretical basis." However, only days earlier, Pound had applauded Kasper for turning his trial for sedition into an opportunity to get "a little publicity for the NAACP being run by kikes not by coons."[52]

What is certain is that Pound had a profound influence in shaping the intensity and focus of his young acolyte's prejudices. The letters that Kasper wrote to Pound during the early 1950s suggest that his actions in Clinton advanced the interests of his mentor even if he had not based them on actual instruction.

The most important influence that Pound had on Kasper was to impart his conspiratorial interpretation of history. Pound believed that a cabal of Jews covertly manipulated the course of world events to their own political and financial advantage. Only a small number of people possessed the insight to see how this secret hand shaped history. It was the responsibility of these enlightened individuals to reveal the truth to others. Kasper assumed this role when he claimed to his supporters that school desegregation was part of a "communist-jewish-international finance conspiracy against white America."[53]

Pound also exposed Kasper to the influence of other intellectuals, most importantly, the nineteenth-century Swiss naturalist Louis Agassiz. In the 1840s, Agassiz moved to the United States, where he took up a teaching position at Harvard University. Having never met a black person in his homeland, Agassiz was shocked and repelled by his first encounters with African American servants. The experience shaped his theory of polygenesis, which, contrary to Darwinism, maintained that blacks and whites were separate species who evolved from different centers of origin. Although Agassiz insisted he based his ideas on a dispassionate analysis of scientific fact, his personal fear of miscegenation was a profound influence. "Social equality I deem at all time impracticable," he stated. "The production of halfbreeds is as much a sin against nature, as incest in a civilized community is a sin against purity of character."[54] Kasper published a collection of writings by the naturalist as part of his Square Dollar Series.[55] Explaining the influence of Agassiz on his own racial philosophy, the segregationist recited his aphorism "You must not trifle with nature."[56] The spirit of Agassiz also appears to have guided his pen when he wrote his polemic "Segregation or Death," with its references to the emasculating impact that miscegenation would have on future generations. Any attempt to "obscure or obliterate natural distinctions in Nature," Kasper warned, would precipitate racial catastrophe, "sterility, physical weakness and sloth, and finally effacement from life's intricate patterns."[57]

Pound's influence is further apparent in the imitative language publicly adopted by Kasper. One of the handbills he distributed during the Clinton desegregation crisis directly imitated the *Blast* manifesto issued by Pound and Wyndham Lewis in 1914: "Now damn all race-mixers/The stink: Roose, Harry and Ike/God bless Jeff/Jax and John Adams/Also Abe/Loathe carpet-bag/Despise scalawag/Hate mongrelizer."[58] A pamphlet published by the Seaboard White Citizens' Council similarly emulated the distinctive style of Pound. In it, Kasper poured scorn on an elaborate array of persons whom he blamed for the problems besetting American society. The banes of his existence included "freaks, golf players, poodle dogs, hot-eyed Socialists, Fabians, scum, mold on top of the omelette . . . liars for hire, the press gang, degenerate liberals crying for the petrefaction of putrefaction." Kasper plagiarized extensively from Pound in constructing this list of targets, particularly *Cantos XIV* and *XV*:

> n and the press gang
>   And those who had lied for hire . . .
>   . . . a circle of lady golfers . . .
> And the Fabians crying for the petre-
> faction of putrefaction . . . [59]

By the time Kasper arrived in Clinton, he had already garnered a reputation as a racial agitator. His skills as an orator soon established him as a popular speaker at Ku Klux Klan rallies across the Southeast, although he never actually became a member of the hooded order. Instead, Kasper enlisted the support of Asa Carter in chartering his own organization, the Seaboard White Citizens' Council.[60] The council wasted no time in taking the fight to its political enemies. In July 1956, only a month after it was founded, Kasper and his associates became the principal suspects in an FBI investigation of cross burnings at the homes of political figures, including Chief Justice Earl Warren, Solicitor General Simon Sobeloff, and New York Senator Herbert Lehman.[61] By then, Kasper had also embarked on a series of "brief scouting trips" in the Upper South, searching for an ideal target to launch an attack on school integration.

His choice was Charlottesville, Virginia.[62] Kasper established a local chapter of the Seaboard White Citizens' Council there in the summer of 1955. He also made his presence known by distributing a pamphlet entitled "Virginians on Guard" to every member of the state general assembly. The pamphlet included a fifty-point program for resisting desegregation, the centerpiece of which was a call to abolish compulsory school attendance laws. Working alongside Asa Carter, Kasper also launched a campaign of intimidation against black and white civil rights activists. Interrupting a meeting of the Virginia Council on Human Relations, he proclaimed to its startled members, "We in the Citizens' Council have declared war on you." When a cross was burned on the lawn of liberal activist Sarah Patton Boyle, Kasper became the primary suspect. Although he was never charged for that offense, police did arrest him for distributing hate literature.[63]

While in Charlottesville, Kasper chanced upon a newspaper story about the imminent desegregation of the high school in Clinton, Tennessee. He sensed an ideal opportunity to mount a resistance movement that would inspire the rest of the South to rise up against racial reform.[64]

Within days of his arrival, Kasper had aroused an apparently peaceable community into violent rebellion. Although the people of Clinton opposed integration in principle, they initially felt there was no alternative but to accept it in practice. A white student interviewed by the CBS show *See It Now* articulated this sense of fatalism in reciting the counsel of his football coach: "All through your life you're going to come up against things you don't like, but . . . you're going to have to accept them anyway and just make the best of them that you can."[65]

Kasper was able to convince the white citizens of Clinton otherwise. The reason for his success in mobilizing grassroots resistance to integration is not immediately apparent. Kasper did not cut a particularly impressive or imposing figure. Although he stood six feet four inches tall, he had a tendency to stoop. The intensity of his gaze was offset by the softness of his speech—audiences had to lean close to hear him—and his sometimes faltering and repetitive use of language. "To hear on the platform this man," observed one reporter, "call the Supreme Court justices Communists and traitors is like hearing an angel-faced boy mutter obscenities behind teacher's back."[66]

Kasper's appeal therefore rested as much in his political doctrine as in the charisma of his personality. Despite the influence of Pound, he drew inspiration from not only European fascism, but also American political tradition. The politics he preached can be defined as a form of reactionary populism. His rhetoric comprised three core elements: anti-elitism, class resentment, and anti-Semitism.[67]

Numerous commentators, both at the time and in retrospect, claimed that class rather than racial issues were the real cause of the Clinton school crisis. Journalist David Halberstam asserted that "the hatred of Negroes is only a superficial symptom of the deeper resentment" of working-class whites toward the political and civic leadership of the town, citing the opinion of one Kasper supporter that they had ruled "the roost too long" and "thought they were better than we are." Political author Stan Opotowsky concurred with this assessment, attributing the disorder to an impoverished populace taking out its frustrations on a commercial elite "who were so tough on credit in their stores and so fancy in their dressed-up ways." Later historians of the crisis have similarly minimized the importance of race, interpreting the admission of black students to the high school as little more than a pretext for poor whites to vent their bitter hatred of the local elite.[68]

Class tensions were a serious issue in Clinton. White employees had twice struck in recent times for improvements in wages and working conditions, first at the local hosiery factory in 1941 and little more than a year before the school crisis at the town telephone exchange. A downturn in the mining industry had led to the layoff of many workers. Some members of the laboring class were therefore spoiling for an opportunity to exact revenge on the business elite they blamed for their misfortunes.[69]

The social order may have been unstable before the school crisis, but it had not collapsed into complete chaos. While some commentators treated class and race as mutually exclusive factors, it was the interaction of these unstable elements that created an explosive chemical reaction in Clinton. Many local whites possessed deep racial prejudices toward African Americans. The construction of the Oak Ridge atomic energy center in the 1940s lured thousands of workers to Anderson County. Most of them were migrants from the Deep South who brought their fear and hatred of blacks with them. The racial anxieties of these whites became more acute because of an economic recession. As their economic status declined, all that separated them from African Americans were the social privileges that whiteness conferred. Desegregation therefore threatened to eliminate whatever advantages poorer whites believed they still had over blacks. It was this combination of actual economic hardship and anticipated social injury that made them so willing to support Kasper.

Kasper may not have been the most charismatic political leader but he did understand how to channel the anger and resentment of ordinary people. His mobilization of a grassroots movement empowered a white working class that was otherwise without political representation. Segregationist leaders in Tennessee repudiated a strategy of massive resistance. The Tennessee Federation for Constitutional Government—the state's equivalent to a Citizens' Council—recruited its members from the middle class to guard against infiltration from "undesirable elements."[70] Although this policy limited its power base, it represented a rational strategic decision on the part of Federation leaders. The ease with which a marginal outsider like Kasper stirred violent unrest against school desegregation shows that many working-class whites were prepared to take the law into their own hands. By restricting its membership, the Federation attempted to protect the segregationist resistance from spinning out of control.

At the same time, many working-class whites felt betrayed and alienated by massive resistance leaders. Kasper positioned himself as a political rival to the Tennessee Federation for Constitutional Government by cultivating the very people it sought to exclude from its ranks. Most of his support came from the lower classes of the local community, "hard, desperate work-bitten" men and women who toiled as mill hands and farm laborers.[71] A survey of local white parents conducted at the time of the school crisis underlined the scale of their deprivation. Twenty-one percent of parents did not have even an elementary school education, only 21 percent had graduated from high school, and a paltry 6 percent had a college degree.[72] At his trial, Kasper referred affectionately to his followers as "hillbillies" and "rednecks" who were oppressed by the cultural superiority of "highbrows."[73] He also articulated the theme at a White Citizens' Council meeting in Kentucky. "They underestimated the intelligence and the resistance power of the mountain folk here. They thought, well maybe they were dealing, with a group of hillbillies, rednecks, crackers, but those are the real people of the United States, make no mistake about it."[74] This rhetoric resonated with the resurgence of anti-intellectualism in American political culture during the 1950s. Kasper tapped into a broader public discourse that disparaged the educated elite as "eggheads" who had little grasp of the practical realities of life and subscribed to treasonous political philosophies.[75] The fact that Kasper had an Ivy League education was an irony apparently lost on his audience and himself.

Kasper nonetheless had a more immediate appeal to working-class whites than the rather aloof segregationist leadership offered by the Tennessee Federation for Constitutional Government. In contrast to the defensiveness of mainstream segregationist leaders, Kasper spoke in a language that resonated more immediately with his supporters. Instead of abstract arguments about states' rights, he made raw appeals to the racial pride and prejudice of ordinary whites. Rather than being defensive about white supremacy, he was openly defiant. Kasper represented the school crisis as a life or death struggle that necessitated "every type of resistance." His fighting talk instilled many ordinary whites with the conviction that they could defend their community against federally enforced reform. Kasper provided a people otherwise lacking social capital with a sense of inclusion, connectedness, and purpose. "Before he came I knew I didn't like it," Earl Bullock observed of school desegregation, "but I didn't know what I could do." Kasper convinced him that there was an alternate course of action: Bullock became one of the eighteen people later arrested for disobeying the injunction against interfering with the admission of the black students to the high school.[76]

Kasper emboldened the white citizens of Clinton to believe that they had not only the political strength but also the moral right to resist desegregation. His appeals to popular sovereignty were a recurrent theme of the rallies in the courthouse square. In speech after speech, Kasper emphasized the importance of direct democracy, calling on his supporters to reclaim political power from the forces of tyranny and oppression: "We need all the rabble rousers we can get. We want trouble and we want it everywhere. We need a band of roving patriots. A collapse of law and order is near at hand."[77] This rallying cry suggests that, while he stood at the opposite end of the political spectrum, Kasper shared with civil rights strategists the conviction that the creation of a dramatic political crisis was the surest means of accomplishing his political goals. In a manner reminiscent of Bryant Bowles in Milford, Kasper also manipulated the insularity of a remote small town by emphasizing the external threat to local autonomy. Integration, he insisted, was a conspiracy by the northeastern urban elite to impose their own cultural norms on the rural folk of the South. This cadre of liberal politicians and unelected judicial officials was attempting to exclude white southerners from the political process and thereby impose autocratic control over the entire country. According to Kasper, the ordinary decent citizens of southern communities such as Clinton must resist these despots and return power to the people. As he asserted, "more than 75% of the present Federal judiciary should be tried for treason to the American people, for treason to the Constitution of the United States."[78] Kasper therefore encouraged his supporters to see their parochial self-interest in protecting racial segregation as a patriotic endeavor to restore democracy to the nation.

One of the most astute tactical moves Kasper made was to mobilize white students in opposition to the admission of African Americans. Entrusting responsibility for white resistance to the students made strategic sense since they were the people most immediately threatened by desegregation. Kasper anticipated that "If the white kids will run the Negroes out as they appear in the schools, there will be no integration regardless to the mandates of Federal courts."[79] To this end, in November 1956 he chartered the Tennessee White Citizens' Youth Council. Under the leadership of seventeen-year-old Carolyn Hutton, it mustered a membership of more than one hundred students. With the black students already admitted to classes, the council assumed responsibility for making conditions so unbearable that they would withdraw their enrollment. It launched a campaign of verbal and physical intimidation, tripping and pushing the students in corridors and defacing their desktops and books.[80]

There was a paradoxical element to the use of white students. On the one hand, Kasper took advantage of the antiauthoritarianism of 1950s youth culture to encourage the students to defy the federal court and the town authorities who ordered them to comply with its decision. Kasper succeeded in enlisting the support of the students by according them a respect that they did not receive from their elders, encouraging them to give voice to their resentment at the imposition of racial reform. On the other hand, the rebellion of the students served a socially reactionary agenda. For several weeks, the Tennessee White Citizens' Youth Council succeeded in making conditions miserable for the African American students. However, its fortunes relied on the strength of segregationist resistance in the larger community. The arrest of white adult leaders and the reaction against the assault on Reverend Turner in December 1956 fatally undermined it.

The second core element of Kasper's political philosophy was anti-Semitism. Kasper attempted to persuade his credulous audience that the principal members of the corrupt overeducated elite that threatened their autonomy were all Jewish. The notion that a secret cabal of Jewish Communists covertly masterminded the civil rights movement was a common strain in segregationist rhetoric. Kasper was nonetheless incomparable in terms of the sheer violent intensity of his animus toward Jews.

As soon as Kasper arrived in Clinton, there followed a massive influx of anti-Semitic hate sheets such as the *American Nationalist*.[81] In a caustic diatribe of his own entitled "Segregation or Death," Kasper claimed that Jews had clandestinely assumed control of the apparatus of political power in the United States, which they were using as a means to promote the mongrelization of the races. A cartoon of a snake with the head of a stereo-typically Jewish male illustrated the supposedly surreptitious character of the Zionist plot against the United States, its body slithering through the White House, Congress, and the Supreme Court and wrapping around the headquarters of the United Nations. According to Kasper, the individuals, organizations, and institutions that promoted racial integration were either Jewish or under the financial and political control of Jews. The NAACP, he insisted, did not represent the opinion of African Americans, most of whom accepted segregation as the natural social order, but rather acted on the instructions of its Jewish paymasters. Judge Taylor and Principal Brittain were also part of the Zionist conspiracy; so too was President Dwight Eisenhower. The sheer scale of this plot to undermine the democratic foundations of the United States necessitated drastic measures. Kasper asserted that three-quarters of the federal judiciary attempting to force integration on the South were Jews who should be hanged for treason in front of the White House. The region and indeed the entire country would not be securely protected until it had ensured "the complete legal disenfranchisement and legal expulsion of the Jew from American national life."[82]

Why were so many people willing to believe the absurd accusations made by Kasper? One explanation is that many of the men and women who supported him had never met a Jew. In the absence of a local Jewish community, most people based their understanding of Jews on cultural stereotypes. Working within an ethnically homogeneous community, it was relatively easy for Kasper to portray Jews as an insidious alien force that threatened Clinton from the outside. Another reason why the anti-Semitic rhetoric of Kasper resonated with the crowds in the courthouse square is that it provided them with a sense of empowerment. Kasper appeared to impart a secret truth to the white citizens of Clinton that the political and civic leadership had concealed. Far from protecting ordinary whites against racial integration, southern politicians were "for political reasons, fear of economic reprisals (probably mortgaged to the hilt to Jews personally) and red-newspaper smear" deliberately "suppressing, either through ignorance or fear, the facts concerning the jewish peril."[83] In claiming to have uncovered the hidden truth about a Jewish plot, Kasper successfully exploited the alienation from mainstream political power felt by local whites.

Ironically, while the immediate focus of the crisis in Clinton was the integration of the local high school, Kasper made little direct reference to the supposed racial threat that African Americans posed to the white community. Kasper attributed school desegregation to a conspiracy by Jewish Communists. By contrast, he assumed that most blacks accepted their place within the racial hierarchy. This conviction that blacks also believed in the separation of the races is illustrated by a handbill distributed by Kasper, which included a doctored photograph of African American GIs kissing white women as a warning of the dangers of integration. Underneath were the words, "Genuine White Folks don't want it. Civilized Nigras don't want it. White people, this could be your daughter. Colored people, this could be your son!"[84] Since, according to Kasper, most African Americans accepted segregation, it followed that the minority who were involved in civil rights activism had been lured into doing so by an outside force. Kasper denied black activists any agency by claiming that they were nothing more than political instruments manipulated by Jewish conspirators.

Although African Americans who attempted to integrate public facilities were only the pawns of Jews, this did not, in the opinion of Kasper, prevent them from being a danger that had to be stopped, by whatever means were necessary. "I do not hate Negroes," Kasper once claimed, "but I believe that for the progress of the white and Negro races this is best accomplished by separate institutions, based on a particular destiny of the separate races." African Americans who understood their subordinate status within the southern social order therefore need not fear whites. As Kasper coarsely asserted, "We don't hate the good nigger." However, the "bad" African American who dared to transgress the racial boundaries imposed by whites faced brutal reprisal.[85]

For all his success in rousing white resistance, Kasper had created more enemies than allies. His trial exposed the opposition of many segregationists to the militant tactics he employed in Clinton. Massive resistance leaders perceived Kasper as a more serious political threat than Bryant Bowles. The fact that Bowles had led a rebellion against school desegregation outside the South was a significant factor. Kasper was an outsider who had, by crossing the Mason-Dixon Line, intruded on what southern segregationists perceived as their jurisdiction. The threat he posed to the political credibility of the massive resistance movement was therefore more immediate than was the case with Bowles.

The tension between militants and mainstream segregationists had a potentially destabilizing impact on massive resistance. Yet segregationist leaders turned the situation to their political advantage by citing the arrest and imprisonment of the lawless radical Kasper as evidence that most white southerners were responsible citizens with the highest regard for law and order.

Segregationist leaders assiduously cultivated an image of public respectability by moderating the rhetoric of racial extremism and disavowing violent opposition to the law. They appealed to issues of high political principle by placing their emphasis on constitutional arguments about states' rights. The name of the foremost segregationist organization within the state—the Tennessee Federation for Constitutional Government—clearly reflected this strategy. The anarchic lawlessness of Kasper therefore threatened to compromise them politically. Segregationists such as the Federation feared that his confrontational tactics could prove disastrously counterproductive, alienating the northern public and provoking the federal government into more forceful implementation of racial integration. Desperate to protect their already tenuous ability to operate within legitimate political discourse, they attempted to purge the dangerous militant from their ranks.

Kasper endeavored to enlist support for his defense by portraying himself as the political victim of state censorship. "Our struggle here," he asserted, "is to regain free speech, freedom of assembly, right to petition for redress of grievances guaranteed by the U.S. Constitution." Kasper made political capital out of cold war tensions. The political establishment feared that the Soviet Union would use southern racism to condemn as hypocrisy American claims to leadership of the free world. Kasper inverted this argument by claiming that the deliberate abuse of segregationists' constitutional rights had turned the United States into a Soviet-style dictatorship: "There's no difference between that and what exists behind the Iron Curtain."[86]

These claims met with a positive response among militant white supremacists. Racial extremists honored Kasper as a martyr who had suffered arrest for his fearless leadership against federal tyranny. The Seaboard White Citizens' Council used the example of its leader's political sacrifice to recruit new members: "They had to call out the U.S. Army with fixed bayonets and their TANKS to prevent the rise of the Christian American people in their wrath when John Kasper did HIS bit to alert them to the menace of Jew-Communist integration!!"[87] According to this interpretation, Kasper was a daring advocate of democracy who had inspired the white citizens of Clinton to use their constitutional rights to free speech and assembly in protest at the judicial dictatorship of the Supreme Court. The real enemy to individual freedom was not the man who threatened and intimidated black students, but the state authorities who sanctioned military force to suppress segregationist dissent. Another radical publication, *The White Sentinel*, evoked bitter memories of the southern past to condemn the repressive use of troops and unwarranted arrest of Kasper. Above an image of National Guardsmen using bayonets to restrain white civilians it ran the headline "Reconstruction Days Are Here Again."[88]

However, most southern politicians and newspapermen approved the use of troops to contain the rioting. Governor Clement eased concerns by emphasizing that the National Guard was installed to restore law and order, not to enforce integration.[89] According to the *Memphis Commercial Appeal*, the disturbances in Clinton were "a disgrace to Tennessee and a challenge to its sovereign authority."[90]

Southern political leaders moved promptly to repair the public relations damage Kasper caused. While reaffirming their opposition to the Supreme Court decision, they disavowed violence as a solution. The inflammatory rhetoric of Kasper, they feared, would provide political ammunition to their opponents who wanted to portray all segregationists as irrational bigots. As one prominent segregationist asserted, "The day John Kasper crossed the Mason-Dixon line, it set the cause of white supremacy back twenty years."[91] Another segregationist leader, Jack Kershaw, vice president of the Tennessee Federation for Constitutional Government, had traveled to Clinton in an attempt to dissuade the townspeople from taking up arms. On the day that the tanks drove into town, "the folks had gone after their guns & were getting ready to fight," a situation that would have caused not only personal injury but also public relations damage to the segregationist movement. Kershaw succeeded in persuading local whites to leave their weapons at home, although this still did not prevent violence.[92] In reaction to the unrest, Kershaw attempted to reclaim the moral high ground by asserting that until Kasper appeared in Clinton, "Our relations with Negroes have always been peaceful," far more so than violent racial confrontations in northern cities such as Chicago and Detroit.[93]

Political leaders in other parts of the South also moved swiftly to contain the trouble Kasper caused within Tennessee. Citizens' Councils across the region issued public statements dissociating themselves from him. Mississippi Governor James P. Coleman invoked a law prohibiting "fomenting and agitation of litigation" to prevent Kasper from speaking in his state. Alabama state senator Sam Engelhardt took similarly preventive action by imposing close surveillance on Kasper and his associates.[94] Segregationist leaders were also at pains to emphasize that Kasper was not a citizen of Clinton, nor even of the South, but was instead an "outside agitator" who used the integration crisis to advance his own personal agenda. So determined were some southern leaders to distance themselves from Kasper that they accused him of being a double agent planted by the NAACP to discredit the segregationist movement.[95]

It was therefore clear from the outset of the district court trial that the segregationist leadership saw Kasper as a serious political liability. The Tennessee Federation for Constitutional Government established a Freedom for Clinton Fund to pay for the defense costs of all the accused with the exception of Kasper. The defense team financed by the Federation also moved unsuccessfully for a separate trial. Their clients, they insisted, had no political affiliation with Kasper and should not be publicly associated with him lest it prejudice their defense.[96] Despite this deliberate attempt to isolate him, Kasper appeared confident that he would be acquitted. "When we're free here," he told reporters, "we're going to move on." The inclusive language with which he referred to the segregationist movement concealed his own marginalized status within it. Interviewed by a television reporter, Kasper asserted that he had the covert support of senior politicians in Washington. "There are some so-called big shots, if you want to put it that way, who are friendly to our cause." When asked to identify these individuals, however, he suddenly became evasive.[97]

Ironically, it was northern liberals rather than southern conservatives who offered their legal support to Kasper. The American Civil Liberties Union (ACLU) had intervened in the conflict between Kasper and the authorities following his conviction for defying a restraining order in August 1956. ACLU activists defended the constitutional rights of white racists on the grounds that any infringement of freedom of speech and assembly constituted a potential threat to the personal autonomy of all American citizens. The ACLU deliberated whether the language of the restraining order had been so "dangerously broadened" that it infringed on Kasper's First Amendment rights to freedom of speech and assembly. It focused in particular on the prohibition that the court imposed on participation in a picket line outside the school and on membership in the White Citizens' Council. However, on this occasion the ACLU decided not to take action. It concluded that the court had not violated the constitutional rights of Kasper since he had declined his entitlement to a jury trial.[98]

During his second contempt of court case, Kasper faced the same judge who had convicted him ten months earlier. He therefore calculated that his best chance of acquittal was a trial by jury. This removed the obstacle that had prevented the ACLU from participating in the first case. The organization issued a statement that the injunction against Kasper violated his freedom of speech and assembly. Its criticisms concentrated on the ban against picketing outside the school, which the ACLU claimed was a legitimate form of protest so long as the demonstrators did not take overt action to obstruct the admission of the black students. "Without direct incitement to definite acts of individual or joint obstructiveness or interference, coupled with a clear and present danger that these acts will take place immediately, the injunction is too broad and interferes with free speech."[99]

The decision of the ACLU to represent Kasper drew strong criticism from numerous leaders within the civil rights movement, most conspicuously A. Philip Randolph, who accused it of having gone "too far."[100] The ACLU appeared not to have understood the extent to which white picketers outside the school used intimidation and force to impede the admission of the African American students. Whatever the merits of its decision to support Kasper, the resultant controversy piqued even greater public interest in the case.

The trial commenced on July 8, 1957. By the time the case reached court, one of the original eighteen defendants had died and charges against six others had been dismissed.[101] The occupational status of the men and women who did stand alongside Kasper in the dock underlines the working-class character of white protest in Clinton.

Lawrence J. Brantley, fifty, used car dealer
William Brakebill, forty-one, service station operator
Alonzo Bullock, fifty, carpenter/preacher
Clyde Cook, thirty-five, fireman
Clifford Carter, thirty-five, unemployed truck driver
Mary Nell Currier, thirty-nine, housewife
Edward Henson Nelson, twenty-two, grocery clerk
Zella Nelson, nineteen, housewife
Virgil Cleo Nelson, twenty-three, carpenter
W. H. Till, forty-three, machinist
Raymond Wood, thirty-five, house painter[102]

The court case was of particular political significance since it was the first time a southern jury had tried segregationists accused of disobeying a federal injunction.[103] U.S. Attorney John C. Crawford, using an extended metaphor, alleged that Kasper "was the hub of a conspiracy and that from him a spoke radiated out to each of the other defendants; that each defendant acted in response to impulses received from Kasper; that the hub and the spokes and the impulses and the responsive acts made of them conspirators and perpetrators of conspiratorial offenses."[104]

It was not only the nature of the case but also its timing that focused the attention of politicians and the news media. The trial started on the same day that Congress began debate on a civil rights bill. Section III of the bill empowered federal judges to try without juries those accused of violating injunctions against the obstruction of civil rights. Southern politicians interpreted this as a judicial coup d'état that would suppress legitimate political protest against racial integration. Senator Richard Russell of Georgia proclaimed that the South was "prepared to expend the greatest effort ever made in history to prevent passage of this bill in its present form."[105] The Clinton case was of considerable importance to the political debate on the bill. Should the jury convict the accused, it could be construed as a setback for the segregationist cause. Conversely, a conviction could also be seen as evidence that a southern jury was capable of reaching a dispassionate decision in the most sensitive of cases. It would also remove the continued threat of John Kasper.

On July 23, the court reconvened to hear the judgment of the jury. The ten men and two women had deliberated for a little more than two hours. Their decision caused a minor sensation not only in the court, but across the South. The jury found Kasper and six other defendants guilty of contempt. Released on bail, the convicted felons later returned to court for sentencing. Kasper received a six-month prison term; his associates escaped with probated sentences of between fifteen months and two years.[106]

To some segregationists, the case threatened to establish a dangerous precedent of federal action against those who dared oppose school integration. One southern newspaper compared the "tyranny" of Washington to centralized state power in the Soviet Union. The federal government had willfully interpreted a minor disturbance that could have been dealt with by the local police as an act of criminal conspiracy.[107]

On the other hand, the decision strengthened southern opposition to the civil rights bill. Senators William Fulbright and Richard Russell asserted that the decision undermined arguments against the use of juries in civil rights cases. According to Russell, the outcome "completely refutes the charge that Southern people are unworthy of trust and perjure themselves in this type of case." In truth, the decision did nothing of the sort.

The circumstances of the trial were far from characteristic of other incidents in which white southerners violated the civil rights of African Americans. Clinton was a community in the Upper South with a history of relatively peaceful race relations and Kasper was a northerner with no roots in the region. By contrast, in the Deep South, where racial hostilities were more intense and local whites led the resistance to reform, it was much less likely that juries would convict those accused of abusing black persons' civil rights. Between 1955 and 1957, southern juries tried thirteen other cases in which whites stood accused of infringing the rights of African Americans. Not one of these cases resulted in a conviction.[108] Although the Clinton case was atypical, it nonetheless assisted southern Democrats in securing an amendment to the civil rights bill that allowed for the use of juries in contempt cases concerning the infringement of civil rights. This seriously undermined the impact of the new legislation since southern juries still proved very reluctant to convict whites who illegally resisted racial reform.

Kasper's conviction therefore represented a political triumph for segregationist leaders since it simultaneously strengthened their assault on the civil rights bill and neutralized the threat that the young political firebrand posed to their political legitimacy. The massive resistance leadership attempted to promote their cause through an appeal to intellect and reason; extremists like Kasper manipulated the baser instincts and emotions of his supporters. Southern newspapers of the time included numerous cartoons that conveyed a sense of relief that the white southern political establishment had eliminated the public relations menace posed by Kasper. These included a rat bearing the name of the militant activist caught in the claws of a cat branded with the words "Tenn. Jury Conviction"; a stereotypical antebellum gentleman combing the troublemaker out of his hair; and a boot labeled "law and order" being applied to the backside of an individual identified as "outside agitator." As these cartoons implied, Kasper's personal loss was ironically a great political gain for the massive resistance movement.[109]

The white citizens of Clinton reacted with relative calm to the conviction of Kasper. Other than a number of threatening telephone calls to some of the jurors, there were no reprisals.[110] The crisis appeared to have passed. In September 1957, eight black students reported for school without any public protest. Yet for some, the past twelve months had proved too much. The man who steered the school through the crisis, Principal David Brittain, announced his resignation. Several other members of staff also handed in their notices. Nonetheless, the school year subsequently passed peacefully. By

September 1958, the number of African American students had increased to thirteen.[111]

There was one more act in the Clinton drama, however. On October 5, 1958, three dynamite explosions tore through the predawn calm in Clinton. The blasts ripped through the high school, causing damage estimated at $300,000. Kasper became the focus of the subsequent FBI inquiry. Having served one prison sentence, he was at the time awaiting trial for further acts of resistance against school desegregation. According to one informant, Kasper had hired professional explosive handlers for the task shortly after his release from prison. Interviewed in connection with the attack, Kasper denied all knowledge but declared that it was "a great victory for the white people of Tennessee." Without sufficient evidence, the FBI abandoned its pursuit of the principal suspect. However, in November federal agents did arrest two of Kasper's associates, Avon Nolan and Clifford Lowe. The following month, a court convicted them of conspiring to destroy the school.[112]

Despite the efforts of the FBI to secure the arrest of those persons responsible for the bombing of the school, the response of federal authorities to the Clinton crisis merits serious criticism. The Eisenhower administration insisted that it did not have the constitutional authority to challenge segregationist resistance to the admission of the black students. According to the president, "until the states show they cannot handle matters we had better be very careful about moving in."[113] While this statement shows that the administration was less than proactive on civil rights, it is possible to see it as a politically astute move since it was far less inflammatory for the governor of the state to send in troops than it was for the federal government. Yet while the tactic succeeded in Tennessee, the administration did nothing when Frank Clement's counterpart in Texas, Allan Shivers, defied federal demands to desegregate a school in Mansfield. Attorney General Herbert Brownell toed a similar line to the president when he turned down a petition from the Anderson County board of education for federal protection of the students, despite its assertion that it would otherwise have to close the school. The board was therefore forced to take the initiative in applying to a federal judge for an injunction restraining Kasper. Although a local U.S. attorney participated in the case, the Justice Department declined to become involved and made no attempt to enforce the restraining order. Not until the assault on Reverend Turner threatened a renewed state of chaos did Brownell announce that the federal government would prosecute any person who obstructed the desegregation of the school.[114] As historian

Oscar Handlin observed, the pusillanimous attitude of the Eisenhower administration provided lawless fanatics such as Kasper with generous space for political maneuver. In his opinion, "Every sign of weakness stimulated the extremists, who did not hesitate to attack the law and the social institutions of the community."[115]

The bombing of the high school elicited a similarly indifferent response from the administration. When the board of education learned that its insurance covered less than one-third of the total cost of repairs, it appealed to Washington for financial assistance on the grounds that the damage occurred as a result of its compliance with a federal order to desegregate. Eisenhower refused. The president informed a press conference that the federal government could not "step in with money every time something goes wrong with a school from a water faucet on up." To compare school desegregation with basic building maintenance suggests a certain failure to comprehend its moral and political magnitude.[116] While the board of education attempted to raise the remaining money needed to restore the high school, the students attended classes at a disused institution in Oak Ridge. A new school building was eventually opened in September 1960.

Despite threats to the contrary, John Kasper did not return to Clinton. His incarceration not only curtailed his activism but also failed to make him a martyr. Moreover, his career never completely recovered from public revelations about his former life.

In early 1957, a Florida state senate committee subpoenaed Kasper to answer accusations of his involvement in an intended bombing campaign against civil rights activists. Kasper first traveled to Florida in January 1957. Governor LeRoy Collins had in his recent inaugural address stated that African Americans were "morally and legally entitled to progress more rapidly." Kasper sensed he could ride the resultant wave of white conservative reaction. At the invitation of Klan leader Bill Hendrix, Kasper and fellow Seaboard White Citizens' Council member Fred Hockett conducted a speaking tour of the state, cultivating particular support among the inhabitants of "'cracker' country."[117]

State authorities took preventive measures to ensure Kasper did not precipitate the sort of chaos that had accompanied his sojourn in Tennessee. Governor Collins entrusted the responsibility for neutralizing Kasper to his Advisory Committee on Bi-Racial Problems. The choice ironically underlined how counterproductive Kasper was to the massive resistance movement since the purpose of the committee, established in March 1956, was to recommend means of resisting racial integration. Committee members advised that state authorities circulate Kasper's license number and a description of his car so "he can be tailed and apprehended, if necessary, before he starts trouble." They also contacted Governor Clement in Tennessee for advice on how he had handled Kasper and his supporters and to "learn all they can about them and about their methods of travel and operation."[118] When the committee learned that Kasper was scheduled to speak in Miami—requesting but being refused the right to be accompanied by thirty armed riflemen—it further proposed that "a transcript should be made of one of his speeches—or some of them—as grounds for securing an injunction against him."[119]

The authorities anticipated that Kasper would play into their hands by publicly inciting racial violence. What they could not predict was that he would incriminate himself in an altogether different way. The revelations about Kasper's past proved more politically damaging than the evidence unearthed about Bryant Bowles a few years earlier.

In late February, Miami police uncovered one hundred boxes of explosives stored on the outskirts of the city. Kasper had only days earlier asserted at a local segregationist rally that whites must "maintain racial integrity, even at the point of a shotgun."[120] State authorities sensed the opportunity to arrest Kasper and his supporters for criminal conspiracy. Police arrested and a court later convicted four members of the Seaboard White Citizens' Council for a related incident in which a cross was burned on the lawn of a local black activist. Kasper also received a subpoena to appear before an investigative committee of the state legislature on the morning of March 11.[121]

The committee must have anticipated that it would implicate Kasper in a campaign of criminal violence. It had weeks earlier issued a resolution condemning him as the leader of a conspiracy planned by persons from outside the state "to agitate and foment racial dissension."[122] However, it was a surprise line of questioning by Chief Counsel Mark Hawes that nullified the threat posed by Kasper.

Rumors had circulated for some months about his former association with African Americans. The *New York Amsterdam News* published a story as early as September 1956 that claimed Kasper had once shared a bed with a black male dance instructor named Ned Williams and that he was the godfather of an African American child. These accusations led the paper to conclude that Kasper was insincere in his support of segregation and instead courted controversy out of a desperate need for public attention. African

Americans who had once considered Kasper their friend expressed their incomprehension at his sudden conversion to the white supremacist cause. In the words of one of his "former intimate girl friends," if Kasper was "putting on an act" in fraternizing with African Americans, "he sure deserves the Academy Award."[123] Black poet LeRoi Jones (later Amiri Baraka) even testified in verse to the former lifestyle of the segregationist firebrand:

Oh, I knew
John Kasper when he hung around with shades . . . [124]

Months after the stories about Kasper first circulated, the *Miami Herald* picked up the story. It was on the basis of this source that Hawes now pressed Kasper on the nature of his past relationships with African Americans. Kasper initially denied the truth of the accusations. However, after four hours of relentless cross-examination, he finally conceded that he had associated with blacks "socially and without distinction" at his New York bookshop. He also admitted that he had dated an African American woman named Florette Henry who, among other things, taught him how to perform a West Indian dance called the Shango.[125]

These revelations caused irreparable damage to Kasper's political credibility among the extreme right. His claim that he had associated with African Americans only in order to convince them they were "being duped and used as instruments of the Jews" appeared disingenuous to many of his supporters.[126] The public exposure of his past alienated Kasper by emphasizing his cultural distance from the southern segregationist movement. To many white supremacists, Kasper appeared to be one of the same northeastern intellectuals he denounced in his speeches. If the uncovering of an affair with an African American woman was harmful to his reputation, then the intimation of a homosexual relationship with a black man, although never proven, was even worse. As Asa Carter observed, "That will about fix it for Kasper in the South." Kasper's other associates also abandoned him. Bill Hendrix denounced him as a hypocrite; Fred Hockett announced that their alliance was over.[127]

In the files of the Mississippi State Sovereignty Commission is an unusual document that illustrates how far Kasper's political stock had fallen among segregationists. It is a spoof NAACP membership application form. The document invites applicants to check a number of boxes, including how many legitimate and illegitimate children they have and how much they earn from paid employment, welfare, or theft. Signatories are also asked to pledge, "niggers is better than White Folks is" and are entitled to "more and MORE WELFARE." The form also requests applicants to choose from a list of people who can provide them with a reference. The list includes Earl Warren, Eleanor Roosevelt—and a certain "J. Kasper."[128]

However, while Kasper had been forced into retreat he was by no means defeated. In the fall of 1957, he once again grabbed the front pages when he led a violent campaign against school desegregation in Nashville. What follows is the story not only of that segregationist counterattack but also of how the authorities finally curtailed the political career of this incendiary white supremacist.

3. Into the Abyss

The Nashville School Crisis

John Kasper struggled during the summer of 1957 for an opportunity to restore his tattered personal and political reputation. Skeptical of him from the outset, few segregationists offered him a second chance now that he had been exposed in their minds as a fraud.

Kasper had in fact attempted to create new battle fronts in his war against racial integration while he was still in Clinton. However, he had soon been forced to retreat. In December 1956, while still free on bond pending appeal of his conviction for the Clinton disorder, the militant segregationist had traveled northwest to Louisville, Kentucky, in the hope of mobilizing opposition to school desegregation. He was much too late. When Kasper turned up in Clinton, the pervasive sense of unease about school desegregation among the white townspeople provided him with a window of opportunity. In Louisville, any such window had already been sealed shut, if it was ever actually open.

The city board of education had spent two years planning the abolition of the dual public school system. During that time, it enlisted the support of civic leaders, ministerial associations, and the press to encourage community acceptance of the change. On September 10, 1956, the integrated school system launched without incident. Why Kasper should choose Louisville as the location for a renewed assault on school desegregation is therefore something of a mystery. He did have some local connections through his association with Millard Grubbs, chairman of the Citizens' Council of Kentucky. The two men had met some months earlier, when Kasper attended a rally protesting the desegregation of schools in Clay and Sturgis. Now he and Grubbs sensed a belated opportunity to disrupt school integration in Louisville by exploiting the controversy over Billy Branham.[1]

Branham was a seventeen-year-old white high school student who, along with his mother, had recently arrived from Detroit. The family had moved into temporary accommodations while they waited for Branham's father, still working in Michigan, to join them. Branham had attempted to enroll at Male High School. However, education authorities had used his non-resident status to deny his registration when they learned he was plotting a campaign to oust black students from the school.[2] On December 12, Kasper appeared alongside Branham at a public meeting to protest the action of school officials. His speech included many of his standard tropes, especially his populist assault on corrupt city authorities who had sold out the white community. Kasper received a rapturous reception from the audience; the problem was there were only thirty-five people in the room.[3] The faltering flame of protest soon flickered out altogether. On January 16, 1957, police arrested Branham and eleven other youths at a club where they were holding a meeting, citing a state law that forbade minors from establishments licensed to sell alcohol. The arresting officers found a letter in Branham's possession offering him "bed and board indefinitely" if he came to Knoxville to help set up a Knox County White Youth Council. Its author was Kasper. The invitation to Branham intimates that he had already decided to cut his losses in Louisville and search for a more amenable community.[4]

That search became more elusive because the authorities were more aware of his intentions and many segregationists were no longer willing to trust him. This was certainly the case in North Carolina, the location chosen by Kasper to relaunch his career. On learning that Kasper intended to rally public opposition to school desegregation in the state, Governor Luther Hodges dryly remarked, "I don't think we need him." Most white North Carolinians agreed. When Kasper arrived in Greensboro on August 31, three days before the scheduled desegregation of local schools, few people turned out to hear him. Later that same day, spectators heckled him during a speech in Winston-Salem. That these experiences created a sense of mounting desperation in Kasper is clear from an incoherent speech he delivered at the Greensboro Courthouse on August 31. "We want a heart attack, we want nervous breakdowns, we want suicides," he proclaimed to a bemused audience who wanted nothing of the sort. When Kasper denounced evangelist Billy Graham as a "nigger lover" because of his opposition to segregation, the crowd turned on him completely. Whites in Charlotte were equally unwelcoming.[5]

Political expediency rather than principle informed the opposition of white North Carolinians to Kasper. The white supremacist Patriots of North Carolina, Inc., warned that the presence of Kasper "would result in great harm to the cause of segregation" because his lawless behavior impaired the public reputations of local communities and encouraged the use of military power to enforce the admission of black students to white schools.[6] These criticisms of Kasper, as with earlier condemnation of Bryant Bowles, contained an element of hypocrisy since local segregationists proved more than capable of damaging the image of their cities without the assistance of an outside agitator. The white racists who hounded fifteen-year-old Dorothy Counts from the Harding High School in Charlotte four days after she had first been admitted could not hold Kasper or Bowles responsible for the rise of mob rule.[7]

Kasper also considered the possibility of his leading popular opposition to the integration of the Central High School in Little Rock. However, segregationists there had mobilized more effectively than the directionless white citizens of Clinton and did not need outside assistance. Amos Guthridge of the Capitol Citizens' Council denounced Kasper as an irresponsible extremist who would undermine legitimate protest to the admission of African American students.[8] Given the mob violence that later brought the city to the brink of anarchy, these criticisms of Kasper were disingenuous. The scale of the disorder in Little Rock ironically precipitated a far more powerful response from federal authorities than any racial disturbance Kasper ever created.

Despite these setbacks, Kasper had already made plans for further protests against desegregation. His choice of location was Nashville, Tennessee. As was the case with Milford and Clinton, the violent reaction to school desegregation in Nashville caught many people by surprise. Local authorities complacently assumed they had prepared the ground for peaceful compliance with a federal court order to admit black pupils to formerly all-white schools. Yet Kasper once more acted as a conduit for otherwise directionless grassroots rage. The young firebrand imbued a white working class who otherwise fatalistically accepted reform with the confidence that they could withstand federal authority. Riotous insurrection consequently shook a city proud of its reputation for racial progressivism. Although their resistance

Chapter Three

ended in failure, white mobs came closer to obstructing the integration process than has been acknowledged. The violence Kasper unleashed nonetheless had the same impact in Nashville as it had in Clinton, strengthening the pragmatic acceptance that school desegregation was essential to the maintenance of community order.

The political barometer did not indicate a coming storm over school desegregation in Nashville. On the contrary, the white community reacted to the Supreme Court ruling with relative composure. Although the political and civic leadership did not explicitly endorse the *Brown* decision, it asked for a calm and reasoned response from ordinary citizens. As Mayor Ben West affirmed, "We have no other thought except to conform to the law of the land."[9] The two local newspapers expressed similar sentiments. Although *The Tennessean* opposed the West administration on other grounds, it accepted the authority of the Supreme Court and promoted popular compliance with its ruling. By contrast, the *Banner* deplored desegregation but placed its faith in the mayor to provide a peaceful solution.[10] Further illustration of the climate of political moderation was the failure of the principal instrument of segregationist opposition, the Tennessee Federation for Constitutional Government, to attract grassroots support.[11]

A number of factors facilitated the temperate reaction in Nashville to the prospect of desegregation. First, the city proudly cultivated its reputation as a progressive center for religion, education, and the arts. The political establishment understood that an outbreak of mob violence in response to the *Brown* decision could irreparably damage the public image of Nashville as the "Athens of the South." Second, the numerous institutions of higher education in the city provided an important forum for public dialogue between both races. Fisk University in particular fostered interracial communication through its annual Race Relations Institute conferences, which by the time of the *Brown* ruling had been running for a decade. The three white private institutions of higher education—George Peabody College for Teachers, Scarritt College, and Vanderbilt University—had also voluntarily opened their doors to black students.[12] Third, restrictive city boundaries excluded many white voters who had relocated to the suburbs and provided African Americans with an unusual and disproportionate influence on municipal elections. Blacks represented less than one-quarter of the population of Davidson County but more than one-third of the electorate. Their political muscle secured the election of black officials Z. Alexander Looby and Robert Lillard to the city council and Coyness Ennix to the board of education. It also proved crucial to Ben West, both in 1951 when he successfully campaigned for mayor and four years later when he won a second term of office. West acknowledged his debt to black voters by appointing more African Americans to the police and fire departments. His administration also oversaw the integration of several public facilities, including the bus system, the public library, and city golf courses. African Americans therefore had reason to expect that the mayor would take a similarly forward stance on school desegregation.[13]

Private institutions once more assumed the initiative for the admission of African American students. The Nashville diocese of the Roman Catholic Church responded to the *Brown* decision with the announcement that it would desegregate its elementary and secondary schools from the start of the 1954 fall term. By contrast, the Nashville board of education interpreted the delay before the court issued its implementation decree as an excuse to do nothing. Not until *Brown II*, when the justices ordered school districts to make a "prompt and reasonable start" toward compliance with its initial decision, did the board establish a committee to study the problems posed by desegregation.

Local blacks concluded that the school board was being neither prompt nor reasonable in its approach toward desegregation. On September 23, 1955, Alfred Z. Kelley, a black barber from East Nashville, filed a class action suit against the board of education to allow the admission of African American students to the public school of their choice. Kelley claimed it unreasonable that his son Robert had to take a bus across town to the all-black Pearl High School when he lived within easy walking distance of East High School. While Bobby Kelley was the principal plaintiff, there were a total of twenty-three children named in the suit, twenty of them African Americans and two of them whites whose parents taught at Fisk University and wanted their children admitted to black schools closer to their homes. On March 28, 1956, a three-judge panel permitted the school board more time to prepare a desegregation plan pending a hearing before a federal district court. Dismissing a petition by the Tennessee Federation for Constitutional Government to intervene in the case, Judge William E. Miller ruled on October 15 that the board of education must provide the court with a desegregation plan no later than January 21, 1957.[14]

The plan submitted by the board received the approval of Judge Miller despite the objections of the plaintiffs. An assessment of the plan shows why they did not hail it as a victory. The board of education proposed to desegregate the public school system starting with all first-grade pupils in

September 1957 and then proceeding at the rate of one further grade per year. It would therefore take an additional eleven years to eliminate the existing dual school system, guaranteeing that thousands of black students would graduate without ever having sat in a mixed classroom. Z. Alexander Looby, who represented the plaintiffs, observed that the plan would also fail to provide relief to his clients since all of them were older than first graders. The plan further permitted black and white parents to transfer a child out of a school where the other race predominated. This transfer plan showed that the board of education was willing to observe the letter rather than the spirit of the law. It ensured minimum compliance with the Supreme Court ruling since white parents would seize the opportunity to withdraw their children from schools where the student body was mostly black. In yet another move calculated to restrict racial integration, the board in an act of cynical racial gerrymandering redrew the school zone boundaries. As a result, only 115 of a potential 1,400 black first graders became eligible for admission to formerly all-white institutions. It was, concluded the *Nashville Globe and Independent*, the city's black newspaper, "pitifully little."[15]

Although the tactics of the school board were deliberately intended to restrict the scale and speed of desegregation, there was much optimism that the admission of the black first graders would pass without incident. Superintendent of Schools William A. Bass attempted to address the concerns of parents and teachers through a series of meetings that started as early as April 1957. Secular and religious leaders also labored to mobilize popular support for school desegregation. In April 1956, white moderates formed the Nashville Community Relations Conference as a means of promoting mutual understanding between the races. The appointment of banker and industrialist Maclin P. Davis, Sr., as chairman reflected the fear of city boosters that racial disorder precipitated by school desegregation would deter the investment of northern capital. Also prominent within the ranks of its members were a number of clerics who performed a particularly public role in preparing the ground for the start of the new school year. As the first day of classes approached, the Nashville Association of Churches and the Nashville Ministers Association distributed a letter to clergymen across the city, encouraging them to offer sermons on the morality of racial reform.[16]

Racial fault lines nonetheless ran deeper in Nashville than the surface calm implied. As school desegregation drew nearer, there was a growing prospect that something or someone would set off serious political tremors. During the summer of 1957, whites worried about the probability of their sons and especially daughters attending classes with black children established the Parents School Preference Committee. The committee sent a petition with six thousand signatures to the school board imploring it to comply with a school preference law enacted by the state legislature in January. This law provided for the creation of a triple-school system that would allow parents to send their children either to a segregated black or white institution or to an integrated facility. Although Judge Miller ruled the law unconstitutional, the committee continued to attract popular support for its proposal, not least from the *Nashville Banner,* which in reaction to the imminent reality of school desegregation abandoned its earlier caution and assumed an ever more reactionary editorial line. While the Parents School Preference Committee worked within the law to resist racial change, some segregationists were prepared to use more extreme tactics. The most dramatic expression of militant opposition was the resurgence of the local Ku Klux Klan under the leadership of construction worker Ernest Carr. "The resentment is deep," concluded Superintendent of Schools Bass, "much deeper than many of us had supposed."[17]

The temptation to tip the delicate political balance into chaos was too much for an opportunist desperate to resuscitate his ailing career. Five days before students were scheduled to register for the start of the new school year, a 1950 gray Chrysler four-door sedan cruised into the city. Behind the wheel was John Kasper. Over the course of the next three weeks, Kasper addressed forty public meetings under the auspices of the Tennessee White Citizens' Council, primarily on the east and west sides of the city. At his side during many of these speeches was Asa Carter, with whom he had evidently reconciled his differences.[18]

Kasper succeeded through the energy of his actions and urgency of his words in galvanizing militant opposition to desegregation. The Tennessee White Citizens' Council launched a campaign of intimidation against African Americans, including anonymous telephone warnings and a motorcade that passed through black neighborhoods. Confronted by these threats, the parents of ninety-six of the African American children due to be admitted to formerly white schools accepted the offer to transfer them to black institutions. This resulted in a mere nineteen children who now faced the daunting challenge of desegregation.[19]

The black pupils registered for classes at five formerly all-white schools on the morning of Tuesday, August 27. A boycott by white parents led to the number of children who registered for school falling one-third short of the estimated total. Many of those same parents assembled outside the schools in protest at the admission of the black pupils. Kasper led some of them into each of the schools in an attempt to coerce the principals into obstructing the desegregation process. He relentlessly sustained the pressure during the two weeks before the start of classes, summoning angry whites to gather around the schools during the day and speaking at rallies on the steps of the Davidson County Courthouse by night. His rhetoric assumed an increasingly inflammatory tone. In a speech on August 28, Kasper announced a plan to intimidate the black families who had enrolled their children at the white elementary schools. He also authored and circulated a sheet that prophesied the "Last Days of Peace Between White and Nigra Races" unless the school board abandoned its desegregation plan. "Straighten your backbone," Kasper ordered his supporters. "When they put the niggers in school with your kids in September, load your shotgun to defend your wife and home—be prepared for the worst race riots, hangings, anything."[20]

City authorities attempted to take preventive measures against mob violence. On the eve of the first day of classes, Sunday, September 8, Police Chief Douglas E. Hosse issued a public statement threatening the arrest of anyone who tried to intimidate children or parents from entering the desegregated schools. All police leave was cancelled in anticipation of trouble and a guard of 115 officers stationed around the 5 campuses. It would not be enough to stem disorder.[21]

On the morning of Monday, September 9, the nineteen black children arrived for the start of classes at the five formerly all-white schools. Despite his name, Charles Battles attended classes at Jones Elementary School without incident.[22] However, the other black students faced a tougher ordeal. Police had to escort the children and their parents through crowds of outraged whites who swore, spat, and hurled stones at them. Officers had to restrain a mob outside Glenn Elementary School after some of its members started to shove M. J. Griffith, a black father escorting his daughter Lasuanda to classes. They also made a number of arrests near Caldwell School after a throng of whites chased and beat William Jackson, a black teenager who simply happened to be in the area.[23] The ugly brutality of the mob was too much for some to bear. Grace McKinley, a black woman who walked her grandchild to Fehr School, pulled a knife on her assailants as she screamed, "If any of you jump me, I'm going to use this." Although there were no serious incidents, several skirmishes broke out between pickets and the police, resulting in a number of arrests. An angry crowd also coursed through the halls of Caldwell School, demanding an audience with Principal Jack Stanfill. A boycott by white parents resulted in only 25 to 30 percent of pupils attending the affected schools.[24]

The public demonstrations during the day were only a prelude to a more dramatic display of segregationist resistance. That evening, Kasper addressed a rally of more than five hundred men and women on the steps of the War Memorial Building. "The Constitution gives you the right to carry arms," he declared. Kasper then brandished a rope above his head and proclaimed that many people would like to see it tied around the neck of black councilman Z. Alexander Looby. "If one of these niggers pulls a razor or a gun on us, we'll give it to 'em! When they fool with the white race they're fooling with the strongest race in the world, the most bloodthirsty race in the world!" No sooner had Kasper concluded his oration than a mob marched on Fehr School and proceeded to smash several of its windows.[25]

When the mob finally dispersed, an uneasy calm settled over the city. It was not to last. According to one nearby resident what followed was "A hellish explosion—just like God had whispered in my ear." The noise was in reality the sound of dynamite. At 12:33 a.m., while most of Nashville slept, a bomb detonated at the Hattie Cotton Elementary School. The blast tore doors off hinges, cracked plaster, and scattered debris across the schoolyard. "It sounded like the whole world ended," exclaimed a city patrolman. Earlier that day the school had opened its doors for the first time to a solitary black child, six-year-old Patricia Watson.[26]

City authorities moved vigorously to prevent the violence from escalating out of control. On the morning of Tuesday, September 10, police erected barricades restricting access to the streets surrounding the desegregated schools. They also made thirty-nine arrests. Twenty-six of those persons detained in custody were white; thirteen were black, several of whom the police arrested for illegal possession of firearms.

The prime target of the police dragnet was Kasper. Officers arrested him on four charges: one relating to vagrancy, one to loitering, and two to disorderly conduct. No sooner had Kasper been released on bond than officers rearrested him for parking his car without a permit outside police headquarters. Kasper posted a further $500 bond and finally walked free. However, his reprieve proved short-lived. At 12:35 a.m., police hauled him from his bed and arrested him for inciting a riot. The arresting constables committed Kasper to the county jail, holding him without bond pending an investigation. Later that day, they transferred their prisoner to the city court, where he stood trial on the four charges on which the police arrested him the previous day. Kasper pleaded not guilty but the court convicted him on all charges and fined him $200. When he failed to pay the fine, Judge Andrew Doyle committed him to the city workhouse. Although a benefactor secured his release, the police continued to hold him at the county jail until September 13, when a Davidson County grand jury indicted him on the charge of inciting a riot. Three days later, Judge Miller granted city authorities a restraining order against Kasper and nine other persons forbidding further interference with school desegregation. Kasper posted the bond set after his indictment by the grand jury and retreated from Nashville in his battered sedan.[27]

Fear of further disorder led many parents to keep their children out of school during the first week of classes. Average attendance remained as low as 40 percent. The departure of Kasper eventually restored confidence and, following a long weekend to allow children to attend the state fair, the elementary schools reopened on Tuesday, September 17. School desegregation continued at an incremental but unimpeded pace.

On October 14, 1957, police returned Kasper to custody after the U.S. Supreme Court rejected his appeal against his conviction for the Clinton disorders. Four days later, he started serving a one-year sentence at the federal penitentiary in Tallahassee, Florida. Nashville had weathered the storm that caused such destruction to other southern communities.[28]

"That damn Kasper found more support here than we expected," conceded one school official after the emergency had receded, "and he capitalized on it."[29] The *Nashville Globe and Independent*, which on the eve of school desegregation had confidently informed its readers the menace posed by Kasper was "a false alarm," also later admitted he had come close to thwarting local authorities. "No invader of this peaceful city ever before got as far along in his defiance of law and order and with threats to promote outrages calculated to overthrow a municipal government like John Kasper did during his sojourn here."[30] Anna Holden of the Congress of Racial Equality was more succinct. When hordes of white protesters gathered at the schools to obstruct the admission of the black pupils, she declared, Kasper had "seemed close to victory."[31]

The key issue is how Kasper succeeded in precipitating this crisis. A comparison of the rhetorical and tactical methods utilized by Kasper first in Clinton and twelve months later in Nashville reveals both continuity and change.

A common thread that weaves through Kasper's speeches in both communities is his antiestablishmentarianism. Kasper accused Nashville authorities of being little more than marionettes whose strings were pulled by the federal government. Their decision to implement school desegregation demonstrated that they acted not in accordance with the democratic will of the local electorate but rather on the direct orders of a dictatorial administration in Washington. These "Broadbottomed, Pot-Bellied Politicians" who used the spoils of public office for their personal advantage could afford to transfer their own children to private institutions while forcing poorer whites to send their children to school alongside African Americans. This insensitivity toward the aspirations of poor but hardworking white parents marked them out as "SNOBS who have only contempt for ordinary folks trying to give their kids at least the same opportunity for personal character development that they had from their fathers and mothers."[32]

Such harangues against the civic and political elite show how Kasper used class resentment to mobilize support among lower-class whites. His speeches pandered to the sense of political marginalization shared by many ordinary whites, resentful at the racial compromises made by elected officials and their unresponsiveness to segregationist protest.

The success with which Kasper mobilized working-class opposition is consistent with the theory of collective efficacy devised by the social psychologist Albert Bandura. According to Bandura, the limited resources and political influence of poorer communities creates a sense of powerlessness. The underprivileged do not believe they have the capacity to organize and implement the course of action needed to address their problems and resentments. They therefore assume a fatalistic attitude toward the world. As Bandura argues, "The disconsolate and fragmented character of disadvantaged communities impedes effective unified action." What the poor need is the inspirational leadership of a person able to convince them that through collective action they do have the capacity to influence the political process. Kasper assumed this role as a community enabler in Nashville.[33]

Segregationist leaders had deliberately excluded poor whites because they feared their supposed susceptibility to lawlessness. The middle-class composition of the Tennessee Federation for Constitutional Government and the Parents School Preference Committee therefore denied many ordinary whites a participatory voice in anti-integration protest. By contrast, Kasper portrayed himself as "an intellectual Robin Hood" who would empower poor and underprivileged whites by helping them to understand their constitutional right to protest the admission of blacks to the public schools. Film footage of Kasper speaking at a rally on the outskirts of Nashville shows him donned in a smart suit and tie while around him his supporters dress in T-shirts and plain cotton dresses. His appearance and demeanor at once communicates a sense of respect for a people he described as "the real salt of the earth" while also setting him apart as a figure of authority who would give voice to their otherwise unorganized opposition to school desegregation.[34]

One intriguing aspect of the segregationist demonstrations in Nashville was the conspicuous presence of women. Photographs of white protesters are filled with the angry faces of white females such as those who spat at police officers escorting three black children to the Caldwell Elementary School or who confronted Superintendent of Schools W. A. Bass.[35] It is difficult to determine either the identities of these women or with which organization, if any, they were affiliated. Some were presumably members of the Parents School Preference Committee, but others were probably supporters of Kasper. Two of the defendants convicted of violating an injunction against interference with school desegregation in Clinton were also women.

The absence of sources means it is only possible to speculate about the women who were drawn into the ranks of the militant segregationist movement. Kasper did not specifically attempt to recruit women to his cause. His rhetoric instead emphasized how white men could redeem their masculinity by protecting their families and communities from the threat of racial integration, encouraging them in one speech to straighten their backbones and arm themselves in defense of their wives and homes. This assertion of masculinity through activism implicitly reduced women to the status of passive victims. However, historians have shown how in other southern communities white women attempted to legitimize their participation in segregationist protests as an extension of their maternal responsibilities.[36] Further research is nonetheless needed on how women involved in acts of mob violence reconciled their espousal of socially conservative values with their own transgressive behavior.

The other persistent line of argument pursued by Kasper in Clinton and Nashville was that the federal officials who forced desegregation on white southerners were part of a communist Jewish conspiracy. While Kasper produced some of his own propaganda, he also acted in both communities as a nexus for the loose network of anti-Semites across the country, many of whom used him to distribute their own hate sheets. Lou Silberman of the Nashville Jewish Community Relations Committee reflected that along with the arrival of Kasper came an influx of anti-Semitic literature from all parts of the United States. "All of a sudden," he observed, "the old-time anti-Semite who is always looking for new gimmicks and gadgets and ways to sell his wares and make a dishonest dollar thus doing, decided that the South was ripe for picking in terms of joining the Jewish question, which in their mind was always there, with the problem of segregation and integration."[37]

Nashville provided Kasper with more potential ammunition than Clinton to support his accusation that Jews were the secret masterminds of school desegregation. While there were no Jews in Clinton, there was a substantial community of around 2,700 in Nashville.[38] Moreover, some Jews had performed a publicly conspicuous role in the desegregation process. One of the members of the board of education was a Jew and the rabbi of Congregation Ohabai Sholom, William Silverman, was at the forefront of ministerial action in support of racial reform.[39]

While Silverman in particular provided Kasper with a specific target, he nonetheless chose not to spit his anti-Semitic venom at local Jews, relying instead on abstract generalizations about an international Jewish conspiracy. It seems implausible that Kasper was unaware of what the rabbi was doing to support desegregation, which begs the question why his accusations never moved beyond the level of generic stereotypes. The answer may relate to the distinction that many white Gentiles drew between what Jonathan Sarna describes as the "Mythical Jew" and the "Jew Next Door."[40] The stereotype of the stateless Jew conspiring to subvert indigenous governments had considerable currency in southern political culture. However, most white Gentiles differentiated between the fabled Jew who inhabited the popular imagination and the actual Jew who lived in their neighborhoods. Like many of their coreligionists across the South, Nashville Jews had adapted almost completely to the cultural norms of the white Protestant majority. One illustration of this is the establishment line taken by the local Jewish newspaper, *The Observer*, which refrained from editorializing on controversial political issues, particularly race. The public behavior of the Jewish community made it difficult for many people to identify them with a supposed plot to subvert the social order. Despite his support for desegregation, Rabbi Silverman also had a strong standing in the larger white community, which may have deflected some of the criticism he would have otherwise endured. In the circumstances, it may have been a tactically shrewd move on the part of Kasper not to target specific individuals but rather to place his emphasis on unnamed conspirators.[41]

While his attacks on Jews lacked a clearly defined target, Kasper was more direct in the accusations he made against African Americans. Kasper had not attributed the desegregation of Clinton High School to the political initiative of African Americans, but instead claimed that they were the unwitting pawns of communist Jews. By contrast, his speeches and pamphlets in Nashville explicitly blamed blacks for breaching the color line and pandered to the basest racial fears of whites. In addition to the doctored photograph of black GIs kissing white women that he had distributed in Clinton, Kasper produced a handbill that warned of the sexual threat that black male students would pose to white girls, emphasizing "the high crimes and venereal disease rates of the colored" and their "earlier physical maturity."[42]

There are several possible explanations why Kasper shifted his rhetorical emphasis toward white fears of miscegenation. First, his experience of fighting and losing the battle to maintain segregation in Clinton may have hardened his racial attitudes. Second, his experiences in Clinton had demonstrated to him the strength and depth of white working-class racism, a power that he hoped to tap in Nashville. Third, the public exposure of his personal relationships with African Americans may have compelled him to reassert his integrity as a segregationist. Fourth, African Americans were a more conspicuous political force in Nashville than in Clinton and therefore a more palpable threat to many whites.

What was also new about the political philosophy espoused by Kasper in Nashville was his use of religious doctrine as intellectual sanction for the separation of the races. His enlistment of fundamentalist churches demonstrated, as had been true of the similar tactics used by Bryant Bowles in Milford, the enduring strength at a grassroots level of a racist folk theology. Kasper enlisted the support in Nashville of two fundamentalist preachers, an unemployed evangelist named John Mercurio and Reverend Fred Stroud of the Bible Presbyterian Church.[43] This was not simply a pragmatic move motivated by the need to enlist whatever allies he could. Kasper had first started to articulate a religious defense of racial segregation some months earlier, informing an audience in Florida that it was "a plan of nature established by the Creator in the heavens."[44] Moreover, he had close ties through his mother to the Bible Presbyterian Church. She was a member of its main congregation in Collingswood, New Jersey, and, while it is unclear whether Kasper accompanied her to services, he did share many of the church's values.

The Bible Presbyterian Church was founded in 1937 by fundamentalist members of the Presbyterian Church of the United States, who denounced the theological liberalism of its leadership as a refutation of biblical doctrine. Delegates at its first General Synod in September 1938 agreed that the "great battle" of the new church was against the corrupting forces of "modernism, compromise, indifferentism, and worldliness."[45] The notion that an aloof denominational leadership had betrayed the fundamental tenets of belief held by ordinary members would have resonated with Kasper since it was analogous to his condemnation of politicians who sold out their electorate by supporting desegregation. Moreover, the Bible Presbyterian Church espoused opinions on the race issue that were entirely consistent with those of Kasper. Carl McIntire, the pastor of the Collingswood church, founded the American Council of Churches in 1941 in opposition to the more liberal National Council of Churches. This separatist organization strictly enforced the color line, proclaiming: "Segregation within the church on racial, linguistic, and national lines is not unchristian nor contrary to the specific demands of the bible." McIntire also toured the South to denounce the civil rights movement as a communist plot. While he denied accusations of anti-Semitism, his diatribes were regularly reprinted in the pages of Jew-hating publications.[46]

Nashville Baptist Presbyterian Church minister Fred Stroud was a strict adherent of the theological racism formulated by McIntire. Stroud, a stoutly built Georgian, had graduated from Columbia Theological Seminary in 1933. Appalled by what he perceived as the apostasy of the Presbyterian Church of the United States, he had convinced his flock of four hundred souls to become one of the founding congregations in the new movement led by McIntire.[47] According to Stroud, segregation had divine authorization; God "had created a servant race and that is the way He wants it." Asked for evidence of the Lord's will, he referred imprecisely to "Sixth Corinthians." This was probably a reference to 2 Corinthians 6:17: "Wherefore come out from among them, and be ye separate, saith the Lord, and touch not the unclean thing; and I will receive them." Although the passage contains no explicit mention of race, it is possible to see how Stroud interpreted it as sanctioning segregation. The preacher also used his interpretation of specific biblical texts to substantiate the claim that the civil rights movement was a communist conspiracy. One of the handbills he distributed during the school crisis exclaimed:

COMMUNISTS!
infiltrated our churches
now it integrates
our schools

The statement concluded with a reference to the Second Epistle of Peter, which warns of "false prophets" who "will secretly introduce destructive heresies." Stroud apparently construed this as confirmation of communist conspirators attempting to enforce desegregation. Moreover, he also alluded to the fate of African Americans who attempted to send their children to all-white schools, citing the warning of Peter that the "unreasoning animals, creatures of instinct to be captured and killed" that followed the false prophets would be destroyed along with them.[48]

The influence of Stroud on Kasper is apparent from his decision to include a clause in the membership application for the Tennessee White Citizens' Council that the signatory must "believe in the separation of the races as ordained by the CREATOR." The form also mandated that members must accept "the divinity of Jesus Christ," an implicit act of anti-Semitism on the part of its author.[49]

Stroud was important to Kasper in a number of other respects. First, his church provided Kasper with a local institutional base from which to build support for his campaign. Second, Stroud had the potential to recruit not only members of his own congregation but also other whites who were disaffected with their own ministers. The clergy in Nashville had provided conspicuous leadership in promoting popular acceptance of school desegregation. As historian Paul Harvey argues, many southern laypeople experienced a sense of betrayal by their ministers because of their stance on the race issue. Stroud had the capacity to offer religious leadership to otherwise alienated laypersons in the same manner that Kasper recruited whites excluded by secular organizations such as the Tennessee Federation for Constitutional Government. Certainly, the placards held by white picketers outside the elementary schools included a slogan that apparently bore the imprimatur of Stroud: "God is the Author of Segregation."[50] Third, Stroud's status as a local pastor conferred the militant segregationist movement with at least some degree of respectability. This connection also allowed Kasper to deflect some of the criticism that he was an outsider who had no reason to be in the city other than to create trouble. Interviewed about the violence that had broken out in Nashville over school desegregation, Stroud insisted that Kasper "had nothing to do with that." Instead, he asserted that the cause was "outside sources and it may have been NAACP sources coming down here into this land to make people think that those of us who were Americans and who were Christians were doing it." In defining the NAACP as the alien "them," Stroud by implication made Kasper appear more like "us" to local whites.[51]

Evangelical churches were not the only means by which Kasper financed his campaign. Although perceived as a lone agitator, he commanded the support of many patrons who represented extremist organizations across the country. This hidden financial network included many stalwarts of the far right such as Elizabeth Dilling and Lyrl Van Hyning, critics of the New Deal and cofounders on the outbreak of World War II of the anti-interventionist organization We the Mothers Mobilize for America.[52] Kasper also secured financial support from the Arab-Asian Institute, based in Washington, D.C., under the leadership of the right-wing and rabidly anti-Semitic Salem Bader.[53]

In addition to his emphasis on race and religion, there was an increased intensity to the violent tactics that Kasper espoused in Nashville. Although his rhetoric in Clinton had been confrontational, it had lacked a clear focus. He had not identified any immediate target for the mob to turn its wrath on, but rather issued broad threats against the federal judiciary. By contrast, in Nashville Kasper specifically advocated acts of retributive violence against the families of the black children who desegregated the schools and their lawyer Z. Alexander Looby.

It is impossible to determine conclusively why Kasper would have threatened death or injury to particular individuals. One can speculate that this strategy was symptomatic of the manner in which political fanaticism feeds on itself. The failure of his other campaigns and his humiliation by the Florida legislative committee may also have caused Kasper to take reckless measures in an attempt to restore his political credibility. However repugnant his tactics may have been, there was an element of rational choice to them. Intimidating the black families into removing their children from the schools represented one of the surest means to stop desegregation. Given that the school board had instituted a transfer plan in an attempt to restrict the numbers of African American children admitted to white schools, it is unclear what action the authorities would have taken in the event that the families applied to send their sons and daughters to black institutions.

It is uncertain whether Kasper also provided his supporters with precise instructions to dynamite the Hattie Cotton Elementary School. The police had found a car covered in Klan stickers near the scene of the attack. Inside were a number of weapons and wire identical to that used to detonate the bomb. Three days later, on Friday, September 13, a local Klansman named Charles Reed surrendered to FBI agents, who handed him over to the police. Reed informed detectives that he and Kasper had hidden a cache of dynamite in an abandoned house on the Saturday night before the bombing, but that it had then disappeared. The police, who already considered Kasper their prime suspect, brought him in for questioning but he refused to confirm or deny the claims made by Reed. In addition to Kasper, the police also arrested six other persons, three of whom they considered to have carried out the bombing. However, the absence of sufficient evidence allowed all of them to walk free from custody. Although the authorities could not determine if Kasper was personally responsible for planting the bomb at the school, his inflammatory speeches had at the very least fostered a climate of violent lawlessness that encouraged such acts of terrorism. His arrest for inciting a riot was the most convenient charge that the authorities could bring against him.[54]

Kasper's terrorist tactics did not have a durable impact on school desegregation in Nashville. Within a week of the bombing of Hattie Cotton School, attendance had returned almost to normal. Nashville lacked sufficient dramatic interest for a news media lured instead to the scenes of violent racial disorder that accompanied school desegregation in Little Rock. The city nonetheless teetered more precariously on the precipice of chaos than many contemporary narratives implied. Historians recognize that many African Americans did not instinctively embrace the nonviolent philosophy of Martin Luther King, Jr. Some members of the black community in Nashville believed that the use of arms was a legitimate form of self-defense. Some African Americans, including friends and relatives of the families whose children desegregated the elementary schools, armed themselves in retaliation against white mobs. The arrest of Grace McKinley for threatening to stab white pickets outside Fehr School demonstrates how close tensions came to the snapping point. Police also detained a black clergyman, Reverend Edward Jackson, for drawing a pistol on the protesters who pelted stones at McKinley and her granddaughter. The potential for serious racial conflict increased further following the bomb attack on Hattie Cotton School. Kelly Miller Smith, pastor of the black First Baptist Church, recalled attending a meeting after the bombing at which "speaker after speaker" stood up and "demanded some kind of reprisal." Some of those in the audience were willing to act on these words. A short time later, police arrested ten African Americans and seized a cache of arms at the home of one of the black children admitted to a white school.[55]

If the situation was so unstable, why was Kasper unable to make more political capital out of it? The response of state and local authorities to the school situation was perhaps the most important factor. Governor Frank Clement resisted segregationist pressure to deploy troops in order to obstruct the desegregation process. In August 1956, Governor Allan Shivers of

Texas ordered state troopers to block the admission of black students to a high school in Mansfield. Just over twelve months later, in September 1957, his counterpart in Arkansas, Orval Faubus, called out the National Guard to prevent the Little Rock Nine from gaining entrance to Central High School. Only days later, Clement issued a public statement that he would not use similar tactics in Nashville, emphasizing that he had no authority to intervene at a community level unless "law and order has completely broken down." In contrast to the defiant stand of Faubus that facilitated mob violence in Little Rock, Clement fostered a climate of public acceptance of desegregation.[56]

Local authorities also took decisive measures to restrain mob elements within the city from creating chaos. The entire police force in Clinton amounted to no more than nine men. In comparison, Nashville Police Chief Douglas Hosse had a much larger and more professional body of men under his command. Hosse placed Kasper under close surveillance almost from the moment that he arrived in the city. In Clinton, Kasper had at least initially been able to operate under the cloak of anonymity. By contrast, by the time he set foot in Nashville he was a known quantity. The authorities knew precisely what he was capable of and took measures to preclude his precipitating a crisis.[57]

Several other factors conspired to frustrate Kasper. It was possible for one man to rouse the resistance of an entire community when it was as small as Clinton. But Kasper found it no easier to replicate these tactics in a larger metropolitan area than had Bryant Bowles when he moved from Milford to Baltimore and Washington. While it was possible in a small town such as Clinton to create a state of paralysis with relatively little organizational effort, the greater size of Nashville made it more difficult to dramatize the power of white opposition to school desegregation. The simultaneous admission of black students to five different schools in Nashville also forced segregationists to disperse their strength. This contrasted with conditions in Clinton, where racial conflict centered on a single focal point, the local high school, which allowed whites to marshal their minimal resources to maximum impact.

Even had the Nashville board of education restricted desegregation to one school, segregationists could not agree on a common strategy of protest. Both the Parents School Preference Committee and the Tennessee Federation for Constitutional Government repudiated the political militancy of Kasper's Tennessee White Citizens' Council. Dr. Clyde Alley, chairman of the Federation's Davidson County chapter, insisted that "we do not endorse his methods" but rather "propose to accomplish our ends by education and through ... peaceful means." Moreover, the militants suffered from bitter factionalism within their own ranks. The local Ku Klux Klan resented what it considered the incursion of Kasper into its territory and refused an alliance. Kasper did little to anticipate these problems. In a manner ironically reminiscent of the failed Southern Christian Leadership Conference campaign in Albany, Georgia, he appears to have relied, like Martin Luther King, Jr., more on his personal power to inspire than proper long-term planning.[58]

The combination of these forces ensured that Nashville avoided the fate of Little Rock, where the public school system had been closed in a futile effort to resist desegregation. Admission of African American students to formerly all-white schools proceeded at an incremental pace in Nashville. In September 1958, thirty-four black first- and second-grade pupils gained admittance to previously segregated institutions. Desegregation of the other grades proceeded on the basis of one per year so that by 1963 there were 773 African American pupils in 7 grades.[59]

Yet while city authorities had reason to congratulate themselves on the speed and efficiency with which they enforced desegregation, they were in part responsible for having fostered white resistance in the first place. Public commemorations of the fiftieth anniversary of school desegregation in Nashville proudly emphasized the calm and controlled measures of local officials in explaining why the city did not descend into the same chaos as had Little Rock.[60] It is certainly the case that the civic and political leadership of Nashville shunned the demagoguery of Arkansas Governor Orval Faubus. However, the historical reality is more complex than recent public remembrances of school desegregation suggest.

The official line from city authorities at the time was that desegregation would have been accomplished peacefully, were it not for the unwelcome intrusion of a dissident outsider. In truth, they had done much to prepare the ground for Kasper to launch his offensive. The board of education in particular failed to provide public leadership by emphasizing the moral imperative of racial reform. On the contrary, it had reluctantly accepted its legal responsibility to meet the terms of a court order and even then had conspired to curtail the number of black pupils admitted to white institutions. As School Superintendent William A. Bass informed a meeting of white Parent-Teacher Associations, "Your school board adopted this system with regret. They felt that the community is not yet ready for this step, but they were under compulsion to comply with the Supreme Court's decision."

Although it was not his intention, many parents interpreted the unenthusiastic tone of the speech as implicitly legitimating their opposition to desegregation. When whites terrorized black parents into requesting that their children be transferred from desegregated schools, the board also appears to have willfully misinterpreted this as an indication that African Americans supported the maintenance of Jim Crow policies. According to Assistant Superintendent W. H. Oliver, the transfer applications proved "that the Negroes in Nashville are pretty well satisfied with educational facilities we have made available to them over the years." This assessment of the situation can only have encouraged segregationists to coerce more black parents into making "voluntary" applications. Moreover, when some of the black parents who applied for transfers under pressure later petitioned to cancel their requests, the board refused them. The obstructionist policy pursued by the board of education had the net impact of reducing the number of black children still enrolled at formerly white institutions by the end of the first half of the school year from nineteen to nine.[61]

While their intentions were more honorable than those of the school board, the actions of white liberals also compromised the integration process. Baptist minister Will D. Campbell attempted to facilitate community acceptance of school desegregation as director of the Department of Racial and Cultural Relations of the National Council of Churches. Campbell tried to eliminate the threat posed by Kasper by circulating photographs of the segregationist leader "dancing with his black girlfriend in New York to suggest that he wasn't serious about racial segregation." The irony of this tactic is that it pandered to the very prejudices about miscegenation that underpinned white opposition to school desegregation. Moreover, as Campbell conceded, this ploy proved counterproductive since it provided the extremist Kasper with an opportunity to reposition himself along with the supposedly more respectable forces of massive resistance. The pictures, Kasper claimed, showed only "that he was acting as a strict constructionist, trying to preserve state's rights, and was not a bigot."[62]

Although Nashville authorities had neutralized Kasper, he was only the most conspicuous public face of segregationist protest in the city. Other, more anonymous, conspirators continued to plot in his absence. They bided their time until the equilibrium of everyday life had returned to the city before creating renewed unrest.

In the early evening of Sunday, March 16, 1958, Detectives J. W. Stinnett and Tom Campsey sat in a patrol car at Thirty-Third and West End. Their

Chapter Three

conversation came to a sudden halt at the sound of an explosion that, in the words of Stinnett, "nearly blew us out of the car." The two detectives raced in the direction of the local Jewish Community Center on West End Avenue. On reaching the Center, they discovered that it had suffered serious damage. Broken fragments of glass lay scattered across the ground and the ceiling and walls in the entrance wall had collapsed. The windows of houses along the street had also been shattered. Stinnett and Campsey soon found the cause of the destruction: a length of detonating wire in one of the doorways. Police calculated the cost of damage to the Center at $6,000.[63]

Rabbi William Silverman was at home with his wife when the bomb detonated. Minutes later, the telephone rang. The caller claimed he was a member of "the Confederate Underground," which had carried out the terrorist attack. "Next will be the Temple," whispered the anonymous voice, "and next will be any other nigger-loving place or nigger-loving person in Nashville." The caller identified William E. Miller, the federal judge who ordered implementation of school desegregation the previous fall, as the first target his associates intended to shoot "in cold blood."[64]

The authorities could not directly implicate Kasper in the bombing since he was at that time five months into his prison sentence. However, circumstantial evidence indicates that the Confederate Underground consisted of some of his closest political associates. The Nashville bombing was one of a series of dynamite attacks on Jewish institutions that occurred in late 1957 and early 1958. As Rabbi Silverman observed, the terrorist attacks occurred in communities where Kasper had established at least some support base. "Notice the plan and the pattern—wherever John Kaspar [sic] has incited against the Jews: Miami, Charlotte, N.C., Gastonia, N.C. and Nashville, there have been bombing and dynamiting of Jewish institutions."[65]

Kasper had found it difficult to associate the acculturated Jewish community of Nashville with the stereotype of the communist subversive conspiring to destroy the democratic order. The bombing of the community center represented a belated effort on the part of his associates to connect local Jews with school desegregation, driven by both desperation and a determination to avenge their imprisoned leader. That the terrorists sought to expose the Jewish community as the secret force responsible for desegregation is clear from the hundreds of anti-Semitic leaflets circulated throughout Nashville on the day of the bombing.[66] Kasper's allies also attempted to make political capital out of the incident by accusing Jews of having planted the bomb themselves as a means of discrediting militant segregationists as dangerous fanatics.[67]

Despite this attempt to stir renewed unrest, the bombing proved counterproductive. State and federal authorities launched an extensive investigation that focused on a possible interstate conspiracy. The mobilization
of resources in support of the FBI manhunt underlined a serious determination on the part of the authorities to protect Nashville Jews against
anti-Semitic extremism. The civic and religious leadership of the city also
publicly condemned the bombing. As Rabbi Silverman asserted, "There
has been an outpouring of messages, telegrams, and resolutions from the
Governor, ministerial associations, ministers, churches, civic groups, and
citizens of our community expressing a sense of outrage and indignation."[68]
Significantly, the bombing also elicited outspoken criticism from local segregationist leaders. "Revulsion to the violence has become so great in Nashville," affirmed the American Jewish Committee, "that the segregationists
would rather not go counter to this mass-sentiment." Alarmed that the
attack would brand all segregationists with the same label of extremism, the
Tennessee Federation for Constitutional Government publicly denounced
the perpetrators and raised funds for the repair of the community center.[69]

This outpouring of public sympathy also emboldened Rabbi Silverman
to take a stronger stand in support of racial desegregation. In a sermon
entitled "We Will Not Yield," he scorned those "jittery Jews" who sought
to protect themselves against segregationist reprisals by avoiding any association with the civil rights cause. Silverman claimed, on the contrary, that
African Americans and Jews shared a common fate. A political climate that
tolerated the repression of one minority fostered potential prejudice against
all minorities. The board of trustees issued an immediate vote of confidence
in the rabbi.[70]

The moment of crisis that facilitated the militant protest of Kasper
had therefore long since passed when prison authorities released him four
months before the completion of his sentence.[71] Although Kasper wasted
little time in attempting to renew the momentum of his political career, his
efforts stalled for lack of a clearly defined plan. He initially announced his
intention to resist the admission of African American students to Memphis
State University, but then recanted when local police threatened him with
immediate arrest.[72] His efforts to recruit supporters near West Palm Beach
in Florida also ended in failure when local Klansmen verbally assaulted
him.[73] Unable to find a fresh crisis that would allow him to take control of
segregationist resistance, he returned to Nashville, attending an interracial
meeting at the Clark Memorial Methodist Church to discuss desegregation of the second grade of the public school system. Police had to evacu-

ate the people in the church when they received a bomb threat. Although it proved a false alarm, fear and suspicion focused on the renewed threat Kasper posed.[74]

However, Kasper had to concentrate too much on his continuing legal battles to foment further disorder. The authorities had postponed his trial for inciting a riot in Nashville pending the completion of his sentence for flouting an injunction in Clinton. Kasper finally came before a criminal court on November 3, 1958. He tried and failed to secure the dismissal of the trial on the grounds that the panel of prospective jurors consisted of "big silk stocking muckety mucks," people who "are economically and socially ahead of my defense witnesses and the persons I am accused of inciting to riot." The same professional middle class he accused of having betrayed their birthright by accepting racial integration now stood prepared to convict him for protecting the constitutional rights of white working-class people. Invoking the rhetoric of the class warrior, Kasper condemned the "executive-type people who live in exclusive, restricted, sub-divisions, with Negro maids and yard boys" who were to cast verdict on him. It did him little good. On November 5, the court found Kasper guilty, and sentenced him to serve six months in the Davidson County workhouse and pay a $500 fine. Released on a $2,000 bond, Kasper launched a series of appeals for a retrial.[75]

Kasper used the time that the appeals process made available to resume his agitation on the race issue. The prospect of further prison sentences did not serve as a disincentive to his endorsement of deliberate acts of lawlessness. In November 1958, Kasper hosted a meeting with supporters in Washington, D.C., presumably the remnants of the Seaboard White Citizens' Council, at which he called for the creation of a new terrorist underground network to combat the federal government.[76]

Kasper also launched a renewed rhetorical tirade against establishment politicians such as Tennessee Governor Buford Ellington, whom he accused of having betrayed ordinary whites by accepting even token desegregation. In answer to his own call to remove "sorry politicians in office much too long," Kasper acted as campaign manager for two hard-line segregationists in the Nashville mayoral election of May 1959. His mayoral candidate, Bessie May Williams, suffered a crushing defeat to the incumbent, Ben West, losing by 1,192 votes to 20,542. Henry A. Jarrell also came in a poor third in the vice mayoral contest, securing only 1,106 votes. Not only did the incumbent, Sanders Anglea, win an emphatic 13,830 votes, but Jarrell received less than half the number of ballots cast for the African American challenger, Leo Lillard.[77] Kasper also suffered the personal humiliation of being pelted with eggs at one public meeting by students from Vanderbilt University, who then tried to throw him into a pond in Centennial Park.[78]

On June 29, 1959, the U.S. Supreme Court refused a petition for a writ of certiorari against the court that convicted Kasper a second time for his part in the Clinton disorders. A little more than two weeks later, U.S. marshals took him into custody before transporting him to the federal penitentiary in Tallahassee.[79] Released on December 16, Kasper remained free on bond for only four weeks. The U.S. Supreme Court refused to review his conviction for inciting a riot in Nashville and, on January 16, 1960, he started his prison sentence at the Davidson County workhouse.[80]

Prison bruised his body and broke his spirit. The notoriety he had attained as an opponent of racial integration made Kasper an obvious target for retributive violence by black prisoners. He suffered his first assault from a black inmate while serving his second sentence at the federal penitentiary in Tallahassee. When an African American punched Kasper in the face in the Davidson County workhouse, his fellow black convicts took up a collection in his honor. A fearful Kasper petitioned for a transfer to the county jail but prison authorities refused him.[81] A letter written by Kasper to Floyd Fleming of the Seaboard White Citizens' Council demonstrates his defeatism, not least in its indifference about the future of the organization he had founded. Kasper had surrendered leadership of the council to Dale Birdsell, a former member of the Louisiana-based Southern Gentlemen, but in his absence it had soon imploded. "Scared, yes, definitely I am scared. If you are so utterly selfish as to worry about what effect the dissolution of the Seaboard charter will have on segregationists, then go to hell. I don't know you and thanks for nothing."[82] A still more wretched appeal for pity came shortly before his release from the workhouse, when Kasper placed himself on a self-imposed fast so that his emaciated appearance would "gain sympathy for himself and from his admirers." However, by the time Kasper performed this last act of showmanship the stage lights had long since been dimmed. When he walked out of the workhouse on July 15, 1960, only a small band of his most loyal allies were there to meet him. The press paid even less attention. Kasper retreated to his mother's home in New Jersey.[83]

There is no clearer indication that Kasper had lost his appetite for political controversy than the decline and end of his correspondence with his erstwhile mentor, Ezra Pound. Pound had returned to Italy after his release from the St. Elizabeths Hospital in 1958. The extent to which Kasper had performed a role stage-managed by Pound may be unclear, but the final correspondence between the two offers further clues about their relationship. At times Kasper seems like an actor in need of direction. In May 1962, he wrote to "Grampaw," offering to publish any of his material and to provide financial support for his medical care. A decade earlier Kasper had exuded enormous excitement in his correspondence with Pound. "Hurry hurry hurry, the Gasp gasps," read one letter, "RUSH! special extra." Now he made no attempt to emulate the style of the poet. The demotic tone of the prose in the later letter intimates his sense of disappointment and defeat. Other than a criticism of the "extreme nepotism and ruinous taxation" policies of the Kennedy administration, Kasper makes no mention of politics but focuses on the mundane details of his domestic life. He also admitted that he had lost contact with the other people who had gathered around the poet and given such purpose and vitality to his life in the 1950s. His faith in the poet nonetheless remained undimmed. Kasper signed the letter "your humble and obedient servant." However, Pound did not reciprocate. In November 1962, Kasper attempted to visit his erstwhile mentor during a vacation to Europe. A terse note written by Pound's mistress, Olga Rudge, states that the poet's wife had invited Kasper to lunch but "E.P. did not want to see him." Kasper wrote to Pound some weeks later. While he still idolized the poet, the snub can only have confirmed his decision to abandon the massive resistance cause.[84]

Civil rights leaders remained on alert for any indication that Kasper was attempting to resume his terrorist activities. In March 1964, the Allied Organizations for Civil Rights liaised with local, state, and federal authorities to ensure that Kasper did not attempt to interfere with a march on the Kentucky state capitol building in Louisville.[85] There was, however, no need for such concern. Interviewed by the FBI, Kasper insisted that "he was still opposed" to desegregation, but that he also "desired to start a new life." His notoriety, he conceded, made him more a liability than an asset to segregationist resistance and "he could be of no further use to this sort of movement."[86] However, some of his supporters sought to convince him otherwise.

In August 1958, Kasper had been the keynote speaker at the founding convention of the National States' Rights Party (NSRP), a far-right organization that amalgamated a number of fringe political parties. One of its leaders, Jesse B. Stoner, had briefly assisted Kasper during his Nashville campaign.[87] Firm in his principle that he was "not a joiner," Kasper maintained only a loose affiliation with the party. Following his release from prison, he attempted to dissociate himself completely from it, but this proved harder than he anticipated. His successive terms of imprisonment had made him the most celebrated martyr of the militant segregationist movement. As one segregationist publication asserted, "No other white patriot in the South has suffered as much persecution for the sake of our cause than has John Kasper."[88]

At its annual convention in February 1964, the NSRP nominated Kasper as its candidate in the forthcoming presidential election. Kasper had not attended the convention. When his running mate, Jesse Stoner, telephoned him to ask whether he would accept the nomination, he neither withdrew his name nor consented to campaign in support of his own candidacy.[89] Pressed by reporters, he preferred to give his backing to the Republican candidate Barry Goldwater. Kasper was adamant that he had not abandoned his opposition to civil rights reform but stated that he had lost faith in his ability to withstand the force of federal activism. Referring to the number of his convictions for resisting school desegregation, he remarked that "any man who runs his head against a wall three times without moving the wall one inch would not be courageous or heroic to do the same thing a fourth time."[90] The names of Kasper and Stoner appeared on the ballot in only three states: Arkansas, Kentucky, and Minnesota. On election day, they polled only 6,957 votes.[91]

John Kasper attained no more than momentary infamy. Within only a few years of first appearing on the public stage, he had retreated into obscurity, marrying his Norwegian girlfriend and pursuing a number of professions— baker, vacuum-cleaner salesman, car mechanic—that intimated nothing of his past life. The FBI closed its file on him in 1967. He died forgotten on April 7, 1998.[92]

Many commentators at the time when Kasper was front-page news dismissed him as an unsophisticated political opportunist. Some claimed that his motivation was financial profit. Journalist Murray Kempton supported this assertion by citing Nashville Judge Andrew Doyle who had concluded, when passing sentence on Kasper, "Yer purpose was to cause trouble and fatten yer pocketbook with the dimes and dollars of irresponsible and uneducated people."[93] Others insisted that the principal impetus for Kasper's political career was a neurotic desire for public adulation. The pathological model of right-wing extremism commanded considerable intellectual credibility at the time and many writers found sufficient evidence to conclude that Kasper was afflicted with some form of psychosis. His treatment for "general neurotic behavior" during the late 1940s, for instance, suggested an unstable mind. The conclusion of most authors who studied Kasper was that he wanted to attain public notoriety as a means of compensating for his failure to pursue a more conventional career. Journalists Wilma Dykeman and James Stokely depicted Kasper as a socially maladjusted individual, desperate for attention, who would enlist in "any cause that seems to further irresponsible rebellion at the moment." In their opinion, Kasper became a segregationist not out of sincere political conviction but simply as a means to pursue his own personal ambition. Other reporters shared the assessment that Kasper suffered from a narcissistic personality disorder. According to Stan Opotowsky, Kasper was a "floundering misfit starving for attention." He cited a remark Ezra Pound is purported to have made to his young acolyte that "To become famous a man must DO SOMETHING—it doesn't matter on which side, just so you DO SOMETHING."[94]

Neither the desire for financial reward nor the need for public notoriety provides an adequate explanation for why Kasper became a segregationist. Having claimed that what inspired Kasper was the prospect of making a fast buck, Murray Kempton unwittingly contradicted himself by disclosing that the young agitator was so poor he "lives nowhere except in the back of old cars with a pile of leaflets as his pillow." Nor could he raise the $200 bail imposed by Judge Doyle. If money was the sole motivation for Kasper, he would have abandoned racial agitation for a more profitable career much sooner.[95]

The accusation that Kasper acted out of an impulse for public recognition contains a greater element of truth. Any person who composes songs in celebration of his own political heroism ("John Kasper was a young man/ A young man were he/When he went to fight the battle/Of Clinton, Tennessee") must be considered something of a self-publicist.[96] At the same time, as an outsider with limited resources Kasper understood that the new media provided the fastest means by which to attract attention to his cause and mobilize a popular support base. It was an irony lost on many reporters that their stories provided Kasper with the publicity they criticized him for seeking.

The attempt to pathologize Kasper is also problematic. Those authors who used such an interpretive model to explain his political actions relied on a reductionist line of reasoning that individualized his behavior and decontextualized him from the broader society in which he was born and raised. Although Kasper was under psychiatric care as a teenager, few contemporary experts would diagnose disobedience and homosexuality as mental illnesses. Moreover, even if, for instance, Kasper were gay, it does not follow that his political extremism was a symptom of his homosexuality.

To dismiss Kasper as a crank does not help us to understand why so many people supported him. It also in some sense diminishes the seriousness of the challenge faced by the black students who braved the threat of violent mob retaliation in attending formerly white schools. The claim that Kasper had no inherent interest in the race issue ultimately reflected the racial bias of reporters unable or unwilling to accept that anyone could convert to the cause of white supremacy. While his political opinions were repugnant, this should not blind us to the possibility that he reached them out of a rational decision. Kasper was no charlatan. On the contrary, he was a successful graduate of Columbia University. Kasper was also much more than an opportunist. His willingness to suffer arrest and imprisonment underlines a sincere conviction in the segregationist cause. There were surely other means by which a young man craving public attention could achieve his ambition. As Bruce Hoffman contends, a political terrorist is not motivated only by the prospect of personal aggrandizement, "the wish to line his own pocket or satisfy some personal need or grievance." On the contrary, in his own mind the extremist is "fundamentally an *altruist*: he believes that he is serving a 'good' cause designed to achieve a greater good for a wider constituency—whether real or imagined."[97]

Kasper stated in numerous interviews that what inspired his actions was less an inherent hostility toward African Americans than their manipulation as pawns in a conspiracy by Jewish Communists to destroy the social order. As he told the FBI, "his segregationist activities actually resulted from anti-Semitic philosophy and not because he is primarily opposed to the Negroes in the United States."[98] This explanation does not account for his earlier fraternization with African Americans at interracial functions. To acknowledge that Kasper may have been inconsistent in his line of political thought is not, however, to dismiss the sincerity of his conversion to the far right.

John Kasper eludes easy analysis. One of the principal problems rests in the fact that he committed so few of his thoughts to paper. He never honored his repeated promise to write a book about his political career. As a result, other than his letters to Ezra Pound and a few pamphlets, he produced little written work that would allow us a clearer insight into why he violently resisted racial change. It is impossible ever to see clearly into the mind of another and in the case of Kasper the veil of mystery can be raised but not entirely removed.

Bryant W. Bowles, president of the National Association for the Advancement of White People, Inc. Library of Congress, Prints and Photographs Division, NYWT&S Collection, LC-USZ62-126462.

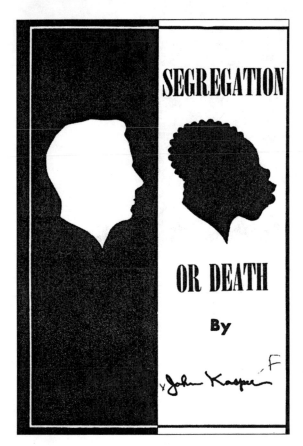

John Kasper, "Segregation or Death" pamphlet. Columbia Rare Book and Manuscript Library, New York.

"WE DARE DEFEND OUR RIGHTS"
Motto State of Alabama

CLEAN THE TRAITORS OUT

Safeguard The White Race and the Nation's Security

ELECT

Native Alabamian

★

Lifelong Democrat

★

REAR ADMIRAL
JOHN G.
CROMMELIN
USN RET.

JOHN G. CROMMELIN

to the

UNITED STATES SENATE

Subject to Democratic Primaries of May 1 and 29, 1962

7 (Paid Political Adv. by John G. Crommelin Headquarters - P. O. Box 441 - Wetumpka, Alabama)

Nashville Superintendent of City Parks F.W. Perkins informs segregationist John Kasper that he cannot hold a rally in Centennial Park without a permit. Library of Congress, Prints and Photographs Division, NYWT&S Collection, LC-USZ62-126457.

J. B. Stoner at a Klan rally in St. Augustine. Florida State Archives.

PART TWO

Never-Ending War

John Crommelin and Edwin Walker

4. Fighting the Hidden Force

John Crommelin and the Defense of Alabama

In October 2003, an audience assembled to celebrate the post-humous induction of a former war hero into the Alabama Military Hall of Honor. The man whose patriotic service the crowd had come to mark was Navy Rear Admiral John G. Crommelin. The United States had marked the half century since the end of World War II with an upsurge of public nostalgia for what one bestselling book described as *The Greatest Generation*: the men and women who, as soldiers and civilians, safeguarded democracy for the future. It was guided by this spirit that public officials and the press memorialized Crommelin following his death on November 2, 1996. An obituary in the *Montgomery Advertiser* praised him as an exemplar of the wartime generation, a "true American patriot" whose distinguished naval career demonstrated an "unwavering love of the service."[1]

That, however, was only half the story. Although the obituary mentioned that on returning to civilian life Crommelin had "embarked on a series of unsuccessful campaigns for the U.S. Senate," it did not elaborate further. Nonetheless, some people were determined to restore the details the paper erased. Two weeks later, the *Advertiser* published a letter from a reader that cited some of the campaign literature used by Crommelin. This material included a commitment to eliminate the "Communist-Jewish Conspirators" who were attempting to use the power of the United Nations to create "a slave-like world population of copper-colored human mongrels." The reason why the newspaper had attempted to bury this information along with the body of the rear admiral was, concluded the correspondent, because "some of the most influential people in Montgomery" wanted to conceal their own pasts as supporters of his far-right campaigns.[2]

It is perhaps fitting that the issue of how to represent publicly the life of a late war hero should become a battlefield. On one side were those persons who—like others who oppose the recent prosecution of former white terrorists for the murder of civil rights activists—considered it inappropriate at a time when the South had supposedly put its racist past behind it to reopen old wounds. It was far better, in their minds, to emphasize those aspects of Crommelin that appealed to popular notions of southern tradition such as masculine heroism and honor. On the other side were those whose historical injuries had never healed. Civil rights activists condemned Crommelin's induction, claiming his racial and religious bigotry offset his wartime service. "This is not a man who you would just consider a sign of the times," asserted Anti-Defamation League activist Deborah Lauter. "He was a leader in the hate movement."[3]

Both sides in the debate about how best to remember Crommelin drew on distinct facets of his personality and career. What they did not address was whether these aspects could be reconciled into a coherent narrative of his life. How and why did Crommelin undergo the transformation from war hero to political villain? Was it in the process of transition from military service to civilian life that he became converted to the cause of the far right, or was he awaiting an opportunity to articulate opinions to which he had long subscribed? Determining how Crommelin became a militant white supremacist is important because he does not conform to the stereotypical portrayal of right-wing extremists as isolated loners on the social and economic margins of society. As one Jewish activist observed, Crommelin was not one of "the kind of men likely to become anti-Semitic agitators" because he boasted of "social position and recognition." In contrast to the conventional wisdom about those who embrace political radicalism, Crommelin had little to gain but a lot to lose.[4]

During the postwar era, Crommelin was a perennial candidate for public office in Alabama. He pushed a far-right agenda that included commitments to maintain racial segregation, secure American withdrawal from the United Nations, and prohibit the fluoridation of water which, he believed, was a means of brainwashing innocent civilians. The common thread with

Chapter Four

which Crommelin tied these disparate campaign issues together was his claim that the source of these threats was a powerful cabal of communist Jews conspiring to crush the security and welfare of white Alabamians. His home state was the battlefield on which would be fought a final clash of civilizations, the forces of Christianity against the hordes of godless atheism.

Crommelin failed, however, to convince the electorate of the threat he claimed they faced. Today those studies of the civil rights struggle that mention him are rare and dismiss him as an inconsequential figure on the lunatic fringe. Yet his impact on state politics was greater than is usually recognized.

Crommelin's inability to win election is itself significant because of what it reveals about the complicated and contradictory intraregional dynamics of massive resistance. Bryant Bowles and John Kasper provoked fierce conflict in communities that had not anticipated trouble over desegregation. Both men succeeded despite being outsiders with limited connections and resources. Crommelin by contrast failed to benefit from what appeared to be many personal and political advantages. Not only was white opposition to integration more intense in Alabama than in Delaware or Tennessee, but as a decorated war hero from a socially prominent family Crommelin also had the credentials for political leadership. Comparing Crommelin with Bowles and Kasper allows us to unravel the apparent paradox that the far right made more political capital in moderate border states than in the reactionary Deep South.

A study of Crommelin also affords insight into the failure of moderate white political leadership. Crommelin had his best chance to win election when he challenged incumbent Lister Hill in the Democratic senatorial primary of 1956. Although racial tensions in Alabama were at their most acute, Hill offered only anemic support for segregation. Crommelin by contrast stood as an uncompromising champion of white privilege. Yet it was Hill who won by a landslide. The senator had secured lucrative federal contracts that created new economic opportunities in his impoverished state. Despite the challenge of black activism, white voters feared that the militant resistance advocated by Crommelin would lead to violent disorder that would stem the flow of federal largesse. Although Crommelin overestimated the strength of white intransigence, so too crucially did Hill. Crommelin campaigned with such conviction that he intimidated Hill into adopting a more racially reactionary stance. Hill's reaction to

Crommelin emphasizes the importance of historical contingency. Had he retained more faith in his own moderation then racial extremism may not have come to dominate electoral politics in Alabama in the way it did for the next decade.

Crommelin is important in a number of other respects. First, while Bryant Bowles and John Kasper burst spectacularly on the political scene but then soon disappeared, Crommelin represented a longer-term menace to racial and ethnic minorities. The strength and persistence of his anti-Semitism led to his being labeled the most serious threat to the security of Jews in the southern states. His enduring impact is underlined by the bitterness of the protests over his public commemoration decades after he retired from political life. Second, the implementation by civil rights groups of a quarantine strategy to contain the threat he posed also illuminates the development of policies to combat hate speech. Third, Crommelin was highly influential in facilitating the infrastructural growth of the far right, the impact of which endures to this day.

John Geraerdt Crommelin was born October 2, 1902, in Montgomery, Alabama. On graduating from high school, he enrolled first at the University of Virginia and then at the U.S. Naval Academy in Annapolis, Maryland. He completed three years of sea duty before training as an aviator, receiving his navy wings in November 1926.[5]

Crommelin received numerous commendations for his service. By the time the United States intervened in World War II, his four brothers had all followed him into the navy. Small boys too young to serve their country could still experience the vicarious thrill of reading in comic books about the exploits of the "Dixie Demons," as the Crommelins became known. Adults were no less in awe, the fearless heroism of the brothers inspiring *Time* magazine to hail them "The Indestructibles."[6]

None seemed to have more superhuman powers than John. As an officer aboard the aircraft carrier *Enterprise*, he participated in every major naval engagement in the South Pacific, earning a commendation for "consistently outstanding performance and distinguished achievement."[7] Following his promotion to captain, the navy assigned him to the flagship *Liscome Bay*. While on a mission to the Gilbert Islands, a Japanese submarine torpedoed the ship. Crommelin, who was showering when the attack occurred, ran naked through the flames to the flight deck, where he coordinated the operations to abandon ship. He then plunged forty-five feet into the sea and clung to a piece of flotsam while he awaited rescue. Awarded the Purple Heart and the Legion of Merit, Crommelin continued to rise through the ranks, culminating with his reassignment to the Joint Chiefs of Staff in April 1949.[8]

It was ironically this devotion to the navy that led to the downfall of Crommelin's career. In 1949, the federal government announced its intention to replace naval aircraft carriers with a fleet of long-range strategic bombers under the command of the newly independent air force. This policy provoked a backlash from senior naval officers referred to by the press as "The Revolt of the Admirals." The foremost dissident was Crommelin. In September 1949, he enlisted the support of Cedric Worth, a civilian assistant to Under Secretary of the Navy Dan A. Kimball, in preparing a memorandum that accused senior army and air force officials of undermining naval aviation in order to accentuate their own power. The memo concluded that unless these conspirators were stopped, the navy would be "nibbled to death" by the Pentagon.[9] Crommelin also released classified documents to the press, including a confidential letter from Vice Admiral Gerald Bogan to Secretary of the Navy Francis Matthews that claimed the Pentagon had sold the country "a false bill of goods."[10]

Although Crommelin secured a hearing for the navy before the House Armed Services Committee, his career was ruined. Secretary Matthews accused him of being "faithless, insubordinate and disloyal," and suspended him from duty. Concerned that court-martialing Crommelin could lead to his becoming a martyr in the minds of other discontented naval men, Chief of Naval Operations Admiral Forrest P. Sherman instead issued an official reprimand.[11] In a letter to Sherman that offers the first evidence of his political paranoia, Crommelin accused a "small, powerful military group" of cynically sabotaging naval aviation, and asked that he either have his reprimand wiped from his record or that he be court-martialed, so he could put his case to the American public. Confronted by this continued insubordination, Sherman issued an order placing Crommelin on indefinite furlough. Under mounting pressure, Crommelin accepted an offer of advancement to the rank of rear admiral in return for his resignation from the navy.[12]

Crommelin accepted his departure because he had by that time decided to run for public office. On April 30, 1950, he announced his intention to campaign as an independent candidate in the Alabama senatorial election the following November. His opponent was Democratic incumbent Lister Hill.[13]

Hill had been a member of the Senate since 1938. An ardent New Dealer, he voted for a series of reform measures that resulted in the unprecedented expansion of federal power into the southern states. His economic liberalism aroused the enmity of a conservative coalition of Black Belt cotton planters and Big Mule industrialists. Industrial leaders regarded his advocacy of the Fair Labor Standards Act of 1938 as an assault on labor and race relations because it established a minimum wage and maximum working week, weakening their control of the workforce and undermining their competitive advantage over northern rivals.[14]

Hill had become even more closely associated with the liberalism of the national Democratic Party during its 1948 convention. When southern activists failed to soften the strong civil rights plank adopted as part of the party platform, many of them stormed out of the convention, reconvening in Birmingham, where they established the breakaway States' Rights Democratic Party with Senator Strom Thurmond of South Carolina as their presidential candidate. Hill's leadership of southern loyalists strengthened the hostility of conservatives in his home state.[15]

Crommelin became the candidate of the industrialist-planter elite in the 1950 election. While his policy commitments were conservative, he did not yet espouse the conspiratorial fantasies that would tarnish his later campaigns. Rather than pander to the racial prejudice of the electorate, he instead attempted to smear Hill as a socialist because of his support of liberal reform programs administered through centralized government. Why Crommelin did not emphasize racial issues is unclear, but tactical considerations probably played a part. State Senator James Simpson had tried and failed to exploit race in his campaign against Hill six years earlier. Not until the later rise of massive resistance would race once more become the primary issue in Alabama politics. Crommelin endured a resounding loss on election day, winning only 38,477 votes compared to 125,534 for Hill.[16]

Following his defeat, Crommelin retreated to his Elmore County plantation. He reappeared on the political scene four years later, running as a candidate in the Democratic Senate primary of June 1954. Three other candidates, including incumbent John J. Sparkman, entered the race. The result was a resounding endorsement of Sparkman, who secured more than 60 percent of the vote. Crommelin came in a distant third, winning only 16,370 votes—little more than 3 percent—out of a total of 496,251.[17]

It is indicative of the initially muted response to the *Brown* decision that Crommelin, now emerging as a more identifiable figure of the far right, tried and failed to make race a central issue of the campaign. In April 1954, he sent a telegram to Chief Justice Earl Warren, urging the Supreme Court to issue an immediate decision in the case which, he claimed, was being postponed to protect the racially moderate Sparkman from having to take a public position on school desegregation. Although the Court announced its decision shortly before the primary, it did not influence the outcome.[18]

Crommelin was also unable to surmount the problem created by the withdrawal of support from the Big Mules who, having unsuccessfully backed him before, chose instead to endorse Congressman Laurie Battle. The rear admiral reacted bitterly by denouncing Battle as a stooge of corporate interests. According to one newspaper, the vitriol Crommelin spat at rival candidates revealed he knew his cause was hopeless and felt free to speak his mind.[19]

Others would later repeat the assertion that Crommelin eschewed caution because he understood he had no chance of winning public office. According to one report on his activities, he "doesn't expect election to public office, but relishes the opportunity to use the platform, press and television to air his bigotry."[20] There is nonetheless reason to doubt such evaluations. The persistence with which Crommelin pursued public office suggests, no matter how misguided, a sincere conviction that he could win.

Unperturbed by his failure to win public office in Alabama, Crommelin made his first foray into national politics in the fall of 1954. Earlier that year, the notorious red-baiting politician Senator Joseph McCarthy had suffered humiliation when he attempted to prove communist subversion of the U.S. Army. Crommelin joined an alliance of retired military officers that formed the lobby group Ten Million Americans Mobilizing for Justice, a name that represented the number of people they intended to recruit in support of a petition protesting a move in the Senate to censure McCarthy.[21]

Ten Million Americans publicized its campaign with a rally at Madison Square Garden on November 29. Crommelin was one of the keynote speakers. His address warned ominously of "some Hidden Force or some Hidden Power" that, he claimed, was attempting to undermine national security by impeding "all congressional inquiry into communist and subversive infiltration of the government."[22]

Although Crommelin did not elucidate who or what he meant by a "Hidden Force," the implicit meaning of the speech soon became clear. In February 1955, Ten Million Americans disbanded when some of its board members protested what they claimed was an attempt by Crommelin to turn it into "an overtly anti-Semitic organization." According to Crommelin, the "Hidden Force" was a secret council consisting of "300 top Jew Zionists" whose efforts "to control the world" had resulted in their seizing control of both the political establishment and the press. Roy Cohn, the Jewish lawyer who served as chief counsel to McCarthy, was a secret agent planted by the council to deflect suspicion from its nefarious activities.[23] Amid this acrimony, Ten Million Americans imploded, with less than 350,000 people actually having signed the petition defending McCarthy.[24]

On returning to his home state, Crommelin attempted in the spring of 1956 to unseat Lister Hill a second time. The outcome of the Democratic senatorial primary had profound implications for Crommelin specifically and Alabama politics more broadly. There was no better opportunity than in 1956 for Crommelin to win public office, riding the cresting wave of massive resistance in the state. Yet it was Hill who scored an overwhelming victory. His decisive defeat of Crommelin denoted a strong sense of political realism on the part of Alabama voters, who recognized that intractable opposition to integration could prove counterproductive. Crommelin's confrontational tactics threatened to provoke the federal government not only to withdraw the investment Hill had secured for the impoverished state, but also to impose racial reform through force. However, the election result was a pyrrhic victory for racial moderates. Hill overestimated the strength of his opponent, shifting to the right in an attempt to deflect criticism that he was soft on the race issue. His actions served to strengthen the hand of racial hard-liners, steering Alabama farther down a route of massive resistance.

The political temper in Alabama altered significantly between 1954 and 1956. Newspaper editors and public officials initially reacted with relative calm to the *Brown* decision. While the white press uniformly opposed the ruling, some newspapers encouraged state politicians to circumvent the court without need of direct confrontation by equalizing conditions in black and white schools.[25] State authorities similarly attempted to suppress grassroots opposition before it had an opportunity to spread. Governor Gordon Persons resisted pressure to call a special session of the state legislature to discuss the ruling. Persons was succeeded in 1955 by racial moderate Jim Folsom, whose landslide victory underlined the limitations of organized resistance to the Court decision. Folsom signaled his political intentions shortly before his inauguration by refusing to sign a statement of opposition to school desegregation. "If there was ever a time on the American educational front," he announced, "when we needed wisdom and tolerance and objective thinking—it is certainly now."[26]

Wisdom and tolerance were, however, in short supply. Historians dispute the precise catalyst for the mass opposition to school desegregation that swept through Alabama. Some place their emphasis on the "with all deliberate speed" decision in *Brown II*, an apparent admission of federal government weakness that encouraged white resistance. Others point to the Montgomery bus boycott, which awakened whites to the increasingly militant assertiveness of African Americans.[27] What is most probable is that a chain of events in 1955 and 1956 had the cumulative impact of turning white Alabamians toward a policy of massive resistance. One of these incidents was the attempt of black student Autherine Lucy in February 1956 to enroll at the University of Alabama, an event that simultaneously demonstrated to whites the threat to their social hegemony and their ability to withstand it through collective action.

Alabama rose to the front ranks of massive resistance. Political reactionaries wrestled control of the state legislature from Governor Folsom, enacting a series of measures to obstruct school desegregation. Alabama politicians led the way in repressing black activism, demanding that the NAACP turn over its membership lists and then banning the organization when it refused to comply. The Citizens' Council also attracted more substantial support, with the exception of Mississippi, than in any other southern state.[28]

Crommelin therefore entered the senatorial race of 1956 in the most auspicious circumstances of his political career. The prospect of a successful challenge to Lister Hill also attracted the interest of militant segregationists from within and outside the state. In a rare moment of political cohesion, they set aside their mutual hostility and suspicion to work in common cause for the Crommelin campaign.

One of the most enthusiastic volunteers was a young man named John Kasper. When Kasper hit the front pages during the Clinton crisis, he told journalists that it was Crommelin who had opened his eyes to the existence of a communist Jewish conspiracy against the South. Kasper also introduced Crommelin to Ezra Pound. Kasper and his associates enlisted the support of a number of military figures sympathetic to the reactionary politics of the poet, presumably in the belief that they possessed the power and influence to secure his release from the mental hospital.[29] These recruits included several veterans of Ten Million Americans Mobilizing for Justice, including Crommelin and Lieutenant General Pedro del Valle. What influence Pound had in shaping the political philosophy of Crommelin is less clear than with Kasper, but the poet did include a reference to the valor of the rear admiral in *Canto CV*:

> With a Crommelyn at the breech-block
> > Or a del Valle,
> This is what the swine haven't got
> > With their
> > > πανουργία ["knavery"][30]

The poet not only flattered Crommelin's ego, but also compounded his conspiratorial anti-Semitism, a role that underlines his status as an éminence grise of the American far right.

Pound's influence is also apparent in one particular aspect of Crommelin's Senate bid. The rear admiral used his campaign to promote popular opposition to the Alaska Mental Health Enabling Act of 1956, claiming that the law was a plot by communist Jews. According to Crommelin, the new mental health facilities were actually prison camps. The conspirators' plan was to incarcerate patriotic Americans in these remote detention centers on the pretext that they were insane and then to brainwash them into accepting racial integration. As he asserted some years later, "By means of an injection and/or lobotomy, the Citizens patterned after our Founding Fathers will be Zombies and utterly useless in this worldwide Life and Death Battle between the forces of Christ and the Anti-Christ."[31] Crommelin accused Hill specifically of hoping to use the new legislation as a means to silence his political opponents. He also picketed the Montgomery branch of the National Institute of Mental Health, which he saw as a local holding center for political prisoners scheduled for transportation to Alaska.[32]

Massive resistance leaders concerned to distance themselves from extremists such as Crommelin were swift to dismiss his claims as hysteria. Many of them nonetheless shared his unease that psychiatric discourse had the potential to mute public opposition to desegregation. Psychiatric research published in the 1950s produced a mounting consensus that the root cause of racism was ignorance, anxiety, and mental instability. Authors such as Gordon Allport contrasted the liberalism of "enlightened people" with the "irrational human behavior" of those who sought to preserve segregation.[33] Labeling segregationists unreasoning and deluded eliminated the need for liberals to engage them in dialogue. Southern political leaders feared that their exclusion from public discussion on the race issue would undermine their ability to plead their case to the rest of the nation.

The Citizens' Councils were especially defensive in the face of accusations that their support of segregation was irrational since it compromised their claims to be a responsible and respectable political organization. A cartoon in the councils' newsletter showed a team of psychiatrists evaluating a segregationist. "He believes in segregation. He must be crazy!" exclaims one analyst. "We'd better brainwash him again!" concludes one of his colleagues. The same newsletter also included an editorial warning how the courts could suppress segregationists' freedom of speech by ordering them to submit to psychiatric testing. Despite the efforts of Citizens' Council leaders to distance themselves from Crommelin, such alarmism was in truth not far removed from the fantastical claims made by the rear admiral.[34]

Crommelin also received crucial support from Asa Carter, another political activist whose relationship with, and influence on, the rear admiral reached far beyond the campaign. A native of Oxford, Alabama, Carter served in the navy during World War II, an experience that may have fostered his later friendship with Crommelin. Following his demobilization, Carter took a journalism degree at the University of Colorado, going on to work as a radio station announcer. He attained notoriety in 1955 when WILD in Birmingham fired him for inflammatory remarks about Jews.[35]

This incident was the first of many that set the militant Carter apart from the more sober and supposedly respectable ranks of massive resistance. The *Montgomery Advertiser*, for instance, saw Carter as being as much a threat to the social order as the National Association for the Advancement of Colored People (NAACP), describing him as a "loathsome fuehrer" leading "a crude and repellent organization wallowing in malevolent prejudice against the Negro and the Jew."[36]

That organization was the North Alabama Citizens' Council that, along with its paramilitary wing, the Original Ku Klux Klan of the Confederacy, Carter founded in October 1955. Over the next several months, he and his followers implemented a campaign of repressive violence against African Americans, inciting rioting at the University of Alabama in reaction to the enrollment of African American student Autherine Lucy, beating black singer Nat "King" Cole on stage at the Birmingham Municipal Auditorium, and assaulting civil rights leader Fred Shuttlesworth and his wife.[37]

Crommelin enlisted support for his senatorial bid by sharing the stage with Carter at numerous North Alabama Citizens' Council rallies.[38] Carter influenced Crommelin ideologically as well as tactically. Rhetorically, he espoused a reactionary populism similar to that of John Kasper. He condemned the self-professedly respectable leaders of massive resistance as elitists out of touch with the needs and interests of ordinary whites. As was the case with Kasper, Carter considered the white political establishment to be as much, if not more, of an adversary as the civil rights movement. To Carter, the temporizing response of the "political big shots" to racial reform represented a betrayal of their birthright. "They have been the enemy," he concluded, "they and their cowardly political kin, for twenty-five years."[39] In sharp contrast, Carter praised the virtues of lower-class whites, whom he characterized as honest and hardworking. Like Kasper, he attempted to transform derogatory terms such as *hillbilly* and *hick* into emblems of honor and personal empowerment. "For 'redneck' takes mind of the toil beneath God's Sun and with His good earth, of that he feels no shame," he wrote effusively in his newsletter, *The Southerner*.[40]

In collaboration with Kasper and Carter, Crommelin constructed a campaign that emphasized the need to protect segregation against the unconstitutional incursions of the federal government. The *Brown* decision, he asserted, embodied "the accelerated trend of the federal government to arrogate power to itself and to deny the constitutional right of the several states to govern in accordance with the will of the people."[41]

This defense of states' rights was consistent with the rhetoric of most southern politicians; what set Crommelin apart was his emphasis on biological racism. His rhetoric stressed that the southern racial hierarchy represented an innate order determined by the hereditary characteristics with which God had imbued blacks and whites. "Segregation is natural," he asserted in a televised broadcast, "its perpetuation is natural to man, and essential to the survival of Western civilization."[42]

Since he believed that segregation had divine sanction, Crommelin interpreted the *Brown* decision not only as a usurpation by the Supreme Court of its constitutional authority, but also as an act of satanic influence. "Anti-segregation," he asserted, "is the pasture of the devil." The godless forces responsible for influencing the ruling were, he concluded, communist Jews. Their intention was "to set up a world government in the framework of the United Nations and take all the national boundaries and erase them and all the racial distinctions and erase them, so that we will have one world without any national boundaries and without any races."[43] This perception of the United Nations as an instrument of the Jewish conspiracy was characteristic of the far right, stemming from an assumption, which endured despite the establishment of the state of Israel, that Jews were a rootless people with no allegiance to any nation. The United Nations therefore provided Jews with the means to attain global power by undermining the sovereignty of individual nation-states.

Crommelin maintained that his opponent was not only too weak to resist this threat, but that he too had conspired to undermine the autonomous regulation of race relations by state government. The rear admiral falsely accused Hill of having introduced a resolution at the Democratic Party convention in 1936 that led to the abolition of the two-thirds vote needed to secure nomination of candidates, a device that traditionally provided southern members with veto power over who ran for the presidency and on what platform. Hill had not introduced the resolution; in fact, he had not even attended the convention. Crommelin also claimed the senator had undermined segregation by sponsoring the Hospital Survey and Construction Act of 1946, which provided for federal loans to improve state health care facilities. He also vowed he would force the senator to take a clearer stand on the race issue by pressuring him "to join the Citizens' Council or tell us why he won't."[44]

On May 3, 1956, Hill won an overwhelming victory with 244,567 votes compared to 112,579 for his opponent.[45] The result represented an improvement on the 1950 race for Crommelin, who increased his share of the vote from 23.5 to 31.8 percent. This arguably had less to do with the personal appeal of the candidate, however, than with the changing political situation, which was now much more conducive to a challenge to Hill.

What had gone wrong for the Crommelin campaign team? The answer is rich in contradiction and irony, but also revealing about the dynamics of massive resistance in Alabama.

Hill not only possessed the advantage of incumbency, but also retained the loyalty of many ordinary voters who had benefited from the federal largesse the New Dealer had secured for his state. His position as a Washington insider could also have benefited him because the electorate hoped he would use his influence to obstruct civil rights reform.

While these circumstances were beyond Crommelin's control, he also bore responsibility for the failure of his campaign. Even with the political winds blowing in the direction of massive resistance, most voters believed they needed a steadier helmsman than the erratic rear admiral. During the late 1950s, the FBI secured a notebook owned by an associate of Crommelin named Matthias Koehl, who had researched the causes of the rear admiral's election defeat. Koehl identified two principal factors. First, voters perceived

Crommelin as a "negative character" who had no constructive proposals for how to resolve the racial crisis. Second, since he had no legal strategy to resist desegregation, the electorate feared that "drastic action and violence" would occur if Crommelin were elected to power. While many whites saw Hill as weak on the race issue, they also recognized that it was tactically misguided to pursue a bloody confrontation over desegregation. Such disorder would not only play into the hands of liberal critics, but also destabilize the security and order of their own communities.[46]

This analysis implied that the main disagreement voters had with Crommelin was over means rather than ends. There was, however, also an ideological element. Crommelin's anti-Semitism was a particular electoral liability. Mainstream massive resistance leaders disavowed anti-Semitism for reasons of both principle and political expediency. Some feared that broadening their campaign to include attacks on Jews would weaken their focus on the defense of Jim Crow. However, most simply did not perceive that Jews were responsible for the desegregation crisis. Only ten communities in Alabama had a Jewish population of more than one hundred. According to a report by the American Jewish Committee, Jews had succeeded, in part because of their small numbers, in being unobtrusively absorbed into the white middle class. One illustration of the acculturation of Alabama Jews was their membership in the Citizens' Councils. A survey of seventy-seven council-type organizations disclosed that sixteen had Jewish members, most of them in the Deep South, and in particular Alabama. The economic strength of Alabama Jews also attracted the interest of politicians such as George Wallace, who were keen to cultivate close ties with the community in the hope of attracting financial support.[47]

Sensitivity over the issue of Jewish membership led the Alabama Association of Citizens' Councils to expel anti-Semites from its ranks. In March 1956, the Association politically excommunicated Carter because of his rhetoric about a communist Jewish conspiracy. It also later expelled the Elmore County Citizens' Council, of which Crommelin was a member, for circulating anti-Semitic material.[48]

Crommelin himself seems to have sensed that anti-Semitism was not an electoral asset. A case in point is his failure to make an issue of the fact that Lister Hill had Jewish ancestry. The family of Hill's mother had converted from Judaism to Catholicism in the nineteenth century. Crommelin, however, may have been unaware of Hill's heritage, since the senator suppressed it from the public.[49] It is nonetheless significant that the rear admiral did not accuse more identifiable Jews in his home state of secretly masterminding the civil rights movement. Instead, he relied on the same tactic as had John Kasper of trading in generic stereotypes or, even when he did single out specific members of the supposed Jewish communist conspiracy, making sure they were from outside of the South and therefore more suspiciously alien. His roster of conspirators therefore included men such as Supreme Court Justice Felix Frankfurter and New York Senator Herbert Lehman, whose outsider status and association with federal power made them more credible threats to the political sovereignty of Alabama than the Jewish neighbor who owned a downtown dry goods store.[50]

The other factor that reduced Crommelin's political fortunes was his failure to cultivate the support of lower-class whites. Despite the presence of Kasper and Carter on his campaign team in the 1956 election, Crommelin did not develop a strategy to exploit the politics of class resentment. Kasper and Carter couched their rhetoric in an earthy language that emphasized the virtues of hard work and decency they believed ordinary whites embodied. Both men aroused working-class anger by arguing that the civic and political leaders who accepted racial reform were themselves protected from its impact because of their social and economic status. These elites did not share the same prospect as workers at the lower end of the economy of competing with African Americans in an integrated job market. Nor did they risk having their sons and especially daughters sitting in the same classroom as black students since they could afford to enroll their offspring at private academies.

While Kasper and Carter spoke of seizing control of government from corrupt and unrepresentative elites, Crommelin attempted to establish his fitness for office by emphasizing his own status as a member of Alabama's social aristocracy. His campaign literature stressed his patrician credentials, stating that he was a descendant of pioneer stock whose antecedents had served in the state legislature and fought for the Confederacy.[51] Far from advocating a grassroots insurgency that would restore government to common people, Crommelin simply promoted replacing one top-down regime with another. His failure to tap into the strong populist tradition in his native state seriously curtailed his electoral campaign.

While Crommelin endured a decisive defeat in the primary, the election result still constituted a victory of sorts for the extremist politics that he espoused. The 68.2 percent share of the vote won by Hill represented his widest ever margin of success in an electoral race. However, the statistics did not tell the entire story. This was no triumph of moderation over fanaticism. The rear admiral succeeded in spooking his opponent into abandoning a position of racial moderation and adopting one of steadfast support for segregation. The outcome of the race paralleled the Arkansas gubernatorial election that same year in which Jim Johnson suffered an emphatic defeat at the hands of Orval Faubus but succeeded in forcing his rival to the right.[52] In accepting that a more forceful defense of Jim Crow was the price of political survival, Hill contributed to a broader rightward shift in Alabama politics that stifled public debate on the race issue and steered the state on a disastrous course of massive resistance.

The impact of the election on the broader political discourse in Alabama was attributable as much to the weakness of Hill as the strength of Crommelin. Historian Tony Badger argues that the ability of southern racial moderates to retain public office during the desegregation crisis demonstrates that they overemphasized the strength of hard-line resistance to civil rights reform.[53] The election result demonstrates that Hill had more room for political maneuver than he appreciated. Hill initially believed his best electoral strategy was simply to ignore Crommelin, rather than dignify his wilder accusations by responding to them publicly. However, when the Crommelin campaign gathered momentum, he panicked. According to one newspaper report, Crommelin's relentless emphasis on the race issue resulted in his performing "surprisingly well." While the rear admiral failed in his efforts to force his opponent to join the Citizens' Council, he raised sufficient doubts about his opponent's commitment to white supremacy that Hill issued a series of press releases stressing his segregationist credentials. It was, he insisted, something he "had to do . . . to get elected."[54] White moderate Virginia Durr commented scornfully how Hill made "the most abject statement, pointing to his record against Civil Rights Bills and the Poll Tax Bill!!" His office also called attention to the fact that the Hill–Burton bill mandated the preservation of segregated hospital care.[55] Hill's decision to sign the Southern Manifesto without even reading it is also clear evidence of his having walked into a trap he himself helped to set. Having capitulated to the forces of racism, there was no way for Hill to reassert his moderate position without the risk of alienating the electorate.[56]

Moreover, in giving so much ground to the forces of political reaction, Hill ensured that any person who subsequently sought public office in Alabama would need to convince voters of her or his unequivocal commitment to segregation. As one author asserts, "segregation was not just the main issue; it was the only one that voters paid attention to."[57] When State Attorney General John Patterson won the gubernatorial election two years later, it was on a platform of uncompromising opposition to racial change.

The impact of this renewed emphasis on race continued to spiral outward for many years. Once Patterson had demonstrated the electoral advantage to be gained from a race-baiting campaign, the only option was to outdo him. As one of his defeated opponents, George Wallace, told his supporters: "Well boys, no other son-of-a-bitch will ever out-nigger me again." When Wallace ran for governor four years later, he proved true to his word.[58]

There is further irony in the fact that Crommelin could not benefit from the new political climate he helped to create. He had no means to compete with candidates more closely linked to the political establishment who not only tapped into superior connections and resources, but also co-opted much of his rhetoric. In contrast to John Kasper in Tennessee or Bryant Bowles in Delaware, he could not make a credible case that mainstream politicians had sold out the electorate by soft-pedaling the race issue. While Crommelin's campaign literature proclaimed that he alone was "The Whiteman's Candidate," in reality every one of the political hopefuls who ran for higher public office claimed the title as his own.[59] The 1958 gubernatorial race is a case in point. John Patterson won the election after soliciting the support of both the Citizens' Council and the Ku Klux Klan, an otherwise natural element of Crommelin's constituency.[60] Although he ran an energetic campaign that included 15 television appearances and more than 100 stump speeches, Crommelin won only 2,245—or 0.36 percent—of the 618,000 votes cast, coming in 11th in a field of 14 candidates.[61] The paradoxical conclusion is that it was in those states where political leaders took a more moderate stand on the civil rights issue that racial extremists had an opportunity to flourish. Their power and influence was in direct proportion to the strength of massive resistance sentiment among local and state authorities. Kasper created disorder in Tennessee but was thwarted in his efforts to cultivate grassroots support in Mississippi and Arkansas. Crommelin similarly struggled to convince white voters in his home state that their elected officials had sold them out. In contrast to the people Kasper stirred into revolt, many ordinary segregationists in Alabama believed they had a representative voice in state government.

Following his defeat, Crommelin shifted his focus from state to local politics. Although his efforts to win office in Montgomery also failed, as had been the case during the senatorial race, he succeeded in exerting some influence on the tone and direction of political discourse. In March 1958, Crommelin came in third of the four candidates who competed in the Montgomery Democratic primary race for mayor, winning 1,760 of the 17,330 votes cast.

While he missed out on a place in the runoff election, Crommelin did help to determine its outcome. Earl James, an uncompromising segregationist who polled second in the primary, won victory over incumbent candidate William Gayle. What tipped the balance in his favor were the votes that went to Crommelin in the first round of balloting.[62] Jewish defense agencies expressed profound alarm that the rear admiral should have assumed the role of political power broker. "This is almost as disturbing as the size of the Crommelin vote itself," exclaimed American Jewish Committee activist Charles Wittenstein, "i.e., that the Crommelin forces are exercising a considerable influence on the choice of Montgomery's next Mayor."[63] The national press affirmed that while Crommelin was "not a potent force in state politics," his role in determining the outcome of the mayoral election meant he "cannot be dismissed in Montgomery" because he would demand a representative voice in the new James administration.[64]

While he remained active in local and state politics, Crommelin nursed greater ambitions. In 1958, he attended the founding convention of the extremist National States' Rights Party (NSRP) in Louisville. Two years later, the party selected him as the running mate of their presidential candidate, Arkansas Governor Orval Faubus. Although Faubus was not a party member, he had attained an honored status among white supremacists for his defiant stand against federal authority during the Little Rock school crisis.[65] The governor, however, neither sought the nomination nor, once he had it, made any attempt to promote his candidacy. Indeed, he persuaded election officials in Florida to remove his name from ballot papers. The governor also later denounced the NSRP for its anti-Semitism and, specifically, its denial of the Holocaust, telling reporters how as a soldier in the 35th Infantry Division, he had witnessed the corpses of concentration camp victims. Faubus nonetheless allowed his name to remain on ballot papers in those states where the NSRP secured the requisite number of signatures.[66]

On election day, Faubus and Crommelin attracted only 44,977 votes.[67] While this was a less than impressive performance, the presence of Faubus on the ticket enhanced the public profile of the NSRP. As one civil rights activist observed, the governor "conferred upon this segment of the lunatic fringe a certain stamp of acceptance which, to date, it has not even begun to have."[68] It was not a mutually beneficial relationship, however. While Faubus had serious misgivings about being associated with the NSRP, its decision to nominate him as a presidential candidate demonstrated he was no longer in control of the political forces he helped to unleash during the Little Rock school crisis.

Chapter Four

Following this foray into national politics, Crommelin resumed his bid for public office in Alabama. He came in a distant second to John Sparkman in the Democratic senatorial primary of May 1960, winning 51,591 votes, or 13 percent of the total.[69] Crommelin was also one of two candidates to challenge Lister Hill in a Democratic senatorial primary two years later, the other being Citizens' Council official Donald Hallmark. Even though the candidacies of Crommelin and Hallmark divided the vote of racial hard-liners, their combined total was still little more than one-third of the ballots cast for Hill. The incumbent senator polled 363,613 votes; Hallmark, 72,855; and Crommelin, 56,822. The *Montgomery Advertiser* articulated the mounting sense of frustration with racial militants. Hallmark's political opinions, it asserted, were "well-meaning but misplaced"; Crommelin was simply "misplaced."[70]

Crommelin continued to campaign tirelessly in spite—or precisely be-cause—of the federal civil rights legislation enacted during the 1960s. His performance in the Alabama Democratic Senate primary of May 1966—narrowly missing second place with 17.3 percent of the total vote—demon-strated an enduring hard core of segregationist resistance. By the late 1960s, however, even many racist whites recognized that minimum compliance rather than massive resistance was the surest means to restrict racial reform. Crommelin's militant tactics appeared all the more anachronistic. Following a futile candidacy as a Democratic candidate in the New Hampshire presidential primary of March 1968, he made a further bid for the Senate but won only 2 percent of the vote. After a run for the lieutenant governorship two years later netted a miserable 1 percent of the vote, Crommelin finally retired from electoral politics.[71]

Reflecting on his resounding defeat in the gubernatorial election of 1958, Crommelin concluded he had been the victim both of a deliberate policy by the press to deny his campaign public exposure and of vote-rigging by the "Communist-Jewish controlled machine."[72]

Although these accusations were attributable in part to paranoia, they were not entirely unwarranted. While civil rights activists did not directly challenge his right to free speech, they were determined to restrict the im-pact of Crommelin's public broadcasts by resisting open dialogue with him. Privately, they perceived the rear admiral as a serious political threat. By publicly paying little or no attention to him, however, they aimed to create the impression of a harmless crank who did not merit the serious attention of the electorate.

During the postwar decades, civil rights organizations struggled to resolve the moral and political contradictions at the core of the debate on
hate speech. Rabble-rousing extremists such as John Kasper and Bryant
Bowles had emphasized the pertinence of the issue by using radio in particular as a means to mobilize opposition to desegregation. Although civil
rights organizations expressed their unease at the amount of media exposure Kasper and Bowles received, they did not devise a strategy on how to
contain the problem.[73] The common conviction of civil rights groups was
that First Amendment freedoms of speech and association were inviolable.
They based this belief on both ideological and strategic considerations. In
particular, they understood that the power to censor political debate was a
sword that cut both ways. Authorities could use it not only to silence hate
speech, but also to suppress civil rights protest. During the 1950s, black and
Jewish activists therefore deduced that in order to promote their own civil
rights they must, paradoxically, protect the civil liberties of their political
opponents. Restricting the rights of white racists to freedom of speech and
assembly on the grounds that their language caused offense might rebound
on the civil rights movement since the courts could use the same criteria to
prohibit any form of political demonstration. The outlawing of the NAACP
in Alabama in the late 1950s showed that it was civil rights activists who
had most to fear from any incursion on constitutional freedoms of speech
and assembly.[74]

When confronted by Crommelin, however, civil rights organizations
reconciled the tensions between personal desire and political reality through
the implementation of a strategy that curtailed the impact of hate speech
without infringing on the constitutional freedom of public debate. As a
persistent candidate for public office, Crommelin regularly broadcast over
the Alabama airwaves. Ironically, it was under the protection of federal law
that the rear admiral continued to publicize his fanatical states' rights message. The Communications Act of 1934 required radio stations to permit
political candidates equal time on air and forbade them from interfering
with the content of campaign commercials. Hence, when the Federal Communications Commission received some complaints about Crommelin, it
ruled decisively in his favor. As an outsider candidate who could not draw
on the power of a party political machine, the rear admiral benefited con-
siderably from the access to the electorate that radio provided.[75]

Jewish defense groups orchestrated the campaign to contain Crommelin.
His tirades about a communist Jewish conspiracy, coupled with his increas-
ing proclivity for violence, created a climate of fear among Alabama Jews.

According to a report by the American Jewish Committee, "Because of Crommelin, the Jews of Alabama felt more threatened than those of other Southern states."[76] The strength of support commanded by Crommelin in his home city convinced the council that "in terms of anti-Semitism, Montgomery was probably the hell-hole of the nation."[77]

The first strategy pursued by Jewish defense agencies was to enlist the support of the U.S. Defense Department. Crommelin made strong use of his military record as a means of promoting his personal integrity. Some Jewish activists believed they could strip the rear admiral of one of his principal political assets by lobbying the Defense Department for his court-martial.[78] However, although the American Jewish Committee drafted a public letter to Secretary of Defense Neil H. McElroy, it withdrew the petition. To use the power of the federal government to force Crommelin into silence, they concluded, compromised the commitment of the American Jewish Committee to uphold the First Amendment right to freedom of speech. Court-martialing Crommelin could also prove counterproductive since it would provide him with an opportunity to use the national publicity as a means of promoting his political martyrdom. In the words of one committee member, "Do you suppose the next time he gets on a public platform that he will not use the action taken against him to make himself out as even a greater hero?"[79]

Having discounted direct confrontation, Jewish activists adopted a more insidious approach to countering the danger posed by Crommelin. American Jewish Committee activist S. Andhil Fineberg used a false name and address to request that the rear admiral add him to his mailing list. The ruse succeeded and the information was used by the American Jewish Committee to anticipate further political action by Crommelin.[80] The committee also implemented a longstanding policy to contain the threat of extremists by publicly paying no attention to Crommelin. Referred to alternately as "the silent treatment" or "the quarantine strategy," the plan was based on the assumption that publicly engaging with political extremists conferred them with greater legitimacy in the minds of the public than would be the case by simply ignoring them. As one committee activist affirmed of Crommelin, "his irrational maunderings should not be dignified and publicized by joining issue."[81] To this end, the council successfully encouraged John Sparkman and Lister Hill not to respond to Crommelin in their campaign speeches.[82]

Jewish defense agencies further sought to counteract the anti-Semitic propaganda of Crommelin through community education programs. This represented an effort to cut off racial and religious bigotry at the root by creating a more tolerant and pluralistic political culture. S. Andhil Fineberg explained the process with a colorful metaphor: "It is far better to drain the swamps where mosquitoes breed than to try and swat every mosquito."[83] In a less high-minded manner, Jewish activists also searched for incriminating evidence that would compromise Crommelin. As the authors of one internal memorandum concluded: "if we could really get something on the Admiral, something preferably involving moral turpitude, that would be a big help."[84] The rear admiral's closet was empty of skeletons, however. "He is not," lamented Solomon Fineberg, "going to consort with Negroes ala Kasper."[85] Despite their failure to discredit Crommelin, the defense agencies were content with the efficacy of the quarantine strategy.

Civil rights organizations may have succeeded in containing the impact of Crommelin's words, but they were also confronted by his increasingly aggressive actions. In an address to a Florida chapter of the Daughters of the American Revolution, Crommelin declared that the "hidden force" threatening the United States must be overcome "in a bloodless way, if possible."[86] While the rear admiral persisted in campaigning for public office, his repeated failure to win election nonetheless shook his faith in the democratic process. By the late 1950s, Crommelin had concluded that the protection of his southern homeland made bloodshed inevitable.[87]

Crommelin attempted to construct a paramilitary movement capable not only of resisting racial reform in his home state, but also deposing the federal government. He used his professional experience and personal reputation as a military leader to coordinate a series of strikes against civil rights activists. Crommelin was a wealthy man who bankrolled white terrorist activity across the South.

Crommelin first started to engage in direct action against desegregation shortly after he met Asa Carter and John Kasper. While Kasper was the principal catalyst for the Clinton crisis, Crommelin provided him with practical and inspirational support, raising finances for his legal defense and serving as a character witness.[88] "You may not see it, and your children may not see it," Crommelin informed local whites, "but some day a statue will be erected on this courthouse lawn to John Kasper."[89]

Although some segregationists used militaristic metaphors to describe the desegregation crisis, Crommelin believed he was actually fighting another war. He interpreted in particular the use of troops to enforce school desegregation as evidence that the civil rights struggle had become an armed conflict. The imposition of a military curfew to suppress the protests led by Kasper in Clinton demonstrated to him the dictatorial infraction of white citizens' constitutional rights.[90] When President Dwight Eisenhower deployed troops to integrate Little Rock Central High School in September 1957, Crommelin construed the action as a declaration of war. "Pearl Harbor! Little Rock!" he declared. "The communist-jewish conspiracy or 'Invisible Government' of the United States dictates the use of federal bayonets to force commingling of white and colored children."[91] This assertion inverted Eisenhower's televised statement rationalizing the use of troops on the grounds of the "harm that is being done to the prestige and influence, and indeed to the safety of our nation and the world" because of the school crisis. Far from protecting the national interest, Crommelin accused the president of advancing communist interests by oppressing the rights of American citizens.[92]

Having crushed the constitutional rights of freedom of speech and assembly in the Upper South, the forces of totalitarianism were, according to Crommelin, now training their sights on a final showdown in Alabama. Crommelin espoused the apocalyptic rhetoric characteristic of right-wing extremism, arguing that his home state was the setting of the decisive conflict between the forces of Christian morality and the communist Jewish conspiracy. "I am convinced," he asserted, "that Alabama is the real battleground in the cold civil war now in progress in the United States, and that Montgomery, our capital, is the major impact town."[93] The use of troops to implement desegregation in Little Rock persuaded Crommelin that the federal government had constructed National Guard armories "located at central points on the arterial highways leading to the major communication and population centers of Alabama."[94]

The rear admiral attempted to mobilize white Alabamians for war under his leadership by emphasizing his distinguished military credentials. His public addresses attempted to capture the "martial spirit" of a state that, according to historian Wayne Flynt, was unparalleled in its public commitment to the traditions of "honor, patriotism, and national military service."[95] Crommelin espoused an ultramasculinist rhetoric that encouraged white males to redeem their pride by fulfilling their traditional role as protectors of their homes and families. Those who failed to do so would suffer shame and disgrace. "I was a naval aviator . . . in the Pacific during twelve major engagements in World War II," he proclaimed in one campaign pamphlet. "I learned that there is no such thing as 'combat fatigue.' So called 'combat fatigue' is in reality 'non-combat fatigue.' The men who really fought become stronger and stronger with each clash with the enemy." In speech after speech, Crommelin ridiculed the complacency and cowardice of white men who failed to answer his call to arms. As he asserted in one televised broadcast, "Historians of the future will marvel most of all at the non-resistance of those who had the most to lose."[96]

This rhetorical emphasis on honor, sacrifice, and redemption tapped into a cultural mindset with deep historical roots in the South. Crommelin in many ways embodied the values of an honor culture that had pervaded the region since antebellum times. The rear admiral's self-conscious assertion of his family lineage and military and social rank was a clear articulation of this cultural attitude. His exhortations to white southern males to protect their southern homeland from a hostile outside force also drew on a historical tradition of personal sacrifice forged during the Civil War.[97]

Crommelin led by example in performing what he believed was the duty of all white southern males to fight for their freedom. He first launched a campaign of intimidation against white moderates struggling to promote biracialism. Significantly, his principal targets were women, presumably because he considered them more susceptible to a show of segregationist machismo. Crommelin lobbied for the dismissal of liberal activist Juliette Hampton Morgan from the staff of the city public library.[98] He also focused his ire on white female activists who formed the interracial prayer group United Church Women. While the women gathered in prayer, Crommelin recorded the license numbers of their cars and, having identified the owners, published their names and telephone numbers in a newsletter circulated throughout the city. The women received so many threatening telephone calls from angry whites that they were frightened into disbanding. According to one of their leaders, Virginia Durr, the situation became so alarming that "Several husbands took out notices in the papers disassociating themselves from their own wives."[99]

That Crommelin could act with impunity in persecuting white moderates reveals much about the political environment of his hometown. Historian J. Mills Thornton III observes of racial politics in Montgomery that "any hint of deviation from white supremacist orthodoxy would incur both active harassment and social ostracism." Militant white supremacist publications such as the *Montgomery Home News* were widely circulated in the city. While the paper enthusiastically supported Crommelin, all candidates for public office courted its readers by placing campaign advertisements in its pages. More mainstream publications also maintained an uncompromising position on the race issue, differing from the *Home News* only in terms of their rhetorical tone.[100] While some whites may therefore have mistrusted the methods used by Crommelin, they did not doubt his motives. Their reluctance to censure the rear admiral provided him with implicit approval to pursue his hounding of white moderates. Virginia Durr affirmed that "there is a great deal of fear, and fear keeps people silent, so the Crommelin crowd, who apparently have no fear at all, keep the good people cowed."[101]

Crommelin's influence soon spread beyond his home state. On October 12, 1958, a bomb blast tore through the Reform Temple in Atlanta. The Confederate Underground—the terrorist network that first came to public attention after the dynamite attack on the Nashville Jewish Community Center a year earlier—claimed responsibility. Within forty-eight hours, police arrested five men, all members of the NSRP.

Circumstantial evidence tied Crommelin to the terrorist plot. One of the arrested men, George Bright, had in his possession a checkbook that included entries for recent payments to Crommelin. The rear admiral was also the first person whom the wife of one of the other men detained by authorities, Wallace Allen, telephoned for help. When FBI agents called on the rear admiral, he proved uncooperative, claiming never to have met Bright.[102] The relationship between Crommelin and the arrested terrorists was sufficiently close that he assumed responsibility for organizing a fund to pay for their legal defense.[103] Although the authorities could not prove Crommelin had helped to plant or detonate the bomb, as an active member of the NSRP hierarchy, it is improbable that he was unaware of the plot. Perhaps, like Kasper, he preferred others to leave their fingerprints on the detonating fuse. What is certain is that Crommelin attempted to turn the bombing into a propaganda coup for the far right. The real admiral used a common rhetorical tactic of segregationists when confronted by an atrocity directed against African Americans, claiming the victims had staged the incident as a means to bring into disrepute the defense of Jim Crow. Crommelin wrote an open letter to J. Edgar Hoover in which he accused Jews of blowing up their own synagogue in order to create public sympathy, discredit their political opponents, and encourage federal authorities to extend their influence over local and state affairs.[104]

Crommelin concentrated for the next few years on campaigning for political office, but resumed his involvement in political violence in September 1962 when he and a squad of NSRP foot soldiers became embroiled in the bloody conflict over the enrollment of black student James Meredith at the University of Mississippi. Local authorities uncovered the intentions of the NSRP when police discovered a cache of illegal weapons in a car owned by one of its activists. While the NSRP performed only an ancillary role in organizing the demonstrations on the university campus, this renewal of direct confrontation was a portent of the next phase of Crommelin's political career.[105]

As black protesters and the federal government focused their concentration on Alabama during the spring and summer of 1963, it seemed to Crommelin that the apocalyptic confrontation he had long prophesied was about to come true. Attempting to incite whites into action by evoking their bitterest historical memories, he warned, "We are headed for a Reconstruction Period that will make the post-Civil War era seem a Sunday School picnic by comparison."[106] Invoking the spirit of Confederate resistance during the Civil War was a common trope of massive resistance rhetoric. As a means to mobilize support it was nonetheless problematic since the South had after all been defeated in battle. Crommelin was therefore astute in encouraging southern whites to emulate the more successful efforts of their forebears in "redeeming" the region from the supposed tyranny of Republican rule.

Crommelin launched his rearguard action in March, leading a violent demonstration in Birmingham against the inauguration of moderate segregationist Albert Boutwell, who had defeated hard-line rival Eugene Connor in the recent mayoral election. Three months later, the FBI expressed its concern that Crommelin might intervene in the already "extremely tense situation" created by the imminent admission of two African American students to the University of Alabama. The apprehension owed in part to a picket the rear admiral organized outside the state capitol when Attorney General Robert Kennedy traveled from Washington to discuss the issue with Governor George Wallace. Concerned that Crommelin could precipitate "rioting, bloodshed and loss of life" on the university campus, Kennedy authorized the FBI to tap his telephone.[107]

The person who eventually persuaded Crommelin and other members of the NSRP not to provoke violence over the admission of the black students was Asa Carter.[108] Carter had shifted from the margins to the center of political power in Alabama (or the center had shifted to the right) when Wallace hired him as a speechwriter during his gubernatorial campaign in 1962. Carter's status underlines the assimilation of extremist elements into the political mainstream. The line separating lawless fanatics from more reputable political leaders was often very thin in the Alabama of the late 1950s and early 1960s. Carter maintained close ties with Crommelin even while serving in the Wallace administration. In January 1963, the two men founded a paramilitary group named Volunteers for Alabama and Wallace. While most terrorists claim to represent the oppressed in a struggle against tyrannical state power, the name of this new organization shows that Carter and Crommelin had the exact opposite intent. Volunteers for Alabama and Wallace represented an effort on their part to create an unofficial state militia. Crommelin established a firearms practice range on his plantation and attempted to drill recruits in the art of guerrilla warfare. However, within little more than five months the organization had split into two competing factions. While the cause of the rift between Carter and Crommelin is not known, the incident illustrates how tempestuous egos tore apart the already slender ranks of the far right.[109]

With or without Carter, Crommelin remained convinced of the need for armed resistance to racial reform. The FBI discovered, for instance, that Crommelin had attended a secret meeting of white supremacists in Birmingham in September 1963, only a week before the bombing of the Sixteenth Street Baptist Church. Whether this was a coincidence is unclear.[110]

What is more certain is that in the spring of 1964 the FBI received reports that Crommelin was planning the most audacious criminal conspiracy of his career. According to numerous sources, a cabal of former military officers was planning "to forcibly overthrow" the federal government. The conspirators included Crommelin and his longtime associate Pedro del Valle, together with Colonel William Potter Gale and former American Nazi Party member Richard Anderson. Their inspiration was the John Frankenheimer film *Seven Days in May*, in which a faction of senior military officials attempt a coup d'état. It was a peculiar instance of life imitating art imitating life. The authors of the novel on which Frankenheimer based the film tapped into public fears that the army could use cold war tensions to engineer a takeover of the U.S. government.[111]

Although the conspiracy did not constitute a serious threat to the government, it casts significant light on the fractious nature of the far right. When FBI agents interviewed Edward Fields, who as a founding member of the NSRP was closely associated with Crommelin, he dismissed the plot as the deluded enterprise of a "couple of crackpots."[112] George Lincoln Rockwell, the self-styled fuehrer of the American Nazi Party, in turn claimed that the FBI should give little credence to Fields since he was "a congenital liar." The conflicting statements of Fields and Rockwell were either an elaborate scheme to throw the authorities off the scent, or evidence of intense mutual animosity within the ranks of the white supremacist movement.[113]

While the authorities continued to monitor Crommelin closely, he did not in the end deliver on his commitment to lead an armed insurrection. In contrast to John Kasper or Bryant Bowles, he failed to precipitate open revolt against racial reform. One particular factor conspired to frustrate his ambitions. Civil rights protest succeeded best when black activists focused their efforts on the attainment of a clearly defined set of goals. As the failure of the Southern Christian Leadership Conference campaign in Albany demonstrated, attempting to fight segregation simultaneously on many fronts was a strategic mistake. White supremacists needed to make similar calculations. Kasper and Bryant showed how a lone agitator with limited resources could accomplish much by concentrating on a single focal point. Crommelin focused on elaborate plans to fight a war against a fantastical enemy—the UN forces who he believed were preparing to invade Alabama at any moment—rather than more immediate threats to white supremacy such as school desegregation. His financial underwriting of numerous conspiracies shows that he had much stronger resources at his disposal than either Bowles or Kasper. For a former military officer, he nonetheless seems to have possessed a surprising lack of strategic acumen.

It is easy to dismiss Crommelin as a crackpot. However, while Robert Sherrill ridiculed Crommelin as a "right-wing nut," he also conceded that the rear admiral consistently won the vote of "100,000 or more" people in statewide elections.[114] His principal base of support was in the Black Belt counties in the south-central part of Alabama and the industrial areas in and around Birmingham.[115]

Although Crommelin never came close to winning election, the sheer persistence of his campaigning was a source of constant alarm to racial and religious minorities. As one assessment of his political career concluded, "The fact that he was notoriously unsuccessful in the end does not diminish the unhappiness he caused."[116] His election campaigns also exposed extremist tendencies that were not so explicit in more "moderate" politicians who nonetheless shared elements of his political agenda.

Crommelin was also a political networker who created common links between the diverse and often competing factions within the far right. Reporter William Peters observed that there was "an informal interlocking directorate which extends loosely from top to bottom of the seemingly haphazard and cumbersome hierarchy of segregationist organizations."[117] Crommelin was one of the foremost members of this affiliation, both as an orator and as a financier, using his substantial personal resources to underwrite numerous political initiatives. His outspoken political campaigns made him a totem of the far-right press, which heralded him as a patriotic hero.[118] In contrast to a controversial and divisive figure such as John Kasper, Crommelin was one of the rare breed capable of creating consensus among militant segregationists. The rear admiral worked so tirelessly to weave together the disparate strands of the far right that it is difficult to determine all of the organizations with which he was associated. However, even an incomplete list shows the scale of the connections he made.

Crommelin maintained his closest ties with the National States' Rights Party, acting as a "father-confessor and den mother" to other party members, most of whom were a generation younger than him.[119] But he also created new political alliances at every opportunity. He was, for instance, a close associate of Gerald L. K. Smith, regularly appearing as the keynote lecturer at public meetings sponsored by the white supremacist.[120] Crommelin was also a keynote speaker at the Ultimatum Conference of Loyal Americans, an umbrella organization that brought together the Klan and more militant elements within the Citizens' Councils.[121] While the far right remained a fractious political force during the 1960s, Crommelin's involvement in numerous organizations provided an important element of connection and continuity. In July 1962, he addressed members of the Defensive Legion of Registered Americans, who had assembled at Stone Mountain in Georgia to demonstrate their opposition to the NAACP.[122] Around the same time, an anti-UN organization named the United States Day Committee, Inc., appointed Crommelin to its advisory committee. In 1964, the rear admiral assumed the additional post of eastern regional director of the white supremacist Christian Defense League.[123] Two years later, Crommelin and Pedro del Valle became members of the board of directors of the American Association for Justice, Inc., an ultranationalist organization that offered legal support to "patriots" facing trial.[124] The former military officers also founded the obscure Sons of Liberty in 1967.[125] In addition to these activities, Crommelin found time in his seemingly relentless schedule to address the annual meeting of the Congress of Freedom in Omaha, Nebraska.[126]

Crommelin further influenced the far right by molding its racialist discourse and mentoring younger activists. His claim that Jews were conspiring to mongrelize the races was a specific inspiration in shaping the political ideology of other militant white supremacists, including John Kasper and George Lincoln Rockwell. Rockwell developed many of the ideas he would later espouse as leader of the American Nazi Party while working on one of Crommelin's electoral campaigns.[127]

As his own activism started to wither, Crommelin nourished the grass-roots of the far right in the hope of growing a new generation of leaders. He served on the adult advisory board of the National Youth Alliance, a right-wing extremist movement that attempted to supplant the influence on college campuses of New Left organizations such as Students for a Democratic Society.[128] His efforts to recruit students to the far-right cause led at an unspecified point to his making contact with David Duke, who had established the White Youth Alliance while an undergraduate at Louisiana State University. The two first collaborated in the Sons of Liberty. In 1976, Crommelin accepted an offer from Duke, who had by this time become Grand Wizard of the Knights of the Ku Klux Klan, to act as associate editor of his monthly newsletter, *The Crusader*.[129] While there is little documentation to provide insight into the precise relationship between the two men, the cultivation of Duke was a potent legacy for Crommelin to bequeath.

Yet perhaps the most important contribution Crommelin made to white supremacy was entirely unintentional. As journalist Harrison Salisbury observed, his political opinions had "a wider acceptance than many Alabamans will admit."[130] While most political leaders in the state eschewed his anti-Semitism, they shared with Crommelin the same cold war fears of communist infiltration of the federal government and an uncompromising opposition to racial integration. Likewise, although Citizens' Council leaders condemned Crommelin as irresponsible for his militant call to arms, their own organization also repressed black protest through such coercive methods as firing employees, withdrawing credit, and evicting tenants. While massive resisters in Alabama claimed Crommelin harmed the reputation of their cause, his extremism did serve a useful political function. The rear admiral was the perfect foil for a segregationist leadership seeking public respectability. In condemning him as fanatical and irrational, they were by implication able to present themselves as lawful and reasonable. George Wallace, for instance, attempted to legitimate his opposition to civil rights reform by dissociating himself from the "nut-cases" of the far right.[131]

In reality, it was often difficult in the Alabama of the late 1950s and early 1960s to distinguish the line that separated the supposedly respectable forces of massive resistance from lawless extremists. Asa Carter retained his membership in the NSRP throughout his tenure as George Wallace's speechwriter. He publicly shared a stage with Crommelin during the gubernatorial election that swept Wallace to power, the two men delivering keynote addresses at the NSRP annual convention.[132] Although Crommelin criticized Wallace, he was relatively mute in comparison with his caustic denunciations of other Alabama politicians, believing that the governor shared his political agenda. When Wallace announced his intention to obstruct the admission of two black students to the University of Alabama in June 1963, Crommelin distributed handbills across the state encouraging public support for his defiance of federal authority. "White men unite," he proclaimed. "Back Governor Wallace." In contrast to Bowles and Kasper, this undermined Crommelin's ability to define himself as a radical alternative to the temporizing political establishment, rendering him all but redundant.

5. Assumption of Command

Military Officers and Massive Resistance

It is tempting to attribute John Crommelin's delusional belief in an omnipotent political adversary to an individual psychosis. That certainly was the opinion of many of his opponents. As one civil rights activist affirmed, "The general opinion is that he is irresponsible and mentally disturbed."[1] The rear admiral certainly appeared to conform to the classic Freudian diagnosis of paranoia. His forced resignation from the navy was a catastrophic personal event that fragmented the order and meaning of his life. Crommelin's inability to accept responsibility for his own downfall arguably led him to project his fear and despair onto an imaginary other. Ascribing the blame for the sudden termination of his military career to a "hidden force" allowed him to recover a sense of stability. One assessment of Crommelin therefore ascribed his motives to "An ingrained frustration arising out of his retirement from active Naval duty as the result of an intra-service dispute."[2] Crommelin also exhibited the megalomania commonly associated with the clinically paranoid. He insisted that his expulsion from the navy was part of a larger conspiracy to precipitate the collapse of American society. In placing himself at the heart of this imaginary crisis, he claimed a personal importance that compensated for the feelings of insignificance he suffered when his military career collapsed. His assertion that he was one of the chosen few who could see the scale of the conspiracy also bolstered his fragile ego.[3]

Plausible as this interpretation is, it does not tell the entire story. This is because it places too much emphasis on the internal mental state of Crommelin at the expense of assessing the external cultural and institutional forces that also shaped him. Crommelin was a product of the political culture of his home state. He may have been delusional in some respects, but his core beliefs were shared by many white Alabamians, including some of the most prominent members of the Alabama political establishment. A conspiratorial paranoia gripped the popular consciousness. In June 1955, for instance, the Alabama Senate adopted a resolution urging Congress to reveal the role of communists in writing the *Brown* decision. Local and state newspaper editorials also promoted the idea that communists had selected Alabama as the target site for an assault on the southern racial order. In 1950, Birmingham Public Safety Commissioner Eugene "Bull" Connor cited a local newspaper editorial warning that fifth columnists had selected his city, "the industrial hub of the South," for military takeover.[4] Even the idea that white civilians who defied federal tyranny would be transported to Alaska had some political currency.[5]

It is also impossible to understand Crommelin without recognizing the role of his military background. Crommelin was not the only former senior military official associated with militant opposition to racial integration. On the contrary, following World War II a conspicuous number of retired officers who had once fought for their country now turned on the federal government, rallying to the front lines in defense of Jim Crow. This raises the issue of whether, on the one hand, the military attracted a disproportionate number of individuals with white supremacist convictions, or, on the other hand, the experience of serving in the armed forces radicalized the racial convictions of these officers. An assessment of other military men active in massive resistance, specifically Pedro del Valle and Edwin Walker, helps provide answers to these questions and places Crommelin in a broader historical context.

In many respects, a career in the armed forces undermined parochial prejudices. The transient nature of military service, which saw men moved from one location to another, both within and outside the United States, exposed them to new cultural and intellectual perspectives. This induced an apolitical mindset that allowed most high-ranking military officials on their retirement to retreat into the anonymity of civilian life.

While few members of the military top brass decided on retirement to run for public office, many did become involved in pressure-group politics.[6] Moreover, those erstwhile officers who entered the world of social protest and electioneering tended toward a position that social scientist Albert Biderman describes as "political deviance."[7] Three factors merit particular emphasis in attempting to account for this phenomenon.

First, the tensions of the cold war induced an apocalyptic outlook in the minds of many military officials. Their attitude was that the fate of the world rested on the result of a decisive clash of civilizations. With the stakes so high, they remained on constant alert to any threat to U.S. national security.

Second, the institutionalized racism of the military had a powerful influence on the men who served in it. White southerners were overrepresented within the senior ranks of the armed forces. In 1950, only 24 percent of the white population of the United States was born in the South. White southerners nonetheless represented 31 percent of all naval officers and 34 percent of all army officers. The numbers were still higher when they included men not born but nonetheless educated in the South. Most of those southern whites who served in the military elite were also from small towns and rural areas rather than metropolitan communities. The racial attitudes of these men reflected their social origins. According to sociologist Morris Janowitz, their upbringing predisposed them toward "a provincial and status quo outlook."[8] Moreover, some of those officers raised outside the southern states became acculturated to their racial mores while serving time on military bases in the region. Dwight Eisenhower, who had been born in Texas but raised in Kansas, was one such officer whose exposure to southern social customs and practices left its mark.[9] This acceptance of the racial stratification of southern society may have been influenced by the fact that it shared similarities with the hierarchical structure of the military. Moreover, the military itself enforced racial separation within its ranks. Those former officers who assumed command positions within massive resistance had spent their years of service in a strictly segregated military. Most retired shortly before or after President Harry Truman issued Executive Order 9981 in July 1948, establishing the right to equality of treatment and opportunity within the armed forces.

Third, anti-Semitism was also a pervasive political force within the military. The wartime fight against fascism had devalued the political currency of anti-Semitism. Senior military officials became much less tolerant of claims from within the ranks of a communist Jewish conspiracy. Historian Joseph Bendersky has nonetheless demonstrated that many senior officers maintained opinions about Jews that "lagged far behind changes in societal attitudes."[10] Addressing a Senate Internal Security Committee on what he saw as the causes for the failure of the American war effort in Korea, General George E. Stratemeyer warned: "There is some hidden force or some hidden power or something that is influencing our people. They don't act like Americans, Americans are supposed to have guts, and our policy . . . is wishy-washy and appeasing."[11] What is so arresting about this statement is that Stratemeyer should use the same euphemism as Crommelin to describe what he perceived as the Jewish threat to national security. Far from being the strange idiom of a madman, the political opinions of the rear admiral were common parlance among many of his fellow officers.

The combination of cold war fears with racial and ethnic prejudice encouraged some military officers to believe that the civil rights movement was part of a communist Jewish conspiracy to subvert the social stability and internal security of the United States. According to John M. Swomley, Jr., "Their domestic criticism is linked to their criticism of foreign policy in that all the things they dislike anywhere are, they are convinced, caused by the Communist enemy or by people who are subverted or duped by that enemy or else are soft on Communism."[12]

One other crucial component that motivated retired military officers to lead massive resistance forces was that they had been conditioned to command. Accustomed as they were to the unquestioning loyalty of those who served under them, they had little respect for the negotiation and compromise demanded by the democratic process. While they held politicians in low esteem, the military elite had, in the estimation of Morris Janowitz, come to believe that they had a solemn mission to act as the "standard bearers and conservators of great traditions in a changing social environment."[13] That assumption was rooted in grandiose notions of masculine bravery and honor. As historian K. A. Cuordileone has shown, the rhetoric of cold war military leaders was highly gendered. Senior officers contrasted their own supposed virility with what they saw as a "corrupt, feckless, and effeminate" political establishment whose impotence had undermined the security and vitality of the nation. In their estimation, the only means by which the United States could recover was through a reassertion of masculine strength. The hypermasculinist oratory of Crommelin, with its emphasis on redemption through warfare, is, while still extreme, more understandable when placed in the broader context of U.S. military culture.[14]

While it is difficult to compile details of all the senior-ranking military figures implicated in massive resistance, even a partial list provides a strong impression of their prominence. The support of these retired officers was an important political asset to massive resisters because of the prestige that their military rank and record commanded in a region with a strongly martial culture and tradition. Marine Colonel Mitchell Paige ran an educational forum called Project Alert that claimed Supreme Court Chief Justice Earl Warren was "guilty of sabotage in the first degree" and that "he should be hanged."[15] General Levzin Campbell and Admiral Ben Morrell ran their Campaign for the 48 States from Memphis, with the aim to reduce federal power and restore state sovereignty. Memphis was also the location of a National States' Rights Conference held in September 1956. Among the delegates were Lieutenant Generals Edward M. Almond and Albert C. Wedermeyer. Also in attendance was Merwin K. Hart of the National Economic Council, a far-right organization that claimed the United States was in the grip of "Marxist-Zionist forces." The council included numerous retired officers on its executive, among them, Major General Charles A. Willoughby and Vice Admiral C. A. Freeman.[16]

One of the sponsors of the National States' Rights Conference was Crommelin, and it is clear that throughout his political career he secured support and advice by tapping into the extensive network of disaffected former officers. His relationship with one officer merits particular attention.

Crommelin collaborated throughout his political career with Lieutenant General Pedro Augusto del Valle. Del Valle was an unusual white supremacist. He was born on August 28, 1893, in San Juan, Puerto Rico. His family immigrated to the United States seven years later, settling in Maryland. In later life, del Valle made a determined effort to reconcile the contradiction between his racialist politics and his own status as a member of a marginal immigrant community by emphasizing his white European ancestry. Referring to himself in the third person, he wrote, "The General is the descendant of a pure Castilian family who moved to Puerto Rico when that island was under Spanish control."[17] Del Valle nonetheless succeeded in spite of his Catholic Latino background in becoming a leader of the far right during the postwar decades.

Like Crommelin, del Valle was a decorated war hero. During World War II, he received the Legion of Merit and a Distinguished Service Medal for leading the marine assaults that resulted in the occupation of Guadalcanal and Okinawa.[18] Unlike Crommelin, his reputation remained untarnished at the time he retired from the military in 1948. It is therefore more difficult to attribute his racial fanaticism to a personal crisis. His political philosophy appears rather to have evolved over the course of his military career. During the 1930s, for instance, he served as an assistant naval attaché in the American Embassy in Rome and also accompanied as an observer the

Italian armed forces that invaded Ethiopia, experiences that imbued him with a strong admiration for the fascist government of Benito Mussolini.[19]

Following the war, del Valle became convinced that the internal security of the United States was under threat from a global Jewish conspiracy. He used his influence to arrange a meeting with officials from the CIA and the Defense Department, at which he attempted to convince them of the need to organize guerrilla combat forces to fight behind Soviet and Chinese lines. When his audience turned down the idea, del Valle decided to form an independent body to coordinate the recruitment of militia groups across the United States, armed with the purpose of rooting out alien forces that had infiltrated the country. A host of other former military officers collaborated with del Valle: Air Force Major General Claire Chennault; Brigadier Generals Bonner Fellers, Bill Lemly, and Clyde Watts; Colonel Matthew McKeon; and Lieutenant Colonels John Coffman and Eugene Cowles Pomeroy. In 1953, these men announced the formation of the ultrapatriotic Defenders of the American Constitution, spreading their message through the newsletter *Task Force*, first published in May 1954.[20]

The political opinions espoused by del Valle in the pages of *Task Force* could have been penned by Crommelin, so similar were they in both tone and content. "WE, THE PEOPLE OF THE UNITED STATES ARE AT WAR!" he exclaimed. "The war I have mentioned is a civil one, a struggle between the powers that be, who believe not in the Constitution, but in centralized power, versus the vast but voiceless majority of the citizens who put their faith in God and the Constitution and do not believe in the surrender of our States' rights and Sovereignty to the Federal power."[21] Issue after issue, *Task Force* documented what it described as the escalating acts of aggression by the federal government against its own citizens: the *Brown* decision, the Civil Rights Act, and, above all, the use of troops to enforce the desegregation of the Central High School in Little Rock. The latter incident in particular demonstrated to del Valle, as it did to Crommelin, that civil war had broken out on the streets of the United States. In the estimation of both men, the citizens of Little Rock were in effect under the military occupation of an enemy power.[22]

Del Valle concurred with Crommelin that this "enemy power" was a cabal of communist Jews who had seized control of the federal government. While del Valle substituted the phrase "Hidden Force" for "Unseen Power," his meaning was the same. These conspirators had reduced the federal government to a puppet regime, pulling the strings of the president. Like Crommelin, del Valle believed that Washington had ceded its power to a United Nations controlled by communist Jews intent on creating a "One World Order." He also shared with Crommelin the conviction that Jews were not white but rather a mongrelized race who wanted to reinvent the world in their own image. Del Valle similarly framed his hatred of Jews in gendered as well as racial terms, contrasting the masculinity of white men with the effeminacy of "the boys with the tinted lips, mincing steps and high-pitched vocal equipment" who conspired to enforce "social mixing and intermarriage."[23]

Another intellectual connection between del Valle and Crommelin was their common conviction that the country was not only at war but also that their home state was the main battleground.[24] Del Valle placed himself on the front line by running for public office against the forces of the communist Jewish conspiracy that he claimed had overrun Maryland. In 1954, he ran for the Republican nomination for governor but proved no more adept a politician than Crommelin, coming in last of the four candidates with only 5 percent of the vote. In contrast to Crommelin, who paradoxically appears to have drawn strength from defeat, del Valle abandoned his interest in electoral politics.[25]

The political paths of Crommelin and del Valle not only ran in parallel but also crossed repeatedly. Their partnership first took shape when the two men defended Senator Joseph McCarthy as founding members of Ten Million Americans Mobilizing for Justice.[26] They also collaborated in lobbying for the release from mental hospital of Ezra Pound and the repeal of the Alaska Mental Health Enabling Act, which del Valle considered a "means of disposing of anti-Communist American Patriots who dare disagree with socialism and internationalism."[27]

Del Valle and Crommelin continued to aid and abet one another for more than two decades. They assumed executive positions in the American Association for Justice, Inc., in 1966 and the following year established the short-lived Sons of Liberty. Disaffected with the democratic process, del Valle and Crommelin saw the Sons of Liberty as a central element in the terrorist strategy they devised during the 1960s. According to del Valle, if it was not possible "to vote the traitors out," then there was "yet another course of action left; the organization of a powerful, armed resistance force to defeat the aims of the usurpers and bring about a return to Constitutional government."[28] The Sons of Liberty was intended to coordinate a network of paramilitary cells that would seize control of government from the civilian authorities. Like so many of the initiatives with which Crommelin was associated, it collapsed because neither he nor del Valle could recruit an armed force to serve under their command.

The former military officer most infamously associated with massive resistance was Major General Edwin A. Walker. Historians have devoted more attention to Walker than Crommelin because of his role in precipitating one of the most dramatic crises of the civil rights struggle, the riot at the University of Mississippi in the fall of 1962. A comparative analysis of Walker and Crommelin provides a further perspective on the political activism of the two former military officers. Although the parallels between the two men are not precise, there were significant similarities in terms of their unceremonious departure from the military, their radical right-wing ideology, and their militant tactics. Both acted on beliefs shared by many within the upper echelons of the military brass that the southern states had a right to legislate racial separation, a right that must be upheld, if necessary, through violence. For both men, the Little Rock school crisis was a seminal moment in their embrace of extremism. However, while Crommelin watched events from afar, Walker was caught up in the crisis. What makes his later career all the more remarkable is that he should have been in command of the troops of the 101st Airborne Division who secured the desegregation of the high school.

Walker was at the time a celebrated military hero. He had been born on November 9, 1909, in Center Point, a small community in central Texas. After his graduation from the New Mexico Military Institute, he attended the West Point Academy from 1927 to 1931. Walker gained his reputation as a military officer first during World War II, when he led a command squad named the First Special Service, and then in Korea as head of artillery forces at the Battle of Heartbreak Ridge. On returning home, he assumed command of the Arkansas Military District in Little Rock.[29]

Journalist Harry Ashmore described Walker as "a model of aloof correctness" in his handling of the school crisis.[30] On the morning of Wednesday, August 25, 1957, Walker addressed more than one thousand white students in the auditorium at Central High School with a firm warning not to obstruct the desegregation process. "We are all subject to all the laws," he informed his audience, "whether we approve of them or not, and as law-abiding citizens, we have an obligation in conscience to obey them. There can be no exceptions; if it were otherwise, we would not be a strong nation but a mere unruly mob."[31]

Despite his publicly dispassionate demeanor, Walker disclosed something of his private thoughts in his inclusive use of the word *we* to describe those who must perform their lawful duty, whether they approved of it or not. When first ordered to command the troops he had demurred, maintaining that it was the responsibility of the police to enforce domestic law and order. Only when President Eisenhower refused to accept his resignation did he relent.[32] Walker carried out his orders in Little Rock because he believed his obligations as a soldier outweighed his convictions as a private citizen. His reservations about school desegregation were not, however, restricted simply to matters of jurisdiction.

In the understated words of one author, Walker was "a Southerner with a parochial view" of race relations.[33] He believed that the use of troops to enforce the admission of black students to the Central High School was part of a communist conspiracy to create civil war within the United States. One of the principal sources on which he based these claims was Conde McGinley's *Common Sense*, the same publication that inspired Bryant Bowles to lead the resistance to school desegregation in Milford, Delaware.[34]

Walker had struggled in Little Rock to resolve his personal abhorrence of desegregation with his professional responsibilities as a soldier. It was a dilemma he would not have to live with for long. In 1958, the National Security Council issued a directive authorizing military officers to instruct troops on their role in protecting the United States from communism.[35] Walker welcomed the initiative because he believed the United States had ceded much of its global supremacy to China and the Soviet Union. First, he attributed the failure to secure victory in the Korean War to American forces having to fight under the banner of the United Nations which, he believed, restricted their movement in the field of combat.[36] Second, and more disturbingly, Walker deemed many American soldiers mentally unfit for the harsh realities of modern warfare. The susceptibility of American POWs to brainwashing by their Korean captors demonstrated to him the need for stronger psychological conditioning of trainee soldiers. In emphasizing the deficiencies of American soldiers, Walker conspicuously made no reference to race. Although the Korean War was the first conflict in which black and white troops had fought together, he does not appear to have identified this as one of the causes of the military stalemate. In any event, Walker responded to the National Security Council directive by formulating a program to improve troop preparation for combat with the communist enemy. The Pro-Blue program included a series of lectures and discussions and a list of recommended reading.

So great was the zeal with which Walker set out to indoctrinate his troops that he soon overstepped the mark. His first blunder was to distribute extremist literature such as Robert Welch's *The Life of John Birch* to his troops. He also made the error of breaching army regulations by advising the men under his command to vote for certain candidates in national elections. Walker compounded these mistakes by giving a speech to soldiers and their wives in which he claimed that Harry S. Truman was "definitely pink" and made similar assertions about the supposed communist loyalties of such public figures as Eleanor Roosevelt and Adlai Stevenson.[37] These accusations led to the exposure of the Pro-Blue program by the *Overseas Weekly*, a tabloid newspaper popular with American soldiers stationed abroad, which claimed that his promotion of partisan politics made Walker unfit for military service. The scandal led Secretary of the Army Elvis J. Stahr to order that Walker be relieved of his command, pending the results of a military tribunal.[38]

On June 12, 1961, the Department of Defense issued a press release announcing the conclusions of the inquiry. The tribunal acquitted Walker of the charge of distributing John Birch Society propaganda but found him guilty of making "derogatory remarks about certain prominent Americans" and of "participating in controversial activities which were contrary to long-standing customs of the military service." Rather than accept the offer of a reassignment to a training post at a Pacific outpost, Walker resigned from the army.[39]

Walker had time to reflect on the causes of his professional ruin. Five months later, on April 4, 1962, he appeared before a Special Senate Subcommittee investigating a directive from the Defense Department restricting the promotion of right-wing politics by military officers. Walker had already attributed the Little Rock crisis to a "fifth column conspiracy."[40] Now he testified that senior government officials were acting as members of a "hidden control apparatus" intent on undermining the sovereignty and national security of the United States.[41] The parallels with Crommelin are clear. In common with his fellow senior officer, he also became convinced that it was his responsibility to lead the fight against this unseen foe.

Like Crommelin, Walker first attempted to wage that fight through the ballot box. On February 3, 1962, he announced his candidacy for the governorship of Texas. Addressing a news conference in the state House of Representatives, he declared in millenarian terms that his purpose was "to defend the United States under God in a struggle for survival against international communism."[42]

Walker's electioneering bore notable similarities in terms of both style and substance with the political campaigns of Crommelin. His speeches placed a comparable emphasis on the threat the United Nations posed to U.S. sovereignty. Both men believed the UN had surreptitiously seized control of the American military with the intention of forcing troops to turn on the civilian population. The brutal imposition of integration would destroy American society and bring about the rise of a mongrelized race ruled by a one world government.[43] Just as Crommelin was convinced that the main battleground between the forces of American civilization and the communist hordes was his home state of Alabama, so too Walker claimed that Texas was the location of the decisive conflict. Texas was of the greatest strategic importance to the United States, owing to its being "the location of most of the major military, naval, air, and atomic installations of the country." However, "the presence of racial situations" rendered the state unstable and vulnerable to attack.[44]

The electorate remained unmoved by this warning. For reasons similar to those of Crommelin, Walker failed to cultivate a constituency in support of his cause. Although he attracted sizable audiences to his public speeches, he proved an uninspiring political candidate. Like Crommelin and del Valle, he lacked the populist touch and assumed that leadership was something he deserved rather than needed to earn. In common with his fellow former officers, in his campaign literature Walker traced his family lineage back through Confederate war heroes to Founding Fathers Charles Pinckney and Charles Cotesworth Pinckney, in a manner that implied his election to public office was a right of heredity.[45] Walker also shared with Crommelin the serious political impediment of being a poor public speaker. In private, he could be clear and concise. When forced to stand on a podium, however, his movements became nervous, his voice became flat, and he stumbled over his words.[46] These shortcomings contributed to Walker's feeble performance in the Democratic primary, in which he finished last of the six candidates with only 134,000 of the 1,400,000 votes cast.[47]

Walker's failure to win public office led him, like Crommelin, to embrace more extreme measures in the fight against integration. Reflecting on his role in enforcing the admission of African American students to Little Rock Central High School, Walker later confessed he had "led forces on the wrong side." Liberated from his responsibilities as a military officer to follow orders from the federal government, he fervently confirmed that he was now "happy to be on the other and right side."[48] Walker issued this declaration in response to the escalating crisis over the admission of African

American student James Meredith to the University of Mississippi. True to his word, when Meredith arrived on the university campus accompanied by federal marshals, Walker performed a command role not in repelling, but rather in rallying, segregationist resistance.

Walker had started to champion the cause of white Mississippians some months earlier, in December 1961, when he delivered an address at the Jackson city auditorium. Accompanied on stage by such massive resistance luminaries as Mayor Allen Thompson, Congressman John Bell Williams, and Governor Ross Barnett, Walker addressed his civilian audience as though they were troops preparing to take the field of combat. "I came here to meet the Communists on their battlefield right here in Mississippi," he proclaimed. "We are at war. Man your weapons and attack."[49] The speech paralleled similar calls to arms by Crommelin. It also became a recruiting tool for massive resistance leaders. The Citizens' Council used parts of the speech in a thirty-minute propaganda film it distributed to television stations across the country, trading on the reputation that Walker had gained among ultraconservatives as a defender of American values.[50]

It was another nine months before Walker would lead the fight against the communist forces he believed responsible for desegregation. James Meredith had first applied to the University of Mississippi in January 1961, but it was not until September 10 the following year that the Supreme Court upheld his right to enrollment. State authorities orchestrated a determined campaign of defiance. With the battle lines drawn, Walker attempted to recruit a white resistance army. On September 26, he appeared on a radio show broadcast by station KWKH in Shreveport, Louisiana. "We have listened and we have been pushed around by the anti-Christ Supreme Court," he declared. "It's time to rise ... Ten thousand strong from every state in the nation." Asked afterward by reporters whether he was attempting to mobilize an armed militia, Walker responded that white citizens must use "whatever is necessary" to withstand federal tyranny.[51]

Walker flew by private plane to Jackson on September 29.[52] Although he believed he was coming to the aid of state authorities, the following day Governor Barnett accepted a deal offered by Attorney General Robert Kennedy to register Meredith in secret. Such was the escalation of racial tension, however, that when the black student arrived under armed escort at the campus the following day, a crowd of several hundred had already gathered. As their numbers swelled from hundreds to thousands, the mood of the crowd became more aggressive. The marshals found themselves besieged by a mob that pelted them with a barrage of stones, bottles, and homemade explosives. Walker appeared among the swarming rioters, urging them on with a rousing speech delivered from under a towering Confederate monument. This moment had an immense symbolic resonance. Here was a contemporary southern military hero summoning the spirit of the Civil War dead in the fight against the old Yankee foe.

Although Crommelin also played an active role in fomenting the violence, there is no evidence of collaboration between the two military men. What is certain is that by the time the army had arrived from Memphis to restore order, 375 people, including 160 marshals, had suffered injuries and 2 more had died.[53]

Following the riot, Assistant Attorney General Nicholas Katzenbach authorized the arrest of Walker on charges of insurrection and sedition.[54] Before Walker stood trial, District Judge Claude Clayton ordered his commitment to a medical center in Springfield, Missouri, for psychiatric evaluation. Those authors who have studied Walker assume he was not only deluded but actually deranged. Jonathan Schoenwald maintains that Walker was "unbalanced" and "unhinged," while William Doyle asserts that he was essentially "a clinical madman."[55] The problem with these opinions is that they contradict the conclusions of the psychiatric professionals who assessed Walker. The decision to commit Walker to a mental ward came on the recommendation of Dr. Charles F. Smith, medical director and chief psychiatrist of the Federal Prison Bureau. Smith had never met Walker but rather drawn the assumption from newspaper reports that the former military officer might be suffering from "paranoid mental disorders."[56] Test results exposed the speculative nature of this diagnosis. The mental health experts who examined Walker deemed him fit to stand trial. On November 6, Judge Clayton ordered Walker's release from the hospital. The Justice Department later dropped its charges against him.[57]

These experiences led many white Mississippians to see Walker as a martyr persecuted by the federal authorities he had so heroically resisted. Crommelin had warned that federal authorities were conspiring to incarcerate segregationists in mental asylums in Alaska. Although the ordeal Walker endured was far less onerous than the indefinite detention in "Siberia usa" Crommelin claimed awaited outspoken opponents of civil rights reform, his experience confirmed the fears of many segregationists that the federal government intended to use accusations of insanity as a pretext to imprison political dissidents. The denial of due process to Walker set a dangerous precedent in the opinion of the southern press. As one segregationist newspaper asserted, "The General became the first political prisoner in the U.S. On arrest he was denied bail, ordered by a Federal judge to a Federal mental prison for 60 to 90 days and denied a writ of habeas corpus for five days. Walker was not even in the judge's jurisdiction and had no lawyer present."[58]

While moderate segregationists dismissed Crommelin's claims about the political misuse of Alaskan mental asylums as paranoid delusion, they saw the psychiatric detention of Walker as genuine evidence of federal tyranny. The State House of Representatives gave him a standing ovation when he paid a surprise visit in December 1962.[59] Walker was also feted as a folk hero by the Citizens' Council of America, which invited him to address its leadership conference in Jackson the following year.[60] The political fortunes of Walker and Crommelin could not in this respect have been more contrasting, one of them enduring ostracism while the other enjoyed adulation. One explanation for this disparity is that while racial hard-liners such as John Patterson and George Wallace rendered Crommelin obsolete, the capitulation to federal authorities by Ross Barnett undermined his prestige and authority, allowing Walker to claim credit as the uncompromising champion of white southern resistance. As was the case with Bryant Bowles and John Kasper, Walker gained political capital from the perceived weakness of state authorities.

Crommelin curiously did not attempt to exploit the experiences of Walker for his own political advantage. The fate of his fellow military officer appeared to prove his accusation that the federal government was intent on discrediting and incarcerating its segregationist opponents. Why Crommelin did not attempt to take advantage of the Walker case is unclear, especially when other military officers on the far right seized it as an opportunity to denounce federal tyranny. Pedro del Valle ran an article in *Task Force* that decried the unconstitutional mistreatment of Walker.[61] Crommelin, by contrast, missed the chance to win some reflected glory. Whether there was any rivalry between Crommelin and Walker is unclear, although there is a possibility that the rear admiral feared that his fellow military officer posed a threat to his own status as a standard bearer of the far right. The National States' Rights Party, for instance, started to cite Walker in its publicity material around the time he announced his candidacy for the Texas governorship. In contrast to the perennially unsuccessful Crommelin, Walker was at the time still an untested political candidate and therefore appeared to possess more electoral potential.[62]

Despite the rapturous support Walker received from Mississippi segregationists, his resounding defeat earlier in the year dissuaded him from launching a further campaign for public office. Although Walker did not run for office a second time, he remained politically active. Like Crommelin, his prestige as a patriotic hero allowed him to act as a bridge between disparate groups on the far right. He made connections with numerous segregationist groups, including the American Loyal Rangers, Americans for the Preservation of the White Race, the Christian Anti-Communist Crusade, the Citizens' Council, and, responding to their overtures, the National States' Rights Party.[63] Walker was also, like Crommelin, rumored to be one of the conspirators in a planned coup d'état, this time in collaboration with Alabama and Mississippi Klansmen. His involvement in these extremist organizations denoted a conviction that the southern political establishment had failed to safeguard against federally imposed race reform.[64]

Walker also came close to crossing from the margins to the mainstream of national politics. For all their success in stirring dissent, the rabble-rousing rhetoric of far-right activists such as Bryant Bowles and John Kasper preached to the converted. Walker, by contrast, threatened to build a constituency that cut across regional and party political lines. In February 1963, he joined forces with fundamentalist preacher Billy James Hargis on a coast-to-coast speaking tour. Hargis, a fellow Texan, had founded his outreach organization Christian Crusade in 1950, attracting a national audience through his daily radio sermons broadcast on more than 270 stations. The two men titled their tour Operation Midnight Ride in an attempt to portray themselves as latter-day Paul Reveres, warning of the threat posed not by the British but the forces of international communism. Hargis affirmed that their purpose was "to alert the public to the enemy within and without."[65]

Operation Midnight Ride drew enthusiastic crowds in the South, Walker even being presented with the key to the city of Birmingham.[66] Yet their largest audiences, sometimes in the thousands, were on the West Coast. Walker and Hargis most impressed listeners with their warnings of the threat China and the Soviet Union posed to American security. However, their anticommunist message also contained a racial element. Civil rights activists were, they insisted, fifth columnists working in the interests of the Kremlin to destroy the social fabric of the United States. Hargis proclaimed to supporters in Los Angeles that Communists controlled the National Association for the Advancement of Colored People (NAACP),

Chapter Five

pointing as evidence to the fact that the organization had not appointed a black president "in a coon's age." Civil rights activists reacted by picketing the tour.[67]

Although West Coast audiences responded less positively than white southerners to such racist rhetoric, they shared a similar commitment to protecting white privilege. Many of the migrants who settled in the Greater Los Angeles area during and after World War II were from the South and conservative Midwest. As historian Lisa McGirr observes, they brought with them "deep-seated racial biases." While most of these whites eschewed explicitly racist argument, they fought tenaciously to protect such practices as residential segregation, overturning a state open housing act by a margin of more than two-to-one. Southern California was also a breeding ground for white racial militancy. The National States' Rights Party, for instance, established a state chapter in Garden Grove, Orange County.[68]

Walker failed, however, to capitalize on the prejudice and fear of white South Californians. While Hargis was an "emotional spellbinder," the tongue-tied performances of Walker dampened the flames lit by the evangelist.[69] What Operation Midnight Ride demonstrated was nonetheless that white southerners espousing ultraconservative politics could potentially recruit a support base beyond their native region. This understanding of the latent power of a national white conservative backlash led Walker and Hargis five years later to promote the presidential candidacy of Alabama Governor George Wallace. The enthusiasm of West Coast Republicans for Walker, a registered southern Democrat, is also indicative of a process of electoral realignment that would later impact on American politics.[70]

Frustrated not only with politicians but also with a civilian population they saw as too weak and directionless to resist the forces conspiring against their country, former military officers such as John Crommelin, Pedro del Valle, and Edwin Walker tried to assume the mantle of leadership in the massive resistance movement. The fact that they entered politics at a time when the president was himself a former military leader rendered their sense of betrayal by the government all the more acute. Walker accused Eisenhower of capitulating to U.S. foreign enemies when he ordered the use of troops to enforce school integration in Little Rock. Crommelin went so far as to accuse the president of being one of the communist Jewish conspirators who sought to destroy the United States.[71] What set these military men apart from rabble rousers like John Kasper and Bryant Bowles was their autocratic personalities. The strategy of Kasper and Bowles was to build their movements up from the grassroots with themselves as the supposed representatives of the popular will. By contrast, the military officers were elitists who promoted a top-down model of leadership. Paradoxically, their common sense of patriotic purpose led them to trample on the Constitution and conspire against their own democratically elected government.

PART THREE

Southern Fuehrer

J. B. Stoner

6. "We Don't Believe in Tolerance"

Terrorist Responses to Civil Rights Reform

"I've been fighting Jews and niggers full time more or less since starting in 1942." So declared J. B. Stoner, perhaps the most violently fanatical racist spawned by massive resistance.[1] He was the nexus of a terrorist network that the authorities held responsible for many of the bomb attacks on homes, schools, and houses of worship that occurred during the desegregation struggle. Stoner recruited members, raised finances, and represented suspected criminals in court.[2]

Southern segregationists during and after World War II dissociated themselves from the racial doctrines of European fascism, sensing no contradiction between their support of the Allied war effort abroad and the oppression of African Americans at home. Public exposure of Nazi concentration camps shattered the credibility of biological racism, forcing white southerners to emphasize other issues such as states' rights in their defense of Jim Crow. Not so Stoner. A self-proclaimed fascist, he saw it as his mission to fulfill the promise of the defeated Nazi regime and found a white supremacist order through the relocation or eradication of racial and religious minorities. Adolf Hitler, concluded Stoner, had been too moderate. He would not make the same mistake.

In contrast to John Kasper and Bryant Bowles, no observer seems to have doubted that, however repellent, Stoner was completely sincere in his political opinions. The endurance of his political activism over the course of more than a half century is testimony to his obsessive sense of purpose. Decades after most white southern politicians had bowed to the new realities shaped by the black freedom struggle, Stoner maintained an uncompromising conviction that he could reverse the civil rights revolution. He was an inspiration to a new generation of far-right activists who revered him as "the patriarch of the White supremacist movement."[3]

Although Stoner was one of the most active and influential figures on the American far right for more than fifty years, the outrage he still arouses has precluded a rigorous assessment of his political career. When Stoner died, historian Ralph Luker produced a short editorial piece wishing him a "Happy Deathday."[4] While the tone of moral condemnation was entirely appropriate to the occasion, the passing of time may allow for more methodical analysis. The persistence of hate groups in contemporary politics provides a purpose to our greater understanding of what motivates them and how they attempt to accomplish their aims. A dispassionate consideration of Stoner's career, specifically his involvement in violence against civil rights activists, is therefore overdue.

Jesse Benjamin Stoner, Jr., was born April 13, 1924, in Walker County, Georgia. His father, Jesse, Sr., worked across the state border in Tennessee as owner of Rock City, a tourist attraction that provided visitors with spectacular views from the peak of Lookout Mountain. The family was sufficiently wealthy to enroll their son at the exclusive McCallie School in Chattanooga. Although raised in the comfort of a relatively prosperous household, Jesse endured personal tragedy in childhood. First, at the age of only two-and-a-half years, he suffered an attack of polio that crippled one of his legs. Three years later, his father died. By the time Stoner was seventeen, he had also lost his mother to cancer. These setbacks did not inhibit his ambition and he enthusiastically pursued a career in law, gaining admittance to the Georgia bar in 1951.[5]

Most reporters who later met Stoner made little attempt to understand what motivated him. Those who sought an explanation for his racial fanaticism found it in an embittered outlook on life brought on by his physical affliction and the loss of his parents. According to such reasoning, Stoner displaced the responsibility for his personal misfortune onto a convenient scapegoat. As one journalist asserted, "Because of the bad leg, he rarely competed with other boys in athletics, so he tried to excel at something else: fighting blacks and Jews."[6]

This line of reasoning is far too reductionist. A polio attack does not turn its victims into vengeful adversaries of racial and religious minority groups. More convincing are the explanations that Stoner himself offered for his conversion to the white supremacist cause. Stoner appears to have been unusually self-reflective for a far-right activist. His account of the childhood experiences that informed his adult worldview is an unusually revealing document.

Historians emphasize how African Americans mastered the art of dissembling as a means of shifting the dynamics of power in their relationships with whites. Blacks allowed whites to assume their outwardly compliant behavior was an expression of their inner acceptance of the racialized social order.[7] Stoner nonetheless claimed he saw through this pretense when he was still only a child. African Americans, he observed, had learned as slaves "how to kowtow to whites, how to put on a false front to white people." This strategy succeeded in deceiving most whites, who "will tell you that their nigger servants love them." The young Jesse, however, possessed greater powers of perception. "They say, 'Yes, sir' and 'Yes, mam,' when you tell them what to do; and if somebody cusses them out they used to say, 'Thank you, boss.' But I've always known that that wasn't their real attitude." On the contrary, he concluded, African Americans had "a strong resentment and antagonism toward white people."[8]

The fact that Stoner became a far-right activist while still in his youth suggests that this was not simply a retrospective evaluation reached from the perspective of adulthood. However, it is not clear why he could see behind what he perceived as the mask of black deference when others could not. Other members of his family did not share his convictions about African Americans; some indeed ostracized him as a result.[9] Nor does it make sense that an existing prejudice predisposed him to see what he wanted to see in black behavior. While not discounting the possibility of genuine bonds of affection between black laborers and their white employers there was, as scholars point out, an attempt to deceive on the part of many African Americans.

While Stoner's opinion of African Americans stemmed from personal contact and observation, the same was not true of his attitude toward Jews. Chattanooga had a small and assimilated Jewish population too inconspicuous to create much of an impression on the young Jesse. It was the mythical Jew rather than the merchants who traded on Main Street that captured his imagination. Jesse was a serious youth less interested in childhood play than adult politics. According to Stoner, "I started taking an interest in politics and what was going on when I was about eight years old." It was through his study of world affairs that the precocious Jesse came to believe in the malign influence of Jews. "The Jews were on the wrong side of every issue, and even when I was a child, I had enough brains to observe that." Stoner cited the support of Jews for Republican forces during the Spanish Civil War as one example. Closer to home, he claimed that Jews were on "the wrong side" of the race issue. Stoner believed that while African Americans resented their subordinate status, they lacked the intelligence and enterprise to challenge white supremacy. Jews therefore were the real masterminds of the civil rights movement. "Of course, the niggers want it," Stoner asserted, "but they don't have the brains or the power to do it." African Americans were, in his opinion, the pawns of Jews, manipulated into fighting for a freedom they did not possess the capacity to benefit from.[10]

Motivated by his deep racial and religious antipathies, Stoner became a member of the far right while still in his teens. In 1940, he wrote to Fred Kaltenbach, a former high school teacher from Iowa fired for attempting to organize a Hitler Youth movement who had fled to Germany, where he became a Nazi radio propagandist. The letter praised the superiority of German medical science and raised the possibility of Stoner traveling overseas for an operation on his crippled leg. Although the trip never occurred, the Nazis used the letter for propaganda purposes, the broadcaster Lord Haw-Haw reading it over the airwaves in a radio broadcast of May 1940.[11]

Stoner's enthusiasm for Nazi Germany extended beyond the skills of its surgeons. By the time the United States had become embroiled in World War II, he believed that the real enemy was not fascism, but rather a global conspiracy by Jews to undermine Western civilization. Resolved to awaken his fellow Americans to this threat, in 1942 he became a Kleagle of the Association of Georgia Klans (and, after its disbandment, the Associated Klans of America). His conviction that the Axis powers did not constitute the real danger to American democracy led, two years later, to his filing a petition with the U.S. House of Representatives, urging its members to approve a resolution that "Jews are the children of the devil" and should be expelled from the country.[12]

In addition to his adulation of Hitler, Stoner cited two public figures closer to home who inspired his political activism. The first of the two personalities was Colonel Eugene Nelson Sanctuary, whom Stoner lauded as the greatest living American.[13] Sanctuary is a further example of a senior military officer implicated in far-right politics. Founder of the anti-Semitic

American Christian Defenders, he also penned numerous pamphlets warning of a Marxist Zionist conspiracy against American democracy, including *Is the New Deal Communist?* and *Are These Things So?*, which equated Judaism with Satanism. His efforts to form a united fascist movement in the United States eventually led to his indictment for sedition in January 1942.[14]

Stoner also sought to emulate Mississippi Senator Theodore G. Bilbo, a reactionary racist characterized by one source as "the most anti-Jewish, pro-Nazi voice in the American Senate."[15] Bilbo's treatise on race relations, *Take Your Choice: Separation or Mongrelization*, published shortly before his death in 1947, was a clear influence on the later writings of Stoner, particularly its claim of divine sanction for segregation and emphasis on the supposedly innate biological differences between blacks and whites.[16] The Mississippi politician also inspired Stoner's plans to create a white republic by repatriating the black population of the United States. In April 1939, Bilbo introduced a bill to the Senate that would have authorized the deportation of African Americans to Liberia.[17]

Journalist Stetson Kennedy saw Stoner deliver a speech at a Klan rally around this time. He could barely believe what he heard. Having publicized his petition to Congress, Stoner disclosed that his ultimate purpose was not simply to repatriate Jews but to eliminate them. This, he declared, was an act of mercy. "I think we ought to kill all Jews just to save their unborn generations from having to go to Hell!" Working undercover, Kennedy had witnessed Klan activity at close hand. Even so, he was unprepared for the visceral hatred espoused by Stoner. "I sat up on the edge of my chair," stated the reporter. "This guy must be stark raving crazy, I thought to myself."[18]

Stoner was all too serious about his intentions to exterminate Jews. In 1945, he established an independent organization, the Stoner Anti-Jewish Party, dedicated to the singular purpose "to make being a Jew a crime, punishable by death." As its name suggests, this new political entity was little more than an extension of his personality, a fact not disguised by the change of its first name to "Christian" seven years later. By that time, the Associated Klans of America had expelled Stoner from their ranks because of his efforts to pass a motion ordering the forced removal of all Jews from Chattanooga. Stoner later responded by appointing himself Imperial Wizard of his own Christian Knights of the Ku Klux Klan.[19]

Stoner further promoted his anti-Semitic crusade through the publication of a pamphlet titled *The Gospel of Jesus Christ Versus the Jews*. Published in 1946, this diatribe constitutes the most thorough articulation of

Stoner's political philosophy that he ever made; he obdurately adhered to the ideas espoused in the pamphlet for the rest of his life. The pamphlet is an early articulation of the Christian Identity theology that later became a dominant ideological force within the far right. Dedicated to "MY LORD, MASTER, AND SAVIOR, JESUS CHRIST," it contained one central claim: that Christians, rather than Jews, are God's chosen people. Stoner asserted that Christians deserved this designation since they alone accepted Jesus as their savior. Jews, by contrast, were "Satanically insane" for spurning the redeemer and God would "punish and destroy" them for their infidelity.[20] Having established the innate sinfulness of Jews, Stoner proceeded to catalogue their many crimes against humanity, including circumcision, divorce, and abortion, claiming the latter was part of a genocidal conspiracy by a Jewish medical profession to decimate the Christian population and claim world domination.[21]

In delineating the scale of the danger Jews represented, Stoner conformed to a common pattern of behavior among conspiracy theorists. Although the threat posed by the Jewish conspiracy was immense, it remained unseen by all but those with rare powers of perception. *The Gospel* therefore imbues its author with a profound sense of importance since he must be the one to warn others of the perils they face. Moreover, having uncovered the conspiracy, Stoner became its central target. "The Jews, those archliars, will probably try to smear, scandalize, and libel me for writing this book that tells the truth," he contended. Although nothing of the sort happened, *The Gospel* demonstrates the missionary-like purpose with which Stoner attempted to publicize his cause.[22]

Stoner enlarged on the themes of *The Gospel* in a sequel published in the 1970s. The title, *Christ Not a Jew and Jews Not God's Chosen People,* is self-explanatory. Stoner draws on an assortment of biblical quotations to support his assertion that the divine blessing bestowed on the Israelites is one of the "biggest lies ever spawned." Jews, he concluded, were a threat to national security and the federal government should revoke their American citizenship.[23] The book is most significant for demonstrating how little, if any, development there was in Stoner's thinking.

Despite his association with terrorist organizations, Stoner also sought legitimacy for his political opinions through the democratic process. In 1948, he attended the convention of the States' Rights Democratic Party—the white southern splinter group that had deserted the national Democratic Party over the civil rights issue—to enlist support for his first congressional campaign. His failure to secure an affluent benefactor did not dissuade him from running as an independent candidate for the Third Congressional District of Tennessee. His feeble performance, winning less than 1,000 of the 30,000 votes cast, may have caused another man to wonder whether he was destined for a career in politics. Stoner, however, was not about to surrender.[24]

The historical record reveals little of Stoner's political activities from the late 1940s to the early 1950s.[25] His career gathered new momentum in August 1958, when he helped found the political organization with which he tied his fortunes for almost half a century, the National States' Rights Party (NSRP). Since Stoner became synonymous with the party, a study of its ideology and tactics offers essential insight into his political career.

The NSRP emanated from a merger of several smaller far-right splinter groups.[26] One of the most prominent activists within the latter organization was Edward Fields. His relationship with Stoner dated back to 1952, when the two men met at law school in Atlanta. The personal and political alliance between Fields and Stoner bound their fates together for three decades, but later descended into bitter acrimony.

Edward Reeds Fields was born September 30, 1932, in Chicago. Photographs of Fields from the time of the civil rights revolution show that while he shared with the conservatively attired Stoner a predilection for gentlemanly bow ties, he also sported an elaborately pomaded ducktail more in keeping with the rebellious spirit of James Dean. The two men were a study in physical contrasts, the clubfooted and somewhat corpulent Stoner comparing unfavorably with his more handsome partner.[27]

While still a child, Fields had moved south with his family to Atlanta. He started to exhibit the first signs of his political fanaticism as a teenager. Officials at the Catholic academy he attended reprimanded him after he attempted to recruit fellow students to a Nazi organization named the Black Front. In 1946, still only age fourteen, he became a member of the Columbians, Inc., a radical racist group that launched a brutal terror campaign against African Americans.[28] By the time the authorities had cracked down on the Columbians, imprisoning their leader Emory Burke and confiscating a huge cache of arms and explosives, Fields had graduated from the academy and enrolled in law school. Like his classmate Stoner, he appears not to have seen any contradiction between training as a lawyer by day while participating in political violence by night. However, he soon abandoned his original career plans in order to enroll at a chiropractic college in Davenport, Iowa. Fields remained active within the far right, however, and the establishment of the NSRP brought him back south to battle the civil rights movement.[29]

Journalist Drew Pearson described the inaugural meeting of the NSRP as a gathering of the "dirty collar crowd."[30] This was an inaccurate assessment of those who assembled in Louisville. In contrast to this characteristic stereotyping of the far right, Arnold Forster of the Anti-Defamation League conceded of the NSRP that "the leadership seems to be of slightly higher caliber than Klan elements and the membership appears to be somewhat more articulate."[31] NSRP rhetoric identified with a southern white working class that, it claimed, lacked a representative voice. A list of the foremost NSRP activists compiled in the early 1960s nonetheless revealed that several of them were members of the professional middle class.[32]

There was nonetheless a contrast between the class status of the party leadership and its grassroots supporters. A publication by the Baltimore NSRP chapter identified three main sources of recruitment: youth, rural and small town communities, and union workers disaffected with their national leaders' support for racial integration.[33] The principals within the party hierarchy were themselves relatively young. According to the inventory mentioned earlier, three of the ten primary NSRP activists were twenty-five years old or younger. In staging counter-demonstrations against civil rights activism, the NSRP enlisted the support of many whites who were not actual members, most of whom were indeed from less urban or affluent areas. As one team of reporters coarsely put it, the audiences at NSRP rallies consisted of "men in shirtsleeves and overalls," "women in calico," and "barefoot children."[34] The party also recruited industrial union workers, principally in Birmingham and Jacksonville. Its success in attracting blue-collar laborers affirms the position of scholars such as Bruce Nelson and Robert Norrell that the entrenched racial prejudice of white southern workers prohibited any possibility of a proletarian revolt against Jim Crow.[35]

The NSRP based its operations first in Jeffersonville, Indiana, and later in Birmingham, Alabama. The party operated along military lines. Members wore a uniform consisting of a white shirt and black trousers and decorated with a black tie, Sam Browne belt, and armband bearing the party emblem, a thunderbolt superimposed on a Confederate battle flag. The NSRP chairman was Ned Dupes, a former disciple of John Kasper.[36] At the pinnacle of its political influence, the NSRP claimed to have thirty-six chapters in thirteen states, not only in the South, but from across the United States. However, many of these local branches existed in little more than name and estimates of external sources suggested that NSRP membership never exceeded five hundred. Although most of these members were men, women occupied a number of prominent positions within the party hierarchy, including Vice Chairperson Anne Bishop and Secretary Treasurer Bernice Settle. In a clear concession to Edward Fields, the NSRP also included Catholics within its otherwise exclusively white Protestant ranks.[37]

The influence of the NSRP was far greater than the paucity of its official membership implies. During the late 1960s, the party newsletter, *The Thunderbolt*, reached a circulation of 25,000, the largest readership of any far-right publication in the United States. Moreover, its use of direct action tactics ensured that the NSRP had an impact on the political scene out of all proportion to the actual number of its members.[38]

Although the name of the NSRP may seem oxymoronic, it accurately articulated the political philosophy of its members. Contemporary commentators considered the party as antithetical to the principles of American political culture. The self-perception of NSRP members was nonetheless that they were patriots rather than traitors. Stoner and his associates saw themselves as inheritors of the ideals of the American Revolution. The title of their party emphasized that federalism was less a political expedience used to protect the parochial self-interest of white southerners than one of the defining principles of American governance. In protecting states' rights to practice segregation, the NSRP therefore claimed to honor the axiom of the Declaration of Independence that governments derive their power from the consent of the governed.

NSRP rhetoric underlined this point by portraying members as guided by the spirit of American Revolutionary heroes. During the 1960s, when Stoner toured the trouble spots of the South to aggravate grassroots resistance to civil rights reform, the NSRP newsletter described him as a "Paul Revere" who had surrendered his "worldly possessions to ride across the land awakening and uniting our people."[39] Another NSRP publication included a photograph of the monument to the Lexington Minute Men, on which was inscribed the command of Captain John Parker: "Stand your ground/Don't Fire Unless Fired Upon/But If They Mean to Have a War/ Let it Begin Here."[40]

In claiming to have inherited the principles of the Founding Fathers, the NSRP hoped to reposition itself from the margins to the mainstream of political life. Its reading of American constitutional history nevertheless inverted conventional interpretations of a country founded on egalitarian ideals. On the contrary, the NSRP claimed inequality as a central ethos of American political tradition. NSRP propaganda emphasized that the signatories of the Declaration of Independence included many slave owners and that the Constitution defined African Americans as three-fifths of a human being. This rhetoric echoed that of southern secessionists a century earlier, who also attempted to legitimate their opposition to the federal government by comparing themselves with the patriotic heroes of the War of Independence. Yet the NSRP also attempted to appeal to northerners who did not recognize the nobility of the Lost Cause by showing that none other than Abraham Lincoln shared their conviction that only whites had a full claim to citizenship. The party claimed Lincoln as one of their own by reproducing the statement he made during his debates with Illinois Senator Stephen A. Douglas in 1858: "I am not nor ever have been in favor of bringing about in any way the social and political equality of the white and black races."[41] This appropriation of Lincoln demonstrates the enduring influence on Stoner of Theodore Bilbo, who had also cited the speech to support his claim that integration was a negation of the Founding Fathers' vision.[42]

Although the NSRP continually adapted to changing political conditions, its core philosophy was a fanatical determination to resist racial reform by any means necessary. In the words of the party constitution, "We dedicate ourselves to the task of saving America and the White race and the preservation of the pure blood of our forefathers."[43] The NSRP emphasized the strength of its members' convictions by stating that African Americans were not simply a lesser race than whites, but an entirely different species. As Stoner asserted, blacks had no souls.[44] "Scientists Say Negro Still in Ape Stage," asserted a leaflet published by the party, which included a diagrammatic comparison emphasizing their common features. Since African Americans were not human, according to the NSRP, miscegenation would result in an inferior mongrel race.[45] African Americans were nonetheless but a biological weapon in the hands of the real adversary of the white race. In the words of Stoner, "the negro is not the enemy. The Jew is THE enemy . . . using the negro in an effort to destroy the White Race."[46]

Stoner and his associates claimed biblical authority for their racial dogma. The NSRP attempted to legitimate its position through the appointment of a party chaplain. The first person to hold the position was Christian Identity minister Gordon Winrod, whose evangelist father Gerald had been at the forefront of the far right a generation earlier. Winrod resigned in September 1962 on the dubious grounds that NSRP members were insufficiently fundamentalist in their religious beliefs.[47] His successor was Oren Potito, author of a tract entitled "Segregate or Integrate: What, as a Christian, should you do?" The NSRP chaplain was in no doubt as to the answer. "GOD IS A SEGREGATIONIST!" he exclaimed and, as evidence, cited the instruction of Paul in 2 Corinthians 6:17: "Therefore come out from them and be separate, says the Lord. Touch no unclean thing, and I will receive you."[48]

The NSRP advocated numerous tactics to protect white racial purity. In the short term, it advocated economic sanctions against African Americans involved in civil rights activism, the crassly titled Fire Your Nigger Campaign.[49] Its longer-term solution to the race problem was the creation of a National Repatriation Commission to administer the resettlement of minorities: blacks to Africa, Asians to Hawaii, and Jews to Madagascar. The NSRP intended to redistribute the property of these expelled peoples to poorer whites.[50]

NSRP activists also embraced terrorist violence. On October 12, 1958, a bomb blast tore through the Reform Temple in Atlanta. Police arrested five members of the NSRP but juries twice failed to convict them.[51] Although state authorities failed to uncover evidence directly connecting Stoner with the incident, they later deduced that he was the intermediary in a terrorist network named Nacirema ("American" backward) responsible for more than sixty bomb attacks in the South during the late 1950s and early 1960s.[52]

Stoner served for six years as general counsel to the NSRP. He assumed higher status in March 1964 when party members met at the Sheraton Hotel in Louisville to nominate their candidates for the forthcoming presidential election. Delegates nominated John Kasper as their presidential candidate and Stoner as his running mate. The resultant campaign was a shambles because Kasper, broken and beleaguered after serving his prison sentences, refused to canvass voters. However, the party rewarded Stoner by appointing him vice chairman.[53]

Stoner also gained a reputation as the leading defense counsel of white racial terrorists. To what extent he owed his courtroom successes to his prowess as a lawyer or the prejudice of all-white juries is unclear. His record was nonetheless impressive. In July 1963, for instance, he successfully defended Melvin Bruce against a charge of obstructing U.S. marshals escorting black student James Meredith to the University of Mississippi.[54] Twelve months later, Stoner represented five Klansmen accused of bombing the home of Donald Godfrey, the first black child to enroll at the Lackawanna Elementary School in Jacksonville, Florida. The court acquitted two of the defendants and ruled a mistrial in the cases of the other accused owing to the failure of the jury to reach a verdict; a second trial led to their walking free.[55] Although he did not represent him in court, Stoner also supported Klansman Byron de la Beckwith "morally and financially" following his imprisonment for transporting an explosive device across state lines.[56]

Stoner had since the outset of his political career espoused an intense hatred of African Americans and Jews, but during the late 1950s, he developed a new animus toward Muslims. The rise of the Nation of Islam represented a serious challenge to Stoner's assumption that African Americans were inherently incapable of spearheading a protest movement against white supremacy. Although African Americans were essential to the leadership of civil rights organizations such as the NAACP, the hierarchical prominence of white liberals strengthened Stoner's convictions.[57] However, the Nation of Islam was different. Its racially exclusive membership, as well as its pronounced anti-Semitism, rendered it impossible even for Stoner to claim its leaders were communist Jews. Stoner conceded as much when he paid a backhanded compliment to the Nation of Islam's spiritual leader, Elijah Muhammad, describing him as an "evil genius."[58]

Although they appeared diametrically opposed to one another, the racially separatist objectives of Black Muslims and white extremists led the two parties to entertain a marriage of convenience. Malcolm X, for instance, claimed that the Nation had negotiated mutual nonaggression pacts with the American Nazi Party and the Ku Klux Klan.[59] Stoner strenuously opposed entering such a compact. His ambition to repatriate African Americans had led him during the 1940s to enter a public dialogue with representatives of Marcus Garvey's United Negro Improvement Association. In an insincere act of statesmanship, he encouraged black nationalists to avert racial conflict by encouraging the resettlement of African Americans to their ancestral homeland. According to Stoner, "peaceful leaders like us won't remain in control" of the race situation for long. "The violent element on both sides will take charge and rivers of blood will flow in the streets."[60]

While Stoner considered it possible to find common cause with Garveyites, he perceived the Nation of Islam as desiring not so much separation from, than destruction of, the white race. His abusive bluster toward Black Muslims betrayed a profound fear of their revolutionary potential. Stoner first contacted the Nation in February 1957. His letter to Elijah Muhammad denounced Muslims as "Infidels" because, like Jews, they refused to accept Christ as their savior. Stoner warned Muhammad that he would never win the hearts and minds of African Americans because Islam was antithetical to their cultural and social practices. Blacks, he maintained, were irresponsible hedonists who would, indeed could, not conform to the strict moral code prescribed by the Koran. Only Christianity, he continued, could redeem black people. Whites must "do more missionary work and be instrumental in saving the individual souls of millions of colored people in spite of their racial weakness."[61] These assertions were both inconsistent and insincere. If African Americans were dedicated to a life of sin and corruption, as Stoner insisted, Christianity would hold no more attraction to them than Islam. Moreover, Stoner had on numerous occasions denied that blacks had souls to save. The uncharacteristically defensive tone of the letter demonstrated how the Nation had scored a chink in Stoner's otherwise impenetrable white supremacist armor. Ironically, it was ultimately less of a threat to segregation than the Christian-inspired civil rights movement.

The next several years nonetheless saw a deepening of Stoner's anxieties about the Black Muslims. In August 1959, he contacted New York City Police Commissioner Stephen Kennedy to offer his support in neutralizing the Nation. The NYPD had closely monitored the Nation since an incident in August 1957, when Malcolm X led a demonstration over law enforcement officers' beating of Black Muslim Hinton Johnson.[62] Stoner sought to capitalize on the apprehensions of the police about the grassroots influence the Nation commanded in Harlem. His alarmist tone exposed an acute anxiety about the recruiting potential of the Nation, at odds with his earlier declaration that Islam was anathema to ordinary African Americans. "If we fail to stop the Muslims now," Stoner warned, "the 16,000 niggers of America will all soon be Muslims and you will never be able to stop them."[63] Stoner could help avert this cataclysm if the New York Police Department provided him with sufficient guns and ammunition. Commissioner Kennedy unsurprisingly chose not to enlist his services.[64]

Undeterred, Stoner contacted Elijah Muhammad directly, threatening him to disband the Nation of Islam voluntarily or suffer its dissolution through force. "If you will dissolve your temples of Islam and publicly say that the great White Race is a superior race and that all niggers should stay in their place," offered Stoner, "I will help you get a good job on a farm."[65] A traumatized Muhammad forwarded copies of the communication to the FBI and the *New York Amsterdam News*, which reprinted it with an announcement that, should the Nation of Islam leader suffer anything untoward, Stoner would be one of the principal suspects.[66]

Nothing came of this attempt to intimidate Muhammad. The Nation of Islam nonetheless elicited a renewed outburst from Stoner when it started to expand its membership base out of northern inner cities and into the southern states. Above all, the establishment of a mosque in Atlanta led Stoner to launch a renewed assault on Muhammad. In a letter of April 1961, Stoner warned that, unless Muhammad closed the mosque, he would launch a boycott of the grocery store the Nation also ran in Atlanta, calling on whites to pressure their black employees not to shop there.[67] However, Stoner's inability to follow through on his earlier threats encouraged Muhammad to ignore the letter. No boycott ever took place.

In contrast to John Kasper and Bryant Bowles, who both scored immediate successes in stirring opposition to school desegregation, Stoner struggled to locate a community responsive to his rallying call. He accompanied Kasper to Nashville in the fall of 1957, appearing at a succession of rallies organized by the young agitator. Two years later, with Kasper now in prison, he collaborated with another member of the Seaboard White Citizens' Council, Fred Hockett, in attempting to obstruct the admission of black students to the Orchard Villa Elementary School. The Dade County School Board had announced in February 1959 its intention to admit four black children to the school in the fall. This announcement had met with a furious retort from white parents, who staged a series of protests. The uproar persuaded Stoner to select Miami as the target for a direct action campaign. However, by the time he arrived in the city, circumstances had changed. On the first day of school, only fourteen white children turned up for classes. Stoner and Hockett stood outside the school in an effort to enforce a systematic boycott, but the absence of so many whites rendered their actions redundant. What undermined the militants was the decision of many white families to move out of the vicinity rather than send their children to an integrated school. Within months of the school board making its announcement, what had once been a predominantly white neighborhood became 90 percent black. The school board decided the only solution was to transform Orchard Villa into a black educational institution, replacing white faculty and transferring in a further four hundred African American children. White resistance had averted the integration of the school without need of the dramatic conflict desired by Stoner.[68]

Stoner assumed greater leadership of local segregationist resistance during the following decade. Scholars have traditionally concluded that massive resistance had receded by the early 1960s as white southerners came to realize that token integration was the price to pay for the social order and economic development of the region.[69] Elite segregationist forces such as the Citizens' Council were in decline, creating a vacuum that was filled by extremist elements. Stoner's success in mobilizing white opposition to civil rights reform demonstrates the residual strength of grassroots racism. In contrast to John Kasper, he was not responsible for planning these counterattacks but rather parasitically attached himself to local insurgencies, using his extensive Klan connections across the South to provide him with a point of entrée. The NSRP was in this sense a segregationist counterpart to the Southern Christian Leadership Conference (SCLC), which similarly used community connections to assume control of local movements. Although whites did not rely on Stoner to resist racial reform, his presence intensified the strength of their counterrevolutionary activism. His cause benefited from the double standards of local and state officials who wanted to maintain segregation without harming their reputations by resorting to force. These officials publicly dissociated themselves from the NSRP, but provided support for Stoner and his associates by failing to crack down on their activities. In the case of Birmingham, Alabama, the NSRP actually profited from the explicit encouragement of state officials.

In August 1963, a federal court ordered the desegregation of the Birmingham public school system. The local board of education responded with a plan of token compliance, scheduling the registration of five African American students to three formerly all-white schools on September 3. Stoner and Fields moved into high gear, presenting state officials with a petition signed by 30,000 people protesting school desegregation and staging a series of open-air rallies. Stoner made his intentions clear to an audience the night before the black students were due to register, announcing that they must "use any and every method" to maintain a dual public school system.[70]

The meaning of that phrase became clear the following morning. Stoner and Fields led 150 placard-wielding protesters to Graymont Elementary School. While some of the demonstrators mounted a noisy motorcade around the school campus, others chanted slogans that claimed local authorities were complicit in the communist Jewish conspiracy: "Eight, six, four, two/Albert Boutwell is a Jew." Despite this show of force, the two black students due to enroll at the school, brothers Dwight and Floyd Armstrong, had actually come and gone fifteen minutes before the demonstrators arrived. Frustration at the failure to obstruct the black schoolchildren led the crowd to charge police officers stationed around the campus.[71] Following the arrest of several of their number, the mob moved on to Ramsay High School. A further melee resulted in the arrest of several NSRP activists, including Fields and Stoner. Although a federal grand jury indicted them for conspiring to obstruct a court order and threatening and assaulting police officers, prosecutors later dropped the charges.[72]

With NSRP members under arrest and driving rain dispelling the remaining demonstrators, it seemed order would return to the streets of Birmingham. The NSRP were not, however, the only white extremists in the city. That night, Klansmen bombed the home of black attorney Arthur Shores. African Americans took to the streets in protest. The ensuing riot resulted in one death and twenty-one injuries.[73] Governor George Wallace ordered the temporary closure of city schools to allow time for the restoration of community calm.[74] Continuing unrest nonetheless culminated in the deaths of four girls attending Sunday school classes at the Sixteenth Street Baptist Church when a bomb tore through its basement on September 15. Although Stoner was one of the principal suspects, the person eventually convicted for the attack was Klansman Robert Chambliss.[75] Stoner and Fields claimed the FBI had planted the bomb to discredit segregationist resistance. While the accusation was absurd, public reaction to the incident abruptly ended the NSRP campaign in Birmingham.[76]

One of the most disturbing aspects of the disorder in Birmingham is that the NSRP created conflict with the consent of public officials. Governor Wallace did not publicly endorse the tactics of extremists but still shared with them a common purpose to oppose racial reform. While disclaiming direct responsibility for racial violence, he created a political climate that facilitated confrontation. Wallace not only supported white parents who sought an injunction preventing the admission of black students to the three schools, but also sent six hundred state troopers to the city to defy the orders of the federal court.[77] Moreover, he publicly fêted the NSRP for their role in resisting desegregation, reserving a table for party members at a fundraiser the week before the Sixteenth Street church bombing.[78] The relationship between Wallace and the NSRP demonstrates how massive resistance assumed an even more radical intensity as it fought its last stand against federal authority. Although their political influence rapidly waned, for a short time a small band of neo-Nazi terrorists had become an unofficial instrument of state power.

Although the NSRP did not enjoy the explicit support of local and state authorities in other parts of the South, it benefited from the hypocrisy of public officials who wanted to maintain segregation but feared being associated with lawless extremism. They provided implicit sanction to the NSRP by refusing to condemn the violence it perpetuated. The willingness of local

Chapter Six

authorities to allow the NSRP to perform their dirty work was most apparent during civil rights demonstrations in St. Augustine, Florida.

St. Augustine appeared to be an auspicious location for Martin Luther King, Jr.'s Southern Christian Leadership Conference (SCLC) to launch a direct action campaign. Although the reactionary city government remained committed to segregation, it was susceptible to economic and political pressure. Civic and business leaders were at the time planning celebrations to mark St. Augustine's four hundredth anniversary. Hoping to use the occasion to attract more tourists, they applied for federal financial support to restore the city's architectural ruins. The SCLC anticipated that city authorities would bow to reform for fear that racial confrontation would attract adverse publicity and a withdrawal of federal funds.

There was, however, a serious element of risk in launching a coordinated assault on St. Augustine. In August 1963, the Florida Advisory Committee to the U.S. Commission on Civil Rights held a hearing in the city. It concluded that St. Augustine was "a segregated superbomb" with an extremely short fuse.[79] The most combustible elements in the city were the militant forces mobilized both in support of and in opposition to civil rights reform. On one side was a large and well-regimented Ku Klux Klan; on the opposing side were black activists under the command of radical NAACP leader Dr. Robert Hayling, who advocated the right to armed self-defense.[80]

Acting in response to a request from Hayling, the SCLC arrived in St. Augustine in March 1964. King hoped the resultant publicity would help maintain pressure on Congress to pass the civil rights bill. The SCLC launched its full campaign on May 26.[81] King led the first in a series of marches to the old downtown slave market, a symbolic focus of protest. The demonstrations initially passed without incident. However, on May 28 a white mob assaulted activists with an arsenal of weapons, including iron pipes and chains. King's appeals to President Lyndon Johnson and Governor C. Farris Bryant for protection went unheeded.[82]

On May 31, Sheriff L. O. Davis obtained an injunction against further night marches. SCLC lawyers petitioned Federal District Judge Bryan Simpson to overrule the order; King agreed to suspend demonstrations pending the decision. On June 9, Simpson ruled in favor of the SCLC and enjoined the police to provide protection for marchers. That evening, SCLC activist Andrew Young led renewed demonstrations in downtown St. Augustine. The marches resulted in violent attacks from whites that necessitated the intervention of state troopers.[83]

The day after this incident, police arrested several SCLC activists, including King, when they attempted to integrate a motel restaurant. Following his arraignment, King secretly testified to a grand jury established to investigate the unrest in St. Augustine that he would discontinue the demonstrations on condition it appointed a biracial committee. King spent a further night in jail before the authorities released him on bail on June 13. The appointment of a biracial committee appeared imminent until the sudden renewed escalation of SCLC demonstrations, including a "wade-in" at the Monson Motor Lodge swimming pool that prompted the owner to pour hydrochloric acid into the water. This dramatic turn of events led the grand jury to impose the condition that King must suspend demonstrations for thirty days as an act of good faith before it would establish a biracial committee. The SCLC leader refused. When activists renewed downtown marches on June 19, Governor Bryant issued an executive order imposing a nighttime curfew. Activists responded by demonstrating at the St. Augustine beach, an event that provoked attacks from angry whites.

The escalating conflict led to renewed negotiations between city officials and civil rights leaders. With Congress having passed the Civil Rights Bill on June 20, King sought to bring to an end a campaign otherwise threatening to drag on interminably. He therefore offered to suspend demonstrations in return for the establishment of a biracial committee. Intractable city officials rejected the proposal. Governor Bryant intervened on June 30 with a public announcement that he had appointed an interim committee that would serve for thirty days until the establishment of a larger and more representative biracial body. The SCLC reciprocated by suspending its campaign. However, there was no committee; Bryant had made his announcement as a means to expedite a resolution of the crisis. Once the SCLC left St. Augustine, city leaders desegregated public facilities in accordance with the Civil Rights Act. The campaign nonetheless failed to remedy the deeper-rooted problems of poverty and deprivation that afflicted the local black community.

Numerous forces conspired to precipitate the brutal backlash to civil rights protest in St. Augustine. One of the principal sources of turmoil was the Ancient City Hunting Club. The club president was former bootlegger Holstead "Hoss" Manucy. Manucy was an imposing figure, weighing 220 pounds and sporting a black cowboy hat.[84] Although Manucy denied any connection between the Ancient City Hunting Club and the Ku Klux Klan, their memberships overlapped to the point that the organizations were indistinguishable from each other.[85]

The Ancient City Hunting Club commanded a powerful influence on the city because of its close association with Sheriff L. O. Davis, a relationship comparable to that between Bull Connor and the Klan in Birmingham. When Davis enlisted club members as special deputies during the SCLC campaign, it was not with any expectation that they would enforce the law impartially.

Local white militants further benefited from the support of Klansmen from the surrounding region, under the leadership of Stoner. Stoner had toured Florida as a Klan circuit speaker since the late 1950s, recruiting members with particular success in and around Jacksonville, less than an hour north of St. Augustine. He now drew on these connections to mobilize a counterattack against civil rights activists.[86] The strength of his support caused the SCLC serious concern. Some of King's advisors tried to dissuade him from traveling to St. Augustine for fear Stoner was plotting to murder him.[87]

Stoner came to St. Augustine with a new accomplice. Their alliance was, for a time, as close as the one he shared with Edward Fields. Starting in St. Augustine, Stoner and Connie Lynch sparked a series of brutal confrontations between civil rights demonstrators and segregationist diehards.

Charles Conley Lynch was born in Clarksville, Texas, on November 15, 1912. He endured considerable hardship as the child of impoverished cotton farming parents, an experience that informed his later championing of poor whites. During the Depression, he was one of the thousands of economic migrants who made their way to southern California in search of employment, finding work first in the citrus and later the building industry before enlisting in the army when the United States entered World War II.[88]

Lynch's political philosophy was principally shaped by his membership in the Church of Jesus Christ, Christian. This organization was a religious sect founded in 1946 by former Klan organizer Dr. Wesley Swift. Ordained as one of its ministers, Lynch served numerous congregations before journeying south in the wake of the *Brown* decision to join the front lines in the fight against integration.[89] His behavior was reminiscent of that of John Kasper, as he lived out of the car in which he toured from one trouble spot to another—in Lynch's case, a 1958 Cadillac. Lynch was a conspicuous presence at many of the flash points of the civil rights struggle, including Little Rock, Albany, Oxford, and Birmingham. It was during this time that he became close friends with Stoner.[90]

Lynch and Stoner made a macabre double act at Klan rallies, trading the microphone with one another as they stirred their audiences into frenzies.

Stoner's inflammatory rhetoric contrasted with his fastidious attire. As he stood before his supporters in suit and bow tie, the NSRP chairman claimed that African Americans were sexually depraved brutes more closely related to apes than humans.[91] While the SCLC symbolically staged its protests at the old slave market, Stoner and Lynch also attempted to use the past as a means to mobilize support for their present struggle. The two men evoked the Lost Cause as a means to rally white males in defense of their wives and daughters. Lynch, wearing his trademark vest cut from a Confederate battle flag, stressed that the white men of St. Augustine were the bearers of a proud tradition of southern resistance to those who threatened their way of life. A century earlier, their forebears had fought to defend their homeland. To honor the Confederate dead, white southerners must now answer the contemporary call to arms. Failure to do so would brand them as weak or cowards.[92]

Although Stoner and his associates were responsible for inciting racial violence in St. Augustine, they would not have done so without the collusion of local authorities. In February 1965, a Florida legislative investigation committee published the report *Racial and Civil Disorders in St. Augustine*. The report attempted to absolve local and state officials of any responsibility for the unrest by blaming "outside militant elements," namely the Klan and the SCLC. To support this assessment, the report included the testimony of Police Chief Virgil Stuart that the whites who assaulted demonstrators were not locals but troublemakers from out of town. More astounding was the assertion that King and Stoner had conspired with news organizations to stage a series of dramatic confrontations for the benefit of television cameras. According to the report, both men had worked "hand in glove with members of the press," accepting bribes to manufacture a conflict between the races. "King's appearances and Stoner's appearances were always perfectly co-ordinated," observed the committee. "Whenever King was in town, Stoner was almost certainly to be." The report intimated that Stoner was less a fanatical segregationist than a fifth columnist intent on the "fragmentation of the community and discreditation of worthwhile patriotic organizations," an accusation reminiscent of massive resistance leaders' contention that John Kasper was an NAACP agent attempting to discredit legitimate protest against desegregation.[93]

The efforts of local and state authorities to dissociate themselves from the racial turmoil in St. Augustine were disingenuous. As reporter Paul Good observed, the intransigence of the city government fostered a climate in which extremism flourished. Local officials did not sanction the violence

Chapter Six

against civil rights activists, but neither did they condemn it. While they did not want to associate themselves publicly with lawlessness, their failure to protect civil rights activists provided white mobs with tacit approval. Not until July 24, almost a month after the SCLC suspended its campaign, did the police arrest Lynch and Stoner, and then only on the relatively minor charge of burning a cross on private property. In a scathing indictment, Good concluded that "The people of St. Augustine, who wouldn't let a Hoss Manucy in their front door, allowed him to run their city."[94] This attitude was similar to that of the more publicly respectable citizens of Milford, whose silence provided implicit approval of Bryant Bowles. Moreover, many whites in St. Augustine made no attempt to conceal their support for the mob. Local restaurateurs raised funds for the Klan and provided Lynch and Stoner with free meals as a token of appreciation for their defense of segregation. As the relationship between Sheriff Davis and Hoss Manucy also demonstrated, the line separating the lawful authorities from the criminal rabble was nonexistent.[95]

Following St. Augustine, Stoner and Lynch roamed from one community to another in the opportunistic hope of imposing their leadership on local grassroots resistance to the civil rights movement. Stoner led a small parade protesting the admission of black students to high schools in Montgomery in September 1964.[96] Four months later, he and a band of NSRP members made a brief appearance in Selma at the start of the SCLC voting rights campaign, long enough for James Robinson to strike Martin Luther King, Jr., in the face.[97]

The most welcome reception Stoner and Lynch received was from whites in Bogalusa, Louisiana. Bogalusa is located sixty miles north of New Orleans, at the state border with Mississippi. In 1965, there were 27,000 residents, 40 percent of them black.[98] The civil rights movement had made little impression on the city, which was still a bastion of white supremacy. Bogalusa boasted the largest per capita concentration of Ku Klux Klan members in the entire South, more than eight hundred within the city and countless more in the surrounding Washington Parish. The Klan recruited well among white workers at the Crown-Zellerbach sawmills, the principal local employer, which feared competition with African Americans in a declining labor market. It also drew strength from a complicit local police force. As pressure to accept civil rights reform mounted, the Klan intensified its brutal campaign of resistance.[99]

Despite the hostile political environment, local blacks endeavored to improve their situation through the establishment of the Bogalusa Voters and

Civic League (BVCL). In January 1965, the BVCL assisted the Congress of Racial Equality (CORE) in coordinating a campaign to test local compliance with the recently passed Civil Rights Act. On January 28, black activists gained admission to a number of restaurants and movie theaters. While the day passed with relatively little incident, racial tensions soon escalated. When CORE resumed its efforts to enforce integration in late February, Klansmen terrorized not only black activists but also white businessmen. Those establishments that had served blacks a month earlier now closed their doors.[100]

The campaign had drawn civil rights activists and segregationists into a cyclical process of radicalism. African Americans' assertion of their rights incited retaliation from the Klan, which in turn bolstered black militancy. On February 21, black radicals formed a local chapter of the armed self-protectionist organization the Deacons for Defense.[101]

On April 8, CORE National Director James Farmer led five hundred demonstrators through the streets of Bogalusa. White violence compelled Farmer to suspend the march before it reached city hall, although there was a second, successful, attempt six hours later.[102] Negotiations between the BVCL and Mayor Jesse Cutrer the following week ended in an impasse. Only on May 16 did city authorities relent, agreeing to enforce integration, improve impoverished black neighborhoods, and hire two black police officers.[103]

Yet white extremists refused to surrender. When African Americans tried to put city authorities' promises to the test, white mobs repelled them. The chaos led Mayor Cutrer to ban all marches. However, the racial turmoil in Bogalusa was out of control. On June 2, the two newly appointed black policemen, O'Neal Moore and Creed Rogers, were traveling in their patrol car when the driver of a pickup truck pulled alongside them, aimed a gun, and fired. Rogers survived a shoulder wound, but Moore died from a head wound. Less than an hour later, police at a roadblock just across the state line arrested a suspect. Ernest Ray McElveen was a forty-one-year-old mill worker. He was also a member of the NSRP.[104]

The presence of the NSRP in Bogalusa was another act of political opportunism on the part of Lynch and Stoner. Local whites had mounted a grassroots insurgency against racial change without need of outside support. As the hostility of segregationists toward John Kasper and Bryant Bowles in Louisville and Charlotte showed, racial militants were usually regarded as unwelcome outsiders in localities where they had no political connections. Stoner was nonetheless able to maneuver into a command role in Bogalusa by drawing on his extensive network of Klan contacts.

Stoner and Lynch increased their presence in Bogalusa following the resumption of demonstrations in early July. More than 1,500 people attended a rally on July 10 at which the NSRP activists performed their now familiar routine. Although there were some women present, Stoner and Lynch addressed the predominantly male audience. Stoner's speech emphasized the danger racial integration posed to traditional white patriarchy. Black males, he asserted, threatened the authority and power that white men commanded as providers for and protectors of their families. The elimination of racially exclusive hiring practices would force white workers into competing with blacks in an ailing local economy. Without enforcement of the color line, black men would also exploit their opportunity to prey on unsuspecting white women. White men must therefore fight or suffer humiliating emasculation. "We don't believe in tolerance," concluded Stoner. "We don't believe in getting along with the enemy, and the nigger is our enemy."[105] Lynch even advocated lynching as a means for white men to reclaim their domestic and social standing.[106]

The following day, Stoner and Lynch led more than five hundred raucous demonstrators through Bogalusa. James Farmer fronted a silent march along the same route shortly thereafter. Four hundred armed policemen monitored both events. Highway patrolmen closed all routes into the city as a means of containing the potentially explosive situation.[107]

Louisiana Governor John McKeithen tried to broker a deal between city officials and the BVCL that included a thirty-day "cooling-off" period in return for the expulsion from Bogalusa of Stoner and Lynch. When black leaders declined this mediation effort, President Johnson dispatched Assistant Attorney General John Doar to the troubled city. The intervention of the Justice Department resulted in the contempt conviction of local police and an injunction against the Klan interfering with integration. Once the curtain came down on the bloody drama enacted in Bogalusa, there was little evidence of any improvement to the lives of local blacks. African Americans still endured limited employment opportunities and political representation. The threat of violence also inhibited enforcement of integration.[108]

The NSRP's reign of chaos finally began to unravel from the mid-1960s. Two factors account for the decline of party influence. First, southern communities took more decisive action to suppress racial violence. The NSRP had benefited in cities such as Birmingham or St. Augustine from the equivocation or even active complicity of local authorities. However, a new realism eventually started to prevail, even on the part of the more intransigent southern communities. The cost of intractable resistance to civil rights reform was, they realized, as damaging to whites as it was to blacks: school closures, a breakdown of law and order, and a disreputable public image that deterred potential investors. White community leaders therefore acted to protect their own interests by removing the racial extremists within their midst. Second, federal authorities also took belated measures to repress racial terrorism. The counterintelligence actions of the FBI proved particularly important in destabilizing the NSRP. Although the Bureau had long insisted it had no authority to intervene in southern law enforcement, the disorder created by the NSRP led it to expand its jurisdiction.

The new determination of racial moderates to reclaim the political initiative from the NSRP first manifested itself in Anniston, Alabama. In May 1961, a white mob had firebombed one of the buses transporting Freedom Riders through the city.[109] Newspapers around the world reproduced a photograph of the burning bus, shaming Anniston with a reputation for racial bigotry. Local authorities understood the need to restore the status of their community in order to attract outside capital investment. Although motivated more by economic self-interest than racial altruism, they attempted to implement the peaceful integration of public facilities. When the NSRP threatened to plunge Anniston into renewed racial chaos, local moderates mobilized against them.

Similar to tactics employed in St. Augustine and Bogalusa, the NSRP used connections with local white extremists to establish its political credibility in Anniston. The party had first collaborated with Klansmen under the leadership of Kenneth Adams when the two forces coordinated the terrorist attack on the Freedom Riders. Stoner defended nine whites, including Adams, accused of bombing one of the buses. When a federal grand jury indicted the accused men, the NSRP organized a solidarity protest at which it hanged in effigy CORE Director James Farmer, Attorney General Robert Kennedy, FBI boss J. Edgar Hoover, and two of his agents.[110]

The NSRP returned to Anniston in October 1964. Racial tensions in the city were riding high. In September, black activists created the Calhoun County Improvement Association with the intention of lobbying for local compliance with the new Civil Rights Act. The organization announced its intentions through publication in the city newspaper of a full-page advertisement entitled "Anniston Manifesto."[111] White supremacists launched an immediate counteroffensive. Their principal target was the biracial Human Relations Council. Established by the city commission in May 1963, the council collaborated with local businessmen to secure gradual desegregation of the downtown commercial district. To assist with their campaign to abolish the council, Kenneth Adams and his cronies reenlisted their NSRP allies. On October 20, Stoner and Lynch staged the first in a series of rallies at which they exhorted whites to take to the streets in defense of segregation. Three days later, the two NSRP leaders accompanied Adams to city hall, where they submitted a petition demanding the immediate dissolution of the Human Relations Council.[112]

Despite persistent acts of intimidation and violence on the part of local white militants and their NSRP allies, the civic and business leadership of Anniston continued their efforts to enforce racial reform. Indeed, the destructive intervention of the NSRP persuaded numerous persons who had hitherto remained publicly silent to proclaim their support for change. Many, if not most, of them acted less out of principled support for racial equality than a pragmatic concern to repair the tarnished reputation of their community and promote the outside investment on which the local economy depended. Whatever their motivation, the result was the relatively orderly desegregation of public facilities. On March 28, 1965, the *Anniston Star* printed a public announcement entitled "Where We Stand!" The five hundred signatories insinuated they had personal reservations about racial integration but nonetheless recognized that reform was in the greater public good. Their statement stressed "the futility of challenging" federal law, stressing that failure to comply would lead to "disruption of our moral and economic fabric." The *Star* endorsed the advertisement in an editorial that emphasized the need for "reason and understanding" on the race issue.[113] One month later, the city school board—reacting to a threatened withdrawal of federal funds—announced plans for the token integration of educational facilities that fall.

The impending prospect of school desegregation provoked a renewed counterattack from the NSRP. On July 15, the party staged a rally at the local courthouse. More than one hundred people turned out in the sweltering heat to hear Stoner and Fields denounce integration as a communist Jewish conspiracy. The rally culminated in a speech by Lynch that proclaimed, "If it takes killing to get the Negroes out of the white man's streets and to protect our constitutional rights, then I say yes, kill them."[114] Inspired by this call to action, three members of the crowd—Damon Strange, Lewis Blevins, and Johnny DeFries—set out in pursuit of an indiscriminate target, a car in which four black foundry workers were traveling home from their shift. Leaning out of the passenger window, Strange fired three gunshots at the car, hitting the driver, Willie Brewster, in the neck. The stricken foundry worker died of his injuries three days later.[115]

The senseless murder of Willie Brewster catalyzed the local community into action. City leaders raised a reward of more than $21,000 for information leading to the arrest of those responsible. Lured by the reward, white construction worker Jimmy Knight testified to the police that he heard Strange, Blevins, and DeFries boast how they had "got us a nigger." With the three men under arrest, Stoner offered his services as their defense lawyer.[116]

On December 2, the all-white jury found Strange guilty of second-degree murder, for which he received a ten-year prison sentence. The verdict was of profound political significance. As the *Washington Post* affirmed, "It was the first time in modern times that a white man has been convicted of murder in the Deep South for the racial slaying of a Negro." Stoner, who forty-eight hours earlier had boasted to reporters of an easy acquittal, burst into tears when he heard the decision.[117]

The second crackdown on the NSRP occurred less than a year later in Baltimore. More than a decade earlier, city officials had demonstrated their determination to repress white militancy when Bryant Bowles attempted to lead white opposition to school desegregation. Now they trained their sights on the NSRP. In early 1966, CORE declared Baltimore its "Target City" for the next twelve months. During the spring and summer, it publicized the problem of ghetto poverty through a succession of rallies in black neighborhoods. In reaction, local NSRP activists Joseph Carroll and Richard Norton persuaded Connie Lynch to rouse white resistance. On July 25, five hundred people turned up at the Riverside Park to hear Lynch rail against civil rights reform. A further rally the following day attracted an audience of eight hundred. By July 27, the crowd had swelled to more than one thousand. Lynch launched an incendiary assault on those he identified as enemies of the white race, including the "nine stooges" on the Supreme Court who, he declared, deserved hanging. "I'm not inciting you to riot," he exclaimed to his audience, "I'm inciting you to victory." Roused by his fighting words, a white mob tore through a black residential area in the eastern part of the city, engaging in a bloody street battle with local youths.[118]

Police arrested Carroll, Norton, and Lynch the following morning. Circuit Court Judge William J. O'Donnell also issued an injunction against the

NSRP holding further demonstrations. In November, a criminal court found the three NSRP members guilty of four offenses, including inciting a riot, and sentenced them each to two years in prison and a fine of $1,000. For Stoner, who had represented the men in court, the decision was a double blow. Not only had he failed a second time to secure the acquittal of party members, but the imprisonment of Lynch meant the loss of one of his closest allies.[119]

The third demonstration of white moderate intolerance toward the NSRP occurred two years later in the small college town of Berea, Kentucky. During the summer of 1968, the Lexington chapter of the party staged a series of public meetings, culminating in a Labor Day rally at which three hundred activists turned out to hear Connie Lynch perform one of his typically incendiary tirades against racial and religious minorities. The recurring presence of the NSRP during the summer had inflamed racial tensions in the town; local blacks decided it was now time to take remedial action. Three carloads of armed African Americans pulled up to the abandoned parking lot where the NSRP was holding its rally. Who fired first remained a matter of controversy, but the resultant shootout claimed the lives of members of both sides: local black laborer John Boggs and NSRP sergeant-at-arms Elza Rucker. Local police rapidly arrested eight whites and six blacks.[120]

The fourteen defendants came to trial in March 1969. In the intervening months, the local community had rallied in support of the arrested African Americans. Mayor C. C. Hensley denounced the NSRP for having "disturbed a century of good feelings between members of both races." Prominent townspeople also set up a biracial committee to raise funds for the black defendants.[121] When the case reached court, the six African Americans pleaded guilty to the minor charge of unlawful assembly and received probationary sentences. Stoner defended his fellow NSRP members. An all-white jury found five of the eight accused men guilty of disorderly conduct; the court fined all of them $500 and sentenced three of the defendants to thirty days in prison.[122] Despite the relative leniency of the sentences, the outcome of the trial reaffirmed that the NSRP could no longer act with impunity. Although Berea had a long tradition of racial liberalism—the city founder was abolitionist John G. Fee—the support white community leaders gave the black gunmen also had considerable symbolic resonance.

As southern community leaders mobilized against the NSRP, federal authorities also launched a crackdown on its activities. From the summer of 1964, the FBI targeted white hate groups, including the NSRP, as part of its Internal Security Counterintelligence Program (COINTELPRO). Bureau agents engaged in the surveillance, infiltration, and exposure of the organization.[123] In January 1965, the Birmingham field office distributed an anonymous letter to black community associations that identified a local white businessman as a member of the NSRP national executive committee. The letter also revealed that the company he managed was "dependent on Negro patronage for a very substantial portion of its business," a disclosure that implicitly encouraged blacks to boycott the firm and thereby curtail its owner's political activism. The same agents also sent unsigned copies of a cartoon to NSRP members that specifically named one of their associates as an FBI informant. Although the exposé was untrue, it planted the seed of doubt and suspicion within party ranks. The most significant act of counterintelligence against the NSRP occurred in Florida, where a television documentary based on sources anonymously supplied by the FBI caused such public concern that it led local law enforcement officials to close down three party chapters.[124] Although it is not possible to calculate the precise impact of COINTELPRO on the NSRP, one measure of its success was the strength of Stoner's anger toward what he denounced as the "Federal Bums of Integration." In the June 1968 edition of *The Thunderbolt*, the NSRP leader declared his intention to "try them all for treason and hang them."[125]

The FBI also supplied information on the NSRP to a congressional investigation of the Ku Klux Klan. At the request of President Johnson, the House Un-American Activities Committee held hearings on the Klan between October 1965 and February 1966. Stoner, who had long sustained collaboration between the Klan and the NSRP, was one of the 187 witnesses called to testify. However, on appearing before the subcommittee on February 24, 1966, he refused to answer questions, citing the First, Fourth, Fifth, Sixth, Eighth, Ninth, Tenth, and Fourteenth Amendments. Although the subcommittee could not prove Stoner had participated in any specific terrorist act, it presented circumstantial evidence pointing to his seditious activities, such as his offering instructions on how to build an explosive device at a NSRP rally in Birmingham in July 1963. More broadly, the subcommittee observed how Stoner's presence in the city coincided with numerous bomb attacks on black institutions. Its conclusion that Stoner and his associates were disloyal to the American way of life was a bitter blow to the NSRP, given how hard its members endeavored to affirm their patriotism.[126]

Although the late 1960s saw the declining impact of the NSRP on southern politics, Stoner's influence within the American far right continued to rise. He accrued power and status by constructing international white supremacist networks and by representing James Earl Ray, the murderer of Martin Luther King, Jr.

Stoner first offered his services to Ray free of charge after British police arrested the fugitive gunman at Heathrow Airport in June 1968. Although Ray hired Arthur Hanes as his defense lawyer, he invited Stoner to visit him in his prison cell. What the two men said to one another is unclear, but Ray had evidently become dissatisfied with Hanes, whom he dramatically fired thirty-six hours before the scheduled start of his trial. The case finally came to court four months later. On March 10, 1969, Ray, represented by new defense attorney Percy Foreman, pleaded guilty. The court sentenced him to serve ninety-nine years in the Tennessee State Penitentiary. In a further twist, Ray recanted his confession only three days later, firing Foreman who, he claimed, had pressured him into the guilty plea as a means to avoid a death sentence. Ray then hired Stoner in an attempt to secure a new trial.[127]

Stoner's appointment fueled conspiracy theories about his possible role in the assassination. He was one of the principal suspects investigated by the FBI. Stoner was speaking at a Klan rally in Meridian, Mississippi, on April 4 when word reached him of King's murder. "He's been a good nigger since then," he snorted. *The Thunderbolt* later editorialized that the assassin deserved a congressional medal, federal pension, and presidential pardon for services to his country.[128] Ray's employment of Stoner raised speculation that the two men were participants in an elaborate white supremacist plot to slay the civil rights leader. While Stoner relished King's assassination, there was no evidence he and Ray had ever met before the prison cell visit.[129]

Stoner worked with fellow lawyers Robert Hill and Richard Ryan to win Ray a new trial. He informed reporters that his Klan associations would prove an asset were he able to argue the case before a white Shelby County jury.[130] Stoner also prepared libel suits against news publishers whose coverage of events, he maintained, had prevented his client from receiving a fair hearing.[131] His efforts were in vain, however. On May 26, 1969, Judge Arthur Faquin, Jr., ruled that Ray had entered his guilty plea in good faith, precluding his right to a retrial.[132] Stoner benefited far more from his relationship with Ray, capitalizing on the publicity to promote his reputation among white supremacists.[133]

Although the domestic influence of the NSRP had waned, Fields and Stoner performed a prominent role in the establishment and expansion of international white supremacist networks. Their ambition and achievement surpassed that of John Crommelin, who had endeavored to unite the disparate forces of the far right within the United States. The political manifesto of the NSRP affirmed the intention of Fields and Stoner to situate their own defense of Jim Crow within a broader international context of white resistance to black insurgency. In its words, "We approve the strengthening of cultural and moral ties among all White nations, in view of the world-wide survival crisis which the White Man faces."[134]

The NSRP initially drew support for its white supremacist politics by citing the apartheid regimes in South Africa and Rhodesia as models of governance. A pamphlet produced by one of the party's chapters cited the success of white rule in both countries as one of its *Forty Reasons for Segregation*. According to the authors, the two governments had demonstrated the superiority of the white race, bringing social order to an otherwise unruly black majority and exploiting the rich natural resources of the region to transform their nations from economic backwaters to international trading and industrial powers. The authors drew a sharp distinction between what they saw as the stability and progress of South Africa and Rhodesia and the situation in decolonized nations such as the Republic of the Congo, where "Chaos, poverty and ignorance are the rules." The contrasting fortunes of these countries held a clear lesson for the future of race relations closer to home. Whites must recognize that blacks did not possess the capacity for self-governance and fight to protect their own place in the racial hierarchy, if they were to avoid the fate of postcolonial Africa.[135]

The prospect of an alliance with southern segregationists was attractive to some white South Africans, who saw it as a means to overcome their international isolation. This was, for example, true of the Pretoria-based *South African Observer*, which reported regularly on race relations in the United States.[136] Despite these overtures, there is no evidence that the rhetorical alliance the NSRP proclaimed with apartheid supporters translated into a practical partnership.

Fields and Stoner were nonetheless successful in founding a loose international federation of far-right groups. From the early 1960s through the late 1970s, the NSRP leaders made several visits to the United Kingdom, where they established alliances with Oswald Mosley's Union Party and the National Front.[137] They later created further connections across other parts of Europe and North America, involving such organizations as the Canadian Western Guard Party, the Polish Freedom Fighters, and other fascist groups in Belgium, Germany, Spain, and Portugal. These coalitions enhanced the reputation and influence of the NSRP, situating the party within a larger global struggle between the races. Moreover, the elaborate international networks that unite the contemporary far right owe much of their origin to the initiatives undertaken by Fields and Stoner.[138]

Analysis of the NSRP informs our understanding of the southern white response to the civil rights movement in a number of ways. Although scholars sometimes assume massive resistance had receded by the early 1960s, the NSRP sustained grassroots opposition to racial reform even after the enactment of federal civil rights legislation. The actions of the NSRP moreover demonstrate an element of collusion between anarchic extremists and more supposedly prudent public officials. Politicians like George Wallace not only failed to secure the arrest and prosecution of NSRP members, but also fostered political conditions in which white racial militancy flourished. The chaos created by NSRP also contributed to southern whites' eventual recognition of the cost to their own communities of uncompromising resistance to reform. By the 1970s, this crackdown on NSRP lawlessness had led Stoner to pursue his political agenda through the ballot box. His notorious electoral campaigns provide important insights into the neglected story of how civil rights groups fought and lost the fight to combat hate speech.

7. Fighting for Freedom by Defending the Enemy

Stoner and the Hate Speech Issue

It lasted only a minute, but elicited a more impassioned public reaction than any other political broadcast aired in the South during the early 1970s. During the first days of August 1972, television audiences across Georgia witnessed the sight of a man in dark suit and bow tie sitting at a desk with a large Confederate battle flag hanging behind him and a smaller version folded in the front pocket of his jacket. The heavy-lidded eyes that stared intently into the camera lens lent him a reptilian appearance and his heavily accented voice was slow and deliberate. "I am J. B. Stoner," he announced. "I am the only candidate for U.S. senator who is for the white people. I am the only candidate who is against integration. All of the other candidates are race mixers to one degree or another." Stoner identified the policies of moderate incumbent, Senator David H. Gambrell, as a particular threat to the racial purity of white voters. Then the aspirant for public office uttered the words that precipitated a political shockwave. "The main reason why niggers want integration is because the niggers want our white women. I am for law and order with the knowledge that you cannot have law and order and niggers too. Vote white."[1]

The commercial was the centerpiece of a radically racist campaign by Stoner. His manifesto pledged that if elected he would "STOP RACE MIXING INSANITY" through a series of measures, including cutting off funds for busing and other federal initiatives to facilitate school desegregation, restricting the access of "lazy drunken Blacks" to public housing and welfare, and campaigning for the repeal of civil rights legislation. Stoner also committed himself to secure a federal law for the forcible repatriation of blacks to Africa.[2]

Throughout his political career, Stoner demonstrated a flair for the inflammatory rhetoric that aroused such controversy during his senatorial campaign. In the aftermath of the genocide committed during World War II, explicitly racist ideology, already on the wane, lost much of its intellectual and cultural legitimacy in the United States. Segregationist leaders increasingly refrained from defending Jim Crow in terms of white supremacy and black inferiority, emphasizing instead the more racially neutral language of states' rights. Stoner, by contrast, reveled in a more atavistic rhetoric that denied the essential humanity of African Americans and advocated the use of extralegal violence to enforce white hegemony. "The nigger is not a human being," he exclaimed at a white supremacist rally in 1965. "He is somewhere between the white man and the ape. We don't believe in tolerance. We don't believe in getting along with our enemy, and the nigger is our enemy."[3]

Stoner's campaign commercial rhetoric posed for liberals the same paradox as that of other demagogues such as John Kasper and John Crommelin. To protect the constitutional freedoms of all citizens, was it necessary to defend the uncensored speech of those who used their public platforms to promote prejudice and inequality? Some concluded that it was. No matter how abhorrent the statements made by Stoner, in their opinion, he had as much right as any other citizen to freedom of speech under the First Amendment. The American Civil Liberties Union (ACLU), whose libertarian philosophy had led it to defend the constitutional rights of white racists throughout the civil rights struggle, issued a statement supporting Stoner's right to unrestricted freedom of speech.[4]

However, other civil rights activists reacted with indignation to the race-baiting language used in the commercial. Access to television and radio was of crucial strategic importance to Stoner. In contrast to mainstream political and civic leaders, he possessed limited resources and relied on the publicity provided by media coverage to reach out to the electorate. Civil rights organizations understood that restricting his access to the airwaves therefore promised to curtail his campaign. Accordingly, black and Jewish civil rights activists launched a collective campaign to silence Stoner. The National Association for the Advancement of Colored People (NAACP) and the Anti-Defamation League of B'nai B'rith (ADL) filed a joint complaint with the Federal Communications Commission (FCC). According to the signatories,

Stoner's public address was not only offensive, but also intended to incite violence against African Americans. In the interests of public decency and safety, the FCC should therefore prohibit further broadcasts.

Pressure on the FCC mounted as other civil rights groups added their voices to the chorus of protest against the Stoner campaign commercial. The Georgia Council on Human Relations, the Atlanta Community Coalition on Broadcasting, and Concerned Citizens all made statements in support of the petition. Atlanta Mayor Sam Massell also issued an executive order that condemned the commercial and encouraged television and radio stations not to broadcast it. The controversy became a national issue when the Congressional Black Caucus added its support to a ban. Hopes were therefore high that the FCC would prohibit Stoner from using racist language on the airwaves.[5]

The attempt to ban further broadcasts exemplified an emerging shift in the policy of some civil rights groups on the constitutional rights of white racists to freedom of speech and assembly. At the height of the black freedom struggle, civil rights organizations had for ideological and strategic reasons refrained from legally campaigning for restrictions on hate speech. Black and Jewish activists certainly spoke out in strong condemnation of hate speech and hate symbols such as burning crosses and the Confederate battle flag.[6] There was, however, an important distinction between mobilizing public opposition to the words and actions of white racists and using the power of law to prohibit them. While the moral case was clear, legally and tactically the situation was more complex.

Civil rights groups were especially worried that their efforts to prohibit racist propaganda would prove counterproductive. First, they feared that hate peddlers would actually gain greater exposure by publicizing themselves as victims of an insidious campaign to deny them their constitutional rights. Second, civil rights activists understood that their own ability to march and demonstrate relied on a broad reading of First Amendment rights by the courts. Restricting the rights of white racists to freedom of speech and association on the grounds that others might find their language offensive could ironically rebound on the civil rights movement since the courts would apply the same narrow interpretation of the First Amendment to civil rights protesters, seriously curtailing their capacity to protest against racial injustice. For these reasons, civil rights organizations had historically eschewed direct challenges to hate speech, favoring instead a more subtle policy of containing its impact by publicly ignoring it. By refusing to bestow any credibility on white racists, they believed that they could confine them to the margins of political discourse.

In the autumn of 1972, black and Jewish activists abandoned their earlier circumspection and became embroiled in a very public controversy over the constitutional rights of hate speakers. The petition filed by the ADL and NAACP revealed a reversal of policy and philosophy and an espousal of the conviction that unrestricted civil liberties constituted a potential threat to civil rights. Much of the historical scholarship on hate speech focuses on the Skokie affair, when members of the National Socialist Party of America attempted to organize a march through a Chicago suburb that was home to a large Jewish community, including many Holocaust survivors. Consistent with its belief in the unrestricted constitutional liberties of all citizens, the ACLU sued for the right of the National Socialist Party to march in Skokie. Jewish defense groups, reacting to grassroots pressure, filed suit to ban the march on the grounds that it would incite violence. Although the Supreme Court upheld the First Amendment rights of the National Socialists, the march never actually took place.[7] Numerous scholars have analyzed the Skokie affair, but hardly any have attempted to situate it within a broader historical narrative of civil rights groups' strategy on hate speech. As a result, most histories of the civil rights movement omit the issue entirely. While the Stoner incident has received little attention, it is significant since it occurred five years earlier than the Skokie case and anticipated what would later prove an acrimonious debate over whether white racists were entitled to the protections of the First Amendment. The outcome of the episode emphasizes the failure of civil rights groups to implement a coherent and effective strategy on hate speech.

Although the petition filed by the ADL and NAACP represented the first coordinated effort by civil rights groups to silence Stoner, newspapers and politicians had sporadically raised the issue of whether he was entitled to unrestricted freedom of speech throughout his career. As early as 1946, author Earl Conrad called on federal authorities to curtail distribution of postcards printed by the Stoner Anti-Jewish Party, stressing that although Allied forces had defeated the Axis powers the fight against domestic fascism remained unfinished.[8] In 1963, Montana Senator Lee Metcalf raised with the U.S. postmaster general the issue of whether the federal government had the authority to restrict circulation of hate literature such as *The Thunderbolt*, but was told no.[9]

These earlier initiatives notwithstanding, the attempt to suppress the Stoner commercial signaled a change in the attitude of civil rights activists who had previously advocated an expansive interpretation of the First Amendment right to freedom of speech. It is essential to contextualize the controversy over the commercial by first providing an overview of how African American and Jewish organizations had historically handled the contentious issue of hate speech.

Black civil rights groups had on occasion challenged the right to freedom of expression when it resulted in racially derogatory representations of African Americans. The NAACP had, most notably, protested movie theater screenings of the D. W. Griffith film *The Birth of a Nation* because of its depiction of hypersexualized black males preying on unsuspecting white women. Black demonstrations occurred during the initial distribution of the film in 1915 and on its reissue shortly after World War II. The protests had a mixed impact: while some theaters withdrew the film, the controversy also attracted curious audiences.[10]

During the era of mass black disobedience, civil rights organizations retreated from the legal censorship of white racists. While the movement was dedicated to the eradication of all forms of racial discrimination, several factors made it a difficult problem to confront directly.

The first of these factors was that civil rights activists understood that for the courts to impose limitations on the freedoms of speech and association would compromise their own cause. Restrictions on First Amendment rights have historically served the political interests of conservative elites who sought to suppress any challenge to their hegemony. The curtailment of free speech as a means to silence dissenting voices occurred consistently from the Alien and Sedition Acts of 1798, through the gagging of antislavery petitions by Congress and the repressive policies of the southern plantation elite during the antebellum era, to the Palmer raids on the radical left following World War I. Traditionally, it is the politically less powerful in the United States who campaign for greater freedom of speech as a means to gaining equality.

This is certainly true of the black freedom struggle. The civil rights revolution relied on the readiness of the federal judiciary to accord demonstrators the protections of the First Amendment. Black political protest depended in part for its success on the safeguarding of speech interpreted by some as inflammatory and offensive. Southern law enforcement officers used the accusation of incitement to assault and arrest civil rights demonstrators. However, the courts continually ruled that these attempts to repress freedom of speech represented unconstitutional acts of censorship. The efforts of African Americans to gain the civil rights guaranteed by the Fourteenth and Fifteenth Amendments therefore relied on enforcement of the civil liberties granted by the First Amendment. As Ira Glasser observes, civil rights activists consequently "saw equality and free speech as mutually reinforcing, twin pillars of a singular value system."[11]

One illustration of how an expansive interpretation of First Amendment rights facilitated civil rights protest is the student sit-ins of 1960. When violence broke out during the demonstrations, law enforcement officers arrested the students for provoking the disorder by intruding on private property. NAACP lawyers attempted to overturn the convictions by claiming that the sit-ins represented something more significant than a simple case of trespass or breach of the peace. The First Amendment, they insisted, permitted the students to protest publicly against racial segregation. While their acts were provocative, the use of violence to suppress the protests represented an infringement of their constitutional rights. The Supreme Court agreed. Between 1961 and 1965, it overturned the convictions of numerous student demonstrators. In the two most important of these cases, *Edwards v. South Carolina* (1963) and *Cox v. Louisiana* (1965), the Court established that even the threat of imminent violence from a hostile audience was insufficient grounds for the suppression of constitutionally protected speech.[12]

The commitment of the Supreme Court to facilitate civil rights protest also led to its decision in *New York Times v. Sullivan* that the First Amendment protection of free speech necessitated a higher criterion of proof in libel actions brought by public figures. Many news organizations had at first been reluctant to report candidly on the repression of civil rights protest in the South for fear that southern public officials would sue them for libel. The enhancement of First Amendment protections in the case led to more aggressive news reporting. This, in turn, heightened public understanding of, and sympathy for, the black freedom struggle.

On March 29, 1960, the *Times* ran a full-page advertisement with the headline "Heed Their Rising Voices." The authors of the advertisement were the Committee to Defend Martin Luther King and the Struggle for Freedom in the South. Their intention was to raise funds for the legal defense of the civil rights leader, whom Alabama authorities had arrested on fallacious charges of tax evasion. "Heed Their Rising Voices" highlighted the brutal repression of black protesters engaged in nonviolent protest. This "unprecedented wave of terror" included "truckloads of police armed with shotguns and tear-gas" ringing Alabama State College in Montgomery and padlocking the doors of its dining hall in an effort to starve student demonstrators into surrender. Although the advertisement did not mention him by name, Montgomery Police Commissioner L. B. Sullivan filed a libel suit against the newspaper and four black ministers named in the advertisement. A Montgomery County jury awarded Sullivan $500,000, a decision upheld by the Alabama Supreme Court. The case then made its way to the U.S. Supreme Court. On March 9, 1964, Justice William Brennan delivered the opinion of the Court, which overturned the earlier ruling. Breaking with historical tradition, the Court ruled that the First Amendment protection of freedom of speech applied to libel cases. According to Brennan, the Constitution sanctioned "uninhibited, robust, and wide-open" speech, including "vehement, caustic and sometimes unpleasantly sharp attacks on government and public officials." The application of the First Amendment led the Court to raise the burden of proof in libel cases through the introduction of the "actual malice" standard. This new standard made it necessary for a plaintiff to prove that the author of a statement knew it was false or acted in "reckless disregard" of the truth. Although the decision applied specifically to statements made about public officials, it demonstrated the commitment of the Warren Court to uphold the First Amendment protection of political debate.[13]

The lessons of recent history also warned civil rights organizations of the need to defend unrestricted constitutional liberties. Only four years before the Stoner controversy, the conservative backlash to the radical black protest of the late 1960s had resulted in the federal government curtailing the rights of freedom of speech and assembly. In July 1967, police arrested H. Rap Brown of the Student Non-Violent Coordinating Committee (SNCC) for inciting a race riot that erupted on the streets of Cambridge, Maryland. Only hours before the outbreak of the disorder, Brown had declared at a political rally that "If Cambridge doesn't come around, Cambridge got to be burned down." The following year, Congress passed an amendment to the new Civil Rights Act that made it illegal to cross state lines and issuing speeches with the intent "to incite, organize, promote, encourage, participate in, and carry on a riot." In criminalizing militant black protest, the Rap Brown Amendment, as commentators labeled it, represented a clear warning even to more moderate civil rights activists that political dissenters were often the first victims of any restrictions on First Amendment rights.[14]

Civil rights activists therefore supported unrestricted freedom of speech because they saw it as essential to the success of their struggle against white racism. Ironically, their assertion that the Constitution allowed all citizens to express publicly ideas or opinions that others might find offensive forced them to defend the rights of their political enemies to the same freedoms. For the courts to impose restrictions on the First Amendment rights of white racists could create a dangerous precedent for the enforcement of similar limitations on black protesters. Civil rights activists tempted to use the judicial system as a weapon to fight hate speech were therefore conscious that it could prove to be a double-edged sword. The need to protect First Amendment rights led in at least one important instance to civil rights organizations publicly upholding the constitutional rights of their own bitterest adversaries.

In 1961, two of Stoner's associates in the NSRP, Robert Lyons and Edward Fields, attempted to hold a rally in the small town of Fairfield, Alabama. A local court granted Mayor Claude Smithson an ex parte injunction—one issued without a hearing—against Lyons and Fields on the grounds that they could incite a race riot. The two men nonetheless attempted to distribute copies of the NSRP newsletter, *The Thunderbolt*, to local townspeople. Arrested by the police, they appeared before the same judge who had issued the injunction against them. The court found them both guilty of violating the injunction and sentenced them to fines of $50 each and five days in prison.[15]

The ACLU appealed to the Supreme Court on behalf of the two NSRP members, claiming that the injunction was an unconstitutional prior restraint on their rights of freedom of speech and assembly. ACLU Executive Director John de J. Pemberton, Jr., emphasized that the primary motivation for the appeal was less a concern for Lyons and Fields than the need to protect against courts issuing similar injunctions against civil rights demonstrations. In his opinion, "if the Supreme Court rules that such injunctions cannot be used to block free speech and association, one of the major obstacles to increased effectiveness of Negro and white opposition to racial discrimination will have been overcome."[16]

Although the actions of the ACLU were in accordance with established policy, what was more surprising was that the NAACP Legal Defense and Educational Fund also filed an amicus brief in behalf of Fields and Lyons. Neither the prosecution nor the NSRP activists—no doubt embarrassed and repelled by the situation—assented to the NAACP acting as a friend of the court. However, the court did grant permission. The brief filed by NAACP lawyer Jack Greenberg stated that, while his organization opposed the NSRP, it worried that should the Supreme Court uphold the convictions it would open the way to other restrictions on the freedoms of speech and assembly, including those of civil rights activists. According to Greenberg, some courts were already citing the case as precedent for the conviction of civil rights demonstrators who violated restraining orders issued without their having an opportunity to contest them. For the Supreme Court to uphold the original ruling could "seriously impede the movement for equal rights now current in the nation." In December 1963, the Supreme Court overturned the convictions of Fields and Lyons on the narrow grounds that their distribution of *The Thunderbolt* did not constitute a violation of the injunction against an NSRP rally.[17] Although the case was not a complete victory for civil rights activists, it demonstrated how their desire to promote liberal interpretations of First Amendment rights paradoxically facilitated the cause of their political foes.

A further factor that curtailed an assault on hate speech was the fear that white racists would turn the situation to their political advantage by portraying themselves to the public as martyrs denied their constitutional rights. In reaction to the civil rights revolution, the postwar decades witnessed the emergence of a new racist discourse that emphasized the victimization of whites. Such rhetoric stressed that racial and religious minorities had improved their condition at the expense of a white majority that had seen its rights systematically eroded. Civil rights organizations worried that racists refused the right to freedom of speech would use the situation to dramatize their claim that whites were the real victims of oppression. "Every hatemonger alleges that attempts are being made to deny him freedom of speech," observed Dr. S. Andhil Fineberg of the American Jewish Committee. "When such a denial actually occurs, it brings to the bigot's support many conscientious citizens who detest his views—genuine liberals to whom freedom of speech is inviolate."[18]

In contrast to black civil rights organizations, Jewish defense groups had long struggled to reach consensus on the appropriate strategic response to hate speech. The issue was a source of both inter- and intraorganizational dissension. In broad terms, activists divided over the cautious tactics of the American Jewish Committee and the more confrontational stance of the American Jewish Congress, the Anti-Defamation League, and the Jewish War Veterans.

The American Jewish Committee had since the 1930s steered clear of direct confrontation with political extremists such as Stoner. Instead, it implemented a policy of containment known as the quarantine strategy. The intention was to avoid public dialogue with the far right that, the committee feared, would confer on the extremists a greater degree of political legitimacy. According to historian Marianne Sanua, the committee was also concerned that restricting its political enemies' freedom of speech could prove counterproductive, impeding the ability of minorities to promote unpopular causes, such as Jewish support for Israel.[19]

During the 1960s, the committee successfully deployed the quarantine strategy against such prominent anti-Semites as John Crommelin and American Nazi Party leader George Lincoln Rockwell. The committee also applied a longer-term plan of promoting community education programs to foster racial and religious tolerance. "In the long run," concluded one of its reports, "the most effective defense against unsound ideas is more speech and more ideas, in the certain knowledge that ultimately truth will triumph."[20]

Scholars usually assume consensus support among Jewish defense agencies for the quarantine strategy. David Hamlin, for example, states that it was the "time-honored and well-tested position" of Jewish groups.[21] This, however, was not entirely true even of the American Jewish Committee. Although the quarantine strategy was an official policy of the committee, circumstances sometimes compelled the organization to take a more interventionist position on hate speech. Apprehension that far-right fanatics would use public forums to incite violence against racial and religious minorities on occasion led the committee to abandon caution. One example of this was John Kasper. The committee collaborated with local and state authorities in Tennessee and Florida to expose his past association with African Americans and thereby ruin his reputation as a segregationist leader.[22]

In contrast to the gradualism of the American Jewish Committee, other defense agencies assumed a more direct stance on hate speech. The American Jewish Congress and the Anti-Defamation League had from their inceptions campaigned for censorship of anti-Semitic literature and speech.[23] Their activities increased immediately after World War II, a time when public exposure of the Holocaust had undermined popular tolerance of anti-Semitism and allowed Jews to establish a more assertive claim to inclusion in American society. The American Jewish Congress, for instance, participated in protests against public addresses by notorious anti-Semite Gerald L. K. Smith in Los Angeles during 1945.[24] In a case that anticipated the later Stoner incident, the ADL filed a petition with the FCC in 1946 protesting radio appearances by Mississippi Klansman Lycurgus Spinks, who was campaigning for the state governorship. Spinks was a theatrical racist who wore his silver hair to his shoulders and proclaimed Jesus was a

Klansman.[25] His verbal assaults on racial and religious minorities included the accusation that the Russian Revolution was caused by "hook-nosed Jews" and "those niggers I'm supposed to sleep with."[26] The ADL argued that Spinks's invective violated the public interest responsibilities of the radio stations on which he appeared. Although the FCC upheld the petition, the ADL declined the opportunity to refute Spinks on air as this would give greater legitimacy to a fringe candidate. When voters went to the polls, Spinks won only 1.5 percent of the vote.[27]

Both the American Jewish Congress and the ADL had also attempted to prohibit the mail distribution of hate literature. In the early 1940s, the Congress sponsored House Bill 2328, which would have empowered the postmaster general to outlaw material containing "defamatory and false statements" based on race or religion.[28] Among the groups that successfully lobbied against the bill was the American Jewish Committee, a clear indication of how hate speech divided defense agencies.[29] The failure of the bill did not dissuade the ADL from later petitioning federal authorities to ban circulation of a newsletter produced by anti-Semitic preacher and former Stoner ally Gordon Winrod, a proposal that also met with rejection.[30]

Although the ADL and American Jewish Congress had on occasion collaborated with the American Jewish Committee in applying the quarantine strategy, they had at best been reluctant partners. During the late 1950s and early 1960s, the two organizations supported quarantine in instances where a more direct approach threatened the security of racial and religious minorities. This was the case, for instance, with George Lincoln Rockwell.[31] The ADL and American Jewish Congress also recognized that support for restrictions on freedom of speech could compromise civil rights activism. During the 1950s, several southern states attempted to repress the NAACP by forcing it to release its membership lists, exposing those whose names appeared to intimidation and violence. When the Alabama NAACP refused to comply, state authorities imposed an outright ban on the organization. To defend the NAACP, with which it had a close alliance, the American Jewish Congress tactically retreated from attempting to censor racist speech, promoting instead the entitlement of all Americans to "the free exercise of the right to speak without fear of retribution, and to the right of voluntary association and free assembly."[32]

Given their earlier caution about censorship of white racists, the confrontational attitude of some civil rights groups toward Stoner represented a tactical shift on the hate speech issue. The effort to ban further broadcasts of the commercial demonstrated an alternative conviction that unrestricted freedom of speech posed a potential threat to, rather than a measure to protect, equality.

The effort to silence Stoner raises crucial issues. First, how do we account for the timing of the decision? Civil rights organizations had wrestled with the hate speech issue for years. Stoner himself had long used public addresses to make abusive statements about racial and religious minorities, so why did the commercial precipitate a shift of policy on hate speech? Second, why did some black and Jewish organizations sign the petition to the FCC while others refrained from confronting Stoner?

The answers to these questions are elusive since neither the organizational records of the NAACP and ADL nor the published scholarship on the two civil rights groups provide much information.[33] The absence of any explicit evidence accounting for the shift in policy is problematic, but it is possible to point toward a tentative explanation. A closer look at both broader shifts in civil rights activism and the distinctive characteristics of the Stoner campaign offer some clues.

The immediate catalyst for the ADL and NAACP petition was Stoner's unprecedented use of explicitly racist language in a campaign commercial. Television provided Stoner with the means to communicate his message to millions of people, the potential impact of which no one could predict. Georgia's senatorial race of 1972 was not the first time Stoner had run for public office, but he had not in the past possessed access to such a powerful medium through which to communicate his message. With little media profile, Stoner did not represent a serious threat. However, with the potential to appear in every living room across the state he posed much more of a menace.

Civil rights groups had refrained from a censorship struggle with Stoner when he stood as a candidate in the Georgia gubernatorial election two years earlier. Stoner's platform stressed his commitment not only to resist further federal intervention in southern race relations, but also to repeal the legislative revolution of the 1960s. As he would later do in his senatorial campaign, Stoner announced his intention to preserve school segregation by opposing busing and improving funding of private academies and to restrict welfare to poor whites. He also declared his determination to resist what he saw as the encroachment of the federal government into other rights and traditions, evidenced by the Supreme Court's prohibition of officially sponsored school prayer in *Engel v. Vitale*. The populist tone of the campaign included condemnation of both federal policymakers and the metropolitan elite in Atlanta who, Stoner claimed, denied rural and small town voters a representative voice in state politics.[34]

State newspapers and television stations reprehended Stoner for his crude racial demagoguery, but recognized his constitutional right to freedom of expression. According to the *Atlanta Journal*, public exposure would only serve to discredit Stoner since "he will sensitize masses of people to just how vulgar and profane their views sound when they are expressed by a real racist."[35] In a separate editorial, the paper also evoked cold war politics by proclaiming that any impingement on constitutional liberties would compromise U.S. leadership of the free world. As the paper histrionically put it, "the Kremlin would be delighted if our country eliminated the right of dissent."[36]

Any apprehension about the Stoner campaign in 1970 eased as a result of his failure to find a public forum for his opinions. The NSRP activist claimed the media conspired to suppress coverage of his campaign. However, the truth was more prosaic: he had no money to publicize his cause. Although Stoner ran a series of newspaper advertisements, he could not raise the funds for a televised campaign commercial. When WAGA-TV broadcast a critical editorial piece on Stoner, the NSRP issued an appeal for financial support so it could advertise on television "a message so dynamic and bold that people will remember it 100 times longer than any Jew propaganda diatribe." The funds were not forthcoming. Edward Fields, who worked as Stoner's campaign manager, conceded "we have run out of money."[37] Stoner did appear on a televised debate between the twelve gubernatorial candidates, but his restrained performance elicited no protest. Civil rights groups closely monitored the election, but realized that any intervention on their part would generate the publicity Stoner had otherwise failed to attract. The outcome of the Democratic primary on September 9 was a resounding success for racial moderates, with Jimmy Carter winning 48.7 percent of the vote. Stoner came in fifth with a feeble 2.2 percent, a position made more humiliating by his loss of fourth place to African American candidate C. B. King.[38]

It is also probable that the change in policy toward Stoner reflected a larger redirection of civil rights activism. The purpose of the direct action protests of the 1960s was to expose the violent racism of white southerners to the rest of the nation, creating public pressure on an otherwise reluctant federal government to intervene in support of the demonstrators. When the police used dogs and fire hoses on black protesters during the Southern Christian Leadership Conference campaign in Birmingham, Alabama, in

1963, it elicited angry condemnations from the press and politicians across the country.[39] By the early 1970s, there was less strategic need for the civil rights movement to publicize white racism. The movement had already demolished the legal foundations of Jim Crow and established many fundamental rights and protections for African Americans. With less immediate need to protect their own freedom of speech, civil rights organizations may have worried less about the repercussions of censoring their political opponents.

The inclusion of the Anti-Defamation League in the coalition against Stoner also demonstrates how changing political circumstances encouraged Jewish defense agencies to take a more direct stand against hate speakers. The quarantine strategy served Jews well during the school desegregation crisis when anti-Semitism reached unprecedented levels in the southern states. Jews were a small and marginal group in southern society—less than 1 percent of the population—and a more direct challenge to racial and religious bigots risked violent reprisal. The terrorist attacks on southern synagogues during the late 1950s were well within the living memory of most Jews in the region.[40] However, by the early 1970s the civil rights movement and the rise to power of white racial moderates had eroded the political strength of militants such as Stoner. The election of Sam Massell, a Jew, as mayor of Atlanta in October 1969 symbolized a new era of social and political inclusion for Jews in the South, encouraging them to take a more public stand against the far right.[41]

The reassertion of a more confrontational policy on hate speech had started in the late 1960s. Two years before the Stoner incident, the FCC revoked the broadcasting license of fundamentalist preacher Carl McIntire in response to protests by numerous groups representing minority interests, including the American Jewish Committee and the NAACP. McIntire had transmitted his racially and religiously reactionary ideology over the airwaves since 1965, when he established the WXUR radio station in Media, Pennsylvania. However, his refusal to present alternate points of view enabled civil rights organizations to challenge his broadcasting license under the terms of the Fairness Doctrine. The success of this campaign may have emboldened black and Jewish activists to confront Stoner shortly thereafter.[42] This shift toward support of political censorship also coincided with the efforts of the Nixon administration to crack down on political extremism. Federal repression of militants provided an opportune moment for civil rights groups to push for restrictions on the First Amendment rights of their adversaries.[43] The societal changes wrought by the civil rights revolution also meant that by the early 1970s explicit expressions of racism were no longer socially or politically acceptable.

Further political developments reshaped policy on hate speech. Civil rights groups were concerned that the Stoner campaign was symptomatic of a resurgence of the far right. The ADL cited the presidential campaign of American Party candidate John Schmitz as evidence.[44] Moreover, the ADL feared that the resurrection of the far right came at a time when the atrocities committed against Jews during World War II were receding in the public consciousness. The generation of Americans who grew to adulthood after the war were less aware, according to the ADL, of what the racial demagoguery of men like Stoner could lead to if not confronted. Even some of those for whom the Holocaust was within living memory were too complacent about the far right. As Arnold Forster and Benjamin Epstein of the ADL asserted, although there was nothing novel about the hatred espoused by Stoner, "what is new is the indifference manifest by so many to the continued existence of this ancient plague." Forster and Epstein concluded that the readiness of the media to provide Stoner with a public forum reflected a "large measure of indifference" to racial and religious prejudice.[45] These concerns led the ADL to conclude it must campaign for censorship of broadcasts "that are incitements, that are inflammatory, that are bigoted." The Stoner campaign commercial presented an opportune moment to test its newly reassertive policy.[46]

The bellicose campaign strategy pursued by Stoner, coupled with the cultural and political shifts of the late 1960s and early 1970s, therefore created the context for a showdown on the hate speech issue. What remained uncertain was the result of that confrontation.

Important as the alliance between the ADL and NAACP may have been, it is no less significant that other civil rights groups opted not to add their support to the petition. The decision of organizations such as the Congress of Racial Equality and the Southern Christian Leadership Conference to maintain their traditional policy of tolerance toward hate speech demonstrates a divergence of opinion emblematic of the broader fracturing of the civil rights coalition in the late 1960s and early 1970s.

The ADL and NAACP faced a difficult task in attempting to censor Stoner for other reasons. First, the power of federal law appeared to protect Stoner from censorship. The Communications Act of 1934 not only compelled broadcasters to provide all political candidates with equal time on air, but also prohibited their imposing conditions on the content of campaign commercials. Its purpose was to facilitate participatory democracy by presenting voters with a panoply of political opinion, including that of candidates outside the main parties. The provisions of the law were strengthened only a year before the senatorial race by the Federal Election Campaign Act, which required broadcasters to offer "reasonable access" to candidates for federal office.[47]

Stoner further benefited from federal protection in the form of the Fairness Doctrine. Established by the Federal Communications Commission in 1949, the Doctrine obliged broadcast licensees to present contrasting points of view on controversial matters of public importance. That the Fairness Doctrine afforded fringe political candidates a disproportionate influence on public discourse is evident from an incident involving Stoner's former ally, John Kasper. During the 1964 presidential election, Lyndon Johnson attempted to arrange a televised news conference publicizing the charitable organization United Fund. All the other candidates waived their equal time rights, with the exception of Kasper, who insisted that the networks broadcast his own United Fund message. Rather than give airtime to the militant racist, broadcasters pulled the president from their schedules.[48] As was true of the Communications Act of 1934, the federal government had fortified the legality of the Fairness Doctrine only shortly before the Stoner campaign commercial, in this case as a result of the Supreme Court decision in *Red Lion Broadcasting, Inc. v. Federal Communications Commission* (1969).[49]

The second reason for the difficulty, as previously discussed, was that the libertarian attitude of the courts toward freedom of speech benefited both proponents and opponents of civil rights reform. The case with the most direct implications for the Stoner incident was *Brandenburg v. Ohio* (1969), in which the Supreme Court overturned the conviction of a Cincinnati Klansman in a case that abolished the "clear and present danger" test for free speech established half a century earlier in *Schenck v. United States* (1919). Justice Oliver Wendell Holmes had attempted to impose a constitutional barrier to the repression of free speech by stating that such action was only legally justified when the words used were "of such a nature as to create a clear and present danger that they will bring about the substantive evils that Congress has a right to prevent."[50] During the decades that followed, however, the broad interpretation of this standard resulted in significant governmental suppression of political dissent, especially during the McCarthyite witch-hunts. However, a series of cases culminating in *Brandenburg* led to a substantial expansion of First Amendment protections. *Brandenburg* had a clear bearing on the Stoner case since it concerned a Klan leader who used the same racially derogatory language and publicly advocated similar policies. The Court overturned his conviction under the Ohio Criminal Syndicalism Law, concluding that the First Amendment protected the right to express racially or religiously inflammatory opinions so long as such language did not serve as a direct means to incite violence.[51]

The ADL and NAACP legal challenge asked the FCC to determine that the Stoner commercial represented a "clear and present danger" to the community, consistent with the criterion to restrict freedom of speech established in *Schenck* but apparently abandoned in *Brandenburg*. Lonnie King of the NAACP evoked Justice Oliver Wendell Holmes's famous opinion in *Schenck* by claiming Stoner's efforts to create public disorder were comparable to "a man falsely shouting fire in a theater and causing a panic." The ADL and NAACP petition significantly emphasized that the language used by Stoner might not only incite white racists into violent acts against African Americans, but might also cause blacks to take retributive measures against the stations that aired the commercial. According to the signatories, the Stoner commercial posed "a serious and imminent threat to the safety and well being of the stations which air it and to the community at large." Indeed, the broadcast later resulted in anonymous threats to bomb both stations.[52]

The petitioners did not attempt to prove that Stoner's use of racial pejoratives and crude stereotyping of black male sexuality constituted an act of group slander. However, they did endeavor to show that the commercial could cause psychological harm. The petitioners included the expert testimony of Dr. Alex Robertson, a pediatrician at Georgia Medical College, who opined that exposure to the racial epithets that Stoner uttered would prove "detrimental to the normal psychological development of children."[53] This strategy was consistent with the NAACP's use in *Brown v. Board of Education* of a study by psychologists Kenneth and Mamie Clark demonstrating the mental harm caused by racism.[54]

On August 3, 1972, the FCC issued its decision on the case. It ruled the petitioners had failed to offer sufficient evidence that the language used by Stoner would directly induce acts of violent lawlessness.[55] The ADL and NAACP contemplated asking a federal court of appeals to overturn the ruling, but concluded this risked generating further publicity for Stoner.[56]

Stoner was understandably elated with the decision, interpreting it as a sign that his segregationist crusade had divine sanction. "I think that God has blessed me," he beamed to reporters. "God has protected me from the Jews and the niggers who were trying to take my constitutional rights of free speech away from me."[57] He seized on the ruling to reaffirm his opinion that, "Even for short pleasure with white women, niggers will risk life and limb."[58] These statements were characteristic of the way Stoner punctuated every remark about African Americans with use of the "N" word and references to their supposedly predatory sexual instincts.

The FCC ruling similarly emboldened Stoner to believe he could act with impunity in employing racial and religious slurs against his political opponents. When WSB-TV in Atlanta broadcast a debate between the candidates in the senatorial race, Stoner refused to shake hands with black activist Hosea Williams of the Southern Christian Leadership Conference and accused him on air of conspiring to deny jobs to white workers. He also retaliated against Mayor Massell by accusing him of being a "Christ-killing, race-mixing, Jew gangster."[59]

Despite his claims to the contrary, the outcome of the Democratic primary demonstrated that Stoner's election to public office was not part of the divine plan. Stoner came in fifth of thirteen candidates with 40,675 votes, 5.7 percent of the total. The overwhelming majority of his support, 27,821 votes, came from rural areas where, in contrast to metropolitan areas, unreconstructed racism remained a potent political force.[60]

While Stoner's election showing was less than spectacular, it represented a substantial improvement on the 18,000 votes he had polled in the Georgia gubernatorial race two years earlier. The ADL considered it "inconceivable" that, "in this day and age," Stoner should attract so many votes.[61] Whether he profited from the public controversy over the campaign commercial is impossible to determine. The efforts of the ADL and NAACP to restrict Stoner's freedom of speech may ironically have provided his campaign with greater media exposure than it would otherwise have received. Local, national, and even international media covered the controversy, generating countless column inches of free publicity for Stoner.[62] Even so, ADL officials insisted with some legitimacy that the commercial "was already a front-page and headline item" before they and the NAACP filed their petition.[63] According to one estimate, television and radio stations had broadcast it more than one hundred times before the intervention of civil rights organizations, meaning that Stoner's message had already reached a mass audience.[64] In the final analysis, the extent to which either of these factors influenced support for Stoner remains inconclusive since the electoral data tells us how, but not why, voters cast their ballots.

While it is unclear whether the intervention of the ADL and NAACP backfired by rousing popular support for Stoner, the controversy surrounding his campaign is replete with irony in other respects. First, the dispute found the two sides in the civil rights struggle reversing their relationship with the federal government. During the desegregation crisis, southern whites pursued a policy of massive resistance against federal law. Segregationists claimed that the Supreme Court had usurped its constitutional authority in handing down the decision in *Brown v. Board of Education*, which they saw as an attempt to impose desegregation in contravention of individual state control of the public school system. These reactionaries similarly resisted the liberalization of the law by the Warren Court in other areas such as school prayer. However, in responding to the protests against the Stoner campaign commercial, the white press and political leadership abandoned their strict constructionist interpretation of the Constitution and supported the unrestricted right to freedom of speech established by the Supreme Court during the preceding two decades. Opposition to the unconditional interpretation of freedom of speech came instead from civil rights activists. The NAACP and ADL wrote to a number of newspapers protesting their freedom of speech editorial line.[65]

Second, the controversy substantiates the argument made by historian Eckard Toy that hate groups paradoxically persecute racial and religious minorities while portraying themselves as victims.[66] During the course of the civil rights revolution, the more politically astute white southern racists started to understand that their best means to defend Jim Crow practices was to shift the terms of public debate away from race. Explicitly racist rhetoric had lost much of its cultural and intellectual legitimacy by the late 1950s and early 1960s. For that reason, segregationists abandoned their emphasis on the supposed inferiority of African Americans and instead attempted to rationalize their resistance to reform by claiming that they were merely protecting their own rights to freedom of choice about who shared classrooms with their children or bought homes in their neighborhood. According to this line of reasoning, the federal government increased opportunity for African Americans only by curtailing the citizenship rights of whites.[67]

While moderate segregationists recognized the need to choose between their emphasis on race on the one hand and the denial of their rights on the other, Stoner attempted to straddle these rhetorical strategies. He saw no contradiction between his incorporation of the language of white victimization and his stress on racist arguments to justify the denial of African Americans' constitutional rights. Stoner used the most offensive of racial epithets to demean African Americans, emphasizing through repetition his hatred of them and rejection of their basic humanity. He also drew on malicious stereotypes of black males as violent criminals and sexual predators to stress that African Americans posed a threat to supposedly civilized society. Although his language abused blacks, his rhetoric represented whites as victims. The political establishment at both the federal and state levels had, in Stoner's opinion, betrayed the electorate they were supposed to represent by implementing laws that undermined white privilege. This legislation, he claimed, rendered whites vulnerable to the predatory advances of African Americans.

Third, although Stoner claimed ordinary whites no longer possessed a representative voice in public life, he communicated his message through the medium of mass communications. While Stoner claimed he was the victim of a tyrannical political establishment, he used the protection of the state to address the electorate without restriction. Stoner ironically relied on the permissive policies of the FCC to make public his claim that the government in Washington was a dictatorship.

Fourth, what allowed Stoner to denounce racial equality in such inflammatory terms was an expansive interpretation of freedom of speech that owed much to the influence of the civil rights movement. It was during the 1950s and 1960s that the Warren Court facilitated black protest by including offensive and provocative language under the protection of the First Amendment. That protection now provided Stoner with the means to employ hate speech against African Americans. In a further twist, one of the members of the FCC board that ruled in favor of Stoner's right to freedom of speech was the future executive director of the NAACP, Benjamin L. Hooks. According to Hooks, African Americans must not let "the emotions of the moment blind them" to the broader importance of protecting First Amendment rights that had proved so important to the advance of racial egalitarianism. Banning the campaign commercial might offer temporary appeasement to African Americans, but in the longer term it was more likely to cause them harm.[68]

The efforts of civil rights organizations to restrict the hate speech of J. B. Stoner ended in failure. During the 1970s, the white supremacist ran for public office on several further occasions, using the protection of federal power to disparage racial and religious minorities in crudely offensive terms. In 1974, for instance, a federal judge ruled that public officials in Macon and Augusta could not prohibit the pasting of posters produced by Stoner, who was running for the lieutenant governorship of Georgia, on city buses. Stoner secured 73,000 votes, around 9 percent of the total, in the election.[69]

Four years later, Stoner ran against incumbent George Busbee for the Georgia governorship. That March, Busbee had signed the Georgia Fair Employment Practices Act into law. Stoner made the repeal of the new legislation the focus of his election bid. One of his television campaign commercials claimed that if Busbee was reelected he would enact further laws that "take from the whites and give to the Niggers."[70] Despite a petition from Atlanta NAACP leader Julian Bond, the FCC reaffirmed that Stoner's use of racially derogatory language in his campaign commercials did not constitute a "clear and present danger" to the community.[71] It is testimony to the residual power of white racism among rural and small town voters that he scored his most impressive result in an election, securing 71,000 votes, or 10 percent of the total.[72]

Although the NAACP attempted to censor Stoner a second time in 1978, further failure led the organization to revert thereafter to its traditionally permissive policy on First Amendment rights.[73] Moreover, the second challenge to Stoner significantly did not receive the support of the ADL. The reluctance of the ADL to renew its partnership with the NAACP suggests its recognition of failure in attempting to censor Stoner. Five years later, when the National Socialist Party of America announced its intention to parade in the Chicago suburb of Skokie, the ADL and other Jewish defense organizations initially recommended a return to their traditional quarantine strategy. Although the protests of local Holocaust survivors eventually led them to petition for a banning order, the lesson they appeared to have learned, but then forgotten, from the Stoner episode was that the courts would protect the unlimited right to freedom of speech.[74]

Despite the persistent efforts of civil rights organizations to silence Stoner, there was never a serious threat that he would win public office. His crude appeals to racial and religious prejudice had appeared anachronistic in the 1950s, when massive resistance leaders attempted to legitimate their opposition to desegregation by framing it in the context of states' rights, let alone the 1970s, when the civil rights revolution had demolished the legal foundations of Jim Crow. Even those who resisted civil rights reform wanted to dissociate themselves from the lawless extremism of radicals such as Stoner. One of the rival candidates in the 1972 senatorial race was Ernest Vandiver, a former governor of Georgia who had threatened to close schools and universities rather than admit African American students through their doors. An archconservative, Vandiver nonetheless understood the need in the new political climate to represent himself as a rational and respectable candidate by ameliorating his language on racial matters. He therefore condemned the Stoner campaign commercial as having "offended the honor and dignity of many Georgians," white as well as black.[75]

Although the coarse language of Stoner did not attract a sizeable share of the white electorate, this did not mean racism was not still an important element in southern politics. An opinion poll conducted a year before the election revealed that 53 percent of Georgia voters believed "public officials don't care what the people want."[76] Their resentment stemmed in substantial measure from federal enforcement of black civil rights. While other white candidates in the primary campaign strategically distanced themselves from the overt racism of Stoner, they espoused a similarly antiestablishment rhetoric rooted in opposition to racial reform. The outcome of the Democratic primary demonstrates that many whites who did not cast their ballots in support of Stoner still shared some of his convictions. Although David Gambrell won the first round with 34 percent of the vote, he lost the runoff election three weeks later to Sam Nunn. Nunn attained 54 percent of the vote by attracting the support of rural and small town voters who had cast their ballots in the first round for Stoner and Vandiver. Even though Nunn eschewed the racist rhetoric of Stoner, his campaign shared a similar agenda. Nunn promised voters that he would "Get Tough in Washington" by restoring states' rights, strengthening law and order, and abolishing the use of busing to facilitate school desegregation. While there were crucial distinctions between Nunn and Stoner—one was a respectable politician, the other a racial extremist—both hoped to use white resentment of federal reforms to win public office.[77]

Although Stoner did not win the election, his campaign indirectly advanced the interests of white racial conservatism. In condemning his extremism, mainstream politicians like Vandiver and Nunn made their own reactionary positions appear more moderate and reasonable. As a letter writer to the *Atlanta Constitution* observed of the 1970 gubernatorial election, the real menace that Stoner posed was that he "makes all the other white racists look good."[78] In an astute commentary on the Stoner incident, white newspaperman Hodding Carter observed, "Hardly anyone preaches it [white supremacy] anymore—not because politicians' hearts are purer, but because that ploy no longer works."[79] What did work, as Sam Nunn demonstrated with his emphases on law and order and states' rights, was the use of racially encoded concepts to legitimize attacks on minorities. The hate speech of political mavericks such as Stoner was ultimately a distraction from this more insidious, and ultimately more successful, danger to civil rights reform. Ronald Reagan's references to "welfare queens" and George H. W. Bush's notorious Willie Horton campaign commercial would demonstrate how, during the 1980s and beyond, mainstream politicians used implicitly racist messages to their electoral advantage.[80]

Stoner did not adopt this new rhetorical strategy. His continued use of racially inflammatory language consigned him even farther to the political margins. However, other far-right activists recognized that the appropriation of racial code words was a means to realign their movement with the political mainstream. This was above all true of John Crommelin's former associate, David Duke. The onetime Grand Wizard of the Knights of the Ku Klux Klan won election to the Louisiana state legislature in 1989, campaigning on a platform that pandered to white resentment at the perceived preferential treatment that federal government policies such as affirmative action accorded to African Americans. The same strategy resulted in Duke winning almost 60 percent of white votes when he ran for the U.S. Senate the following year, although he still lost the election. Duke appealed in particular to lower-class whites who otherwise believed they had no representative voice in the political process. More than three decades earlier, rabble rousers such as John Kasper and Bryant Bowles had exploited the anger and resentment of ordinary whites toward political officials they saw as privileging the interests of African Americans. Duke demonstrated that this reactionary populism was still a potent strain in southern politics. One interesting footnote to the Duke story is that one of his closest allies is Stoner's former political partner, Edward Fields.[81]

Although Stoner was a prominent focus of the debate over hate speech during the 1970s, his political influence gradually waned during the following decades. While he remained an active force within the far right until shortly before his death, the pervasive impact of the civil rights revolution on southern society rendered him an anachronism. His political legacy was nonetheless significant.

Stoner made a further bid for public office in the spring of 1980, when he ran as a Democratic candidate in the Georgia senatorial primary. In addition to his customary calls for the annulment of federal civil rights laws and the forcible repatriation of African Americans, he demanded tighter restrictions on immigration, a response to the recent Mariel boatlift that brought 125,000 Cuban migrants, some of whom the Castro administration had released from correctional and mental health facilities, to American shores.[82]

However, Stoner would have less opportunity to publicize his cause than in the past. What silenced him was not the intervention of civil rights organizations, but his conviction for the bombing more than two decades earlier of the Bethel Baptist Church in Birmingham, Alabama. Georgia Democratic Party officials cited Stoner's status as a convicted felon to remove his name from primary ballot papers. The NSRP leader attempted to secure an injunction preventing the election from taking place unless his name was reinstated, but his lawsuit proved unsuccessful. For the next three years, Stoner would invest his time, money, and energy in an attempt to overturn his conviction.[83]

The story of how the law finally caught up with Stoner is long and elaborate. Ironically, the process started at almost the exact time that federal authorities concluded the NSRP no longer constituted a threat and closed their investigation of its activities.[84] In February 1976, Alabama Attorney General William J. Baxley launched a renewed investigation of the bombing of the Sixteenth Street Baptist Church thirteen years earlier, which resulted in the deaths of four black teenagers.[85] In September 1977, a Jefferson County grand jury indicted former Klansman Robert Chambliss on four counts of first-degree murder. Although Baxley's investigation failed to uncover evidence connecting Stoner with the same crime, the attorney general secured his indictment for the earlier bombing of the Bethel Baptist Church.[86] Stoner appeared before a superior court in Cobb County, Georgia, which released him on $10,000 bail. It was a further fourteen months before he attended the same court to answer an extradition charge from Alabama authorities. The judge ruled Stoner could not be compelled to stand trial in Alabama on the grounds that state officials had failed to prove he was in Birmingham on the date of the bombing. However, the Georgia Supreme Court overturned the ruling.[87]

On May 14, 1980, a mostly white jury found Stoner guilty of the bombing. The NSRP leader remained free on bond pending appeal. On August 13, 1982, the Alabama State Supreme Court upheld his conviction. Freed on bond, Stoner persisted with the appeals process. When the U.S. Supreme Court decided five months later not to hear his case, it seemed time had finally run out for Stoner. However, he still refused to admit defeat. Rather than surrender to the authorities, he went on the run. It took five months before an FBI manhunt secured his arrest. To protect him from possible reprisals, the authorities ordered Stoner to serve his ten-year sentence in solitary confinement at the Kilby Correctional Facility outside Montgomery.[88]

Stoner suffered a series of setbacks as a result of his incarceration. The NSRP imploded when dissident members deposed him as national chairman. Renaming themselves the States' Rights Voters League, the rebels also voted to expel Edward Fields. In May 1984, police arrested Fields when he broke into Stoner's home in an attempt to retrieve some of his possessions. Although Stoner declined to press charges, the incident caused the acrimonious dissolution of their longstanding relationship.[89] Stoner lost not only his party, but also his license to practice law when the Georgia Supreme Court permanently disbarred him.[90]

None of these experiences dampened his spirit. In contrast to John Kasper, Stoner endured prison with no diminution of his commitment to the white supremacist cause. He had served only three-and-a-half years of his sentence when prison authorities released him on October 5, 1986.[91] Still proclaiming his innocence, Stoner pronounced that he was "more determined than ever before" to restore white supremacist rule. He interpreted the recent electoral defeat of his prosecutor William J. Baxley as a sign of divine approval.[92]

Stoner renewed his assault on racial and religious minorities with what he called his "Crusade Against Corruption." The campaign focused on the AIDS epidemic that, Stoner claimed, was an act of divine vengeance against African Americans.[93] Stoner's interpretation of AIDS was a contemporary adaptation of historical discourses on black sexuality and health, specifically the claim that African Americans suffered high disease and mortality rates because of their own innate dirtiness and degeneracy. With the approach of the new millennium, Stoner inferred that the spread of AIDS was a portent of the impending Day of Judgment. "I praise God for AIDS," he affirmed. "We are now certain of White victory."[94]

By the 1980s, such rhetoric had pushed Stoner to the outermost reaches of political debate. However vile his opinions, popular discourses on AIDS revealed that bigotry and intolerance was hardly the preserve of militant racists. As Elizabeth Fee asserts, "Attitudes once expressed toward the black population as sexually promiscuous, sexually threatening, and a reservoir of disease have now been, in revived form, turned against the gay male population."[95] The Christian Right in particular interpreted AIDS as divine punishment of homosexuals for their moral depravity. When Pat Buchanan, director of communications in the Reagan White House, proclaimed that homosexuals had "declared war on nature, and now nature is extracting an awful retribution," his words differed little from those of Stoner other than in terms of their chosen target.[96]

In 1990, Stoner successfully challenged a proposed amendment to the Georgia state constitution that would have prohibited convicted felons from holding public office for at least ten years after serving their sentence. It was a fleeting victory. Having run on a typically bilious white supremacist platform, Stoner secured only 31,000 votes, less than 3 percent of the total. It was to prove his final electoral campaign.[97]

Even as he became more elderly and enfeebled, Stoner maintained an unmatched capacity to cause outrage and offense, necessitating police protection at many of his public appearances.[98] In 1993, for instance, he publicly denounced the opening of the Holocaust Museum in Washington, D.C., claiming the federal government was using taxpayers' money to perpetuate the hoax of the Final Solution.[99] His use of racial epithets ensured that he attracted media attention out of proportion to his much diminished political influence. Rap artist Ice Cube even wrote a song, "My Skin is My Sin," in which he warned "the cracker named J. B. Stoner," after seeing him on television "talking more shit," not to "let me catch you on no corners." Although a liaison with Stoner on the streets of South Central Los Angeles was rather unlikely, Ice Cube welcomed the prospect. "Grand wizard," he asserted, "bring your ass on imperial so we can get physical."[100]

Although he commanded little influence on the larger world of politics, Stoner attained the status of elder statesman within the renascent far right of the 1980s and 1990s. He maintained close ties with the Klan and was a keynote speaker at the annual congresses of the paramilitary hate group Aryan Nations.[101]

While Stoner's mind willed him on in his white supremacist crusade, his body finally forced him to surrender. Following a debilitating stroke in 2001, he moved into a nursing home in LaFayette, Georgia. In his last interview before he died on April 23, 2005, the decrepit racist sounded a note of enduring defiance. "We'll come back," he declared. "We'll come back, better than ever."[102]

Conclusion

According to historian J. Mills Thornton, III, African American protest against segregation and discrimination relied on a perception of "the existence of a historical moment of transition." Blacks' growing awareness of the indecisiveness and division of what had once seemed a monolithic white leadership radicalized their belief in the potential for racial change.[1] A similar argument can be made of white militants. Federal court orders to desegregate schools elicited an uncertain response from many local and state authorities. Although they opposed racial integration in principle, they recognized in practice that the preservation of law and order relied on public compliance. This "historical moment" created an opportunity for extremists to mobilize whites who were frustrated with public officials but uncertain about alternate courses of action. In contrast to the equivocation of conventional leaders, the combative rhetoric of militants convinced their grassroots supporters that resistance was possible.

The violent tactics of these militants was a threat to segregationist leaders who sought to present a respectable front to their resistance of federal law. They nonetheless tried to turn the turmoil created by extremists to their political advantage. When John Kasper precipitated chaos in Clinton, Tennessee, segregationists used the fact that he was a northerner to argue that local townspeople would never have risen in revolt without the malign influence of a silver-tongued outsider. Kasper's conviction for inciting a riot also presented massive resisters with an opportunity to show their northern liberal critics that they did not tolerate violent fanaticism.

There was more than an element of hypocrisy about the reaction of supposedly respectable segregationists to extremists like Kasper. Although they did not sanction violence, their defiance of federal authority embodied in such initiatives as the Southern Manifesto fostered a political climate in which militants believed they could act with impunity. As Ralph McGill of the *Atlanta Constitution* observed after the dynamiting of the Clinton High School, southern political leaders who "have repudiated their oaths and stood against due process of law have helped unloose the flood of hate and bombing."[2]

The attention bestowed on Kasper also obscured another uncomfortable reality for segregationists. At the same time that Kasper was rousing dissent in Clinton, white citizens in the Kentucky mining communities of Clay and Sturgis were also demonstrating against school desegregation. There were clear parallels between events in Tennessee and Kentucky. In Sturgis, whites drove around the black area of town in an attempt to intimidate African American families. When black parents attempted to escort their children to the newly integrated high school, they met an armed mob. In a move that corresponded with the actions of his Tennessean counterpart Frank Clement, Kentucky Governor Albert Chandler dispatched National Guardsmen armed with two M-47 tanks to protect the African American families. A second unit also soon arrived in Clay. Although State Attorney General Jo Ferguson initially ruled that the local school boards could order the removal of black students, a federal court overruled him in December 1956. In Clinton, racists retaliated against the admission of black students by bombing the high school. Sturgis escaped a similar incident but only because explosives planted in the local black neighborhood failed to detonate.[3]

The public focus on Kasper created a smokescreen that concealed the fact that no outsider had led the mobs in Clay and Sturgis. Without a Kasper to blame, segregationists attributed racial disorder either to communist subversives or to the recklessness of a white underclass. South Carolina journalist William D. Workman, Jr., contended that, despite the responsible leadership of the Citizens' Councils, "There remains more than enough of the 'p' white trash' in the South to cause trouble even in times of relative tranquillity."[4] However, although the mobs in Clay and Sturgis primarily consisted of working-class men and women, their leaders were from the upper ranks of local society. The person who coordinated protest in both communities was William Waller, a thirty-four-year-old World War II veteran.

College-educated and the owner of a local farm implement business, Waller was, in the words of a report on the Kentucky school crises, "at least, upper middle class." So too were the other leaders of rebellion, including in Clay not only Baptist Church minister M. L. Clark, but also Mayor Herman Clark.[5] Kasper briefly helped the efforts of segregationists to sustain the illusion (or self-delusion) that white elites were not responsible for the violent repression of black civil rights. The actions of Arkansas Governor Orval Faubus in precipitating the Little Rock school crisis shattered that assumption.

Whatever short-term advantage militants provided segregationist leaders was outweighed by the longer-term damage they inflicted on the massive resistance cause. In a recent study of how white southerners responded to the civil rights movement, historian Jason Sokol asserts that the political conduct and credo of massive resisters provide limited insight into the mindset of ordinary men and women who played no active role in the race struggle. According to Sokol, "While these intransigents often captured headlines and solidified fears, they do not substantially further one's understanding of the majority's plight."[6] Analysis of racial militants nonetheless illuminates the mentality of more conventional white citizens in one important respect. The turmoil fueled by extremists forced southern whites to choose between uncompromising resistance and at least token compliance with racial reform.

The terrorist tactics of rabble-rousing extremists not only failed to reverse the tide of civil rights reform, but actually hastened its forward advance. When John Kasper created turmoil on the streets of Clinton, state authorities used military force to contain segregationist protest. Moreover, the violence led the more responsible townspeople to promote public compliance with the desegregation of the high school. Kasper compelled the townspeople to decide what they valued more: the strict maintenance of the color line or the order and reputation of their community. The rioting, the beating of a local minister, and the bombing of the high school all contributed to a collective acceptance that the price of violent resistance was too high to pay. Journalist Harry Ashmore observed how local whites came to realize that they were the victims of their own violence. As he rather cynically observed, "when a half-million dollars worth of public property disappeared in the dynamiting of the High School, the word went out that this sort of thing had to stop."[7] Fellow newspaperman Anthony Lewis was no less aware of the pragmatic imperatives that persuaded people to accept change, but phrased his words with greater diplomacy: "a southern community has stood resolutely for the law despite its basic sympathy for racial segregation."[8] Other communities learned the lesson of Clinton and took preemptive measures to circumvent violence and ease the orderly transition to a desegregated public school system.

The disorder that Kasper unleashed in Nashville also proved antithetical to his cause. Public outrage at the bombing of the Hattie Cotton School placed segregationists on the defensive and strengthened the hand of city authorities in securing the peaceful and orderly implementation of school desegregation. John Seigenthaler, the future Justice Department official then working as a reporter for the *Nashville Tennessean*, observed that the incident shook public officials out of their complacency. Law enforcement officials, he noted, had taken few preventive measures against racial militants, allowing mobs to intimidate black parents and their children as they tried to enter formerly all-white schools. The bombing, however, galvanized them into action. Once Nashville "became subject to national ridicule, police came out of their lethargy and cracked down on mob violence."[9]

Kasper primarily operated in the Upper South. The success of J. B. Stoner in provoking violent opposition to the civil rights movement in Birmingham, St. Augustine, and Bogalusa showed that whites in the Deep South, where racism was more entrenched, were less willing to recognize the consequences of intractable resistance.

Racial terrorism also resulted in greater federal intervention in southern state affairs. In May 1960, President Dwight Eisenhower signed a new Civil Rights Act into law. As well as measures protecting and promoting black voting rights, the legislation made it a federal crime to use threats or force to obstruct a court order. It also authorized federal authorities to investigate the bombing of schools, churches, and other buildings when there was evidence that the perpetrators had fled across state lines. The terrorist acts committed by members of the National States' Rights Party were instrumental in shaping federal policy. During the Senate debate, Kenneth Keating of New York documented eighty-eight bombing incidents between 1955 and 1960; at least sixteen of these incidents directly or indirectly involved Kasper, Stoner, and John Crommelin.[10]

While some southern politicians saw the new powers assigned to federal investigators as an infringement of states' rights, others conceded that local law enforcement was insufficient to counter racial violence.[11] Although these legislators opposed the voting rights provisions of the bill, they willingly approved the anti-bombing measures. Terrorist brutalities undermined the ability of white southern political leaders to sustain their own resistance to racial integration within the confines of the law. Herman

Talmadge, one of the most outspoken opponents of black civil rights in the Senate, asserted that he had "nothing but contempt and loathing for that type of dementia which motivates a person to destroy with explosives or fire a church, a school, a plant, a house, or any structure."[12] Such declarations were, as already stated, somewhat disingenuous. The defiance of federal law by politicians, including Talmadge, created the context for lawless extremism in the first place. The violence of white extremists nonetheless placed the southern political leadership on the defensive. Their acceptance of increased federal power undercut the states rights' philosophy that impelled their opposition to the civil rights movement.

Although racial militants proved counterproductive to the segregationist cause, it would be wrong to dismiss their historical importance. The 1990s witnessed the resurgence of the far right. Manifestations of this political phenomenon included the electoral campaigns of former Klansman David Duke, the spate of arson attacks on southern black churches, and the bombing of the Alfred P. Murrah Federal Building in Oklahoma City. The far-right activists who conspired against the civil rights movement during the 1950s and 1960s were an important influence on a later generation of political extremists. John Crommelin had, for instance, been a mentor to Duke when he first became involved in radical right-wing politics. The influence of Crommelin also endures in the contemporary militia movement. Half a century after the rear admiral warned of such dangers, militia members claim that Jewish internationalists are attempting to use the power of the United Nations to destroy American sovereignty and create one world government. The militias share with Crommelin the conviction that white citizens must arm themselves to repel the United Nations forces already stationed on American soil in preparation for an invasion. They also believe, as did Crommelin, that the conspirators have constructed concentration camps for the internment of political dissidents.[13]

The persistence of such convictions suggests that the far right is not simply a product of individual pathologies but is more deeply rooted in American political culture. To caricature the far right as a group of irrational lunatics is to ignore the confluence of racial, class, and gender influences that shape the ideology of its adherents. White supremacists in contemporary society share with their antecedents of a half century ago a sense, albeit baseless, of dispossession by minorities who with apparent governmental support claim an equal right to full citizenship. No matter how unwarranted, their perception that they have no other opportunity for political participation is a catalyst for their resort to violence.

Conclusion

Notes

Introduction

1. Lewis, *It Can't Happen Here.* Philip Roth has recently returned to this theme in a novel that creates an alternative past in which the real-life aviation hero and Nazi sympathizer Charles Lindbergh defeats Franklin Roosevelt in the 1940 presidential election and installs a new fascist administration. Roth, *Plot Against America.*

2. Grill and Jenkins, "The Nazis and the American South," 668–69.

3. For more information on domestic fascism during World War II, see Bennett, *Party of Fear.*

4. Myrdal, *American Dilemma,* xlvii.

5. Recent scholarship on massive resistance includes Chappell, *A Stone of Hope*; Kruse, *White Flight*; Lewis, *The White South and the Red Menace*; Lewis, *Massive Resistance*; Webb, *Massive Resistance*; and Woods, *Black Struggle, Red Scare.*

6. Bartley, *Rise of Massive Resistance.*

7. Chappell, *A Stone of Hope,* quotation on 177.

8. Finley, *Delaying the Dream.*

9. *The Citizens' Council,* November 1955, 4. See also Daniel, *Lost Revolutions,* 196.

10. Workman, *Case for the South,* vii, 18–19.

11. Brooks, "Winning the Peace," 587.

12. Novick, *Holocaust and Collective Memory,* 113.

13. X with Haley, *Autobiography of Malcolm X,* 51.

14. Lassiter, *Silent Majority,* 3.

15. Bartley, *Rise of Massive Resistance,* 94–95.

16. Bell, *Radical Right*; Lipset and Raab, *Politics of Unreason.*

17. Zanden, *Race Relations in Transition,* 82.

18. Shafer quoted in Kittrie, *Rebels with a Cause,* 5.

19. Allport, *The Nature of Prejudice,* 419.

20. See, for instance, Pipes, *Conspiracy.*

21. Berkman, *William Dudley Pelley*; Diamond, *Roads to Dominion*; Ribuffo, *Old Christian Right*.

22. Blee, *Inside Organized Racism*, 3.

23. Kazin, "The Grass-Roots Right," 139.

24. Toy, "Right-Wing Extremism from the Ku Klux Klan to the Order," 141.

Chapter One. A Blueprint for Rebellion

1. *Southern School News*, November 1954, 9.

2. *Belton v. Gebhart*, 87 A.2d 862 (Del. Ch. 1952), aff'd 91 A.2d 137 (Sup. Ct. 1952); *Bulah v. Gebhart*, 87 A.2d 137 (Del. Ch. 1953); Shagaloff, "Desegregation of Public Schools in Delaware," 189–90.

3. *Southern School News*, September 1954, 3.

4. *Southern School News*, September 1954, 3; *Report of the United States Commission on Civil Rights 1959*, 185.

5. *Southern School News*, October 1956, 10.

6. [Telerama. 1954 compilation]/WPTZ-TV (Philadelphia: WPTZ-TV, 1954), 54024 PST, Walter J. Brown Media Libraries and Peabody Awards Collection, University of Georgia Libraries, Athens.

7. *New York Times*, October 1, 1954; *Southern School News*, October 1954, 4; Shagaloff, "Desegregation of Public Schools," 195–96.

8. Kee, "The *Brown* Decision and Milford, Delaware," 211, 214–16.

9. Kee, "The *Brown* Decision and Milford, Delaware," 216–18.

10. *Wilmington Evening Journal*, September 27, 1954; *New York Times*, September 27, 1954; *Delaware State News*, September 28, 1954; *Time*, October 11, 1954; Kennedy, *Jim Crow Guide to the U.S.A.*, 99.

11. *New York Times*, September 28, 1954.

12. *U.S. News & World Report*, October 8, 1954.

13. John W. Flamer, Field Secretary, Activity Report to Gloster B. Current, Director of Branches, October 9, 1954, Papers of the National Association for the Advancement of Colored People, Part 3: The Campaign for Educational Equality, Series C: Legal Department and Central Office Records, 1951–1955; Peters, *Southern Temper*, 62.

14. *New York Times*, September 29, 30, October 18, 1954.

15. *New York Times*, October 1, 2, 1954; *Chicago Tribune*, October 1, 1954; *Bridgeport Telegram*, October 1, 1954; *Washington Post*, October 2, 1954; *Time*, October 11, 1954; Sarratt, *Ordeal of Desegregation*, 152.

16. *Washington Post*, October 6, 15, 1954; *Athens* (Ohio) *Messenger*, October 15, 1954; *Chicago Defender*, October 23, 1954; *New York Times*, October 23, 1954; *Southern School News*, November 1954, 6, 9, December 1954.

17. *Evans v. Buchanan*, 149 F. Supp. 376 (D.C. Del 1957); 152 F. Supp. 886 (D.C. Del. 1957); Raffel, *Historical Dictionary of School Segregation and Desegregation*, 100–101.

18. De Santis, *Collected Works of Langston Hughes*, vol. 10, 147.

19. Polk, *Florida State Gazetteer*; Shofner, *Jackson County, Florida*.

20. United States Federal Census 1930, roll 321, page 15B, Enumeration District 157.

21. World War II Army Enlistment Records, Record Group 64, National Records and Archives Administration, College Park, Md.

22. Department of the Navy, Office of the Chief of Naval Operations, Memorandum to J. Edgar Hoover, February 20, 1958, Federal Bureau of Investigation, Bryant W. Bowles, Jr. File (hereinafter cited as FBI/BB); *Tampa Tribune*, December 11, 2005; Kee, "The *Brown* Decision and Milford, Delaware," 224. The FBI file on Bowles offers little insight into his political career because the Bureau has destroyed some of it. David M. Hardy, FBI Records Management Division, to author, October 22, 2007.

23. Baltimore office report, November 11, 1954, Federal Bureau of Investigation, National Association for the Advancement of White People, File Number 105–18867 (hereinafter cited as FBI/NAAWP); *Wilmington Morning News*, January 4, 1954; *Time*, October 11, 1954.

24. Roy, *Apostles of Discord*, 17–18, 118–19.

25. Muse, *Ten Years of Prelude*, 44.

26. Rorty, "Desegregation Along the Mason-Dixon Line," 494; Bryant W. Bowles, president of the National Association for the Advancement of White People, Inc., head-and-shoulders portrait, facing front, LC-USZ62–126462 (black-and-white film copy negative), Prints and Photographs Division, Library of Congress, Washington, D.C.; Peters, *Southern Temper*, 63.

27. Fine and Sloan, *American Jewish Year Book 57*, 183.

28. Committee on Un-American Activities, *Preliminary Report on Neo-Fascist and Hate Groups*, 11–12; McNeil, *Fight for Fluoridation*, 166; Berlet and Lyons, *Right-Wing Populism in America*, 172; McGinley, *Coming Red Dictatorship*.

29. NAAWP rally, October 10, 1954, Milford School Desegregation Recordings, MSNC-2.

30. Ward, *Radio and the Struggle for Civil Rights in the South.*

31. *News Journal* (Wilmington, Del.), November 12, 1978; *Chester Times*, April 21, 1959.

32. Bryant W. Bowles, *Why National Association for the Advancement of Colored People* (Washington, D.C., n.d.), FBI/NAAWP.

33. *The National Forum* 1, no. 3 (November 1954), Hall-Hoag Collection of Dissenting and Extremist Printed Propaganda, John Hay Library, Brown University, Series 2: Radicalism and Reactionary Politics in America, Roll 20; *The National Forum* 1, no. 5 (January 1955), Group Research, Inc. Records 1955–1996, Columbia Rare and Manuscript Library, Columbia University, New York, Series I: Topical, 1955–1996, box 231.

34. One of the first, and still among the best, analyses of the contribution of black churches is Morris, *Origins of the Civil Rights Movement.*

35. Chappell, *A Stone of Hope.*

36. Dailey, "Sex, Segregation and the Sacred after *Brown*."

37. *Southern School News*, October 1954, 4; *The National Forum* 1, no. 5 (January 1955).

38. Citizens' meeting at Harrington, Delaware Airport, September 26, 1954, Milford School Desegregation Recordings, MSDC-4. Record Group #RG9200, Subgroup #M10—Milford Radio Station WKSB, Delaware Public Archives, Dover.

39. Bryant Bowles rally, September 26, 1954, Milford School Desegregation Recordings, MSDC-5.

40. A report on the Milford crisis compiled by Professor Kenneth B. Clark affirmed the importance of churches in the organization of white resistance. "Governor Blamed for Setback in Delaware," press release, October 9, 1954, Papers of the NAACP, Part 3: The Campaign for Educational Equality, Series C: Legal Department and Central Office Records, 1951–1955.

41. For more information on parachurch organizations, see Coleman, "Religious Social Capital," 33–48.

42. *Salisbury Times*, September 29, 1954.

43. NAAWP rally, September 26, 1954, Milford School Desegregation Recordings, MSDC-5. For further information on the involvement of Reverend Lynch in NAAWP activities, see *Wilmington Morning News*, October 11, 1954; NAAWP Rally, October 10, 1954, Milford School Desegregation Recordings, MSDC-2.

44. Kee, "The *Brown* Decision and Milford, Delaware," 221, 225–27.

45. *New York Times*, September 29, 1954.

46. *Brainerd (Minn.) Daily Dispatch*, October 4, 1954.

47. *The National Forum* 1, no. 5 (January 1955).

48. "Radio address by Bryant Bowles in which he endorses segregationist candidates for Milford School Board, May 13, 1955," Milford School Desegregation Recordings, MSDC-6.

49. "Citizens meeting at Harrington Delaware Airport. Bryant Bowles organizes branch of NAAWP, September 26, 1954," Milford School Desegregation Recordings, MSDC-4.

50. "NAAWP Rally, October 10, 1954," Milford School Desegregation Recordings, MSDC-2.

51. Rorty, "Desegregation Along the Mason-Dixon Line," 502; Kee, "*Brown* Decision," 223–24.

52. Jacoway, *Turn Away Thy Son*, 69.

53. Baltimore office report, June 6, 1955, FBI/NAAWP.

54. Fleming, "Resistance Movements and Racial Desegregation," 45.

55. *The National Forum* 1, no. 5 (January 1955); 1, no. 3 (November 1954), FBI/NAAWP. For more on the distribution of anti-Semitic literature in Milford during the school crisis, see interview with Theodore Henry Blum for the Rutgers Oral History Archives conducted by Sandra Stewart Holyoak and Jamie Wang, September 20, 2002, transcript, 27–28, http://oralhistory.rutgers.edu/Interviews/pdfs/blum_theodore.pdf (last accessed August 10, 2007).

56. *Time*, October 25, 1954.

57. Fine, *American Jewish Year Book 56*, 223–24; Fine and Sloan, *American Jewish Year Book 57*, 183; Shagaloff, "Desegregation of Public Schools in Delaware," 200.

58. NAAWP Rally, October 10, 1954, Milford School Desegregation Recordings, MSDC-2.

59. "Bryant Bowles rally, September 26, 1954," Milford School Desegregation Recordings, MSDC-5; *New York Times*, September 27, 1954.

60. "Bryant Bowles rally, September 26, 1954," Milford School Desegregation Recordings, MSDC-5.

61. "NAAWP meeting at Lincoln, Delaware, September 30, 1954," Milford School Desegregation Recordings, MSDC-1. For further information on McCall, see Peters, *Southern Temper*, 213–24.

62. *Wilmington Evening Journal*, September 29, 1954.

63. Selwyn James, "Town That Surrendered to Hate," *Redbook Magazine*, April 1955, 35, 70.

64. "Governor Blamed for Setback in Delaware," press release, October 9, 1954, Papers of the NAACP, Part 3: The Campaign for Educational Equality, Series C: Legal Department and Central Office Records, 1951–1955.

65. Kenneth B. Clark to the Editor, *New York Times*, October 4, 1954, Papers of the NAACP, Part 3: The Campaign for Educational Equality, Series C: Legal Department and Central Office Records, 1951–1955.

66. *Baltimore News Post*, October 5, 1954; *Baltimore Sunday American*, October 10, 1954; *Southern School News*, November 1954, 8; *Life*, October 11, 1954; Mitchell, "Foes of Integration," 533–35.

67. *The Crisis* (November 1954): 551, 555–56; Fleming, "Resistance Movements and Racial Desegregation," 45.

68. Rorty, "Desegregation Along the Mason-Dixon Line," 494–97; Mitchell, "Foes of Integration," 538; Sarratt, *Ordeal of Desegregation*, 153–54; Durr, *Behind the Backlash*, 95.

69. *Washington Post*, October 7, 1954; *Galveston News*, October 9, 1954; *Chicago Defender*, October 16, 1954; *New Republic*, October 25, 1954; Mitchell, "Foes of Integration," 540–41.

70. *New York Times*, October 2, 10, 1954; *Tampa Tribune*, October 1, 1954; *Washington Post*, October 12, 17, 1954; Mitchell, "Foes of Integration," 539.

71. *New York Times*, October 17, 1954.

72. *Wilmington Evening Journal*, October 6, 1954; *New York Times*, October 5, 22, 1954.

73. *Washington Post*, October 10, 11, 1954; *New York Times*, October 10, 11, 1954; *Chicago Tribune*, October 11, 1954; *Bridgeport Post*, October 11, 1954; *Charleston Gazette*, October 13, 1954; *Newport News*, October 13, 1954; *Time*, October 25, 1954.

74. *Washington Post*, December 17, 1954, January 14, 1955; *Southern School News*, February 1955, 3, April 1955, 4.

75. "Radio address by Bryant Bowles in which he endorses segregationist candidates for Milford School Board, May 13, 1955," Milford School Desegregation Recordings, MSDC-6; *Washington Post*, May 16, 1955; *Southern School News*, November 1956, 15.

76. June Shagaloff, memorandum to Thurgood Marshall, December 20, 1954, NAACP Collection, Part 3: The Campaign for Educational Equality, Series C: Legal Department and Central Office records, 1951–1955; Baltimore office report, June 6, 1955, FBI/NAAWP; *Frederick Post*, November 13, 1954; *Salisbury Times*, March 30, 1955; *Reno Evening Gazette*, April 7, 1955.

77. *Wilmington Morning News*, July 18, 1955; *Salisbury Times*, July 18, 1955.

78. *Kannapolis (N.C.) Daily Independent*, October 14, 1955; *Washington Post*, October 27, 28, 1954.

79. Special Agent in Charge, Houston, to J. Edgar Hoover, October 2, 1957, FBI/BB.

80. Special Agent in Charge, Houston, to J. Edgar Hoover, August 7, 1958, May 14, 1958, FBI/BB; *Beaumont Enterprise*, August 6, 1958; *Washington Post*, August 7, 1958. Bowles later filed an unsuccessful petition for a writ of habeas corpus. *Bryant William Bowles, Jr. v. State of Texas* 366 F.2d 734 (September 19, 1966).

81. Bryant W. Bowles, Jr., obituary, *Tampa Tribune*, April 17, 1997.

82. For more information on Miller, see "The Fearmongers," *Life*, February 7, 1964. The literature on Duke is substantial, but a good starting point is Swain, *The New White Nationalism in America*.

83. *Wisconsin Rapids Daily Tribune*, November 14, 1955.

84. Bill Bags, "A House on Sand", reproduction of unidentified Florida newspaper, November 1954, box 8, folder: "Bowles, Bryant, 1954–1955," Jewish Community Relations Council of Minnesota, Minnesota Historical Society, St. Paul.

85. *Florence Morning News*, August 6, 1954.

86. *Florence Morning News*, March 12, 1955, August 18, 1963.

87. *Florence Morning News*, March 1, 1955. For a similar expression of concern about the NAAWP, see the *Gastonia Gazette*, October 25, 1963.

88. Fleming, "Resistance Movements and Racial Desegregation," 45.

89. *Florence Morning News*, August 29, 1955.

90. Charlotte office report, date illegible, FBI/NAAWP; *Washington Post*, September 14, 1957.

91. "Integration Squeeze Play," *The Citizens' Council*, March 1959, 2; "Unbalanced," *The Citizens' Council*, August 1957, 4. See also Don Whelpley, "Brainwashed Southerners Fall for 'Liberal' Bait Then Claim 'Persecution,'" *The Citizens' Council*, August 1958. All in Hall-Hoag Collection, Series 2, Roll 4.

92. *Statesville (N.C.) Record & Landmark*, October 11, 1954.

93. Workman, *Case for the South*, 18–19, 246. For further information about the banning of Bowles, see Papers of the NAACP, Part 18. Special Subjects, 1940–1955,

Series C: General Office Files: Justice Department-White Supremacy, reel 33, frame 737.

94. Clift et al., *Negro Education in America*, 205.

95. Harold C. Fleming and John Constable, "Integration and the Schools," confidential report, November 1956, 15, box A100, folder 6, General Office File, National Association for the Advancement of Colored People Collection, Library of Congress, Washington, D.C.

96. *Chicago Defender*, October 23, 1954. See also the opinion of Arnold De Mills in the same issue.

97. Rorty, "Desegregation Along the Mason-Dixon Line," 502; Miami office report, January 25, 1955, FBI/NAAWP; *Jacksonville Journal*, November 12, 16, 17, 1954.

98. FBI Charlotte, North Carolina Office, Memorandum, March 11, 1958, FBI/BB.

Chapter Two. A Collapse of Law and Order

1. *The Intruder* (Dir. Roger Corman, Los Altos Productions, Inc., 1961). This powerful work of social realism is all the more impressive coming from a director who, at the time, was more well known for such low-budget classics as *Teenage Caveman* (1958), *She-Gods of Shark Reef* (1958), and *Attack of the Giant Leeches* (1959).

2. Garrow, "Foreshadowing the Future," 26–28.

3. See, for example, his report in the *Winnipeg Free Press*, September 8, 1956.

4. *Atlanta Independent*, September 29, 1957. Examples of international news coverage include *London Times*, September 8, 1956; *Le Monde* (Paris), September 4, 6, 1956; *Daily Gleaner* (Kingston, Jamaica), August 31, September 3–8, 1956.

5. *Chicago Defender*, September 15, 1956.

6. McClelland, "A Structural Analysis of Desegregation," 301.

7. *Joheather McSwain v. County Board of Education, Anderson County* [104 F. Supp. 861].

8. *United States of America v. Frederick John Kasper, et al.*, Court's Instructions to the Jury, July 23, 1957, box 51, folder 2, Brainard and Frances Cheney Papers, Special Collections and University Archives, Jean and Alexander Heard Library, Vanderbilt University, Nashville.

9. *Report of the United States Commission on Civil Rights*, 218.

10. Graham, *Crisis in Print*, 63–64. Only one of the eight newspapers in the four main cities of Tennessee, the *Chattanooga News-Free Press*, condemned the *Brown* decision. Bergeron et al., *Tennesseans and Their History*, 293.

11. Bartley, *Rise of Massive Resistance*, 73, 79–80; Greene, *Lead Me On*, 195–96; Redd, "Educational Desegregation in Tennessee," 341–42; John Hope, II, "Trends in Patterns of Race Relations in the South Since May 17, 1954," *Phylon* 17 (second quarter, 1956): 106.

12. Badger, "Southerners Who Refused to Sign the Southern Manifesto," 517–34.

13. *Southern School News*, October 1956, 6, November 1956, 6. The cartoon originally appeared in the *Memphis Commercial Appeal*.

14. Redd, "The Status of Educational Desegregation in Tennessee," 332.

15. Only twelve of the fifteen students actually turned up on the first day of school: Jo Ann Allen, Bobby Cain, Theresa Caswell, Minnie Ann Dickey, Gail Ann Epps, Ronnie Hayden, Alva J. McSwain, Edward Lee Soles, Maurice Soles, Regina Turner, Alfred Williams, and Charles Williams.

16. *Southern School News*, July 1956, 7; Graham, *Crisis in Print*, 92–93; Brittain, "A Case Study of the Problems of Racial Integration," 55.

17. *New York Times*, August 27, September 16, 1956.

18. *New York Herald Tribune*, August 28, 1956.

19. *New York Times*, August 29, 1956; *Clinton Courier News*, August 30, 1956.

20. Adamson, "Few Black Voices Heard," 40.

21. *Memphis Commercial Appeal*, August 30, 1956; *Southern School News*, November 1956, 6; Injunctive and Contempt Proceedings in Clinton, Tennessee: Summary of Facts, January 21, 1957, American Civil Liberties Union Archives, 1917–1995, Series 3, box 1106, folder 22, MC#001, Department of Rare Books and Special Collections, Princeton University Library (hereafter cited as ACLU Archives).

22. *New Orleans Times Picayune*, September 1, 1956; *Memphis Commercial Appeal*, August 31, 1956. The other persons named in the injunction were Tom Carter, Max Stiles, Ted Hankins, and Leo Bolton.

23. *Memphis Commercial Appeal*, September 1, 1956.

24. Anderson, *Eisenhower, Brownell, and the Congress*, 126–27; Holden et al., *Clinton, Tennessee*, 15.

25. Lewis et al., *Second American Revolution*, 41.

26. Greene, *Lead Me On*, 204–6; *Victoria (Tex.) Advocate*, September 2, 1956; *Jackson Daily News*, September 1, 2, 3, 1956.

27. *Clinton Courier-News*, September 6, 1956; *Chicago Defender*, September 5, 11, 1956; *Jackson Daily News*, September 4, 1956; *New Orleans Times-Picayune*, September 4, 1956.

28. *Clinton Courier-News*, September 27, 1956.

29. *Birmingham News*, September 15, 1956; *Oshkosh Daily Northwestern*, September 15, 1956; *Facts* 13 (April–May 1958): 129.

30. Muse, *Ten Years of Prelude*, 99; *Moberly (Mo.) Monitor*, September 25, 1956.

31. *New York Times*, November 9, 21, 1956; *Nevada State Journal*, November 13, 1956; *Nashville Tennessean*, November 21, 1956; ADL Bulletin, December 1956, 6–7; *Southern School News*, December 1956, 5.

32. Anderson, *Children of the South*, 11, 62; *Clinton Courier News*, November 29, 1956; *New York Times*, November 28, 29, December 1, 1956; *Report of the United States Commission on Civil Rights*, 220.

33. *Nashville Tennessean*, December 3, 1956; Burk, *Eisenhower Administration and Black Civil Rights*, 170; Brownell with Burke, *Advising Ike*, 204.

34. *Clinton Courier News*, December 6, 1956.

35. Greene, *Lead Me On*, 209; *The Nation*, December 22, 1956, 531–32.

36. *Nashville Tennessean*, December 6, 1956; *New York Times*, December 11, 1956; Adamson, "Few Black Voices Heard," 37.

37. *New York Times*, February 16, 1957.

38. *Brownsville Herald*, February 20, 1957; *Corpus Christi Times*, February 20, 1957. On the Cole episode, see Ward, "Race, Politics, and Culture."

39. *New York Times*, May 25, 1957; *Southern School News*, June 1957, 15, and September 1957, 3.

40. "Frederick John Kasper," Washington Field Office, April 24, 1959, 2–3, 5, 12, John Kasper Federal Bureau of Investigation File, Section 1 (hereinafter cited as JK/FBI); *Philadelphia Inquirer*, February 5, 1957; William A. Emerson, Jr., "Touring With a Rabble-Rouser," *Newsweek*, March 18, 1957, 38; James Rorty, "Hate Monger With Literary Trimmings: From Avant-Garde Poetry to Rear-Guard Politics," *Commentary* 22 (December 1956): 533–34.

41. Torrey, *Roots of Treason*, 228; John Kasper to Ezra Pound, October 30, 1951, Pound Mss. II, Manuscripts Department, Lilly Library, Indiana University.

42. "Frederick John Kasper," Washington Field Office, April 24, 1959, 12–13, Section 1, JK/FBI.

43. "Frederick John Kasper," Washington Field Office, May 15, 1951, Pound Mss. II.

44. "Frederick John Kasper," Washington Field Office, May 31, 1951, Pound Mss. II.

45. *Bigotry in Action: Organized Anti-Semitism in the United States Today*, 6, Arkansas Council of Human Relations (Manuscript Collection MS Ar4 ACHR), box 18, folder 170, Special Collections, University of Arkansas Libraries, Fayetteville; Rorty, "Hate Monger," 535; Carpenter, *A Serious Character*, 800–801; Hickman, *Geometry of Modernism*, 128–29; Stock, *Life of Ezra Pound*, 430; Tytell, *Ezra Pound*, 307, 312; John Kasper to James Horton, June 30, 1951, Pound Mss. II; ADL Bulletin, September 1956, 7.

46. Elliott Erwitt, "Demonstrators during the trial of Julius Rosenberg and his wife Ethel, the first US civilians to be executed for espionage" (Washington, D.C., 1953), PAR 156665 (EREI953XXX W00189/27); "The Rosenberg trial" (Washington, D.C., 1953), PAR167583 (EREI953XXX W00183/23), www.magnumphotos.com/Archive/C.aspx?VP=XSpecific_MAG.AgencyHome_VPage&pid=2K7O3R1VX08V.

47. *Congressional Record*, Daily Digest of the 84th Cong., 2nd sess., Vol. 102-Part 13, D102; Subcommittee on Territories and Insular Affairs of the Committee on Interior and Insular Affairs, *Alaska Mental Health*, 168; Ellsworth and Harris, *American Right Wing*, 17.

48. Carpenter, *A Serious Character*, 828. See also Mullins, *This Difficult Individ-*

ual, 22, 312. It is important to note that Mullins was a rival for the affection of Pound, who had fallen out badly with Kasper. John Kasper to Ezra Pound, November 7, 20, December 31, 1952, Pound Mss. II.

49. Drew Pearson, "Washington Merry-Go Round," quoted in Washington Field Office, Correlation Summary, April 5, 1961, JK/FBI, Section 3, 139; Stock, *Life of Ezra Pound*, 432.

50. Thayer, *Farther Shores of Politics*, 18; Rockwell, *This Time The World*, 112. See also Arthur Gordon, "Intruder in the South," *Look*, February 19, 1957, 27.

51. Henderson, "Pound, Sweden and the Nobel Prize," 162–63.

52. Tryphonopoulos and Surette, *'I Cease Not to Yowl,'* 236, 235. The actual date of Confederate defeat was not 1864, but 1865.

53. John Kasper, "John Kasper Fine and Costs," January 3, 1960, JK/FBI, Section 2. One of the best assessments of the political philosophy of Pound is Surette, *Pound in Purgatory*.

54. Gould, *Mismeasure of Man*, 42–50, quotations on 46 and 48.

55. Kasper, *Gists from Agassiz*.

56. *Chicago Defender*, August 16, 1958.

57. Kasper, "Segregation or Death," 2.

58. Tytell, *Ezra Pound*, 307; Torrey, *Roots of Treason*, 229. For further observations about the relationship between Pound and Kasper, see Norman, *Ezra Pound*, 250–53.

59. David Rattray, "Weekend with Ezra Pound," *The Nation*, November 16, 1957, 346.

60. Brittain, "A Case Study of the Problems of Racial Integration," 269; *Facts* 11 (September 1956): 88; *Washington Post and Times Herald*, June 6, 1956; *Washington Star*, June 16, 1956; *Chicago Defender*, June 23, 1956; Martin, *Deep South Says Never*, 101. The other founding members of the Seaboard White Citizens' Council were Fred B. Hockett, George Fleming, and Edgar Johnson. *Stevens Point (Wis.) Daily Journal*, March 13, 1957.

61. *New York Times*, July 15, 1956; *Chicago Sunday Tribune*, July 15, 1956; Washington Field Office, "Frederick John Kasper," April 1959, 36–37, Section 1, JK/FBI; "Correlation Summary: Frederick John Kasper, Jr.," May 4, 1961, 8, Section 3, JK/FBI.

62. *Report of the United States Commission on Civil Rights 1959*, 279; Wilma Dykeman and James Stokely, "Failure of a Hate Mission," *The Nation*, April 20, 1957, 342.

63. Friedman, "Virginia Jewry in the School Crisis," 20; Korey and Lubin, "Arlington—Another Little Rock?" 204; Dan Wakefield, "Battle of Charlottesville: Symbol of the Divided South," *The Nation*, September 15, 1956, 212; Dierenfield, "One 'Desegregated Heart,'" 251–53, 276; Boyle, *Desegregated Heart*, 253–54; Lassiter and Lewis, *Moderates' Dilemma*), 83; ADL Bulletin (September 1956): 7; *Nevada State Journal*, February 7, 1957.

64. Knoxville Office report, November 25, 1960, Section 3, JK/FBI.

65. *See It Now*, January 6, 1957.

66. *Miami Herald*, March 2, 1957.

67. I have based my ideas about "reactionary populism" on the interpretation of a number of scholars, including Canovan, *Populism*; Kazin, *Populist Persuasion*; and Lipset and Raab, *Politics of Unreason*.

68. David Halberstam, "The Town That Became 'Everybody's Test Tube,'" *The Report*, January 10, 1957, 33–34; Stan Opotowsky, "Dixie Dynamite: The Inside Story of the White Citizens Councils" (1957; reprint of news stories originally published in the *New York Post*), Papers of the National Association for the Advancement of Colored People, ed. August Meier, 28 parts (Frederick, Md.: University Publications of America, 1982), Part 20: White Resistance and Reprisals, 1956–1965, Reel 13, Group III, Series A, Administrative File, frame 675; McClelland, "A Structural Analysis of Desegregation," 302, 307. See also Clift et al., *Negro Education in America*, 222; Don Shoemaker, "With All Deliberate Speed," *New Republic*, September 23, 1957, 15.

69. Holden et al., *Tennessee*.

70. Daniel, *Lost Revolutions*, 200.

71. Dykeman and Stokely, *Neither Black Nor White*, 127.

72. Lovett, *Civil Rights Movement in Tennessee*, 43.

73. *Miami Herald*, March 3, 1957, 28A; *New York Times*, July 24, 1957, 12. Further references to the class identity of Kasper's supporters can be found in *The Crisis* 64 (January 1957): 35; Halberstam, "The Town That Became 'Everybody's Test Tube,'" 34; Nikitin, *Ultras in the USA*, 186.

74. *See It Now*, January 6, 1957. Kasper expounded on his affinity with working people in one of the newspaper interviews he gave at the time. "I can talk much easier to a person who works with hands and either produces something or transports or helps to grow something, because they have horse-sense and independent thought. They're not—as the intellectual—trying to imitate someone else and someone else's living." *Birmingham News*, September 13, 1956.

75. Hofstadter, *Anti-Intellectualism in American Life*, especially Chapter One.

76. *Nashville Tennessean*, September, 13, 14, 1956; Halberstam, "White Citizens Councils," 302.

77. Dykeman and Stokely, *Neither Black Nor White*, 127.

78. John Kasper, "Segregation or Death" (n.p., n.d.), box 25, folder 269, Anti-semitic Literature Collection 8. Kasper allegedly declared later that it would be "easier to assassinate them than to impeach them." Nathan D. Shapiro to Editor, *U.S. News & World Report*, January 10, 1957, Papers of the NAACP, Part 3: The Campaign for Educational Equality, Series D: Central Office Records, 1956–1965.

79. Unidentified newspaper clipping, Papers of the NAACP, Part 20: White Resistance and Reprisals, 1956–1965, Reel 13, Group III, Series A, Administrative File, frame 481.

80. *Southern School News*, December 1957, 5; *Washington Post*, July 16, 1957.

81. *Facts* 12 (June–July 1957): 105–6.

82. "Anti-Semitism in the South," *Facts* 13 (April–May 1958): 127–34; *The Crisis* 64 (January 1957): 34; Brittain, "A Case Study of the Problems of Racial Integration," 116; Jerome Bakst, "Angry Young Men of Hate," ADL Bulletin (March 1959): 8; Kasper, "Segregation or Death," 8. Kasper focused most of his venom on Judge Taylor, whom he saw as one of the principal architects of the Jewish conspiracy against the white people of Clinton. "In the old days, he would have been hanged, then taken down and drawn and quartered. And then they would have hoisted him on pikes above the city walls and let the crows eat on him for three or four weeks." *Great Bend Daily Tribune*, December 4, 1958.

83. Carter, *South Strikes Back*, 172–73.

84. "LAST DAYS OF PEACE BETWEEN WHITE AND NIGRA RACES," n.d., box 51, folder 5, Brainard and Frances Cheney Papers, Special Collections and University Archives, Jean and Alexander Heard Library, Vanderbilt University, Nashville, Tenn.

85. FBI Washington Field Office, "Frederick John Kasper," May 24, 1959, 24, JK/FBI; Nathan Perlmutter, "Bombing in Miami: Anti-Semitism and the Segregationists," *Commentary* 25 (June 1958): 502.

86. *Telenews Tennessee*, newsreels T16 #7 and T46 #10, MacDonald & Associates Historical Film Archive, Chicago, Ill. Kasper made similar claims about his status as a defender of constitutional freedom in an appeal for funds to cover his legal costs. "John Kasper Fine and Costs," January 30, 1960, JK/FBI.

87. "Are you a Segregationist?" undated publicity letter, JK/FBI.

88. *The White Sentinel*, September 1956, box 18, folder 6, Florida Legislative Investigation Committee Records, 1954–1965, State Archives of Florida, Tallahassee.

89. *Knoxville News-Sentinel*, September 2, 1956.

90. *Memphis Commercial Appeal*, September 2, 1956. See also Graham, *Crisis in Print*, 99–100.

91. "Victory For Little Bob," *Life*, August 5, 1957, 13; Martin, *Deep South Says Never*, 121; Dykeman and Stokely, *Neither Black Nor White*, 125–26.

92. Winchell, *Where No Flag Flies*, 294.

93. Jack Kershaw, "Address to Citizens of Anderson County, Tenn., 9–1–56," box 51, folder 1, Cheney Papers.

94. James N. Rhea, "Farewell to Uncle Tom," *The Nation*, November 2, 1957, 301; Ellsworth and Harris, *The American Right Wing*, 5; Wakefield, "Battle of Charlottesville," 212; *Clarion Ledger*, May 20, 1957; Shoemaker, *With All Deliberate Speed*, 129; *Miami Herald*, March 8, 1957.

95. "Correlation Summary: Frederick John Kasper, Jr.," May 4, 1961, 67, 75, JK/FBI. NAACP Executive Secretary Roy Wilkins actually ordered a check of membership lists to determine whether Kasper had ever been a member of the organization. He had not. George Thurston (*Tallahassee News*) to Roy Wilkins, February 12, 1957; Roy Wilkins to George Thurston, March 12, 1957, Papers of the NAACP, Part 20:

White Resistance and Reprisals, 1956–1965, Reel 13, Group III, Series A, Administrative File, frame 688.

96. *Washington Post*, July 21, 1957; *New York Times*, July 15, 1957.

97. Shoemaker, *With All Deliberate Speed*, 51; *Washington Post*, July 23, 1957; *Telenews Tennessee*, newsreel T14 #12, MacDonald & Associates.

98. Alan Reitman, Assistant Director, to William J. Hodges, September 17, 1956; Rowland Watts, Staff Counsel, to J. Benjamin Simmons, September 13, 1956; Alan Reitman to Irving Ferman, October 8, 1956; Spencer Coxe, Executive Director, to Louis Joughin, December 14, 1956, ACLU Archives, series 3, box 1106, folder 22.

99. Public Statement on Legal Proceedings Arising From Integration Conflict in Clinton, Tennessee, n.d.; ACLU News Release, February 27, 1957, ACLU Archives, series 3, box 1106, folder 22.

100. A. Philip Randolph and B. F. McLaurin, Brotherhood of Sleeping Car Porters, to Ernest Angell, ACLU Chairman, January 14, 1957. See also the opposition of Socialist Party leader Norman Thomas to Patrick Murphy Malin, January 11, 1957, and February 27, 1957, series 3, box 1106, folder 22, ACLU Archives.

101. *New York Times*, March 23, 1957. The *Times* offers the most detailed narrative account of the trial. See its editions of July 10, 11, 17, 18, 1957.

102. *United States v. Alonzo Bullock, et al.*, No. 1555 Civil, United States District Court for the Eastern District of Tennessee Northern Division.

103. *Washington Post*, July 9, 1957; *New York Times*, July 9, 1957.

104. *United States of America v. Frederick John Kasper, et al.*, Court's Instructions to the Jury, July 23, 1957, box 51, folder 2, Cheney Papers.

105. Eisenhower, *Waging Peace*, 157. Russell further asserted that white southerners would resist the Civil Rights Bill even if it became law. "The concentration camps might as well be prepared, because there will not be prisons enough to lock up the inhabitants of the South." Kennedy, *Jim Crow Guide to the U.S.A.*, 163. See also the expressions of opposition by Senators James Eastland of Mississippi and Russell Long of Louisiana. *Congressional Record*, Vol. 103, Part 9, 85th Cong., 1st sess., 11349 and 12139.

106. *Southern School News*, June 1957, 15, and August 1957, 1; *New York Times*, July 23, 26, 29, 1957; *Washington Post*, August 24, 1957. The six defendants convicted in addition to Kasper were William Brakebill, Lawrence Brantley, Alonzo Bullock, Clyde Cook, Mrs. M. N. Currier, and William H. Till.

107. Martin, *Deep South Says Never*, 162; Wilma Dykeman and James Stokely, "In Clinton, Tennessee," *The Nation*, December 22, 1956; *Richmond Times-Dispatch*, July 24, 1957, 14.

108. Belknap, *Federal Law and Southern Order*, 32.

109. *New York Times*, July 28, 1957; *Southern School News*, April 1957, 12; *Memphis Commercial Appeal*, September 4, 1956.

110. *New York Times*, July 25, 1957.

111. Halberstam, "Town," 35; Anderson, *Children of the South*, 21.

112. Govan and Livingood, *Chattanooga Country*, 502; *Washington Post*, October 6, 7, 9, 10, 11, 13, 1958; *New York Times*, October 7, 16, 1958; *Southern School News*, November 1958, 14; "Frederick John Kasper," Washington Field Office, May 24, 1959, 42; J. Edgar Hoover to FBI Knoxville, Memphis and Washington Field Offices, October 7, 1960; Knoxville Office Report, November 25, 1960, JK/FBI; *New York Times*, October 6, 1958; *Chicago Defender*, October 7, 11, 1958; *Nashville Tennessean*, December 14, 1958.

113. *New York Times*, September 6, 1956.

114. *Zanesville Signal*, December 3, 1956; *New Republic*, December 17, 1956; Steamer, "Presidential Stimulus and School Desegregation," 27–28.

115. Oscar Handlin, "Civil Rights After Little Rock: The Failure of Moderation," *Commentary* 24 (November 1957): 394.

116. *New York Times*, October 7, 16, 1958; *Washington Post*, October 11, 1958.

117. Fine, *American Jewish Year Book* 59, 107; Killian, "Purge of an Agitator," 152; *Newsweek*, March 18, 1957, 36–38; Perlmutter, "Bombing in Miami," 502; unidentified newspaper clipping, Papers of the NAACP, Part 20: White Resistance and Reprisals, 1956–1965, Reel 13, Group III, Series A, Administrative File, frame 480. Fred Hockett was a fifty-one-year-old carpenter. *Danville (Va.) Bee*, March 13, 1957.

118. "Notes on Meeting of Bi-Racial Commission, November 20, 1956" (typescript); Joe Grotegut to Governor Collins, September 11, 1956, box 33, folder 4, Race Relations, Governor's Advisory Commission on, Governor LeRoy Collins Correspondence, 1955–1961, Florida State Archives, Tallahassee, Series 776.

119. "Meeting of Governor's Advisory Commission on Bi-Racial Problems, March 5, 1957", box 117, folder 1, Collins Correspondence.

120. *Stevens Point Daily Journal*, March 9, 1957; *Miami Herald*, March 1, 1957; Killian, "Purge of an Agitator," 154.

121. *Miami Herald*, March 1, 1957; Belknap, *Federal Law and Southern Order*, 32.

122. "Resolution of the Legislative Investigating Committee of the Florida State Legislature, February 26, 1957," Papers of the NAACP, Part 20: White Resistance and Reprisals, 1956–1965, Reel 7, Group III, Series A, Administrative File, frame 325.

123. *New York Amsterdam News*, September 29, 1956.

124. "Hymn for Laurie Poo," in Harris, *Leroi Jones/Amiri Baraka Reader*, 9.

125. *Miami Herald*, March 3, 5, 6, 9, 1957; *New Republic*, March 25, 1957; *Stevens Point Daily Journal*, March 12, 1957; Dykeman and Stokely, "Failure of a Hate Mission," 342–43; Newton, *Invisible Empire*, 151–52. It is unclear whether Henry was the same "intimate girl friend" cited in the *New York Amsterdam News* story.

126. *For Your Information* 4 (October 1959).

127. *New York Post*, March 12, 1957; *New York Journal-American*, March 13, 1957; *Newsweek*, March 25, 1957; *Facts* 13 (February–March 1958): 113; "Kasper's Past is Catching Up," *Labor Reports* (Jewish Labor Committee), April 1957.

128. "Membership Application, N.A.A.C.P (National Association for the Advancement of Colored People," SCR ID # 2–79–1–104–1–1–1, Sovereignty Commission Online, Mississippi Department of Archives and History Digital Collections, http://mdah.state.ms.us/arlib/contents/er/sovcom/result.php (last accessed December 1, 2006).

Chapter Three. Into the Abyss

1. *Middlesboro (Ky.) Daily News*, March 7, 1957; *Chicago Defender*, September 12, 1956.

2. *Florence (S.C.) Morning News*, December 3, 1956; *Charleston Gazette*, December 4, 1956; Carmichael and James, *Louisville Story*, 108–12.

3. *Kingsport (Tenn.) Times*, December 13, 1956; Carmichael and James, *Louisville Story*, 112.

4. *Kingsport (Tenn.) Times*, January 17, 1957.

5. Jinks, "A Testing of Ideals," 86. Jinks worked as a reporter for the *Charlotte Observer*.

6. Bagwell, *School Desegregation in the Carolinas*, 108.

7. *New York Times*, August 30, September 2, 1957; *Arkansas Gazette*, September 1, 3, 1957; *Charlotte Observer*, September 2, 1957; Fine and Sloan, *American Jewish Year Book 59*, 57; Dan L. Morrill, "The Civil Rights Revolution in Mecklenburg County," http://www.cmhpf.org/educationcivilrights.htm (last accessed July 31, 2006).

8. *Arkansas Democrat*, August 29, 1957. For similar efforts by Little Rock segregationists to dissociate themselves from Kasper, see *Arkansas Gazette*, August 30, 1957, and *New York Times*, August 30, 1957.

9. Redd, "Educational Desegregation in Tennessee," 339.

10. Redd, "The Status of Educational Desegregation in Tennessee," 331; *Nashville Tennessean*, May 18, 1954; Graham, "Desegregation in Nashville," 140, 142.

11. Doyle, *Nashville Since the 1920s*, 237; Will D. Campbell, memorandum to All Human Relations Personnel in the South, August 20, 1957, Papers of the NAACP, Part 3: The Campaign for Educational Equality, Series D: Central Office Records, 1956–1965.

12. Lewis with D'Orso, *Walking with the Wind*, 80–81; Doyle, *Nashville*, 223–24; Redd, "Status of Education Desegregation," 324.

13. Halberstam, *The Children*, 20, 22, 111–12; Lovett, *Rights Movement in Tennessee*, 54; Muse, *Ten Years of Prelude*, 116; Graham, "Desegregation in Nashville," 137; Doyle, *Nashville*, 224–25, 228; *Southern School News*, April 1957, 12.

14. *Robert W. Kelley, et al. v. Board of Education of Nashville, 139 F. Supp. 578*; Redd, "Status of Education Desegregation," 324, 328; Graham, "Desegregation in Nashville," 135, 143–44.

15. Javits, *Discrimination—U.S.A.*, 191–92; *Southern School News*, December 1956, 5, August 1957, 6; Muse, *Ten Years of Prelude*, 118; Doyle, *Nashville*, 235; *Nashville Globe and Independent*, September 6, 1957.

16. Van Til, *My Way of Looking At It*, 175–77; Powell, *Black Monday's Children*, 59–60; *Southern School News*, September 1957, 3; *Nashville Globe and Independent*, August 2, 1957; *New York Times*, August 24, 26, 1957.

17. Doyle, *Nashville*, 237; *New York Times*, August 23, 24, 1957; *Southern School News*, September 1957, 6, and October 1957, 6; Graham, "Desegregation in Nashville," 142, 150. Quotation from Bass in *New York Times*, August 28, 1957.

18. Washington Field Office, "Frederick John Kasper, Jr., aka, John Kasper, John Rutko, Tom Dooley, Jay," April 24, 1959, 31, John Kasper Federal Bureau of Investigation File (hereinafter cited as JK/FBI), Section 1; *Nashville Globe and Independent*, August 6, 1957; *New York Times*, September 24, 25, 26, 30, 1957.

19. Holden, *A First Step Towards School Integration*, 5, 7–8; Bergeron et al., *Tennesseans and Their History*, 296.

20. *New York Times*, August 28, 29, 1957; Sarratt, *Ordeal of Desegregation*, 161; Toby, "Bombing in Nashville," 388; John Kasper, "Last Days of Peace Between White and Nigra Races," Brainard and Frances Cheney Papers, box 51, folder 1, Special Collections and University Archives, Jean and Alexander Heard Library, Vanderbilt University, Nashville.

21. Graham, "Desegregation in Nashville," 151; *New York Times*, September 8, 1957.

22. Kempton, *America Comes of Middle Age*, 171.

23. Kempton, *America Comes of Middle Age*, 170–71.

24. *Chicago Defender*, September 10, 16, 1957; *New York Times*, September 10, 1957; *Washington Post*, September 10, 1957.

25. *New York Times*, September 10, 1957; Kennedy, *Jim Crow Guide to the U.S.A.*, 103; *Washington Post*, September 11, 1957.

26. *Time*, September 23, 1957; *New York Times*, September 11, 1957; *Southern School News*, October 1957, 6; *Life*, September 23, 1957; *Santa Fe New Mexican*, September 10, 1957; Unknown to A. Rose, November 3, 1958, JK/FBI, Section 1.

27. *Chronicle-Telegram* (Elyria, Ohio), September 11, 1957; *Chicago Defender*, September 12, 1957; *New York Times*, September 13, 1957; *Newport Daily News*, September 13, 1957; *Washington Post*, September 13, 17, 1957; *Southern School News*, October 1957, 6; Unknown to A. Rose, November 3, 1958, JK/FBI, Section 1. The other persons named in the restraining order were Emmett Carr, Vincent Albert Crimmons, Margaret L. Conquest, James Harris, Paul McConnell, John Mercurio, J. A. Stinson, Mary B. Stinson, and Reverend Fred Stroud.

28. *Evening Sentinel* (Holland, Mich.), October 18, 1957; *New York Post*, October 18, 1957; *Arkansas Democrat*, September 17, 1957; *Washington Post*, September 18, 1957; *Chicago Defender*, September 19, 1957; *New York Times*, September 19, 1957; Norris, "Red Roses and Redstones," 187.

29. *U.S. News & World Report*, September 20, 1957.

30. *Nashville Globe and Independent*, August 30, September 27, 1957.

31. Holden, *A First Step Towards Integration*, 3.

32. Kasper, "Last Days of Peace Between White and Nigra Races."

33. Bandura, *Self-Efficacy*, 3, 499–501 (quotation, 501).

34. Newsreel T49 #14, MacDonald & Associates Historical Film Archive, Chicago, Ill.; Wilma Dykeman and James Stokely, "On the Road with John Kasper," *New Republic*, December 1, 1958, 14.

35. *Life*, September 23, 1957; *Southern School News*, September 1957, 1.

36. Cope, "A Thorn in the Side?" 160–90; Godfrey, "Bayonets, Brainwashing, and Bathrooms," 42–67; Anderson, "Massive Resistance, Violence, and Southern Social Relations," 203–20.

37. Dr. Lou H. Silberman, "Report on Nashville: A Community Relations Committee in Action," unpublished typescript, May 4, 1958, Community Relations Committee, 1953–1967, Archives of the Jewish Federation of Nashville and Middle Tennessee. For a further statement that "hate publications from across the country had been distributed in Nashville," see Rabbi William B. Silverman, "We Will Not Yield: The Answer of Prophetic Judaism to Violence, Threats and Dynamite," typescript of sermon, March 28, 1958, Archives of the Jewish Federation of Nashville and Middle Tennessee.

38. Fine, *American Jewish Yearbook 55*, 12.

39. Minutes of meeting to establish a permanent Nashville Community Relations Conference, April 23, 1956, Nelson and Marian D. Fuson Papers, box 3, folder 5, Jean and Alexander Heard Library, Vanderbilt University; Dr. William B. Silverman to Albert Vorspan, October 28, 1957, Papers of the NAACP, Part 3: The Campaign for Educational Equality, Series D: Central Office Records, 1956–1965.

40. Sarna, "The 'Mythical Jew,'" 57–78.

41. For more on the respect that Nashville Jews commanded from the local white community and the compromises needed to attain it, see Spinney, "Jewish Community in Nashville," 225–41.

42. John Kasper, "Annexation Means Integration," reproduced in Special Agent in Charge, Memphis, "Frederick John Kasper, Jr.," memorandum, September 29, 1960, JK/FBI, Section 3.

43. Kasper, Mercurio, and Stroud are among the list of speakers named on a handbill advertising a rally on the day before the admission of black students to formerly all-white schools. Tennessee White Citizens' Council, "Keep Our Schools White," September 8, 1957, Brainard and Frances Cheney Papers, box 51, folder 5.

44. *Stevens Point Daily Journal*, March 9, 1957.

45. Randall Balmer, "Fundamentalist With Flair," *Christianity Today*, May 21, 2002; "History of Bible Presbyterian Church," http://www.bpc.org/synod/minutes/beacon_1939_08_31.html (last accessed September 12, 2006).

46. Martin, *With God On Our Side*, 79; Special Agent in Charge, Newark, to

J. Edgar Hoover, March 18, 1958, Section 1, JK/FBI. For a fuller evaluation of Carl McIntire, see Forster and Epstein, *Danger on the Right*, 100–114.

47. Kempton, *America Comes of Middle Age*, 175. A photograph of Stroud can be found in the *Oxnard Press-Courier*, September 16, 1957.

48. *Southern School News*, August 1957, 6; McGill, *The South and the Southerner*, 272–73.

49. Tennessee White Citizens' Council application form, Cheney Papers, box 51, folder 5.

50. Harvey, *Freedom's Coming*, 239–43; Holden, *A First Step Towards School Integration*, 3.

51. Newsreel T54 #6, MacDonald & Associates Historical Film Archive.

52. *For Your Information* 4 (October 1959). For more information on Dilling and Van Hyning, see Jeansonne, *Women of the Far Right*.

53. Washington Field Bureau, "Frederick John Kasper, Jr.," April 24, 1959, 52–53, Section 1, JK/FBI; *Chillicothe (Mo.) Constitution-Tribune*, February 17, 1959. Bader is briefly mentioned in Horne, *Class Struggle in Hollywood*, 131.

54. Doyle, *Nashville*, 239; *Chester (Pa.) Times*, September 14, 1957; *Gettysburg Times*, September 14, 1957; *New York Times*, September 15, 1957; *Washington Post*, September 15, 1957; *Southern School News*, October 1957, 3; "Frederick John Kasper," Washington Field Office, April 1959, 39, and Knoxville Bureau, memorandum, December 13, 1960, JK/FBI, Section 1. One author claims that seven Klansmen were imprisoned for the bombing of Hattie Cotton School, but I have found no evidence to support this assertion. Newton, *The FBI and the KKK*, 63.

55. *Nashville Tennessean*, September 11, 1957; Halberstam, *The Children*, 55; *New York Times*, September 12, 1957. Anna Holden of the Congress of Racial Equality also recounted how one African American woman turned a shotgun on whites who attempted to break into her home. Holden, *A Step Towards Integration*, 12.

56. *Nashville Banner*, September 9, 1957.

57. *Southern School News*, October 1957, 6.

58. *Southern School News*, August 1957, 6; Muse, *Ten Years of Prelude*, 118.

59. Muse, *Ten Years of Prelude*, 121.

60. See, for instance, E. Thomas Wood, "Nashville Now and Then: An Explosive Moment," *Nashville Post*, September 7, 2007, and John Egerton, "16 'Little Pioneers' Paved Way," *The Tennessean*, September 9, 2007.

61. *Chicago Defender*, May 16, 1957; *Southern School News*, June 1957, 15, October 1957, 6; Holden, *A First Step Towards School Integration*, 11, 13.

62. Campbell, *Forty Acres and a Goat: A Memoir*, 50.

63. *Nashville Banner*, March 17, 1958; *Nashville Tennessean*, March 17, 1958; "Wilkins Asks Funds for Bombed Jewish Center," press release, March 21, 1958, Papers of the NAACP, Part 20: White Resistance and Reprisals, 1956–1965, Reel 12, Group III, Series A, Administrative File, frames 006–007.

64. *Nashville Tennessean*, March 17, 1958.

Notes to Chapter Three

65. Silverman, "We Will Not Yield."

66. Nashville Community Relations Conference, "Report on Nashville 1960: Its Problems and Possibilities", March 30–31, 1960," box 3, folder 7, Fuson Papers.

67. Unknown (name deleted) to John Kasper, n.d., JK/FBI, Section 1. The author of this letter also distributed copies to the FBI, segregationist groups, and civil rights organizations.

68. Rabbi William B. Silverman, letter to congregation, March 21, 1958, Archives of the Jewish Federation of Nashville and Middle Tennessee.

69. Memorandum, "The March 16 Bombings at Miami and Nashville," March 31, 1958, Material on bombings of Jewish institutions in the South and in Illinois, HVBS, Subject Files Collection, American Jewish Committee Archives, http://ajcarchives.org/AJCArchive/DigitalArchive.aspx (last accessed November 19, 2007).

70. Silverman, "We Will Not Yield"; *Intermountain Jewish News* (Denver, Colo.), April 18, 1958.

71. *New York Times*, June 12, August 2, 1958; *Miami Herald*, July 30, 1958; *Miami News*, July 31, 1958; *New York Post*, August 3, 1958; *Zanesville (Ohio) Times Recorder*, August 2, 1958.

72. *Zanesville Times Recorder*, August 2, 1958.

73. "Summary of a Survey on White Citizens' Council, November, 1958," Solomon Andhil Fineberg Papers, Manuscript Collection No. 149, box 4, folder 2, American Jewish Archives, Cincinnati, Ohio.

74. *Nashville Banner*, August 25, 1958; *Southern School News*, September 1958, 9–11; Washington Field Office, "Frederick John Kasper," April 1959, JK/FBI Section 1.

75. John Kasper, "John Kasper Appeal," May 11, 1959, reproduced in Washington Field Office, "Frederick John Kasper, Jr.," August 6, 1959, 13, Section 1, JK/FBI; *Southern School News*, December 1958, 13; January 1959, 7; Dykeman and Stokely, "On the Road with John Kasper," 13.

76. *Denver Post*, December 1, 1958.

77. *Southern School News*, April 1959, 9, May 1959, 5, June 1959, 5; Special Agent in Charge, Memphis, to J. Edgar Hoover, May 5, 1959; Special Agent in Charge, Memphis, to J. Edgar Hoover, May 13, 1959, JK/FBI, Section 2.

78. Washington Field Bureau memorandum, August 6, 1959, JK/FBI, Section 2.

79. *New York Times*, June 30, July 28, 1959; *Montgomery Advertiser*, July 17, 1959; *Washington Post*, July 17, 1959.

80. *New York Times*, January 1, 1960; *John Kasper v. State of Tennessee*, Petition for a Writ of Certiorari to the Supreme Court of Tennessee and Answer to Petition for Writ of Certiorari, Supreme Court, October Term, 1959, JK/FBI Section 2.

81. Special Agent in Charge, Jacksonville, to J. Edgar Hoover, July 28, 1959, JK/FBI, Section 2; *New York Times*, January 17, 1960; *New York Herald-Tribune*, January 17, 1960; Correlation Summary, April 5, 1961, JK/FBI, Section 3.

82. *New York Herald Tribune*, October 13, 1958; *New York Mirror*, April 7, 1960. A copy of the letter made its way into the hands of journalist Drew Pearson, who quoted from it at length.

83. *For Your Information* 5 (June 1960): 2; *Chicago Tribune*, July 16, 1960; *The Post* (Frederick, Md.), July 18, 1960.

84. John Kasper to Ezra Pound, [?] 2, 1952; John Kasper to Ezra Pound, May 25, 1962; Olga Rudge, lettercard, 1974; Ezra Pound Papers Addition, YCAL MSS 53, box 9, folder 210, Beinecke Rare Book and Manuscript Library, Yale University.

85. *Chicago Defender*, March 5, 1964.

86. Special Agent in Charge, Memphis, memorandum, August 1, 1962, Section 4, JK/FBI; Special Agent in Charge, Philadelphia, to J. Edgar Hoover, September 7, Section 3, JK/FBI1960; Special Agent in Charge, Memphis, "Frederick John Kasper, Jr.," September 29, 1960, Section 3, JK/FBI.

87. *Facts* 13 (October–November 1958): 127.

88. "Kasper For President" (Birmingham, Ala.: National States Rights Party, n.d.), Group Research, Inc. Records 1955–1996, Series I: Topical, 1955–1996, box 186, Columbia Rare and Manuscript Library, Columbia University, New York.

89. *Louisville Courier-Journal*, March 2, 1964; *Chicago Tribune*, March 31, 1964; "Kasper for President," petition to Florida county registrars, Florida Legislative Committee, box 18, folder 13, Florida State Archives, Tallahassee; Special Agent in Charge, Memphis, Report: "Frederick John Kasper," June 18, 1964, 4, Section 4, JK/FBI.

90. *Miami Herald*, October 15, 1964.

91. Fine and Himmelfarb, *American Jewish Year Book 66*, 205; *Birmingham Post-Herald*, November 19, 1964; *Elyria Chronicle-Telegram*, December 3, 1958; *Great Bend Daily Tribune*, December 4, 1958.

92. *For Your Information*, March 1962; Special Agent in Charge, Washington Field Office, to J. Edgar Hoover, September 15, 1961, JK/FBI, Section 4; Special Agent in Charge, Richmond, to J. Edgar Hoover, October 7, 1961, JK/FBI, Section 4; John Kasper to Ezra Pound, May 25, 1962, box 9, folder 210, Ezra Pound Collection, Beinecke Library; Laird Wilcox to author, February 2, 2004, and February 4, 2004; Ruthanne Fullerton to author, February 9, 2004, and February 10, 2004.

93. Kempton, *America Comes of Middle Age*, 174. The attempt to convey southern dialect sadly betrayed Kempton's patronizing attitude even toward white moderates in the region.

94. Dykeman and Stokely, "On the Road with John Kasper," 14; Stan Opotowsky, "Dixie Dynamite: The Inside Story of the White Citizens Councils," Papers of the NAACP, Part 20: White Resistance and Reprisals, 1956–1965, Reel 13, Group III, Series A, Administrative File, frame 673. See also the evaluation of Arthur Gordon, "Intruder in the South," *Look*, February 19, 1957, 28, 30.

95. Kempton, *America Comes of Middle Age*, 174–75.

96. "Clinton Ballad," in Brittain, "A Case Study of the Problems of Racial Integration," 281.

97. Hoffman, "Why Is Terrorism So Difficult to Define?" 9.

98. A. Rosen to Mr Belmont, March 12, 1963, Section 4, JK/FBI.

Chapter Four. Fighting the Hidden Force

1. *Montgomery Independent*, October 24, 2003; *New York Times*, January 25, 2004; *Montgomery Advertiser*, November 5, 1996. The book that both reflected and re-inforced wartime nostalgia is Brokaw, *Greatest Generation*.

2. *Montgomery Advertiser*, November 17, 1996.

3. *New York Times*, January 25, 2004. There are a number of excellent studies on the contested meaning of southern history. See Brundage, *Southern Past*; Cobb, *Away Down South*; and Goldfield, *Still Fighting the Civil War*.

4. Solomon Andhil Fineberg, "John O. Beaty and John G. Crommelin," report, August 1972, Series A: Correspondence, 1939–1974, box 2, folder 9, Solomon Andhil Fineberg Papers, American Jewish Archives, Cincinnati, Ohio.

5. Special Agent in Charge, Mobile, Report: "John Geraerdt Crommelin, Jr.," March 17, 1964, John Crommelin Federal Bureau of Investigation File (hereinafter cited as JC/FBI).

6. *Time*, January 24, 1944, August 20, 1945.

7. "John Geraerdt Crommelin, Jr.," JC/FBI; *Washington Post*, October 7, 1949.

8. "John Geraerdt Crommelin, Jr.," JC/FBI; *New York Times*, September 13, 1949; Cook, *Segregationists*, 157–58; Cronenberg, *Forth to the Mighty Conflict*, 134–35.

9. *New York Times*, September 13, 14, 1949; *Washington Post*, October 2, 1949; *Time*, September 5, 26, October 24, 1949; Raymond, *Power at the Pentagon*, 198–200.

10. *Time*, October 17, 1949.

11. *Time*, October 17, November 21, 1949; *New York Times*, April 30, 1950.

12. "Fact Sheet: Rear Admiral John G. Crommelin, Jr. (U.S. Navy, Ret.)" (n.d.), American Jewish Committee John Crommelin File, Jacob and Hilda Blaustein Human Relations Library, New York (hereinafter cited as AJC/JC); *Time*, November 28, 1949, March 27, 1950; *Washington Post*, March 24, 1950.

13. *New York Times*, April 30, 1950; *Washington Post*, May 2, 14, 1950; *Newport (R.I.) News*, November 6, 1950.

14. Webb, "A Southern Liberal Fights for Survival."

15. Fredrickson, *Dixiecrat Revolt*.

16. *Time*, November 6, 1950.

17. *New York Times*, April 11, 1954; Harry Fleischman and Charles F. Wittenstein, "Admiral Crommelin," April 14, 1959, box 2, folder 9, Fineberg Papers.

18. John G. Crommelin, telegram to Earl Warren, April 29, 1954, JC/FBI.

19. *Anniston Star*, April 2, 1954; *Washington Post*, April 25, 1954.

20. Executive Board report, "Anti-Semitism in the U.S. and Problems Dealing With It," October 1960, Anti-Semitism/AJC file, AJC Subject Files Collection.

Reports and memoranda on anti-Semitism in America and AJC's work to combat it, 1960–1962, American Jewish Committee Archives, http://ajcarchives.org/AJCArchive/DigitalArchive.aspx (last accessed November 19, 2007).

21. "Pro-McCarthy Petition Movement entitled TEN MILLION AMERICANS MOBILIZE FOR JUSTICE, November 23, 1954," John Crommelin File, American Jewish Committee Anti-Semitic and Extremist Collection, Jacob and Hilda Blaustein Human Relations Library (hereinafter cited as AJC/Extremist); Norman Jacobs, "Hero to Hatemonger: The Metamorphosis of John G. Crommelin," *ADL Bulletin* (March 1957): 1. The other retired military men who served on the board of Ten Million Americans Mobilize for Justice included Lieutenant General Pedro del Valle, Admiral William H. Standley, and General James A. Van Fleet. *Time*, November 29, 1954.

22. *Chicago Daily Tribune*, November 30, 1954; Turner, *Power on the Right*, 101.

23. Unsigned memos, February 11, 1955, and February 16, 1955, John Crommelin File, AJC/Extremist; Gordon Hall, "Report: Breakfast with Admiral John G. Crommelin, Retired, the Chief-of-Staff of the Ten Million Americans for Mobilizing for Justice, Room 897, Hotel Roosevelt, N.Y. 17, N.Y. Date: Saturday Jan. 15, 1955, Time 9:00 a.m.-12 noon," box 103, Group Research, Inc. Records, Columbia Rare and Manuscript Library, Columbia University, New York.

24. *New York Times*, November 19, 27, 1954; Parmet, *Eisenhower & the American Crusades*, 383.

25. See, for instance, the editorial in *Lee County Bulletin*, December 2, 1954.

26. Norrell, *Reaping the Whirlwind*, 86–87; McMillen, *Citizens' Council*, 41; Jones, "Desegregation of Public Education in Alabama," 167–68.

27. As examples of this interpretative debate, see Grafton and Permaloff, *Big Mules & Branchheads*, 185–86, and Hamilton, *Lister Hill*, 211–13.

28. McMillen, *Citizens' Council*, 45–46.

29. Meacham, *Caged Panther*, 50.

30. Pound, *Cantos*, 751; Terrell, *Companion to the Cantos*, 688.

31. *Montgomery Home News*, January 19, 1961; Memorandum, "John C. Crommelin: Information Concerning," February 6, 1961, JC/FBI.

32. Hamilton, *Lister Hill*, 216; Dan Wakefield, "Eye of the Storm," *The Nation*, May 7, 1960.

33. Allport, *Nature of Prejudice*. See also Lief and Stevenson, "Psychological Aspects of Prejudice."

34. "Mental Health," *The Citizens' Council* (December 1957): 4; "Who's Crazy?" *The Citizens' Council* (December 1957): 2. See also "Head-Docs Say South Is 'Sick'" and "Somebody's Sick, Sick, Sick," *The Citizens' Council* (April 1958): 1, 2.

35. Roche, "Asa/Forrest Carter," 235–36; Sprayberry, "Interrupted Melody," 16–18; Eskew, *But for Birmingham*, 114; McMillen, *Citizens' Council*, 47–48.

36. *Montgomery Advertiser* quoted in *Delta Democrat Times*, July 12, 1956.

37. Ward, "Race, Politics, and Culture," 181–208; *Delta Democrat Times*, December 27, 1956; Roche, "Asa/Forrest Carter," 237–38.

38. *Corpus Christi Caller-Times*, March 11, 1956; *Brownsville Herald*, March 18, 1956; *Anniston Star*, March 25, 1956.

39. Sprayberry, "Interrupted Melody."

40. *The Southerner*, March 1956. Despite his attempts to cultivate the "mountain people" in the northern red hills region of the state, it was actually among the white industrial workforce in and around Birmingham that Carter drew most of his support. In the red hills, African Americans were few in number and posed less of an immediate threat to whites. By contrast, racial tensions rooted in economic competition between black and white industrial workers made Birmingham a significant recruiting ground for militant segregationists. "Fact Sheet: Rear Admiral John G. Crommelin, Jr. (U.S. Navy, Ret.)," American Jewish Committee.

41. John G. Crommelin, "Fellow Americans," May 16, 1956, JC/FBI. Crommelin made a similar point in a letter written to the FBI. John G. Crommelin to J. Edgar Hoover, May 24, 1956, JC/FBI.

42. Transcript of Political Telecast, March 29, 1956, AJC/Extremist; Memorandum, "Rear Admiral John G. Crommelin (Retired)," June 1957, JC/FBI.

43. Transcript of Political Telecast, March 29, 1956, AJC/Extremist; Memorandum, "Rear Admiral John G. Crommelin (Retired)," June 1957, JC/FBI. See also Buswell, *Slavery, Segregation and Scripture*, 52–53.

44. Hamilton, *Lister Hill*, 152, 138, 216–17.

45. *New York Times*, May 4, 1956.

46. Special Agent in Charge, Chicago, to J. Edgar Hoover, December 17, 1959, JC/FBI.

47. S. Andhil Fineberg to Staff Advisory Committee, "The Situation in Alabama—Second Report, July 22, 1960"; Memorandum from S. Andhil Fineberg, "Summary of a Survey on White Citizens Councils and Related Matters" (n.d.), box 2, folder 9, Fineberg Papers; Lesher, *George Wallace*.

48. *New York Times*, March 6, 1956; *Delta Democrat Times*, May 11, 1956; "Fact Sheet: Rear Admiral John G. Crommelin, Jr. (U.S. Navy, Ret.)," 3–4, JC/AJC; Unidentified newspaper clipping, May 11, 1961, Papers of the NAACP, Part 20: White Resistance and Reprisals, 1956–1965, Reel 13, Group III, Series A, Administrative File, frame 922.

49. Elliott, Sr., and D'Orso, *Cost of Courage*, 187.

50. Jacobs, "Hero to Hatemonger," 1.

51. John G. Crommelin, paid political advertisement (n.d.), box 2, folder 9, Fineberg Papers.

52. Jacoway, *Turn Away Thy Son*, 28–45.

53. Badger, "Southerners Who Refused to Sign the Southern Manifesto."

54. *Anniston Star*, May 13, 1956; Crispell, *Testing the Limits*, 115.

55. Sullivan, *Freedom Writer*, 117–18; Hamilton, *Lister Hill*, 217–18.

56. Badger, "The White Reaction to *Brown*," 90.

57. Cheatham, *Bad Boy of Gospel Music*, 141.

58. Carter, *Politics of Rage*, 96.

59. John G. Crommelin to Mr. Finley, March 4, 1960, box 2, folder 9, Fineberg Papers.

60. Bartley, *Rise of Massive Resistance*, 201–2; Thornton, *Dividing Lines*, 99, 108–9.

61. Fine and Sloan, *American Jewish Year Book 59*, 109–10; Fine and Himmelfarb, *American Jewish Year Book 60*, 48; "Crommelin," *Facts* 13 (April–May 1958): 115; Memorandum, "Program to Deal with Organized Anti-Semitic Activity," December 10, 1958, box 2, folder 9, Fineberg Papers.

62. Thornton, *Dividing Lines*, 110–12; *Montgomery Home News*, April 9, 1959.

63. Charles F. Wittenstein to Harry Fleishman, March 23, 1959, AJC/Extremist.

64. *Washington Post*, April 24, 1960.

65. *The Thunderbolt*, n.d., box 1, folder 1, Florida Legislative Investigation Committee Records, 1954–1965, State Archives of Florida, Tallahassee.

66. *Washington Star*, April 13, 1961; Fine and Himmelfarb, *American Jewish Year Book 61*, 43; *New York Times*, October 4, 1960.

67. Fine and Himmelfarb, *American Jewish Year Book 62*, 109. The electoral statistics cited by Fine and Himmelfarb are fractionally different from the data available from the website http://www.ourcampaigns.gov (last accessed May 24, 2007).

68. S. Andhil Fineberg to Edwin J. Lukas, September 39, 1960, box 2, folder 9, Fineberg Papers.

69. *Anniston Star*, January 31, 1960; *New York Times*, May 4, 1960; *Washington Post*, May 4, 1960; *For Your Information* (January 1961).

70. Fine and Himmelfarb, *American Jewish Year Book 64*, 137; *For Your Information* (January 1963); George Kellman to Roy H. Millenson, May 14, 1962, AJC; Hamilton, *Lister Hill*, 242.

71. *Birmingham News*, May 9, 1966; *New York Times*, May 3, 4, 1966; *Birmingham News*, January 31, 1968; *Washington Evening Star*, February 22, 1968; *Portsmouth (N.H.) Herald*, March 11, 1968; Richardson, *A Nation Divided*; "Our Campaigns: NH US President- D Primary," http://www.ourcampaigns.com/cgi-bin/r.cgi/RaceDetail.html?&RaceID=35985 (last accessed January 31, 2004); *Anniston Star*, February 20, 22, 1968; *Atlanta Journal and Constitution*, May 12, 1968; Charles F. Wittenstein to Milton Ellerin, November 20, 1970, AJC/Extremist.

72. John G. Crommelin "Fellow American," campaign newsletter, May 24, 1958, AJC/Extremist.

73. See, for instance, the concerns about Kasper documented in Ward, *Radio and the Struggle for Civil Rights*, 120.

74. For a thorough analysis of these issues, see Walker, *Hate Speech*. Hate speech is discussed in more detail in Chapter Seven.

75. Communications Subcommittee of the Committee on Commerce, United States Senate, *Political Broadcasting*, 151.

76. American Jewish Committee Report, "Southern States: Anti-Semitism," August 1973, box 2, folder 9, Fineberg Papers. Another American Jewish Committee activist corroborated this claim, stating that "The Jews of Alabama are being subjected to an ordeal such as no other Jewish community has experienced in the past dozen years." Irving M. Engel to S. Andhil Fineberg, April 1, 1958, Memoranda and correspondence on anti-Semitic groups, synagogue bombings, letters to President Dwight D. Eisenhower and Senator Clifford Case, HV file, AJC Subject Files Collection, American Jewish Committee Archives, http://ajcarchives.org/AJCArchive/DigitalArchive.aspx (last accessed November 19, 2007).

77. A. Harold Murray and Charles F. Wittenstein, "Field Trip to Montgomery, Alabama, March 16–18, 1959," box 2, folder 9, Fineberg Papers.

78. Edwin J. Lukas, memorandum, July 17, 1957, AJC/Extremist; H. R. Sobel, Rear Admiral U.S. Navy (Re.) to Admiral Arleigh Burke, U.S. Navy, November 18, 1958, AJC/Extremist.

79. Unknown to E. J. Lukas, January 29, 1958, AJC/Extremist; Admiral Arleigh Burke to Admiral H. R. Sobel, December 8, 1958, AJC/Extremist.

80. Solomon A. Fineberg, memorandum, "John O. Beaty and John G. Crommelin," August 1972, box 2, folder 9, Fineberg Papers.

81. Lucien S. Loeb to George Kellman, March 11, 1963; George Kellman to Lucien S. Loeb, March 13, 1963, AJC/Extremist.

82. Edwin J. Lukas to Roy H. Millenson, March 14, 1960, AJC/Extremist; Charles F. Wittenstein to Solomon Andhil Fineberg, March 30, 1962, box 2, folder 9, Fineberg Papers.

83. Fineberg, "Quarantine Treatment," 111–12.

84. A. Harold Murray and Charles F. Wittenstein, "Field Trip to Montgomery, Alabama, March 16–18, 1959," box 2, folder 9, Fineberg Papers.

85. S. Andhil Fineberg to Charles Wittenstein, April 9, 1959, box 2, folder 9, Fineberg Papers.

86. Perlmutter, "Bombing in Miami," 502–3.

87. Special Agent in Charge, Mobile, Alabama, Report: "John Geraerdt Crommelin, Jr.," March 17, 1964, JC/FBI.

88. *Atlanta Journal and Constitution*, November 11, 1956; *Washington News*, June 27, 1957.

89. *Memphis Press-Scimitar*, February 9, 1957; *Knoxville Journal*, March 24, 1957.

90. John G. Crommelin to William F. Knowland, March 8, 1957, W. S. Hoole Special Collections Library, University of Alabama, Tuscaloosa.

91. John G. Crommelin, "Dear Judge," November 1, 1957. Crommelin also sent a telegram with a similar message directly to Eisenhower. See *Wetumpka Herald*, September 26, 1957. The White House did not respond.

92. Nichols, *A Matter of Justice*, 198; Cook, *Segregationists*, 160.

93. John G. Crommelin, "Fellow American," May 14, 1960, AJC/Extremist.

94. John G. Crommelin to William F. Knowland, March 8, 1957.

95. Flynt, *Alabama in the Twentieth Century*, 376, 499.

96. *The Cross and The Flag* (May 1957); John G. Crommelin, "Fellow American," March 7, 1964, September 25, 1970, AJC/Extremist.

97. The best studies of southern masculinity and honor are Wyatt-Brown, *Southern Honor*, and Greenberg, *Honor & Slavery*.

98. Stanton, *Journey toward Justice*, 169–70, 199–200.

99. Wakefield, *Revolt in the South*, 64; Barnard, *Outside the Magic Circle*, 245.

100. Thornton, *Dividing Lines*, 96, 99; Wakefield, *Revolt in the South*, 399.

101. Sullivan, *Freedom Writer*, 190.

102. Special Agent in Charge, Mobile to J. Edgar Hoover, October 31, 1958, and October 24, 1958, JC/FBI; *Denver Post*, December 3, 1958.

103. Edward Fields, "Trial Facts Prove Frame-Up," *Right* (January 1959): 2–3. Crommelin claimed the arrested men were patriots falsely arrested by the authorities and named his campaign to raise financial support for them the Defend America Fund.

104. John G. Crommelin to J. Edgar Hoover, November 1, 1958, JC/FBI. Several southern newspapers reprinted the letter, including *The Public Appeal* (Durham, N.C.), December 31, 1958. See also John G. Crommelin, "Fellow American," February 25, 1959, AJC/Extremist.

105. Doyle, *American Insurrection*, 9; Belknap, *Federal Law and Southern Order*, 92; *Chicago Sun-Times*, September 9, 1963; *New York Times*, September 10, 1963.

106. John G. Crommelin, "THIS IS NOT POLITICS . . . THIS IS SURVIVAL!" 1963, mayoral campaign advertisement, 1963, AJC/Extremist.

107. *Washington Evening Star*, April 25, 1963; *Chicago Tribune*, April 26, 1963; *New York Times*, April 26, 1963; Mr. Belmont to A. Rosen, June 5, 1963, JC/FBI.

108. Carter, *The Politics of Rage*, 139.

109. John G. Crommelin, "THIS IS NOT POLITICS . . . THIS IS SURVIVAL!"; Special Agent in Charge, Mobile, Report: "John Geraerdt Crommelin, Jr.," March 17, 1964, JC/FBI; Memorandum from Richmond Office, March 6, 1964, JC/FBI.

110. U.S. House of Representatives, *Report of the Select Committee on Assassinations: Findings and Recommendations*, 377.

111. Special Agent in Charge, Louisville, to J. Edgar Hoover, March 3, 1964; J. Edgar Hoover to Special Agents in Charge, Birmingham and Richmond, April 3, 1964; Unknown to J. Edgar Hoover, July 3, 1964, JC/FBI.

112. Special Agent in Charge, Birmingham, to J. Edgar Hoover, May 3, 1964, JC/FBI.

113. A. Rosen to Mr. Belmont, March 2, 1964; Memorandum, "William Potter Gale: Racial Matters," March 3, 1964; Memorandum from Richmond Office, March 6, 1964, JC/FBI. The animosity between Rockwell and Fields led later that year to the former filing a $550,000 million libel suit against the latter; he lost.

114. Sherrill, *Gothic Politics in the Deep South*, 268–69.

115. William P. Engel to Charles A. Wittenstein and Edwin J. Lukas, May 16, 1962, box 2, folder 9, Fineberg Papers.

116. National Jewish Community Relations Council, *Combating Anti-Semitism Today*, 63.

117. Peters, *Southern Temper*, 50.

118. Ellsworth and Harris, *American Right Wing*, 31.

119. Wilson and Harris, "Hucksters of Hate," 16.

120. Summary of Meeting held at Embassy Auditorium, Los Angeles, April 11, 1957, John Crommelin File, AJC/Extremist.

121. Fine and Himmelfarb, *American Jewish Year Book 60*, 49–50.

122. For more information on the Legion, see Fine and Himmelfarb, *American Jewish Year Book 64*, 138.

123. D. Boylan, "A League of Their Own: A Look Inside the Christian Defense League," http://cuban-exile.com/doc_026-050/doc0046.html (last accessed July 1, 2004). For further details on the League, see Barkun, *Religion and the Racist Right*, and Sergeant, *Extremism in America*, 159–62.

124. John G. Crommelin to Pedro del Valle, September 15, 1966, and October 5, 1966, Pedro Augusto del Valle Papers, Special Collections and University of Oregon Libraries, Eugene, Ore.

125. Southern Poverty Law Center, "Extremism and the Military: A Timeline," http://www.splcenter.org/intel/news/item.jsp?sid=23 (last accessed May 23, 2007).

126. Epstein and Forster, *The Radical Right*, 66–67.

127. Simonelli, *American Fuehrer*, 73, 117, 160n3; California Bureau of Criminal Identification and Investigation, *Para-Military Organizations in California*, ANP-2–3.

128. *Washington Post*, May 25, 1969, November 15, 1970.

129. Sims, *The Klan*, 112.

130. *Time*, May 16, 1960.

131. Carter, *Politics of Rage*, 297.

132. NSRP convention advertisement, September 1962, Group Research, Inc. Records, Series I, box 246.

Chapter Five. Assumption of Command

1. Lucien S. Loeb to George Kellman, March 11, 1963, box 2, folder 9, Solomon Andhil Fineberg Papers, American Jewish Archives, Cincinnati, Ohio.

2. Executive Board report, "Anti-Semitism in the U.S. and Problems Dealing With It," October 1960, Anti-Semitism/AJC file, AJC Subject Files Collection. Reports and memoranda on anti-Semitism in America and AJC's work to combat it, 1960–1962, American Jewish Committee Archives, http://ajcarchives.org/AJCArchive/DigitalArchive.aspx (last accessed November 19, 2007).

3. For a short but informative introduction to the mental condition of paranoia,

see Bell, *Paranoia*. See also "The Seven Elements of Paranoia," in Robins and Post, *Political Paranoia*.

4. Lewis, *White South and the Red Menace*, 14. This fear was shared by other white southerners. The *Shreveport Journal* published an article titled "The South: Soviet Target," which claimed that the communist conspiracy was focused on the region because it was the location of America's main military defenses. Chmaj, "Paranoid Patriotism," 92.

5. Harris, *Miracle in Birmingham*, 36.

6. Knebel and Bailey, "Military Control," 19.

7. Biderman, "Where Do They Go from Here?" 153–54.

8. Janowitz, *Professional Soldier*, 87, 100–101, 242.

9. Pach and Richardson, *Presidency of Dwight D. Eisenhower*, 139.

10. Bendersky, *Jewish Threat*, xvii.

11. Bendersky, *Jewish Threat*, 405.

12. Swomley, *Military Establishment*, 194.

13. Janowitz, *Professional Soldier*, 251, 80.

14. Cuordileone, *Manhood and American Political Culture in the Cold War*, xiv, xxiii, 46.

15. Swomley, *Military Establishment*, 194.

16. *Washington Post*, October 14, 1956. For further names of retired officers associated with the far right, see Kolkey, *New Right*, 10.

17. Lora and Langton, *Conservative Press in Twentieth-Century America*, 405.

18. Alexander, *Final Campaign*, 28–35; La Bree, *Gentle Warrior*, 81.

19. Del Valle chronicled his Italian experiences in *Roman Eagles over Ethiopia* and *Semper Fidelis*, 75–105.

20. "The Platform of the Defenders of the American Constitution, Inc.: Our Beliefs and Objectives," *Task Force* 7, no. 1 (May 1960), box 15, Jewish Community Relations Council of Minnesota Records, Minnesota Historical Society, St. Paul; Overstreet, *Strange Tactics of Extremism*, 237; del Valle, *Semper Fidelis*, 188–91.

21. Pedro A. del Valle, "Centralized Power Versus Constitutional Government," *Task Force* 5, no. 5 (September 1958), box 15, Jewish Community Relations Council of Minnesota Records.

22. P. A. del Valle, "Calling All Patriots: Defeat the Civil Rights Bill of 1963," *Alert No. 6*, August 27, 1963, box 15, Jewish Community Relations Council of Minnesota Records; A. K. Chesterton, "Little Rock as viewed through British eyes," *Task Force* 4, no. 9 (January 1958).

23. Pedro del Valle, "Regardless of Who Is Elected President Invisible Rulers Govern United States," *Task Force* 2, no. 6 (October 1955); del Valle, "Centralized Power Versus Constitutional Government," box 15, Jewish Community Relations Council of Minnesota Records; Lora and Langton, *Conservative Press*, 407.

24. Pedro A. del Valle, Editorial, *Task Force* 1, no. 1 (May 1954), box 15, Jewish Community Relations Council of Minnesota Records.

25. *Salisbury Times*, April 23, 1954; *Washington Post*, April 13, May 23, 1954; *Frederick Post*, June 18, 1954; *The Capital* (Annapolis, Md.), June 28, 1954; Forster and Epstein, *Cross-Currents*, 145; *Maryland Manual*, 1955–56, Vol. 166, 289, Archives of Maryland Online, http://www.msa.md.gov/megafile/msa/speccol/sc2900/sc2908/000001/000166/html/am166—289.html (last accessed July 25, 2007).

26. Pedro A. del Valle, Editorial, *Task Force* 4, no. 2 (June 1957), box 15, Jewish Community Relations Council of Minnesota Records.

27. Wilhelm, *Ezra Pound*, 317; Chesterton, "Little Rock as viewed through British eyes"; Pedro A. del Valle, "Retribution or Revenge?" *Task Force* 3, no. 1 (May 1956); T. D. Horton, "Ezra Pound Release Endorsed by Defenders; The Background of the Pound Case: Economics," *Task Force* 4, no. 12 (April 1958); Pedro A. del Valle, "An Alaskan Siberia For Mental Health?" *Task Force* 2, no. 10 (February 1956) Pedro A. del Valle, "Another Warning," *Task Force* 2, no. 11 (March 1956), box 15, Jewish Community Relations Council of Minnesota Records. The Pound connection also led to del Valle recruiting John Kasper's former ally David Horton as secretary of the Defenders of the American Constitution. Scott, "Anger in Paradise," 58n38.

28. Cook, *The Warfare State*, 265.

29. *The Handbook of Texas Online*, http://www.tshaonline.org/handbook/online/articles/WW/fwaaf.html (last accessed April 8, 2008).

30. Ashmore, *Hearts and Minds*, 285.

31. *New York Times*, September 26, 1957.

32. Doyle, *American Insurrection*, 13; Levitas, *Terrorist Next Door*, 417n21.

33. Raymond, *Power at the Pentagon*, 120.

34. Ashmore, *Hearts and Minds*, 285.

35. Swomley, *Military Establishment*, 184.

36. "The American Eagle—Vigilant and Undaunted," Los Angeles, January 11, 1962, in Walker, *Walker Speaks . . . Unmuzzled!* 27.

37. *Time*, April 28, November 10, 1961.

38. Courtney and Courtney, *Case of General Edwin A. Walker*, 29.

39. Department of Defense Press Release, June 12, 1961, Group Research, Inc. Records 1955–1996, box 329, Columbia Rare and Manuscript Library, Columbia University, New York; Schoenwald, *A Time for Choosing*, 106.

40. Walker, *Censorship and Survival*, 22.

41. *New York Times*, April 8, 1962; *Time*, April 13, 1962, Bjerre-Poulsen, *Right Face*, 187; Schmaltz, *Hate*, 140–41 (quotation).

42. *New York Times*, February 4, 1962. See also "The American Eagle is Not a Dead Duck," McCormick Auditorium, Chicago, February 9, 1962, *Walker Speaks*, 47–65.

43. "The American Eagle is Not a Dead Duck," McCormick Auditorium, Chicago, February 9, 1962, *Walker Speaks*, 50–51; "The American Eagle—Vigilant and Undaunted," Los Angeles, January 11, 1962, *Walker Speaks*, 29–30, 43.

44. "Platform of Edwin A. Walker, Candidate for Governor of Texas Subject to Democratic Primary May 5, 1962" (Dallas: Walker Campaign Headquarters, 1962), Center for American History, University of Texas at Austin.

45. *Walker Speaks*, front matter.

46. *Time*, December 22, 1961, February 9, 1962; *Kingsport (Tenn.) News*, February 16, 1962; Thayer, *Farther Shores of Politics*, 231.

47. *Time*, May 18, 1962.

48. Special Agent in Charge, Dallas, to J. Edgar Hoover, September 9, 1962, Edwin Walker Federal Bureau of Investigation File (hereinafter cited as EW/FBI). See also the comments about Little Rock in "America's Retreat from Victory," *Walker Speaks*, 18.

49. *Clarion-Ledger* (Jackson, Miss.), December 28, 29, 1961; Doyle, *American Insurrection*, 97.

50. W. J. Simmons to Mississippi Sovereignty Commission, January 1, 1962, SCR ID #7–4–0–56–2–1–1, Sovereignty Commission Online, http://mdah.state .ms.us/arlib/contents/er/sovcom/result.php?image=/data/sov_ommission/images/ png/cd08/059159.png&otherstuff=7|4|0|56|2|1|1|58358| (last accessed October 4, 2007).

51. *New York Times*, September 30, 1962; *Clarion-Ledger*, September 28, 1962; *The Worker*, November 20, 1962.

52. Special Agent in Charge, Dallas, to J. Edgar Hoover, September 29, 1962, EW/FBI.

53. Dittmer, *Local People*, 141; Clowse, *Ralph McGill*, 201.

54. *Chicago Defender*, October 2, 1962; Fleming, *Son of the Rough South*, 281–82.

55. Schoenwald, *Time for Choosing*, 107; Doyle, *American Insurrection*, 97.

56. Herbert J. Miller, Jr., Assistant Attorney General, to J. Edgar Hoover, November 13, 1962, EW/FBI; *Dallas Morning News*, October 6, 1962.

57. *Dallas Morning News*, November 6, 1962; *The Worker*, November 20, 1962; *New York Times*, January 22, 1963.

58. *Aiken Standard and Review*, October 19, 1962. See also *Florence Morning News*, October 8, 1962.

59. *Los Angeles Times*, December 7, 1962.

60. Correlation Summary, Subject: Major General Edwin A. Walker, July 1, 1964, EW/FBI.

61. *Task Force* 9, no. 10 (February 1963), box 15, Jewish Community Relations Council of Minnesota Records.

62. *Arkansas NSRP Newsletter* 1, no. 5 (March 1962), box 18, folder 212, Antisemitic Literature Collection, undated, Series II, American Jewish Historical Society Archives, Center for Jewish History, New York. Further expressions of support for Walker are included in *Arkansas NSRP Newsletter* 1, no. 2 (December 1961), and 1, no. 4 (February 1962).

63. Supplemental Correlation Summary, Subject: Major General Edwin A.

Walker, May 1, 1967; M. A. Jones to Mr. DeLoach, January 18, 1965; Correlation Summary, Subject: Major General Edwin A. Walker, July 1, 1964, EW/FBI.

64. Supplemental Correlation Summary, Subject: Major General Edwin A. Walker, May 1, 1967; Special Agent in Charge, Jackson, to J. Edgar Hoover, November 2, 1964; Memorandum, "Alleged Klan Participation in Insurrection Plot," November 5, 1964, EW/FBI.

65. Redekop, *American Far Right*, 51; Friendly, *The Good Guys, The Bad Guys and the First Amendment*, 4–5.

66. Walker, *Christian Fright Peddlers*, 90n.

67. Walker, *Christian Fright Peddlers*, 90.

68. McGirr, *Suburban Warriors*, 182, 183–85; See also Schuparra, *Triumph of the Right*, 42–52, 104–6.

69. Redekop, *American Far Right*, 33n27.

70. McWhorter, *Carry Me Home*, 317; *The New South Student*, April 1968.

71. *Walker Speaks*, 14, 29; Cook, *Segregationists*, 160.

Chapter Six. *"We Don't Believe in Tolerance"*

1. Raines, *My Soul is Rested*, 321. According to one team of authors, Stoner was "Perhaps the most outspoken and obsessive anti-Semite in American history." George and Wilcox, *American Extremists*, 354.

2. Applebome, *Dixie Rising*, 47.

3. Gerringer, *Terrorism*, 222.

4. Ralph E. Luker, "Happy Deathday, J. B. Stoner," History News Network, http://hnn.us/blogs/entries/115 (last accessed August 5, 2008).

5. *White Extremist Organizations, Part II: National States Rights Party* (unpublished monograph, May 1970), 5, National States Rights Party, Federal Bureau of Investigation File (hereinafter cited as NSRP/FBI); George and Wilcox, *American Extremists*, 354.

6. *Philadelphia Inquirer*, June 29, 1980.

7. Kelley, "'We Are Not What We Seem,'" 75–112.

8. Interview with J. B. Stoner conducted by Janice D. Wilson, May 12, 1981, 2, Kennesaw College Oral History Project, Bentley Rare Book Gallery, Horace W. Sturgis Library, Kennesaw State University.

9. *Los Angeles Times*, March 30, 1969.

10. Stoner, interview with Janice D. Wilson, May 12, 1981, 2, 14.

11. For more on the career of Kaltenbach, see Graves, "Propaganda by Short Wave."

12. *Chicago Defender*, December 8, 1945, August 3, 1946.

13. *Atlanta Constitution*, July 5, 1946.

14. Sanctuary, *Is the New Deal Communist?*; *Are These Things So?*; Committee on Un-American Activities, *Preliminary Report on Neo-Fascist and Hate Groups*, 15.

15. Forster, *Square One*, 59.

16. Bilbo, *Take Your Choice.*

17. Bilbo, *Take Your Choice,* 273–74.

18. Kennedy, *Klan Unmasked,* 70–71.

19. Arthur J. Levin, Anti-Defamation League Atlanta Regional Office, circular, August 15, 1952, box 46, folder 15, Ralph McGill Papers, Manuscript Archives, and Rare Book Library, Emory University; Thayer, *The Farther Shores of Politics,* 35–36, Committee on Un-American Activities, "Activities of the Ku Klux Klan Organizations in the United States," Part 5, 3806–7, 3809–10; *Atlanta Constitution,* July 5, 1946; Newton, *Invisible Empire,* 116; "Clan Rally and Cross Burning, Danville, Virginia, September 3, 1960," poster, John Crommelin File, American Jewish Committee Anti-Semitic and Extremist Collection, Jacob and Hilda Blaustein Human Relations Library (hereinafter cited as AJC/Extremist).

20. Stoner, *Gospel of Jesus Christ,* 1, 11, 12, 48. For more information on Christian Identity, see Barkun, *Religion and the Racist Right.*

21. Stoner, *Gospel of Jesus Christ,* 36, 45, 13, 46, 26 (quotation, 55–56).

22. Stoner, *Gospel of Jesus Christ,* 25.

23. J. B. Stoner, *Christ Not a Jew and Jews Not God's Chosen People* (Marietta, Ga.: Thunderbolt, n.d.), Hargrett Rare Book and Manuscript Library, University of Georgia, Athens.

24. McWhorter, *Carry Me Home,* 71; Starr, "Birmingham and the 'Dixiecrat' Convention," 34; Introduction, box 305, Group Research, Inc. Records, Rare Book and Manuscript Library, Columbia University, New York.

25. The FBI, for instance, destroyed much of its documentation on Stoner.

26. *White Extremist Organizations,* Part II, 5, NSRP/FBI.

27. See, for example, photograph SCR ID # 3–6A-2–34–1–1–1, Sovereignty Commission Online, http://mdah.state.ms.us/arlib/contents/er/sovcom/result .php?image=/data/sov_commission/images/png/cd02/015471.png&otherstuff=3 |6|2|34|1|1|1|15122|A (last accessed February 18, 2008). By contrast, for a physical description of Stoner, see Watters, *Down to Now,* 289.

28. The story of the Columbians is told in Dudley, "Hate Organizations of the 1940s," and Steven Wiesenburger, "Columbians, Inc."

29. California Bureau of Criminal Identification and Investigation, *Para-Military Organizations in California,* NSRP 1–2; *White Extremist Organizations,* Part II, 3, NSRP/FBI.

30. *Denver Post,* December 4, 1958.

31. *Chicago Defender,* November 22, 1958.

32. Alex Rittenbaum, memorandum, April 6, 1964, Jewish Community Council Papers, Department of Archives and Manuscripts, Linn-Henley Research Library, Birmingham, Ala. See also the description of George Bright, one of the suspects in the Atlanta Temple bombing case, as a "brilliant architect" in SCR ID # 1–8–0–16–5–1–1, Sovereignty Commission Online, http://mdah.state.ms.us/arvec/digitial_archives/sovcom/result.php?image=/data/sov_commission/images/png/cd01/000423.png&otherstuff=1/8/0/16/5/1/1/4/15 (last accessed December 1, 2006).

33. *Race & Nation*, n.d., box 18, folder 212, Antisemitic Literature Collection, American Jewish Historical Society Archives, Center for Jewish History, New York.

34. David Watson and Jack McClintock, "Hawkers of Hate," *Florida Accent*, December 3, 1967, 6.

35. Nelson, *Divided We Stand*; Norrell, "Caste in Steel."

36. *Para-Military Organizations in California*, NSRP-4; *Memphis Commercial Appeal*, September 24, 1963.

37. *White Extremist Organizations*, Part II, ii, 2; NSRP membership application form, box 39, Jewish Community Relations Council Papers, Minnesota Historical Society, St. Paul; Committee on Un-American Activities, *Present-Day Ku Klux Klan Movement*, 13.

38. Applebome, *Dixie Rising*, 48; George and Wilcox, *American Extremists*, 358; Supplemental Correlation Summary, May 1, 1967, Edwin Walker Federal Bureau of Investigation File.

39. *The Thunderbolt*, September 1965, box 39, Jewish Community Relations Council of Minnesota Papers. For a similar reading of the contemporary far right, see Mulloy, "Conversing with the Dead," 439–56.

40. Reverend Oren Potito, "Segregate of Integrate: What, as a Christian, should you do?" n.d., box 18, folder 212, Antisemitic Literature Collection, undated, 1869–1993, Series II. This concern to establish the nationalist rather than sectionalist character of segregationist resistance was not unique to the NSRP, as shown by the names of numerous other white supremacist organizations, such as the American Heritage Protective Committee, Defenders of State Sovereignty and Individual Liberty, the Federation for Constitutional Government, and the Patriots of North Carolina, Inc.

41. Ohio National States' Rights Party Newsletter, November 1963, box 18, folder 212, Antisemitic Literature Collection. The *Shreveport Journal* similarly emphasized the "Americanness" of the segregationist position by publishing a pamphlet titled *What Lincoln Said About Integration, Reprinted by Popular Request* (Shreveport, La., n.d.), which quoted the same speech.

42. Bilbo, *Take Your Choice*, 9, 28–32, 100–101.

43. Thayer, *Farther Shores of Politics*, 38.

44. *New York Times*, May 4, 1964.

45. "Scientists Say Negro Still in Ape Stage," 7.48, Birmingham Police Department Surveillance Files, 1947–1980, Department of Archives and Manuscripts, Linn-Henley Research Library, Birmingham, Ala.

46. J. B. Stoner, "The Philosophy of 'White Racism,'" n.d., AJC/Extremist.

47. *ADL Bulletin* 28 (September 1971): 3.

48. Reverend Oren Potito, "Segregate or Integrate: What, as a Christian, should you do?", n.d., box 18, folder 212, Antisemitic Literature Collection. Potito continued to disseminate his racial and religious doctrine through the *National Christian News*, published from 1962 until his death in 1995.

49. *Richmond News Leader*, September 5, 1960; *Kansas City Star*, July 21, 1963; *St. Louis Review*, September 4, 1964; *Houston Post*, February 22, 1967.

50. J. B. Stoner, "Jews Behind Race-Mixing," n.d., box 18, folder 212, Antisemitic Literature Collection; National States' Rights Party Official Platform [n.d.], Jewish Community Relations Council of Minnesota Papers; *White Extremist Organizations*, Part II, 1, NSRP/FBI.

51. Greene, *Temple Bombing*.

52. McMillan, "New Bombing Terrorists of the South," 39–40.

53. Committee on Un-American Activities, *Present-Day Ku Klux Klan Movement*, 13; Committee on Un-American Activities, "Activities of the Ku Klux Klan Organizations in the United States," 3812; "Personal Newsletter" [n.d.], box 39, Jewish Community Relations Council of Minnesota Papers.

54. *Chicago Defender*, July 6, 1963.

55. *New York Times*, July 6, 1964.

56. Massengill, *Portrait of a Racist*, 10.

57. Stoner, for instance, tirelessly emphasized that the president of the NAACP was Arthur Spingarn, a Jewish liberal. Roy, *Apostles of Discord*, 131.

58. Evanzz, *Messenger*, 206–7.

59. Goldman, *Death and Life of Malcolm X*, 253, 308. Willis Carto of the Liberty Lobby, a close associate of John Crommelin, also expressed support for the Nation of Islam. Michael, *Willis Carto and the Far Right*, 52–57.

60. *Chicago Defender*, May 22, 1957. The correspondence between Stoner and black nationalists continued through the editions of May 27, June 10, June 17, June 18, June 19, August 5, 1957.

61. The letter was reproduced in Muhammad, *Message To The Blackman in America*, quotations on 330 and 331.

62. Natambu, *Life and Work of Malcolm X*, 195–98.

63. *Chicago Defender*, September 26, 1959; Evanzz, *Messenger*, 206–7.

64. Central Research Section, report, "The Nation of Islam," October 1960, 45, Nation of Islam FBI File, Part 2, Federal Bureau of Investigation Electronic Reading Room, http://foia.fbi.gov/nation_of_islam/nation_of_islam_part02.pdf (last accessed April 18, 2008).

65. Evanzz, *Messenger*, 207–8.

66. *New York Amsterdam News*, September 19, 1959.

67. J. B. Stoner to Elijah Muhammad, April 10, 1961, box 1, folder 1, Florida Legislative Investigation Committee Records, 1954–1965, State Archives of Florida, Tallahassee; Central Research Section, report, "The Nation of Islam," October 1960, 31–32.

68. Mohl, "Race and Space in the Modern City," 131; *New York Times*, September 9, 1959; *Anniston Star*, September 10, 1959; *Charleston (W.Va.) Gazette Mail*, August 16, 1959; *Aiken Standard and Review*, October 12, 1959; *Tucson Daily Citizen*, October 14, 1959.

69. See, for example, Bartley, *Rise of Massive Resistance*, 341.

70. Manis, *A Fire You Can't Put Out*, 401.

71. Wilson and Harris, "Hucksters of Hate—Nazi Style," 11; *Washington Evening Star*, September 4, 1963; *Washington Post*, September 5, 1963; *New York Times*, September 5, 1963.

72. Fine and Himmelfarb, eds., *American Jewish Year Book* 64, 68–69; *Washington Evening Star*, September 24, 1963; *Anniston Star*, January 16, 1964; *Birmingham News*, June 4, 1964.

73. Thornton, *Dividing Lines*, 342–43.

74. *New York Times*, September 6, 1963.

75. Sikora, *Until Justice Rolls Down*, 45, 55, 155.

76. *Washington Daily News*, September 18, 1963; *Birmingham News*, October 20, 1963.

77. *Washington Post*, September 5, 1963; *New York Times*, September 5, 1963.

78. Carter, *The Politics of Rage*, 173–74; Dorman, *Wallace Myth*, 80, 89.

79. Colaiaco, *Martin Luther King Jr.*, 98.

80. Kallal, "St. Augustine and the Ku Klux Klan," 101–2.

81. Fairclough, *To Redeem the Soul of America*, 181.

82. *St. Augustine Record*, May 28, 1964.

83. Branch, *Pillar of Fire*, 333–35; Abernathy, *And the Walls Came Tumbling Down*, 291.

84. *New York Times*, June 21, 1964.

85. Kallal, "St. Augustine and the Ku Klux Klan," 127–28.

86. "Activities of the Ku Klux Klan Organizations in the United States," 3810–11. For examples of Stoner's relationship with Jacksonville Klansmen, see *New York Times*, May 4, 1964, and *Chicago Defender*, May 5, 1964.

87. Young, *An Easy Burden*, 295.

88. *White Extremist Organizations*, Part II, 6, NSRP/FBI; Armbrister, "Portrait of an Extremist," 80.

89. Branch, *Pillar of Fire*, 344.

90. Colburn, *Racial Change and Community Crisis*, 7; Armbrister, "Portrait of an Extremist," 82.

91. *New York Times*, May 4, 1964.

92. *New York Times*, June 13, 15, 1964; Colburn, *Racial Change and Community Crisis*, 8.

93. Florida Legislature Investigation Committee, *Racial and Civil Disorders in St. Augustine*, 5, 10, 14, 141.

94. Good, *Trouble I've Seen*, 92. On the arrest of Lynch and Stoner, see *Florence Morning News*, July 25, 1964.

95. Warren, *If It Takes All Summer*, 141.

96. *Kingsport News*, September 9, 1964.

97. Levine, *Resolving Racial Conflict*, 52–53; *Washington Post*, January 19, 1965.

98. Fairclough, *Race & Democracy*, 344–45, 347, Simon Wendt, *Spirit and the Shotgun*, 76–77.

99. *Chicago Defender*, April 3, 10, 1965; Paul Good, "Klantown USA," *The Nation*, February 1, 1965, 110–13; Hill, *Deacons for Defense*, 84, 86–87, 101; Fairclough, *Race & Democracy*, 345, 348–52, 356.

100. Fairclough, *Race & Democracy*, 353–54; Wendt, *Spirit and the Shotgun*, 83.

101. Fairclough, *Race & Democracy*, 357–58.

102. Hill, *Deacons for Defense*, 120–22.

103. Wendt, *Spirit and the Shotgun*, 89–90.

104. *Time*, June 11, 1965. The case against McElveen later collapsed owing to a lack of evidence.

105. *Chicago Defender*, July 10, 1965; *New York Times*, July 11, 1965; *Bogalusa Daily News*, July 12, 1965. See also Honigoberg, *Crossing Border Street*, and Sims, *The Klan*, 197.

106. Lipsitz, *A Life in the Struggle*, 111.

107. *The Thunderbolt*, September 1965, box 39, Jewish Community Relations Council of Minnesota Papers; *New York Times*, July 12, 1965; *Rocky Mountain News*, July 12, 1965.

108. *Chicago Defender*, July 15, 1965; Fairclough, *Race & Democracy*, 369–74.

109. Arsenault, *Freedom Riders*, 140–49.

110. *Anniston Star*, May 31, September 6, 1961; O'Reilly, "FBI and the Civil Rights Movement," 208.

111. *Anniston Star*, September 13, 1964.

112. HUAC, *Present-Day Ku Klux Klan*, 13; *Anniston Star*, October 24, 1964.

113. *Anniston Star*, March 28, 1965.

114. Noble, *Beyond the Burning Bus*, 131.

115. *New York Times*, November 30, 1965.

116. For details of Stoner's handling of the trial, see *Anniston Star*, November 18, 29, 1965; *Chicago Defender*, November 23, 1965; *Los Angeles Times*, November 28, 1965.

117. *Washington Post*, December 3, 1965. A second trial resulted in the acquittal of Defries; prosecutors dropped their case against Blevins in return for his testimony.

118. Wes McCune to Jason R. Silverman, February 17, 1967, folder 11, box 246, Group Research, Inc. Records; *Baltimore Sun*, July 26, 28, 29, 1966; *White Extremist Organizations*, Part II, 6, 10, NSRP/FBI; Durr, *Behind the Backlash*, 131–32.

119. *Washington Daily News*, July 9, 1966; *Washington Post*, July 30, 1966; *New York Times*, November 20, 1966; *Baltimore Sun*, November 22, 1966; *Washington Star*, November 22, 1966.

120. *Lexington Leader*, September 2, 4, 1968; *Louisville Times*, September 3, 1968; *New York Times*, September 2, 3, 1968; *Louisville Courier Journal*, September 4, 5, 1968.

121. *Raleigh (W.Va.) Register*, September 3, 1968; *Moberly Monitor-Index*, September 10, 1968.

122. *Chicago Defender*, March 13, 1969; *Berea Citizen*, March 20, 1969; White Extremist Organizations, Part II, 10–11, NSRP/FBI.

123. For a thorough analysis of COINTELPRO-White Hate Groups, see Cunningham, *There's Something Happening Here.*

124. Special Agent in Charge, Birmingham, to J. Edgar Hoover, February 19, 1965; Special Agent in Charge, Birmingham, to J. Edgar Hoover, June 24, 1965; G. C. Moore to W. C. Sullivan, October 12, 1967, FBI Memoranda, 1961–1971, FBI National Headquarters Reading Room, Washington, D.C.

125. Overstreet, *FBI in Our Open Society,* 216. I have found no evidence to support a claim that the FBI actually shared information with the NSRP in order to facilitate its disruption of civil rights demonstrations. See Schultz and Schultz, *Price of Dissent,* 155.

126. House Un-American Activities Committee, "Activities of the Ku Klux Klan Organizations in the United States," 3807–11.

127. Posner, *Killing the Dream,* 48, 62, 353n2; *Chicago Defender,* October 12, 1968; *Edwardsville Intelligencer,* March 21, 1969; *Los Angeles Times,* March 22, 1969; *Washington Post,* March 22, 1969.

128. U.S. House of Representatives, *Report of the Select Committee on Assassinations,* 381; *Los Angeles Times,* March 30, 1969.

129. Posner, *Killing the Dream,* 254. Stoner later claimed to the congressional committee investigating the assassination of King that the FBI had offered first him and later Asa Carter $25,000 to murder the civil rights leader, but both men believed they were being set up and therefore declined. Raines, *My Soul Is Rested,* 322.

130. *Los Angeles Times,* March 24, April 8, 1969.

131. *Syracuse Herald-American,* March 23, 1969; *New York Times,* March 23, 1969.

132. *Los Angeles Times,* May 27, 1969.

133. Weisberg, *Frame-Up,* 320. Stoner continued to collaborate with Ray's brother Jerry, later defending him against a charge of shooting a teenage boy. *Chicago Defender,* July 27, 1970.

134. Platform of the National States' Rights Party, n.d., box 18, folder 212, Antisemitic Literature Collection, Series II.

135. Anonymous, *Forty Reasons for Segregation* (Dayton, Ohio: National States' Rights Party, n.d.), box 18, folder 212, Antisemitic Literature Collection, Series II.

136. The January 1969 edition of the paper, for example, included enthusiastic support for George Wallace's presidential campaign the previous year.

137. Macklin, *Very Deeply Dyed in Black,* 70; Thurlow, *Fascism in Britain,* 239.

138. *Jewish Press,* March 3, 1978; *The Thunderbolt,* November 1981; *White Extremist Organizations,* Part II, NSRP/FBI, 5, 8. Grumke, "Relations Between Right-Wing Extremists," 497.

Chapter Seven. Fighting for Freedom by Defending the Enemy

1. *Atlanta Constitution,* August 3, 1972. A copy of the advertisement is available from the Julian P. Kanter Political Commercial Archive, Political Communications Center, University of Oklahoma, ID 45086.

2. "VOTE FOR The White People's Candidate J. B. Stoner The White Racist For United States Senator From Georgia STOP RACE MIXING INSANITY," campaign pamphlet, box 29, folder 15, Oscar Cohen Papers, Manuscript Collection No. 294, American Jewish Archives, Cincinnati, Ohio; "Stop Busing: Vote for J. B. Stoner for U.S. Senator," campaign pamphlet, American Jewish Committee Anti-Semitic and Extremist Collection, Jacob and Hilda Blaustein Human Relations Library, New York (hereafter cited as AJC/Extremist).

3. "Activities of the Ku Klux Klan Organizations in the United States," Part 5, 3821.

4. *Atlanta Constitution*, August 4, 1972.

5. *Atlanta Journal*, August 4, 1972; *Charleston (W.Va.) Gazette*, August 4, 1972; *Billings (Mass.) Gazette*, August 3, 1972; *Atlanta Independent*, August 6, 10, 1972.

6. See, for instance, Cook, *Troubled Commemoration*, 167.

7. See, for example, Downs, *Nazis in Skokie*, and Strum, *When the Nazis Came to Skokie*.

8. *Chicago Defender*, October 26, 1946.

9. Senator Lee Metcalf to Postmaster General J. Edward Day, June 12, 1963; Louis J. Doyle to Senator Lee Metcalf, July 5, 1963, Group Research, Inc. Records 1955–1996, Series I: Topical, 1955–1996, box 246, Columbia Rare and Manuscript Library, Columbia University, New York.

10. Blight, *Race and Reunion*, 395–96; Biondi, *To Stand and Fight*, 95–97; Benshoff and Griffin, *America on Film*, 78.

11. Ira Glasser, "Introduction" in Gates et al., *Speaking of Race, Speaking of Sex*, 2.

12. Walker, *In Defense of American Liberties*, 263–64; *Edwards v. South Carolina*, 372 U.S. 229 (1963); *Cox v. Louisiana*, 379 U.S. 536 (1965).

13. Belknap, *The Supreme Court under Earl Warren*, 191–92; Garrow, *Bearing the Cross*, 131, 135. The most extensive analysis of *New York Times v. Sullivan* is Lewis, *Make No Law*.

14. For further information on the Amendment, see D'Arcus, "Protest, Scale, and Publicity," 718–41.

15. George M. Snyder, Corporal, Intelligence Unit, Maryland State Police to Wesley McCune, August 21, 1964, box 246, Group Research, Inc. Records; *Denver Post*, October 12, 1961.

16. *Civil Liberties* 211 (November 1963); *Washington Evening Star*, December 12, 1963; *Washington Post*, December 12, 1963; *New York Times*, December 12, 1963; *Birmingham Post-Herald*, December 12, 1963.

17. *Fields v. City of Fairfield*, 375 U.S. 248 (1963) (per curiam); *Labor*, December 28, 1963.

18. Fineberg, "Quarantine Treatment," 114.

19. Sanua, *Let Us Prove Strong*, 254–55.

20. "Anti-Semitism and Problems In Dealing With it," Executive Board Meeting, October 28–30, 1960, Anti-Semitism/AJC file, AJC/Extremist. Reports and

memoranda on anti-Semitism in America and AJC's work to combat it, 1960–1962, American Jewish Committee Archives, http://ajcarchives.org/AJCArchive/DigitalArchive.aspx (last accessed November 19, 2007).

21. Hamlin, *Nazi/Skokie Conflict*, 108. See also *Sanua, Let Us Prove Strong*, 252–53.

22. Cohen, *Not Free to Desist*, 396.

23. The ADL, for instance, participated in protests against derogatory stereotypes of Jews in theater productions during the 1910s. Erdman, *Staging the Jew*, 150–59.

24. Leonard, "'Little Fuehrer Invades Los Angeles,'" 81–102.

25. *Cedar Rapids Gazette*, September 3, 1949; *Lowell Sun*, August 24, 1949.

26. *Chicago Defender*, September 23, 1944.

27. Forster, *Square One: A Memoir*, 83–84.

28. Maslow, "Prejudice, Discrimination, and the Law," 9–17; Anonymous, "Group Libel Laws," 252–63.

29. Walker, *Hate Speech*, 85.

30. *ADL Bulletin* 28 (September 1971): 3–4.

31. On the difficulty of maintaining cross-organizational support for quarantining Rockwell, see Simonelli, *American Fuehrer*, 63–65.

32. *Congress Weekly* 23 (October 22, 1956): 4.

33. Neither of the most recent studies of the NAACP discusses the issue of hate speech. See Gilbert Jonas, *Freedom's Sword*, and Berg, *Ticket to Freedom*. No scholar has to date written an organizational history of the ADL. The absence of any reference to the case in NAACP magazine *The Crisis* may indicate a lack of approval for the petition from national headquarters, which was more conservative than the radical Atlanta branch. Although I contacted the Atlanta offices of the NAACP and ADL on numerous occasions to discuss the Stoner incident, neither organization responded.

34. "The White People's Candidate: J. B. Stoner, 'Champion of White Supremacy for Governor of Georgia,'" campaign flyer, box 1, folder 2, J. B. Stoner Gubernatorial Campaign Collection, 1970, Wilcox Collection of Contemporary Political Movements, Kansas Collection, RH WL MS 21, Kenneth Spencer Research Library, University of Kansas Libraries; *Atlanta Constitution*, January 30, September 2, 1970.

35. *Atlanta Journal*, August 14, 1970.

36. *Atlanta Journal*, July 30, 1970.

37. Edward Fields, "J. B. Stoner for Governor Committee," campaign newsletter, n.d.; Edward Fields, "J. B. Stoner for Governor Committee: Sabotage Plot Fails," campaign newsletter, n.d., box 1, folder 2, Stoner Gubernatorial Campaign Collection. The source of funds for the commercial run by Stoner in 1972 is unclear.

38. *Atlanta Constitution*, September 11, 1970, July 6, 1971.

39. See, for example, Fairclough, *To Redeem the Soul of America*, 137–39.

40. The terrorist attacks on Jewish institutions are the subject of Greene, *Temple Bombing*.

41. For more on the career of Mayor Massell, see Evans, *Provincials*, 225–54.

42. *ADL Bulletin* 29 (November 1972): 4; Hendershot, "God's Angriest Man," 373–96. The American Jewish Committee also drew on the successful campaign against McIntire when it lobbied for the cancellation of *Bridget Loves Bernie*, a comedy show about the marriage between a Catholic woman and a Jewish man. Sanua, *Let Us Prove Strong*, 275.

43. For more information on the federal attack on political dissidents, see Kotlowski, *Nixon's Civil Rights*, and Cunningham, *There's Something Happening Here*.

44. *ADL Bulletin* 29 (December 1972): 5.

45. Forster and Epstein, *New Anti-Semitism*, 303, 307, 324.

46. Benjamin Epstein quoted in "How Free Is Free Speech?" *ADL Bulletin* 26 (March 1969): 4.

47. Orlik, *Electronic Media Criticism*, 198–99.

48. Blundell, "Law Intended to Promote Political Broadcasts Inhibits Them," 129–33.

49. *Red Lion Broadcasting Co., Inc. v. Federal Communications Commission*, 395 U.S. 367 (1969). For more on the Fairness Doctrine, see Krattenmaker and Powe, *Regulating Broadcast Programming*.

50. *Schenck v. United States*, 249 U.S. 47 (1919).

51. *Brandenburg v. Ohio*, 395 U.S. 444 (1969). For a fuller discussion of the liberalization of freedom of speech by the Supreme Court, see Walker, *Hate Speech*.

52. *Billings (Mont.) Gazette*, August 3, 1972.

53. Lonnie King, Rev. Joe Boone, and Stuart Lewengrub to William B. Ray, Chief, Division of Complaints and Compliance, Federal Communications Commission, August 2, 1972, box 29, folder 15, Cohen Papers.

54. Droge, "From Natural to Cultural Inferiority," 91–118.

55. Ben F. Waple, Secretary, Federal Communications Commission, to Lonnie King, August 3, 1972, Stuart Lewengrub memorandum to Arnold Forster, August 8, 1972, box 29, folder 15, Cohen Papers; *Atlanta Journal*, August 3, 1972; *Washington Post*, August 4, 1972.

56. *Atlanta Constitution*, August 4, 1972.

57. *Atlanta Constitution*, August 4, 1972.

58. *Capital Times* (Madison, Wis.), August 4, 1972.

59. Stuart Lewengrub, "The Hate Campaign," *ADL Bulletin* (October 1972): 7–8; *Atlanta Journal*, August 2, 1972.

60. Bartley and Graham, *Southern Elections*, 94, 112–15; *American Jewish Year Book*, 1971, 133; *Jet*, August 24, 1972; *Atlanta Constitution*, August 11, 1972.

61. Alexander F. Miller, memorandum to Benjamin R. Epstein, August 14, 1972, box 29, folder 15, Cohen Papers.

62. For an example of international news coverage, see *The Times* of London, August 4, 1972.

63. Stuart Lewengrub, memorandum to ADL Southeastern Regional Board, ADL Supporters, B'nai B'rith Presidents, ADL Chairmen, Jewish Professionals, August 9, 1972, box 29, folder 15, Cohen Papers.

64. Forster and Epstein, *New Anti-Semitism*, 301.

65. See, for instance, *Atlanta Constitution*, August 11, 1972; *Atlanta Independent*, August 17, 1972. Some northern newspapers also cautiously endorsed the FCC ruling. See, for instance, *Edwardsville (Ill.) Intelligencer*, August 7, 1972.

66. Toy, "Right-Wing Extremism," 131.

67. For a more thorough analysis of how segregationists reframed their arguments in terms of the threat to their own rights, see Kruse, *White Flight*.

68. *Manitowoc (Wis.) Herald-Times*, August 9, 1972; *The Bee* (Danville, Va.), August 9, 1972.

69. "Keep Stoner in Front," *The Thunderbolt*, Adv. Supplement, June 1974; *Kansas City Times*, February 17, 1977; *Atlanta Constitution*, August 3, 1978; *New York Times*, April 29, 2005.

70. J. B. Stoner, "Opposed to Civil Rights Laws," Kanter Political Commercial Archive, ID 45088. For more information on the act signed into law by Governor Busbee, see Looney, "The Politics Behind Georgia's Fair Employment Practices Law," 21–23.

71. Group Research, Inc. Records Series I, box 305; Grant, *Way it Was in the South*, 441; *Frederick (Md.) News*, July 29, 1978; *Pacific Stars and Stripes*, July 30, 1978.

72. *Atlanta Constitution*, August 3, 1978.

73. *Frederick (Md.) Post*, July 29, 1978.

74. Strum, *When the Nazis Came to Skokie*, 17–18, 70–71, 88–92.

75. *Delta Democrat-Times*, August 4, 1972.

76. *Atlanta Constitution*, August 1, 1972.

77. Bartley and Graham, *Southern Elections*, 94; Bartley and Graham, *Southern Politics*, 171–72. Two years earlier, one newspaper had stressed that many whites repelled by Stoner were nonetheless "angered by the jeers of black militants and revolutionary minorities, urging destruction of America and defiling what is held sacred by good citizens." *Savannah Morning News*, May 22, 1970.

78. *Atlanta Constitution*, August 20, 1970.

79. *Delta Democrat-Times*, August 6, 1972.

80. For further discussion of coded racism, see Hardisty, *Mobilizing Resentment*.

81. "David Duke Running for Office—Again," *Southern Poverty Law Center Intelligence Report*, Winter 1999. For further analysis of Duke, see Rose, *Emergence of David Duke and the Politics of Race*, and Kuzenski et al., *David Duke and the Politics of Race in the South*.

82. *New York Times*, May 2, 1980. For further information on the Mariel boatlift, see Skop, "Race and Place in the Adaptation of Mariel Exiles," 449–71.

83. *Washington Star*, June 4, 1980; *Atlanta Constitution*, July 31, 1980.

84. Attorney General to FBI Director, Memorandum, April 22, 1976, NSRP/FBI.

85. *Birmingham News*, February 19, 1976.

86. *Washington Post*, September 28, 1977.

87. *New York Times*, September 29, 1977, December 1, 1978; *Washington Post*, July 18, 1979; "Urgent Bulletin: J. B. Stoner indicted," box 305, Group Research, Inc. Records.

88. *New York Times*, May 16, 1980; *Washington Post*, August 14, 1982, February 12, June 3, 1983; *Atlanta Journal*, June 16, 1983; *Atlanta Constitution*, September 9, 1983.

89. *Atlanta Journal*, June 16, 1983; Edward Fields, *Personal News Letter* (November 1984), RH WL E520, Wilcox Collection; *States' Rights Voters League Quarterly Report* (Spring 1984), RH WL E315, Wilcox Collection.

90. *Atlanta Journal*, April 6, 1984.

91. *Atlanta Constitution*, October 6, 1986.

92. "Christmas Greetings from J. B. Stoner," newsletter, December 1986, Wilcox Collection.

93. J. B. Stoner, "Praise God for AIDS" (August 1987), box 305, Group Research, Inc. Records.

94. J. B. Stoner, "The Miracle of AIDS," (n.d.), box 305, Group Research, Inc. Records.

95. Fee, "Sin Versus Science," 141.

96. Jones, *Bad Blood*, 226.

97. *Atlanta Constitution*, March 24, 1990.

98. See, for example, *Simon Wiesenthal Newsletter* (early 1988), box 305, Group Research, Inc. Records.

99. J. B. Stoner, "Only American Monuments Should Be In Washington" (July 1993), box 305, Group Research Archives.

100. Ice Cube, *Bootlegs & B-Sides* (Priority—539211).

101. *Atlanta Journal and Constitution*, January 18, 1987; *Atlanta Journal*, January 19, 1987.

102. *Washington Post*, April 28, 2005; "Segregationist Calls for 'Standing Up,'" http://www.nationalist.org/news/flashes/2004/stoner.html (last accessed February 8, 2006).

Conclusion

1. Thornton, *Dividing Lines*, 11–12.

2. McGill, *A Church, A School*, 9.

3. *New York Times*, September 7–19, December 13, 1956, September 4, 1957.

4. Workman, *Case for the South*, 139.

5. Griffin, *Sturgis, Kentucky*, 10; Report of Harrison Lilly, Chicago Bureau, FBI report on school integration in Sturgis, Kentucky, September 5, 1957; *New York Times*, September 15, 1956.

6. Sokol, *There Goes My Everything*, 13.

7. Ashmore, *Epitaph for Dixie*, 121.

8. Lewis et al., *Second American Revolution*, 43. See also the editorial assessment of the violence in Clinton in the *Delta Democrat-Times* of December 6, 1956, and *Kingsport News* of October 14, 1958.

9. *Harvard Crimson*, October 16, 1958.

10. *Congressional Record*, Vol. 106, Part 5, 86th Cong., 2nd sess., 5727–28.

11. Southern politicians who opposed an increase in the power of federal authorities included Representatives Robert E. Jones and George W. Andrews of Alabama. *Congressional Record*, Vol. 106, Part 4, 86th Congress, 2nd Session, 5447, 5449.

12. *Congressional Record*, Vol. 106, Part 6, 86th Congress, 2nd Session, 7581. See also the opinion of Representative Prince H. Preston, Jr., of Georgia. *Congressional Record*, Vol. 106, Part 4, 5462.

13. Durham, *Christian Right*, 132–40.

Bibliography

Manuscripts

American Jewish Archives, Cincinnati, Ohio: Solomon Andhil Fineberg Papers.
American Jewish Historical Society Archives, Center for Jewish History, New York: Antisemitic Literature Collection, undated, 1869–1993.
Archives of the Jewish Federation of Nashville and Middle Tennessee, Beinecke Rare Book and Manuscript Library, Yale University: Ezra Pound Collection.
Bentley Rare Book Gallery, Horace W. Sturgis Library, Kennesaw State University: Kennesaw College Oral History Project.
Columbia Rare and Manuscript Library, Columbia University, New York: Group Research, Inc. Records, 1955–1996.
Delaware Public Archives, Dover: Milford School Desegregation Recordings, Record Group #RG9200, Subgroup #M10—Milford Radio Station WKSB.
Department of Archives and Manuscripts, Linn-Henley Research Library, Birmingham, Ala.: Birmingham Police Department Surveillance Files, 1947–1980; Jewish Community Council Papers.
Department of Rare Books and Special Collections, Princeton University Library: American Civil Liberties Union Archives, 1917–1995.
Florida State Archives, Tallahassee: Race Relations, Governor's Advisory Commission on, Governor LeRoy Collins Correspondence, 1955–1961.
Jacob and Hilda Blaustein Human Relations Library, New York: American Jewish Committee Anti-Semitic and Extremist Collection; "Political Broadcast Paid for by the Friends of John Crommelin, Channel 10, Mobile, Alabama, 1961" (sound recording).
Kenneth Spencer Research Library, University of Kansas Libraries: Wilcox Collection of Contemporary Political Movements.
Library of Congress, Washington, D.C.: National Association for the Advancement of Colored People Collection.

MacDonald & Associates Historical Film Archive, Chicago, Ill.: Telenews Tennessee.

Manuscripts Department, Lilly Library, Indiana University, Bloomington: Pound Mss. II.

Minnesota Historical Society, St. Paul: Jewish Community Relations Council of Minnesota Records.

National Records and Archives Administration, College Park, Md.: World War II Army Enlistment Records.

Papers of the National Association for the Advancement of Colored People, ed. August Meier, microfilm, 28 parts. Frederick, Md.: University Publications of America, 1982.

Special Collections, University of Arkansas Libraries, Fayetteville: Arkansas Council of Human Relations.

Special Collections and University Archives, Jean and Alexander Heard Library, Vanderbilt University, Nashville: Brainard and Frances Cheney Papers; Nelson and Marian D. Fuson Papers.

Special Collections and University of Oregon Libraries, Eugene: Pedro Augusto del Valle Papers.

State Archives of Florida, Tallahassee: Florida Legislative Investigation Committee Records, 1954–1965.

Walter J. Brown Media Libraries and Peabody Awards Collection, University of Georgia Libraries, Athens: [Telerama. 1954 compilation]/WPTZ-TV (Philadelphia: WPTZ-TV, 1954), 54024 PST.

W. S. Hoole Special Collections Library, University of Alabama, Tuscaloosa: John G. Crommelin, letter to William F. Knowland, March 8, 1957.

Government Reports and Documents

California Bureau of Criminal Identification and Investigation. *Para-Military Organizations in California*. Sacramento, Calif., 1965.

Committee on Un-American Activities, U.S. House of Representatives, 89th Cong., 2nd sess. *Activities of the Ku Klux Klan Organizations in the United States, Parts 1–5*. Washington, D.C.: U.S. Government Printing Office, 1966.

Committee on Un-American Activities, U.S. House of Representatives. *Preliminary Report on Neo-Fascist and Hate Groups*. Washington, D.C.: U.S. Government Printing Office, 1954.

———, *The Present-Day Ku Klux Klan Movement*, 90th Cong., 1st sess., December 11, 1967. Washington, D.C.: U.S. Government Printing Office, 1967.

Federal Bureau of Investigation Files: Bryant W. Bowles, Jr.; Edwin Walker; Frederick John Kasper; John G. Crommelin; National Association for the Advancement of White People; National States' Rights Party.

Florida Legislature. Legislative Investigation Committee. *Racial and Civil Disorders in St. Augustine: Report of the Legislative Investigation Committee*. Tallahassee, 1965.

Political Broadcasting: Hearings Before the Communications Subcommittee of the Committee on Commerce, United States Senate, Eighty-Seventh Congress, Second Session, on S. 204 [and other] Bills to Amend Section 315 of the Federal Communications Act of 1934, July 10, 11, and 12, 1962. Washington, D.C.: U.S. Government Printing Office, 1962.

Report of the United States Commission on Civil Rights. Washington, D.C.: U.S. Government Printing Office, 1959.

Subcommittee on Territories and Insular Affairs of the Committee on Interior and Insular Affairs, U.S. Senate. *Alaska Mental Health: Hearings Before the Subcommittee on Territories and Insular Affairs of the Committee on Interior and Insular Affairs, United States Senate, Eighty-Fourth Congress, Second Session.* Washington, D.C.: U.S. Government Printing Office, 1956.

U.S. House of Representatives, 95th Cong., 2nd sess. *Report of the Select Committee on Assassinations: Findings and Recommendations.* Washington, D.C.: U.S. Government Printing Office, 1979.

Newspapers and Periodicals

Aiken (S.C.) Standard and Review
Alabama Independent
Anniston Star
Arkansas Democrat
Arkansas Gazette
Athens (Ohio) Messenger
Atlanta Constitution
Atlanta Journal
Baltimore American
Baltimore News Post
Berea (Ky.) Citizen
Birmingham News
Birmingham Post-Herald
Brainerd (Minn.) Daily Dispatch
Bridgeport (Conn.) Post
Bridgeport (Conn.) Telegram
Brownsville Herald
Burlington (N.C.) Daily Times-News
The Capital (Annapolis, Md.)
Charleston (W.Va.) Gazette
Charlotte Observer
Chester (Pa.) Times
Chicago Defender
Chicago Sun-Times
Chicago Tribune

Cincinnati Enquirer
Citizens' Council, The
Clinton Courier News
Corpus Christi Caller-Times
Corpus Christi Times
Danville (Va.) Bee
Delaware State News
Denver Post
Edwardsville (Ill.) Intelligencer
Elyria (Ohio) Chronicle-Telegram
Florence (S.C.) Morning News
Frederick (Md.) Post
Galveston News
Gettysburg Times
Great Bend (Kans.) Daily Tribune
Harvard Crimson
Holland (Mich.) Evening Sentinel
Indiana Evening Gazette
Intermountain Jewish News (Denver)
Jackson Daily News
Jacksonville Journal
Kannapolis (N.C.) Daily Independent
Kansas City Times
Kingsport (Tenn.) News
Knoxville Journal
Knoxville News-Sentinel
Lee County Bulletin (Auburn, Ala.)
Le Monde (Paris)
Lexington Leader
Louisville Courier-Journal
Louisville Times
Manitowoc (Wis.) Herald-Times
Memphis Commercial Appeal
Miami Herald
Miami News
Moberly (Mo.) Monitor-Index
Montgomery Advertiser
Montgomery Home News
Montgomery Independent
Nashville Banner
Nashville Globe and Independent
Nashville Post

Nashville Tennessean
The Nation
Nevada State Journal
New Orleans Times–Picayune
Newport (R.I.) News
Newsweek
New York Amsterdam News
New York Herald Tribune
New York Journal-American
New York Mirror
New York Post
New York Times
Oshkosh (Wis.) Daily Northwestern
Oxnard (Calif.) Press-Courier
Pacific Stars and Stripes
Philadelphia Inquirer
Portsmouth (N.H.) Herald
The Public Appeal (Durham, N.C.)
Raleigh (W.Va.) Register
Richmond News Leader
Richmond Times–Dispatch
St. Augustine Record
St. Louis Review
Salisbury Times
Savannah Morning News
Southern School News
Statesville (N.C.) Record & Landmark
Stevens Point (Wis.) Daily Journal
Tampa Tribune
Time
Tucson Daily Citizen
U.S. News & World Report
Victoria (Tex.) Advocate
Wall Street Journal
Washington Post
Washington Post and Times
Washington Star
Wetumpka Herald
Wilmington Evening Journal
Wilmington Morning News
Wilmington News Journal
Wisconsin Rapids Daily Tribune

Zanesville (Ohio) Signal
Zanesville (Ohio) Times Recorder

Online Sources

American Jewish Committee Archives, Subject Files Collection. http://ajcarchives
    .org/AJCArchive/DigitalArchive.aspx.
Boylan, D. "A League of Their Own: A Look Inside the Christian Defense League."
    http://cuban-exile.com/doc_026–050/doc0046.html.
"History of Bible Presbyterian Church." http://www.bpc.org/synod/minutes/
    beacon_1939_08_31.html.
Morrill, Dan L. "The Civil Rights Revolution in Mecklenburg County." http://
    www.cmhpf.org/educationcivilrights.htm.
Rutgers Oral History Archives. http://oralhistory.rutgers.edu.
Sovereignty Commission Online, Mississippi Department of Archives and His-
    tory Digital Collections. http://mdah.state.ms.us/arlib/contents/er/sovcom/
    result.php.

Secondary Sources

Abernathy, Ralph David. *And the Walls Came Tumbling Down: An Autobiography*.
    New York: Harper & Row, 1989.
Adamson, June N. "Few Black Voices Heard: The Black Community and the De-
    segregation Crisis in Clinton, Tennessee, 1956." *Tennessee Historical Quarterly* 53
    (Spring 1994): 30–41.
Alexander, Joseph H. *The Final Campaign: Marines in the Victory on Okinawa*.
    Darby, Pa.: Diane Publishing Co., 1996.
Allport, Gordon W. *The Nature of Prejudice*. Cambridge, Mass.: Addison-Wesley
    Pub. Co., 1954.
Anderson, J. W. *Eisenhower, Brownell, and the Congress: The Tangled Origins of the
    Civil Rights Bill of 1956–1957*. Tuscaloosa: University of Alabama Press, 1964.
Anderson, Karen S. "Massive Resistance, Violence, and Southern Social Relations:
    The Little Rock, Arkansas, School Integration Crisis, 1954–1960." In *Massive
    Resistance: Southern Opposition to the Second Reconstruction*, ed. Clive Webb,
    203–20. New York and Oxford: Oxford University Press, 2005.
Anderson, Margaret. *The Children of the South*. New York: Farrar, Straus and Giroux,
    1966.
Applebome, Peter. *Dixie Rising: How the South is Shaping American Values, Politics,
    and Culture*. New York: Times Books, 1996.
Armbrister, Trevor. "Portrait of an Extremist." *Saturday Evening Post*, August 22,
    1964, 80–83.
Arsenault, Raymond. *Freedom Riders: 1961 and the Struggle for Racial Justice*. Oxford
    and New York: Oxford University Press, 2006.

Ashmore, Harry S. *Epitaph for Dixie*. New York: Norton, 1958.

———. *Hearts and Minds: The Anatomy of Racism from Roosevelt to Reagan*. New York: McGraw-Hill, 1982.

Badger, Anthony J. "The White Reaction to *Brown*: Arkansas, the Southern Manifesto, and Massive Resistance." In *Understanding the Little Rock Crisis: An Exercise in Remembrance and Reconciliation*, ed. Elizabeth Jacoway and C. Fred Williams, 83–98. Fayetteville: University of Arkansas Press, 1999.

Badger, Tony. "Southerners Who Refused to Sign the Southern Manifesto." *Historical Journal* 42 (1999): 517–34.

Bagwell, William. *School Desegregation in the Carolinas: Two Case Studies*. Columbia: University of South Carolina Press, 1972.

Balmer, Randall. "Fundamentalist With Flair." *Christianity Today*, May 21, 2002, 52–57.

Bandura, Albert. *Self-Efficacy: The Exercise of Control*. New York: W. H. Freeman and Company, 1997.

Barkun, Michael. *Religion and the Racist Right: The Origins of the Christian Identity Movement*. Rev. ed. Chapel Hill and London: University of North Carolina Press, 1997.

Barnard, Hollinger F., ed. *Outside the Magic Circle: The Autobiography of Virginia Foster Durr*. Tuscaloosa: University of Alabama Press, 1985.

Bartley, Numan V. *The Rise of Massive Resistance: Race and Politics in the South During the 1950s*. Baton Rouge: Louisiana State University Press, 1969.

Bartley, Numan V., and Hugh D. Graham. *Southern Elections: County and Precinct Data, 1950–1972*. Baton Rouge and London: Louisiana State University Press, 1978.

———. *Southern Politics and the Second Reconstruction*. Baltimore and London: Johns Hopkins University Press, 1975.

Belknap, Michal R. *Federal Law and Southern Order: Racial Violence and Constitutional Conflict in the Post-Brown South*. Athens: University of Georgia Press, 1987.

———. *The Supreme Court under Earl Warren, 1953–1969*. Columbia: University of South Carolina Press, 2005.

Bell, Daniel, ed. *The Radical Right*. New York: Doubleday, 1964.

Bell, David. *Paranoia (Ideas in Psychoanalysis)*. Thriplow, Cambridge: Icon Books, 2003.

Bendersky, Joseph W. *The "Jewish Threat": Anti-Semitic Politics of the U.S. Army*. New York: Basic Books, 2000.

Bennett, David H. *The Party of Fear: From Nativist Movements to the New Right in American History*. Chapel Hill: University of North Carolina Press, 1988.

Benshoff, Harry M., and Sean Griffin. *America on Film: Representing Race, Class, Gender, and Sexuality at the Movies*. Malden, Mass.: Blackwell, 2004.

Berg, Manfred. *Ticket to Freedom: The NAACP and the Struggle for Black Political Integration*. Gainesville: University Press of Florida, 2005.

Bergeron, Paul H., Stephen V. Ash, and Jeanette Keith. *Tennesseans and Their History*. Knoxville: University of Tennessee Press, 1999.

Berkman, Scott. *William Dudley Pelley: A Life in Right-Wing Extremism and the Occult*. Syracuse, N.Y.: Syracuse University Press, 2005.

Berlet, Chip, and Matthew N. Lyons. *Right-Wing Populism in America: Too Close for Comfort*. New York: Guilford Press, 2000.

Biderman, Albert D. "Where Do They Go from Here?—Retired Military in America." *The Annals of the American Academy of Political and Social Science* 406 (1973): 146–61.

Bilbo, Theodore G. *Take Your Choice: Separation or Mongrelization*. Poplarville, Mass.: Dream House Publishing Company, 1947.

Biondi, Martha. *To Stand and Fight: The Struggle for Civil Rights in Postwar New York City*. Cambridge, Mass.: Harvard University Press, 2003.

Bjerre-Poulsen, Niels. *Right Face: Organizing the American Conservative Movement*. Copenhagen: Museum Tusculanum Press, 2002.

Blee, Kathleen M. *Inside Organized Racism: Women in the Hate Movement*. Berkeley: University of California Press, 2002.

Blight, David W. *Race and Reunion: The Civil War in American Memory*. Cambridge, Mass.: Belknap Press of Harvard University, 2001.

Blundell, William E. "Law Intended to Promote Political Broadcasts Inhibits Them." In *Broadcasting and the Public Interest*, ed. John H. Pennybacker and Waldo W. Braden, 129–33. New York: Random House, 1969.

Boyle, Sarah Patton. *The Desegregated Heart: A Virginian's Stand in Time of Transition*. London: Gollancz, 1963.

Branch, Taylor. *Pillar of Fire: America in the King Years 1963–65*. New York: Simon and Schuster, 1998.

Brittain, David James. "A Case Study of the Problems of Racial Integration in the Clinton, Tennessee High School." Ed.D., New York University, 1959.

Brokaw, Tom. *The Greatest Generation*. New York: Random House, 1998.

Brooks, Jennifer E. "Winning the Peace: Georgia Veterans and the Struggle to Define the Political Legacy of World War II." *Journal of Southern History* 66 (2000): 563–604.

Brownell, Herbert, with John P. Burke. *Advising Ike: The Memoirs of Attorney General Herbert Brownell*. Lawrence: University Press of Kansas, 1993.

Brundage, W. Fitzhugh. *The Southern Past: A Clash of Race and Memory*. Cambridge, Mass.: Harvard University Press, 2005.

Burk, Robert Frederick. *The Eisenhower Administration and Black Civil Rights*. Knoxville: University of Tennessee Press, 1984.

Buswell, J. Oliver, III. *Slavery, Segregation and Scripture*. Grand Rapids, Mich.: William B. Eerdmans Publishing Co., 1964.

Campbell, Will D. *Forty Acres and a Goat: A Memoir*. Oxford, Miss.: Jefferson Press, 2002.

Canovan, Margaret. *Populism*. New York: Junction Books, 1981.

Capeci, Dominic J., Jr. "The Lynching of Cleo Wright: Federal Protection of Constitutional Rights During World War II." *Journal of American History* 72 (1986): 859–87.

Carmichael, Omer, and Weldon James. *The Louisville Story*. New York: Simon and Schuster, 1957.

Carpenter, Humphrey. *A Serious Character: The Life of Ezra Pound*. London and Boston: Faber and Faber, 1988.

Carter, Dan T. *The Politics of Rage: George Wallace, the Origins of the New Conservatism, and the Transformation of American Politics*. New York: Simon and Schuster, 1995.

Carter, Hodding. *The South Strikes Back*. Garden City, N.Y.: Doubleday, 1959.

Chalmers, David M. *Hooded Americanism: The First Century of the Ku Klux Klan, 1865–1965*. Garden City, N.Y.: Doubleday, 1965.

Chappell, David L. *A Stone of Hope: Prophetic Religion and the Death of Jim Crow*. Chapel Hill and London: University of North Carolina Press, 2004.

Cheatham, Russ. *Bad Boy of Gospel Music: The Calvin Newton Story*. Jackson: University Press of Mississippi, 2003.

Chmaj, Betty E. "Paranoid Patriotism: The Radical Right and the South." *Atlantic Monthly* (November 1962): 91–97.

Clift, Virgil A., Archibald W. Anderson, and H. Gordon Hullfish, eds. *Negro Education in America: Its Adequacy, Problems, and Needs*. New York, Evanston, and London: Harper & Row, 1962.

Clowse, Barbara Barksdale. *Ralph McGill: A Biography*. Macon, Ga.: Mercer University Press, 1998.

Cobb, James C. *Away Down South: A History of Southern Identity*. New York: Oxford University Press, 2005.

Cohen, Naomi W. *Not Free to Desist: The American Jewish Committee, 1906–1966*. Philadelphia: Jewish Publication Society of America, 1972.

Colaiaco, James A. *Martin Luther King Jr.: Apostle of Militant Nonviolence*. New York: St. Martin's Press, 1988.

Colburn, David R. *Racial Change and Community Crisis: St. Augustine, Florida, 1877–1980*. New York: Columbia University Press, 1985.

Coleman, John A. "Religious Social Capital: Its Nature, Social Location, and Limits." In *Religion as Social Capital: Producing the Common Good*, ed. Corwin Smidt, 33–48. Waco, Tex.: Baylor University Press, 2003.

Cook, Fred J. *The Warfare State*. London: Jonathan Cape, 1962.

Cook, James Graham. *The Segregationists*. New York: Appleton-Century-Crofts, 1962.

Cook, Robert J. *Troubled Commemoration: The American Civil War Centennial, 1961–1965*. Baton Rouge: Louisiana State University Press, 2007.

Cope, Graeme. "A Thorn in the Side? The Mothers' League of Central High School and the Little Rock Desegregation Crisis of 1957." *Arkansas Historical Quarterly* 57 (1998): 160–90.

Courtney, Kent, and Phoebe Courtney. *The Case of General Edwin A. Walker: A Documented Exposé!* New Orleans: Conservative Society of America, 1961.

Crispell, Brian Lewis. *Testing the Limits: George Armistead Smathers and Cold War America.* Athens and London: University of Georgia Press, 1999.

Cronenberg, Allen. *Forth to the Mighty Conflict: Alabama and World War II.* Tuscaloosa: University of Alabama Press, 2003.

Cunningham, David. *There's Something Happening Here: The New Left, the Klan, and FBI Counterintelligence.* Berkeley, Los Angeles, and London: University of California Press, 2004.

Cuordileone, K. A. *Manhood and American Political Culture in the Cold War.* New York: Routledge, 2005.

Dailey, Jane. "Sex, Segregation and the Sacred after *Brown.*" *Journal of American History* 91 (June 2004): 119–44.

Daniel, Pete. *Lost Revolutions: The South in the 1950s.* Chapel Hill: University of North Carolina Press, 2000.

D'Arcus, Bruce. "Protest, Scale, and Publicity: The FBI and the H. Rap Brown Act." *Antipode* 35 (2003): 718–41.

De Santis, Christopher C., ed. *The Collected Works of Langston Hughes*, vol. 10, *Fight for Freedom and Other Writings on Civil Rights.* Columbia: University of Missouri Press, 2001.

del Valle, Pedro. *Roman Eagles over Ethiopia.* Harrisburg, Pa.: Military Service Publishing Company, 1940.

———. *Semper Fidelis: An Autobiography.* Hawthorne, Calif.: Christian Book Club of America, 1976.

Diamond, Sara. *Roads to Dominion: Right-Wing Movements and Political Power in the United States.* New York: Guilford Press, 1995.

Dierenfield, Kathleen Murphy. "One 'Desegregated Heart': Sarah Patton Boyle and the Crusade for Civil Rights in Virginia." *Virginia Magazine of History and Biography* 104 (1996): 251–84.

Dittmer, John. *Local People: The Struggle for Civil Rights in Mississippi.* Urbana: University of Illinois Press, 1994.

Dollinger, Marc. *Quest for Inclusion: Jews and Liberalism in Modern America.* Princeton and Oxford: Princeton University Press, 2000.

Dorman, Michael. *The Wallace Myth.* New York: Bantam, 1976.

Downs, Donald Alexander. *Nazis in Skokie: Freedom, Community, and the First Amendment.* Notre Dame, Ind.: University of Notre Dame Press, 1985.

Doyle, Don H. *Nashville Since the 1920s.* Knoxville: University of Tennessee Press, 1985.

Doyle, William. *An American Insurrection: The Battle of Oxford, Mississippi, 1962.* New York: Doubleday, 2001.

Droge, David. "From Natural to Cultural Inferiority: The Symbolic Reconstruction of White Supremacy in *Brown v. Board of Education.*" In *Brown v. Board of*

Education at Fifty: A Historical Perspective, ed. Clark Rountree, 91–118. Lanham, Md.: Lexington Books, 2004).

Dudley, J. Wayne. "Hate Organizations of the 1940s: The Columbians, Inc." *Phylon* 42 (1981): 262–74.

Durham, Martin. *The Christian Right, The Far Right and the Boundaries of American Conservatism*. Manchester: Manchester University Press, 2000.

Durr, Kenneth D. *Behind the Backlash: White Working-Class Politics in Baltimore, 1940–1980*. Chapel Hill: University of North Carolina Press, 2003.

Dykeman Wilma, and James Stokely. *Neither Black Nor White*. New York: Rinehart, 1957.

Eisenhower, Dwight D. *Waging Peace: The White House Years, 1956–1961*. London: Heinemann, 1965.

Elliott, Carl, Sr., and Michael D'Orso. *The Cost of Courage: The Journey of an American Congressman*. New York: Doubleday, 1992.

Ellsworth, Ralph E., and Sarah M. Harris. *The American Right Wing: A Report to the Fund for the Republic*. Washington, D.C.: Public Affairs Press, 1962.

Epstein, Benjamin R., and Arnold Forster. *The Radical Right: Report on the John Birch Society and Its Allies*. New York: Random House, 1966.

Erdman, Harley. *Staging the Jew: The Performance of an American Ethnicity, 1860–1920*. New Brunswick, N.J.: Rutgers University Press, 1997.

Eskew, Glenn T. *But for Birmingham: The Local and National Movements in the Civil Rights Struggle*. Chapel Hill and London: University of North Carolina Press, 1997.

Evans, Eli N. *The Provincials: A Personal History of Jews in the South*. New York: Atheneum, 1973.

Evanzz, Karl. *The Messenger: The Rise and Fall of Elijah Muhammad*. New York: Vintage, 2001.

Fairclough, Adam. *Better Day Coming: Blacks and Equality, 1890–2000*. New York: Viking, 2001.

———. *Race & Democracy: The Civil Rights Struggle in Louisiana, 1915–1972*. Athens: University of Georgia Press, 1995.

———. *To Redeem the Soul of America: The Southern Christian Leadership Conference and Martin Luther King, Jr*. Athens: University of Georgia Press, 1987.

Fee, Elizabeth. "Sin Versus Science: Venereal Disease in Twentieth-Century Baltimore." In *AIDS: The Burdens of History*, ed. Elizabeth Fee and Daniel Fox, 121–46. Berkeley: University of California Press, 1988.

Fine, Morris, ed. *American Jewish Year Book 55*. New York and Philadelphia: American Jewish Committee and Jewish Publication Society of America, 1954.

———. *American Jewish Year Book 56*. New York and Philadelphia: American Jewish Committee and Jewish Publication Society of America, 1955.

Fine, Morris, and Jacob Sloan, eds. *American Jewish Year Book 57*. New York and

Philadelphia: American Jewish Committee and Jewish Publication Society of America, 1956.

———. *American Jewish Year Book 59*. New York and Philadelphia: American Jewish Committee and Jewish Publication Society of America, 1958.

Fine, Morris, and Milton Himmelfarb, eds. *American Jewish Year Book 60*. New York and Philadelphia: American Jewish Committee and Jewish Publication Society of America, 1959.

———. *American Jewish Year Book 61*. New York and Philadelphia: American Jewish Committee and Jewish Publication Society of America, 1960.

———. *American Jewish Year Book 62*. New York and Philadelphia: American Jewish Committee and Jewish Publication Society of America, 1961.

———. *American Jewish Year Book 64*. New York and Philadelphia: American Jewish Committee and Jewish Publication Society of America, 1963.

———. *American Jewish Year Book 66*. New York and Philadelphia: American Jewish Committee and Jewish Publication Society of America 1965.

Fineberg, S. Andhil. "The Quarantine Treatment." In *The Hate Reader*, ed. Edwin S. Newman, 111–16. Dobbs Ferry, N.Y.: Oceana Publications, 1964.

Finley, Keith M. *Delaying the Dream: Southern Senators and the Fight against Civil Rights, 1938–1965*. Baton Rouge: Louisiana University Press, 2008.

Fleming, Harold C. "Resistance Movements and Racial Desegregation." *The Annals of the American Academy of Political and Social Science* 304 (1956): 44–52.

Fleming, Karl. *Son of the Rough South: An Uncivil Memoir*. New York: Public Affairs, 2005.

Flynt, Wayne. *Alabama in the Twentieth Century*. Tuscaloosa: University of Alabama Press, 2004.

Forster, Arnold. *A Measure of Freedom: An Anti-Defamation League Report*. Garden City, N.Y.: Doubleday, 1950.

———. *Square One: A Memoir*. New York: Donald I. Fine, Inc., 1988.

Forster, Arnold, and Benjamin R. Epstein. *Danger on the Right: The Attitudes, Personnel and Influence of the Radical Right and Extreme Conservatives*. New York: Random House, 1964.

———. *The New Anti-Semitism*. New York: McGraw-Hill, 1974.

Fredrickson, Kari. *The Dixiecrat Revolt and the End of the Solid South, 1932–1968*. Chapel Hill and London: University of North Carolina Press, 2001.

Friedman, Murray. "Virginia Jewry in the School Crisis." *Commentary* 27 (1959): 17–22.

Friendly, Fred W. *The Good Guys, The Bad Guys and the First Amendment: Free Speech vs. Fairness in Broadcasting*. New York: Random House, 1976.

Garrow, David J. *Bearing the Cross: Martin Luther King, Jr. and the Southern Christian Leadership Conference*. New York: W. Morrow, 1986.

———. "Foreshadowing the Future: 1957 and the United States Black Freedom Struggle." *Arkansas Law Review* 62 (2009): 1–28.

Gates, Henry Louis, Jr., Anthony P. Griffin, Donald E. Lively, Robert C. Post,

William B. Rubenstein, and Nadine Strossen. *Speaking of Race, Speaking of Sex: Hate Speech, Civil Rights, and Civil Liberties*. New York and London: New York University Press, 1994.

George, John, and Laird Wilcox. *American Extremists: Militias, Supremacists, Klansmen, Communists, & Others*. Amherst, N.Y.: Prometheus, 1996.

Gerringer, Arthur E. *Terrorism: From One Millennium To The Next*. Lincoln, Neb.: Writers Club Press, 2002.

Godfrey, Phoebe. "Bayonets, Brainwashing, and Bathrooms: The Discourse of Gender, Race and Sexuality in the Desegregation of Little Rock's Central High." *Arkansas Historical Quarterly* 62 (2003): 42–67.

Goldfield, David R. *Still Fighting the Civil War: The American South and Southern History*. Baton Rouge: Louisiana State University Press, 2002.

Goldman, Peter. *The Death and Life of Malcolm X*. 2nd ed. Urbana: University of Illinois Press, 1979.

Good, Paul. *The Trouble I've Seen: White Journalist/Black Movement*. Washington, D.C.: Howard University Press, 1975.

Gould, Stephen Jay. *The Mismeasure of Man*. New York: W. W. Norton, 1981.

Govan, Gilbert E., and James W. Livingood. *The Chattanooga Country, 1540–1976: From Tomahawks to TVA*. Rev. ed. Knoxville: University of Tennessee Press, 1977.

Grafton, Carl, and Anne Permaloff. *Big Mules & Branchheads: James E. Folsom and Political Power in Alabama*. Athens: University of Georgia Press, 1985.

Graham, Hugh Davis. *Crisis in Print: Desegregation and the Press in Tennessee*. Nashville: Vanderbilt University Press, 1967.

———. "Desegregation in Nashville: The Dynamics of Compliance." *Tennessee Historical Quarterly* 25 (1966): 135–54.

Grant, Donald L. *The Way it Was in the South: The Black Experience in Georgia*. Athens: University of Georgia Press, 1993.

Graves, Harold N., Jr. "Propaganda by Short Wave: Berlin Calling America." *Public Opinion Quarterly* 4 (1940): 601–19.

Greenberg, Kenneth S. *Honor & Slavery*. Princeton: Princeton University Press, 1996.

Greene, Lee Seifert. *Lead Me On: Frank Goad Clement and Tennessee Politics*. Knoxville: University of Tennessee Press, 1982.

Greene, Melissa Fay. *The Temple Bombing*. Reading, Mass.: Addison-Wesley, 1996.

Griffin, Roscoe. *Sturgis, Kentucky: A Tentative Description and Analysis of the School Desegregation Crisis*. New York: Anti-Defamation League of B'nai B'rith, 1956.

Grill, Johnpeter Horst, and Robert L. Jenkins. "The Nazis and the American South in the 1930s: A Mirror Image?" *Journal of Southern History* 58 (1992): 667–94.

"Group Libel Laws: Abortive Efforts to Combat Hate Propaganda." *Yale Law Journal* 61 (1952): 252–63.

Grumke, Thomas. "Relations Between Right-Wing Extremists in Germany and the United States, 1945–1990." In *The United States and Germany in the Era of the Cold War, 1968–1990, A Handbook, Volume 2,* ed. Detlef Junker, 495–501. Cambridge: Cambridge University Press, 2004.

Halberstam, David. *The Children.* New York: Random House, 1998.

———. "The Town That Became 'Everybody's Test Tube.'" *The Reporter* (January 10, 1957): 32–36.

———. "The White Citizens Councils." *Commentary* 22 (October 1956): 293–302.

Hamilton, Virginia Van der Veer. *Lister Hill: Statesman from the South.* Chapel Hill and London: University of North Carolina Press, 1987.

Hamlin, David. *The Nazi/Skokie Conflict: A Civil Liberties Battle.* Boston: Beacon Press, 1980.

Handlin, Oscar. "Civil Rights After Little Rock: The Failure of Moderation." *Commentary* 24 (November 1957): 392–96.

Hardisty, Jean V. *Mobilizing Resentment: Conservative Resurgence from the John Birch Society to the Promise Keepers.* Boston: Beacon Press, 1999.

Harris, W. Edward. *Miracle in Birmingham: A Civil Rights Memoir, 1954–1965.* Indianapolis, Ind.: Stonework Press, 2004.

Harris, William J., ed. *The Leroi Jones/Amiri Baraka Reader.* New York: Thunder's Mouth Press, 1991.

Harvey, Paul. *Freedom's Coming: Religious Culture and the Shaping of the South from the Civil War through the Civil Rights Era.* Chapel Hill and London: University of North Carolina Press, 2005.

Hendershot, Heather. "God's Angriest Man: Carl McIntire, Cold War Fundamentalism, and Right-wing Broadcasting." *American Quarterly* 59 (2007): 373–96.

Henderson, Archie. "Pound, Sweden and the Nobel Prize: An Introduction." In *Ezra Pound and Europe,* ed. Richard Taylor and Claus Melchior, 155–64. Amsterdam: Rodopi, 1993.

Heymann, David C. *Ezra Pound: The Last Rower.* New York: Viking, 1976.

Hickman, Miranda B. *The Geometry of Modernism: The Vorticist Idiom in Lewis, Pound, H.D, and Yeats.* Austin: University of Texas Press, 2005.

Hill, Lance. *The Deacons for Defense: Armed Resistance and the Civil Rights Movement.* Chapel Hill and London: University of North Carolina Press, 2004.

Hoffman, Bruce. "Why is Terrorism So Difficult to Define?" In *The Terrorism Reader,* 2nd ed., ed. David J. Whittaker, 5–10. London and New York: Routledge, 2001.

Hofstadter, Richard. *Anti-Intellectualism in American Life.* New York: Knopf, 1963.

———. *The Paranoid Style in American Politics and Other Essays.* Cambridge, Mass.: Harvard University Press, 1964.

Holden, Anna. *A First Step Towards School Integration.* New York: Congress of Racial Equality, 1958.

Holden, Anna, Bonita Valien, and Preston Valien. *Clinton, Tennessee: A Tentative Description and Analysis of the School Desegregation Crisis.* New York: Anti-Defamation League of B'nai B'rith, 1957.

Hollis, Daniel Webster, III. *An Alabama Newspaper Tradition: Grover C. Hall and the Hall Family.* University: University of Alabama Press, 1983.

Honigoberg, Peter Jan. *Crossing Border Street: A Civil Rights Memoir.* Berkeley: University of California Press, 2002.

Hope, John, II. "Trends in Patterns of Race Relations in the South Since May 17, 1954." *Phylon* 17 (1956): 103–18.

Horne, Gerald. *Class Struggle in Hollywood: Moguls, Mobsters, Stars, Reds, and Trade Unionists.* Austin: University of Texas Press, 2001.

Jacoway, Elizabeth. *Turn Away Thy Son: Little Rock, The Crisis That Shocked the Nation.* New York: The Free Press, 2007.

Janowitz, Morris. *The Professional Soldier: A Social and Political Portrait.* New York: The Free Press, 1960.

Javits, Jacob K. *Discrimination—U.S.A.* New York: Harcourt, Brace, 1960.

Jeansonne, Glen. *Women of the Far Right: The Mothers' Movement and World War II.* Chicago and London: University of Chicago Press, 1996.

Jinks, Larry. "A Testing of Ideals." In *Journalists in Action*, ed. Dean Edward W. Barrett, 84–89. Manhasset, N.Y.: Channel Press, 1963.

Jonas, Gilbert. *Freedom's Sword: The NAACP and the Struggle Against Racism in America, 1909–1969.* New York: Routledge, 2005.

Jones, James H. *Bad Blood: The Tuskegee Syphilis Experiment.* Expanded ed. New York: The Free Press, 1993.

Jones, Lewis W. "Desegregation of Public Education in Alabama." *Journal of Negro Education* 24 (1955): 165–71.

Junker, Detlef, ed. *The United States and Germany in the Era of the Cold War, 1968–1990, A Handbook, Volume 2.* Cambridge: Cambridge University Press, 2004.

Kallal, Edward M., Jr. "St. Augustine and the Ku Klux Klan: 1963 and 1964." In *Martin Luther King, Jr. and the Civil Rights Movement*, ed. David J. Garrow, 93–176. Brooklyn, N.Y.: Carlson Publishing Inc., 1989.

Kasper, John, ed. *Gists from Agassiz, or Passages on the Intelligence Working in* Nature. Washington, D.C.: Square Dollar Series, 1953.

Kazin, Michael. "The Grass-Roots Right: New Histories of U.S. Conservatism in the Twentieth Century." *American Historical Review* 97 (February 1992): 136–55.

———. *The Populist Persuasion: An American History.* Ithaca, N.Y.: Cornell University Press, 1998.

Kee, Ed. "The *Brown* Decision and Milford, Delaware, 1954–1965." *Delaware History* 27 (1997): 205–43.

Kelley, Robin D. G. "'We Are Not What We Seem': Rethinking Black Working-Class Opposition in the Jim Crow South." *Journal of American History* 80 (1993): 75–112.

Kempton, Murray. *America Comes of Middle Age: Columns 1950–1962.* Boston and Toronto: Little, Brown and Company, 1963.

Kennedy, Stetson. *Jim Crow Guide to the U.S.A.: The Laws, Customs and Etiquette Governing the Conduct of Nonwhites and Other Minorities as Second-Class Citizens.* Reprint, Westport, Conn.: Greenwood Press, 1973.

———. *The Klan Unmasked.* Boca Raton: Florida Atlantic University Press, 1990.

Killian, Lewis M. "The Purge of an Agitator." *Social Problems* 7 (Autumn 1959): 152–56.

Kittrie, Nicholas N. *Rebels with a Cause: The Minds and Morality of Political Offenders.* Boulder, Colo.: Westview Press, 2000.

Knebel, Fletcher, and Charles W. Bailey, II. "Military Control: Can It Happen Here?" *Look,* September 11, 1962, 17–21.

Kolkey, Jonathan Martin. *The New Right, 1960–1968.* Washington, D.C.: University Press of America, 1983.

Korey, William, and Charlotte Lubin. "Arlington—Another Little Rock?" *Commentary* (September 1958): 201–9.

Kotlowski, Dean J. *Nixon's Civil Rights: Politics, Principle, and Policy.* Cambridge, Mass., and London: Harvard University Press, 2001.

Krattenmaker, Thomas G., and Lucas A. Powe, Jr. *Regulating Broadcast Programming.* Cambridge, Mass.: MIT Press, 1994.

Kruse, Kevin M. *White Flight: Atlanta and the Making of Modern Conservatism.* Princeton and Oxford: Princeton University Press, 2005.

Kutler, Stanley I. *The American Inquisition: Justice and Injustice in the Cold War.* New York: Hill and Wang, 1982.

Kuzenski, John C., Charles S. Bullock, III, and Ronald Keith Gaddie, eds. *David Duke and the Politics of Race in the South.* Nashville and London: Vanderbilt University Press, 1995.

La Bree, Clifton. *The Gentle Warrior: General Oliver Prince Smith, USMC.* Kent, Ohio, and London: Kent State University Press, 2001.

Lassiter, Matthew D. *The Silent Majority: Suburban Politics in the Sunbelt South.* Princeton: Princeton University Press, 2005.

———, and Andrew B. Lewis, eds. *The Moderates' Dilemma: Massive Resistance to School Desegregation in Virginia.* Charlottesville and London: University Press of Virginia, 1998.

Leonard, David J. "'The Little Fuehrer Invades Los Angeles': The Emergence of a Black-Jewish Coalition After World War II." *American Jewish History* 92 (2004): 81–102.

Lesher, Stephan. *George Wallace: American Populist.* Reading, Mass.: Addison-Wesley, 1993.

Levine, Bertram J. *Resolving Racial Conflict: The Community Relations Service and Civil Rights, 1964–1989.* Columbia: University of Missouri Press, 2005.

Levitas, Daniel. *The Terrorist Next Door: The Militia Movement and the Radical Right.* New York: Thomas Dunne Books, 2002.

Lewis, Anthony. *Make No Law: The Sullivan Case and the First Amendment.* New York: Random House, 1991.

————, et al. *The Second American Revolution: A First-Hand Account of the Struggle for Civil Rights*. London: Faber & Faber, 1966.

Lewis, George. *Massive Resistance: The White Response to the Civil Rights Movement*. London: Hodder Arnold, 2006.

————. *The White South and the Red Menace: Segregationists, Anticommunism, and Massive Resistance, 1945–1965*. Gainesville: University Press of Florida, 2004.

Lewis, John, with Michael D'Orso. *Walking with the Wind: A Memoir of the Movement*. New York: Simon & Schuster, 1998.

Lewis, Sinclair. *It Can't Happen Here; A Novel*. Garden City, N.Y.: Doubleday, Doran & Company, 1935.

Lief, Harold I., and Ian P. Stevenson. "Psychological Aspects of Prejudice with Special Reference to Desegregation." *American Journal of Psychiatry* 114 (1958): 816–23.

Lipset, Seymour Martin, and Earl Raab. *The Politics of Unreason: Right Wing Extremism in America, 1790–1970*. New York: Harper & Row, 1970.

Lipsitz, George. *A Life in the Struggle: Ivory Perry and the Culture of Opposition*. Philadelphia: Temple University Press, 1988.

Looney, Ginney. "The Politics Behind Georgia's Fair Employment Practices Law." *Southern Changes* 1 (1978): 21–23.

Lora, Ronald, and William Henry Langton, eds. *The Conservative Press in Twentieth-Century America*. Westport, Conn.: Greenwood Press, 1999.

Lovett, Bobby L. *The Civil Rights Movement in Tennessee: A Narrative History*. Knoxville: University of Tennessee Press, 2005.

McClelland, Janice M. "A Structural Analysis of Desegregation: Clinton High School, 1954–1958." *Tennessee Historical Quarterly* 56 (Winter 1997): 294–309.

McGill, Ralph. *A Church, A School*. New York and Nashville: Abingdon Press, 1959.

————. *The South and the Southerner*. Athens and London: University of Georgia Press, 1992.

McGinley, Conde J. *The Coming Red Dictatorship*. Union, N.J.: Christian Educational Association, 1953.

McGirr, Lisa. *Suburban Warriors: The Origins of the New American Right*. Princeton and Oxford: Princeton University Press, 2001.

McMillan, George. "New Bombing Terrorists of the South Call Themselves NACIREMA." *Life*, October 11, 1963, 39–40.

McMillen, Neil R. *The Citizens' Council: Organized Resistance to the Second Reconstruction, 1954–64*. Urbana: University of Illinois Press, 1971.

McNeil, Donald Raymond. *The Fight for Fluoridation*. New York: Oxford University Press, 1957.

McWhorter, Diane. *Carry Me Home: Birmingham, Alabama, the Climactic Battle of the Civil Rights Revolution*. New York: Simon & Schuster, 2001.

Macklin, Graham. *Very Deeply Dyed in Black: Sir Oswald Mosley and the Resurrection of British Fascism after 1945.* London and New York: I. B. Tauris, 2007.

Manis, Andrew M. *A Fire You Can't Put Out: The Civil Rights Life of Birmingham's Reverend Fred Shuttlesworth.* Tuscaloosa and London: University of Alabama Press, 1999.

Martin, John Bartlow. *The Deep South Says Never.* New York: Ballantine Books, 1957.

Martin, William C. *With God On Our Side: The Rise of the Religious Right in America.* New York: Broadway Books, 1996.

Maslow, Will. "Prejudice, Discrimination, and the Law." *Annals of the American Academy of Political and Social Science* 275 (May 1951): 9–17.

Massengill, Reed. *Portrait of a Racist: The Man Who Killed Medgar Evers?* New York: St. Martin's Press, 1994.

Meacham, Harry M. *The Caged Panther: Ezra Pound at Saint Elizabeths.* New York: Twayne, 1967.

Michael, George. *Willis Carto and the Far Right.* Gainesville: University Press of Florida, 2008.

Mitchell, Clarence. "Foes of Integration in Baltimore and Washington." *The Crisis* (November 1954): 533–41.

Mohl, Raymond A. "Race and Space in the Modern City: Interstate-95 and the Black Community in Miami." In *Urban Policy in Twentieth-Century America,* ed. Arnold Richard Hirsch and Raymond A. Mohl, 100–158. New Brunswick, N.J.: Rutgers University Press, 1993.

Morris, Aldon D. *The Origins of the Civil Rights Movement: Black Communities Organizing for Change.* New York and London: The Free Press/Collier Macmillan, 1984.

Muhammad, Elijah. *Message To The Blackman in America.* Chicago: Muhammad Mosque of Islam No. 2, 1965.

Mullins, Eustace. *This Difficult Individual, Ezra Pound.* New York: Fleet, 1961.

Mulloy, Darren. "Conversing with the Dead: The Militia Movement and American History." *Journal of American Studies* 38 (2004): 439–56.

Muse, Benjamin. *Ten Years of Prelude: The Story of Integration Since the Supreme Court's 1954 Decision.* New York: Viking Press, 1964.

Myrdal, Gunnar. *An American Dilemma: The Negro Problem and Modern Democracy.* New Brunswick, N.J.: Transaction Publishers, 1996.

Natambu, Kofi. *The Life and Work of Malcolm X.* Indianapolis: Alpha, 2002.

National Jewish Community Relations Council. *Combating Anti-Semitism Today: A Reassessment Conference Report.* New York: NCRAC, 1968.

Nelson, Bruce. *Divided We Stand: American Workers and the Struggle for Black Equality.* Princeton: Princeton University Press, 2001.

Newman, Edwin S. *The Hate Reader.* Dobbs Ferry, N.Y.: Oceana Publications, 1964.

Newton, Michael. *The FBI and the KKK: A Critical History*. Jefferson, N.C., and London: McFarland, 2005.

———. *The Invisible Empire: The Ku Klux Klan in Florida*. Gainesville: University Press of Florida, 2001.

Nichols, David A. *A Matter of Justice: Eisenhower and the Beginning of the Civil Rights Revolution*. New York: Simon & Schuster, 2007.

Nikitin, Vyacheslav. *The Ultras in the USA*. Moscow: Progress Publishers, 1981.

Noble, Phil. *Beyond the Burning Bus: The Civil Rights Revolution in a Southern Town*. Montgomery, Ala.: NewSouth Books, 2003.

Norman, Charles. *Ezra Pound: A Biography*. London: Macdonald, 1969.

Norrell, Robert J. "Caste in Steel: Jim Crow Careers in Birmingham, Alabama." *Journal of American History* 73 (1986): 669–94.

———. *Reaping the Whirlwind: The Civil Rights Movement in Tuskegee*. New York: Alfred A. Knopf, 1985.

Norris, Hoke, "Red Roses and Redstones." In *We Dissent*, ed. Hoke Norris, 169–201. New York: St. Martin's Press, 1962.

Novick, Peter. *The Holocaust and Collective Memory: The American Experience*. London: Bloomsbury, 2000.

O'Reilly, Kenneth. "The FBI and the Civil Rights Movement During the Kennedy Years—From the Freedom Rides to Albany." *Journal of Southern History* 54 (1988): 201–32.

Orlik, Peter B. *Electronic Media Criticism: Applied Perspectives*. 2nd ed. Mahwah, N.J.: Lawrence Erlbaum Associates, 2001.

Overstreet, Harry, and Bonaro. *The FBI in Our Open Society*. New York: Norton, 1969.

———. *The Strange Tactics of Extremism*. New York: Norton, 1964.

Pach, Chester J., and Elmo Richardson. *The Presidency of Dwight D. Eisenhower*. Rev. ed. Lawrence: University Press of Kansas, 1991.

Parmet, Herbert S. *Eisenhower & the American Crusades*. New Brunswick, N.J.: Transaction Publishers, 1999.

Perlmutter, Nathan. "Bombing in Miami: Anti-Semitism and the Segregationists." *Commentary* 25 (June 1958): 498–503.

Peters, William. *The Southern Temper*. Garden City, N.Y.: Doubleday & Company, Inc., 1959.

Pipes, Daniel. *Conspiracy: How the Paranoid Style Flourishes and Where It Comes From*. New York: The Free Press, 1997.

Polk, R. L. *R. L. Polk & Co.'s Florida State Gazetteer and Business Directory*. Jacksonville, Fla.: R. L. Polk and Company, 1918.

Posner, Gerald. *Killing the Dream: James Earl Ray and the Assassination of Martin Luther King, Jr*. New York: Little, Brown and Company, 1998.

Pound, Ezra. *The Cantos*. London: Faber and Faber, 1975.

Powell, Gloria J. *Black Monday's Children: A Study of the Effects of School Desegrega-*

tion on Self-Concepts of Southern Children. New York: Appleton-Century-Crofts, 1973.

Raffel, Jeffrey A., ed. *Historical Dictionary of School Segregation and Desegregation: The American Experience.* Westport, Conn., and London: Greenwood Press, 1998.

Raines, Howell, ed. *My Soul is Rested: The Story of the Civil Rights Movement in the Deep South.* New York: Penguin, 1983.

Raymond, Jack. *Power at the Pentagon.* New York, Evanston, and London: Harper & Row, 1964.

Redd, George N. "Educational Desegregation in Tennessee—One Year Afterward." *Journal of Negro Education* 24 (Summer 1955): 333–47.

———. "The Status of Educational Desegregation in Tennessee." *Journal of Negro Education* 25 (Summer 1956): 324–33.

Redekop, John Harold. *The American Far Right: A Case Study of Billy James Hargis and Christian Crusade.* Grand Rapids, Mich.: William B. Eerdmans, 1968.

Reed, Roy. *Faubus: The Life and Times of an American Prodigal.* Fayetteville: University of Arkansas Press, 1997.

Richardson, Darcy G. *A Nation Divided: The 1968 Presidential Campaign.* Lincoln, Neb.: Writers Club Press, 2001.

Robins, Robert S., and Jerrold M. Post. *Political Paranoia: The Psychopolitics of Hatred.* New Haven and London: Yale University Press, 1997.

Roche, Jeff. "Asa/Forrest Carter and Regional/Political Identity." In *The Southern Albatross: Race and Ethnicity in the American South,* ed. Randal L. Hall and Philip D. Dillard, 235–74. Macon, Ga.: Mercer University Press, 1999.

Rockwell, George Lincoln. *This Time The World.* 2nd ed. New York: Parliament House, 1963.

Rorty, James. "Desegregation Along the Mason-Dixon Line: Some Border Incidents and Their Lessons." *Commentary* 18 (December 1954): 493–503.

———. "Hate Monger With Literary Trimmings: From Avant-Garde Poetry to Rear-Guard Politics." *Commentary* 22 (December 1956): 533–42.

Rose, Douglas, ed. *The Emergence of David Duke and the Politics of Race.* Chapel Hill and London: University of North Carolina Press, 1992.

Roth, Philip. *The Plot Against America.* Boston: Houghton Mifflin, 2004.

Roy, Ralph Lord. *Apostles of Discord: A Study of Organized Bigotry and Disruption on the Fringes of Protestantism.* Boston: Beacon Press, 1953.

Sanctuary, Eugene Nelson. *Are These Things So? Being a Reply to This Question Propounded by a Jewish High Priest of the First Christian Martyr 1900 Years Ago. A Study in Modern Termites of the Homo Sapiens Type. Compiled by the WAAJA, World Alliance Against Jewish Aggressiveness.* Woodhaven, N.Y.: Community Press, 1934.

———. *Is the New Deal Communist?* New York: n.p., 1935.

Sanua, Marianne R. *Let Us Prove Strong: The American Jewish Committee, 1945–2006.* Lebanon, N.H.: University Press of New England, 2007.

Sarna, Jonathan. "The 'Mythical Jew' and the 'Jew Next Door' in Nineteenth Century America." In *Antisemitism in American History*, ed. David Gerber, 57–78. Urbana: University of Illinois Press, 1986.

Sarratt, Reed. *The Ordeal of Desegregation: The First Decade*. New York and London: Harper & Row, 1966.

Scates, Shelby. *War & Politics By Other Means: A Journalist's Memoir*. Seattle: University of Washington Press, 2000.

Schmaltz, William H. *Hate: George Lincoln Rockwell & the American Nazi Party*. Washington and London: Brassey's, 1999.

Schoenwald, Jonathan M. *A Time for Choosing: The Rise of Modern American Conservatism*. New York: Oxford University Press, 2001.

Schultz, Bud, and Ruth Schultz. *The Price of Dissent: Testimonies to Political Repression in America*. Berkeley and Los Angeles: University of California Press, 2001.

Schuparra, Kurt. *Triumph of the Right: The Rise of the California Conservative Movement, 1945–1966*. Armonk, N.Y., and London: M. E. Sharpe, 1998.

Scott, Peter Dale. "Anger in Paradise: The Poetic Voicing of Disorder in Pound's Later Cantos." *Paideuma* 19 (1990): 47–63.

Sergeant, Lyman Tower, ed. *Extremism in America*. New York: New York University Press, 1995.

Shagaloff, June. "Desegregation of Public Schools in Delaware." *Journal of Negro Education* 24 (Summer 1955): 188–204.

Sherrill, Robert. *Gothic Politics in the Deep South: Stars of the New Confederacy*. New York: Grossman, 1968.

Shoemaker, Dan, ed. *All Deliberate Speed: Segregation-Desegregation in Southern Schools*. New York: Harper & Brothers, 1957.

Shofner, Jerrell H. *Jackson County, Florida: A History*. Marianna, Fla.: Jackson County Heritage Association, 1985.

Sikora, Frank. *Until Justice Rolls Down: The Birmingham Church Bombing Case*. Tuscaloosa: University of Alabama Press, 1991.

Simonelli, Frederick J. *American Fuehrer: George Lincoln Rockwell and the American Nazi Party*. Urbana: University of Illinois Press, 1999.

Sims, Patsy. *The Klan*. New York: Stein and Day, 1978.

Skop, Emily. "Race and Place in the Adaptation of Mariel Exiles." *International Migration Review* 35 (2001): 449–71.

Sokol, Jason. *There Goes My Everything: White Southerners in the Age of Civil Rights, 1945–1975*. New York: Alfred A. Knopf, 2006.

Spinney, Rob. "The Jewish Community in Nashville, 1939–1949." *Tennessee Historical Quarterly* 52 (1993): 225–41.

Sprayberry, Gary S. "Interrupted Melody: The 1956 Attack on Nat 'King' Cole." *Alabama Heritage* 71 (Winter 2004): 16–24.

Stanton, Mary. *Journey toward Justice: Juliette Hampton Morgan and the Montgomery Bus Boycott*. Athens: University of Georgia Press, 2006.

Starr, J. Barton. "Birmingham and the 'Dixiecrat' Convention." *Alabama Historical Quarterly* 32 (1970): 23–50.

Steamer, Robert J. "Presidential Stimulus and School Desegregation." *Phylon* 24 (1963): 20–33.

Stock, Noel. *The Life of Ezra Pound.* New York: Pantheon Books, 1970.

Stoner, J. B. *The Gospel of Jesus Christ Versus The Jews: Christianity's Attitude Toward the Jews as Explained from the Holy Bible.* Chattanooga, Tenn.: Stoner Anti-Jewish Party, 1946.

Strum, Philippa. *When the Nazis Came to Skokie: Freedom for Speech We Hate.* Lawrence: University Press of Kansas, 1999.

Sullivan, Patricia, ed. *Freedom Writer: Virginia Foster Durr, Letters from the Civil Rights Years.* New York and London: Routledge, 2003.

Surette, Leon. *Pound in Purgatory: From Economic Radicalism to Anti-Semitism.* Urbana and Chicago: University of Illinois Press, 1999.

Swain, Carol M. *The New White Nationalism in America: Its Challenge to Integration.* Cambridge: Cambridge University Press, 2002.

Swomley, John M., Jr. *The Military Establishment.* Boston: Beacon Press, 1964.

Talmadge, Herman E. *You and Segregation.* Birmingham, Ala.: Vulcan Press, 1955.

Terrell, Carroll F. *A Companion to the Cantos of Ezra Pound.* Berkeley: University of California Press, 1984.

Thayer, George. *The Farther Shores of Politics: The American Political Fringe Today* London: Allen Lane, 1968.

Thornton J. Mills, III. *Dividing Lines: Municipal Politics and the Struggle for Civil Rights in Montgomery, Birmingham, and Selma.* Tuscaloosa and London: University of Alabama Press, 2002.

Thurlow, Richard. *Fascism in Britain: From Oswald Mosley's Blackshirts to the National Front.* London and New York: I. B. Tauris, 1998.

Toby, Jackson. "Bombing in Nashville: A Jewish Center and the Desegregation Struggle." *Commentary* 25 (May 1958): 385–89.

Torrey, E. Fuller. *The Roots of Treason: Ezra Pound and the Secret of St. Elizabeths.* New York: McGraw-Hill, 1984.

Toy, Eckard V., Jr. "Right-Wing Extremism from the Ku Klux Klan to the Order, 1915 to 1988." In *Violence in America*, vol. 2, *Protest, Rebellion, Reform*, ed. Ted Robert Gurr, 131–52. Newbury Park, Calif.: Sage Publications, 1989.

Tryphonopoulos, Demetres P., and Leon Surette. *"I Cease Not to Yowl": Ezra Pound's Letters to Olivia Rossetti Agresti.* Urbana and Chicago: University of Illinois Press, 1998.

Turner, William W. *Power on the Right.* Berkeley, Calif.: Ramparts Press, 1971.

Tytell, John. *Ezra Pound: The Solitary Volcano.* London: Bloomsbury, 1987.

Van Til, William. *My Way of Looking At It: An Autobiography.* Terre Haute, Ind.: Lake Lure Press, 1983.

Wakefield, Dan. *Revolt in the South.* New York: Grove Press, 1960.

Waldrep, Christopher. *Racial Violence on Trial: A Handbook with Cases, Laws, and Documents*. Santa Barbara, Calif.: ABC-Clio, 2001.

Walker, Brooks R. *The Christian Fright Peddlers: The Radical Right and the Churches*. Garden City, N.Y.: Doubleday, 1964.

Walker, Edwin A. *Censorship and Survival*. New York: The Bookmailer, Inc., 1961.

———. *Walker Speaks . . . Unmuzzled!* Dallas: American Eagle Publishing Company, 1962.

Walker, Samuel. *Hate Speech: The History of an American Controversy*. Lincoln and London: University of Nebraska Press, 1994.

———. *In Defense of American Liberties: A History of the ACLU*. New York and Oxford: Oxford University Press, 1990.

Ward, Brian. "Race, Politics, and Culture: The Cole Incident of 1956." In *Race and Class in the American South Since 1890*, ed. Melvyn Stokes and Rick Halpern, 181–208. Providence, R.I.: Berg, 1994.

———. *Radio and the Struggle for Civil Rights in the South*. Gainesville: University Press of Florida, 2004.

Watters, Pat. *Down to Now: Reflections on the Southern Civil Rights Movement*. New York: Pantheon Books, 1971.

Webb, Samuel. "A Southern Liberal Fights for Survival: Senator Lister Hill and the World War II Conservative Backlash." Paper presented at American History Seminar, Clare College, Cambridge, February 20, 2006.

Weisberg, Harold. *Frame-Up: The Martin Luther King/James Earl Ray Case*. New York: Outerbridge & Dienstfrey, 1971.

Wendt, Simon. *The Spirit and the Shotgun: Armed Resistance and the Struggle for Civil Rights*. Gainesville: University Press of Florida, 2007.

Wiesenburger, Steven. "The Columbians, Inc.: A Chapter of Racial Hatred from the Post-World War II South." *Journal of Southern History* 69 (2003): 821–60.

Wilhelm, James J. *Ezra Pound: The Tragic Years, 1925–1972*. University Park: Pennsylvania State University Press, 1994.

Wilhoit, Francis M. *The Politics of Massive Resistance*. New York: G. Braziller, 1973.

Wilson, Joseph, and Edward Harris. "Hucksters of Hate—Nazi Style." *The Progressive* (July 1964): 11–16.

Winchell, Mark Royden. *Where No Flag Flies: Donald Davidson and the Southern Resistance*. Columbia: University of Missouri Press, 2000.

Woods, Jeff. *Black Struggle, Red Scare: Segregation and Anti-Communism in the South, 1948–1968*. Baton Rouge: Louisiana State University Press, 2004.

Workman, William D., Jr. *The Case for the South*. New York: Devin-Adair Company, 1960.

Wyatt-Brown, Bertram. *Southern Honor: Ethics and Behavior in the Old South*. New York: Oxford University Press, 1982.

X, Malcolm, with Alex Haley. *The Autobiography of Malcolm X*. London: Hutchinson, 1966.

Young, Andrew. *An Easy Burden: The Civil Rights Movement and the Transformation of America*. New York: HarperCollins, 1996.

Zanden, James W. Vander. *Race Relations in Transition: The Segregation Crisis in the South*. New York: Random House, 1965.

Index

ACLU. *See* American Civil Liberties Union

Adams, Kenneth, 177

ADL. *See* Anti-Defamation League of B'nai B'rith

Agassiz, Louis, 52–53

AIDS epidemic, Stoner's view on, 208

Alabama, 103–33. *See also* Anniston, Alabama; Birmingham, Alabama; Fairfield, Alabama; Montgomery, Alabama; Selma, Alabama; University of Alabama

Alabama State College, 190

Alaska Mental Health Enabling Bill, 50–51, 112, 140

Alien and Sedition Acts of 1798, 188

Allen, Jo Ann, 48, 222n15

Allen, Wallace, 127, 240n103

Alley, Clyde, 90–91

Allied Organizations for Civil Rights, 97

Allport, Gordon, 9, 112

Almond, Edward M., 138

American Anti-Jewish Party, 157

American Association for Justice, Inc., 131, 140

American Christian Defenders, 157

American Civil Liberties Union, 63–64, 185, 191

American Council of Churches, 86

American Heritage Protective Committee, 247n40

American Jewish Committee, 94, 116, 254n42; and Crommelin, 120, 123; response to hate speech, 192–94, 197

American Jewish Congress, 192, 193–94

American Loyal Rangers, 148

American Nazi Party, 51, 129, 131, 164, 193

American Party, 198

American Revolution, white militants as heirs to, 23, 28, 161, 162. *See also* Founding Fathers, use of

Americans for the Preservation of the White Race, 148

Ancient City Hunting Club, 170–71

Anderson, Richard, 129

Anderson County School District (Tennessee), 39–71 passim

Andrews, George W., 257n11

Anglea, Sanders, 95

Anniston, Alabama, 176–77

Anti-Defamation League of B'nai B'rith, 160, 192, 193–94, 204, 253n23; and Crommelin, 104; and Stoner, 185–86, 187–88, 194–203 passim, 253n23 anti-Semitism, 94, 136, 197, 214; bombing of Jewish Community Center in Nashville, Tennessee, 93; of Bowles, 23, 29; and *Common Sense*, 25, 29; of Crommelin, 104, 106, 110–17 passim, 122–25, 132, 193; "Hidden Force," 109–10, 124, 134, 137, 139; of Kasper, 55, 58–60, 83–84, 93–94, 99–100, 193, 226n82; in Milford, Delaware, 29, 218n55; of the NSRP, 29–30, 36, 120; of Pound, 50, 52, 55, 111–12; presence of in the military, 136–37; segregationists' desire to avoid, 7; of Stoner, 155–56, 157–58, 162, 245n1, 248n57

Arkansas. *See* Central High School (Little Rock, Arkansas)

Arkansas Military District (Little Rock, Arkansas), 141

Armstrong, Dwight, 167

Armstrong, Floyd, 167

Armstrong, Louis, 25, 48

Aryan Nations, 209

Ashmore, Harry, 141, 212

Atlanta, Georgia, 38, 159, 186, 196, 197; bombing of Reform Temple in, 127, 163

Atlanta Community Coalition on Broadcasting, 186

Austin High School (Anderson County, Tennessee), 42

Badger, Tony, 118

Baltimore, Maryland, 22, 31–32, 90, 178

Bandura, Albert, 82

Baptist Presbyterian Church (Nashville, Tennessee), 86

Baraka, Amiri, 70

Barnett, Ross, 145

Bartley, Numan, 4

Barton, Nevie, 49

Bass, William A., 77, 78, 83, 91

Battle, Laurie, 109

Battles, Charles, 79

Baxley, William J., 207, 208

Beaumont, Texas, 35

Belafonte, Harry, 35

Bell, Daniel, 8

Berea, Kentucky, 179

Berkman, Scott, 9

Bethel Baptist Church (Birmingham, Alabama), 207

Bible Presbyterian Church, 85–86

Biderman, Albert, 135

Bilbo, Theodore G., 157, 162

Birdsell, Dale, 96

Birmingham, Alabama, 113, 130, 135, 148, 171; blacks boycotting an NSRP member, 180; demonstrations in, 128, 196; desegregation of schools in, 167–68; recruiting ground for militant segregationists, 129, 160, 167, 176, 213, 237n40; violence in, 128, 129, 168, 207

The Birth of a Nation (movie), 188

Bishop, Anne, 161

Black Belt South, 4, 108, 130

black churches: arson attacks on, 214; bombings of, 129, 168, 207; role of in desegregation, 25

Black Front, 159

Black Muslims, 164, 165

Blast (Pound and Lewis), 53

Blee, Kathleen, 9

Blevins, Lewis, 177, 178, 250n117

B'nai B'rith. *See* Anti-Defamation League of B'nai B'rith

Bogalusa, Louisiana, 4, 11, 173–75, 176, 213

Bogalusa Voters and Civic League, 173–74, 175

Bogan, Gerald, 107

Boggs, J. Caleb, 17, 19, 20, 31–32

Boggs, John, 179

Bond, Julian, 204

Boutwell, Albert, 128
Bowles, Bryant, Jr., 10, 69, 85,
105–6, 130, 142, 148; appeal to
lower/working classes, 16, 206;
in Baltimore, Maryland, 31–32,
90; biographical data, 21–22;
in Charlotte, North Carolina,
36; criminal and trial record of,
33–34, 35, 38, 220n80; and the
FBI, 220nn79–80; and freedom of
speech, 37; in Milford, Delaware,
2–3, 15–35 passim, 38, 57, 85, 119,
219n75; and the NAAWP, 19–20, 22,
24–38 passim; physical description
of, 22–23; segregationists hostile to,
174; use of radio, 122
boycotts: economic sanctions against
blacks, 163; Louis Armstrong
concert by whites, 48; Montgomery
bus boycott by blacks, 111; Nation of
Islam by whites, 166; NSRP member
by blacks, 180; schools by whites,
19–20, 25, 30, 33, 34, 44, 78–79, 166
Brakebill, William, 64
Brandenburg v. Ohio, 199–200
Branham, Billy, 73
Brantley, Lawrence J., 64
Brennan, William, 190
Brewster, Willie, 178
Bright, George, 127, 240n103
Brittain, David, 43, 44, 47, 59, 66
Brown, H. Rap, 190
Brownell, Herbert, 47, 67
Brown II, 21, 111
Brown v. Board of Education, 2, 202;
Alabama Senate resolution on role
of Communists in, 135; compliance
only after implementation decree,
17, 21, 32, 73; Crommelin on, 114;
first mobilizations against, 15, 38;
reactions to in Tennessee, 42–43,
221n10; response to in Delaware,
16–17

Bruce, Melvin, 163
Bryant, C. Farris, 169, 170
Buchanan, Pat, 208
Bullock, Alonzo, 64
Bullock, Earl, 57
Burke, Emory, 159
Busbee, George, 204
Bush, George H. W., 206
BVCL. *See* Bogalusa Voters and Civic
League

Cain, Bobby, 44, 49, 222n15
Caldwell School (Nashville,
Tennessee), 79, 83
Calhoun County Improvement
Association, 176–77
Campaign for the 48 States, 138
Campbell, Levzin, 138
Campbell, Will D., 92
Campsey, Tom, 92–93
Carpenter, Humphrey, 51
Carr, Emmett, 230n27
Carr, Ernest, 78
Carroll, Joseph, 178
Carter, Asa, 53, 54, 70, 78, 251n129;
in Birmingham, Alabama, 48;
in Clinton, Tennessee, 45; and
Crommelin, 113–14, 124, 128–29;
excommunicated from Citizens'
Councils, 116; and the NSRP, 132; as
speechwriter for Wallace, 128, 132;
use of lower-class whites by, 114,
117, 237n40
Carter, Clifford, 64
Carter, Jimmy, 196
Caswell, Theresa, 222n15
Central High School (Little Rock,
Arkansas), 28–29, 41, 74; use of
troops in, 90, 125, 139, 142, 212; and
Walker, 3, 141–42, 144
Chambliss, Robert, 168, 207
Chandler, Albert B., 46, 211
Chappell, David, 4, 25

Charles Carroll School (Baltimore, Maryland), 32
Charlotte, North Carolina, 36
Charlottesville, Virginia, 54
Chennault, Claire, 139
Christian Anti-Communist Crusade, 148
Christian Crusade, 10, 148
Christian Defense League, 131
Christian Identity, 162
Christ Not a Jew and Jews Not God's Chosen People (Stoner), 158
churches: attempts to encourage racial reform, 5–6, 25, 77, 84, 126; black churches, 25, 129, 168, 207, 214; Catholic Church desegregating schools in Nashville, Tennessee, 76; evangelical churches, 5–6, 26, 87; fundamentalist churches, 26, 85–86, 148, 162–63, 197; ideological defense of Jim Crow, 25; justifying segregation as divinely ordained, 6, 25, 27, 85–87, 114, 157–58, 162, 200–201, 208; theological racism, 85, 86; white churches, 25, 218n40
Citizens' Councils, 56, 62–63, 111, 119, 121, 211; Alabama Associations of Citizens' Councils, 116; Capitol Citizens' Council, 74; Citizens' Council of Kentucky, 10, 56, 73; Citizens' Councils of America, 147; condemning Crommelin, 113, 116, 132; decline in, 166–67; Elmore County Citizens' Council, 116; formation of first Councils, 6, 37; and Hill, 115, 118; Jewish membership in, 116; North Alabama Citizens' Council, 113–14; publications, 37, 53, 113; Seaboard White Citizens' Council, 3, 6, 10, 53–54, 61, 68–69, 95–96, 166; Tennessee White Citizens' Council,

62, 78, 87, 90, 231n43; and Walker, 145, 147, 148
Civil Rights Act of 1957, 40, 65, 139
Civil Rights Act of 1960, 213
Civil Rights Act of 1964, 169–70, 174, 176
Civil Rights Act of 1968, 190
civil rights movement: pushing for constitutional rights of civil rights activists, 122, 186, 188–89, 191, 194–95, 197, 202–3; seen as a communist conspiracy, 86, 122; seen as masterminded by Jews, 7, 23, 58–59, 60, 117–18, 122, 137, 156. *See also* desegregation
Clark, Herman, 212
Clark, Kenneth B., 31, 200, 218n40
Clark, Mamie, 200
Clark, M. L., 212
Clark Memorial Methodist Church (Nashville, Tennessee), 94–95
class politics, 82; class divisions over segregation, 4–5, 28; class tensions, 55–56; and the NSRP, 160; use of class resentment, 40, 55–56, 74, 82, 95, 117, 205–6, 225n77. *See also* lower/working-class whites; upper-middle class
Clay, Kentucky, 46, 211–12
Clayton, Claude, 146
Clement, Frank, 43, 45, 62, 67, 69, 89, 211
Clinton, Tennessee, 39–71 passim, 210–11, 212–13
Clinton Committee for Honest, Forthright Government, 48
Clinton High School (Anderson County, Tennessee), 43–44, 66–67, 84, 222n15; and violence, 42, 47, 67, 68, 211
Cobbs, Raymond C., 34
Coffman, John, 139
Cohn, Roy, 110

COINTELPRO. *See* Internal Security Counterintelligence Program

Cole, Nat "King," 48, 113

Coleman, James P., 62

Collins, LeRoy, 68

Columbians, Inc., 159

The Coming Red Dictatorship (McGinley), 23

Commission on Civil Rights, 169

Committee to Defend Martin Luther King and the Struggle for Freedom in the South, 189

Common Sense (magazine), 23, 29, 142

Communications Act of 1934, 122, 198, 199

Communism: segregationists' fear of, 54, 135, 137, 140, 145, 148, 157, 242n4; claim that NAACP was Communist controlled, 148–49; Jewish Communists, 7, 29, 50, 58, 60–61, 100, 103, 121, 137–40, 149, 177

Concerned Citizens, 186

Confederate Underground, 93, 127

Congressional Black Caucus, 186

Congress of Freedom, 131

Congress of Racial Equality, 81, 174, 178, 198, 232n55

Connor, Eugene "Bull," 128, 135, 171

Conquest, Margaret L., 230n27

Conrad, Earl, 187

Constitution of the United States: applied to libel cases, 190; civil rights activists pushing for their rights under, 122, 186, 188–89, 191, 194–95, 197, 202–3; protecting freedom of speech of segregationists, 122, 185, 188, 190–94, 197, 202, 204; segregation as unconstitutional, 42, 78, 114, 202; segregationists pushing for their rights under, 35, 37, 45, 61–63, 82, 125, 139–40, 147, 161–62, 177, 185–92 passim, 196, 200, 226n86

Cook, Clyde, 64

CORE. *See* Congress of Racial Equality

Corning, Hobart M., 33

Coughlin, Charles, 2

Counts, Dorothy, 36, 74

Cox v. Louisiana, 189

Crawford, John C., 64–65

Crimmons, Vincent Albert, 230n27

Crommelin, John, 137, 146–47, 181–82, 206, 236n21; in Alabama, 103–33; call for violence, 213; candidate in local elections, 119–20, 121, 240n109; candidate in national elections, 103–5, 107–10, 111, 113–14, 115–19, 121; and Carter, 113–14, 124, 128–29; and del Valle, 111, 129, 131, 138–41; and Duke, 132, 206, 214; and the FBI, 115, 127, 128, 129; and freedom of speech, 123, 125, 185; and Kasper, 111–12, 124; mental health of, 107, 121, 134–35; and military, 3, 10, 106–7, 123, 134–35, 137–38, 149; and the NSRP, 120, 127–28, 129, 131, 132; and paramilitarism, 124–26, 129; and Pound, 111–12, 140; and Walker, 141, 143–44, 147, 148

Crusade Against Corruption, 208

Cullen, James K., 32

Cuordileone, K. A., 137

Currier, Mary Nell, 64

Cutrer, Jesse, 174

Dagsboro, Delaware, 20

Dailey, Jane, 25

Dance, Jack, 48

Danes, Joseph, 26

Daniels, Billy, 25

Daughters of the American Revolution, 124

Davidson County, Tennessee, 79, 96. *See also* Nashville, Tennessee

Davis, L. O., 169, 171

Davis, Maclin P., Sr., 77
DeBerry, Dave, 21
Deep South, 5, 55, 66, 116, 178; seen as
    likely site for racial confrontations,
    5, 16, 38, 105, 213. *See also* specific
    states
Defend America Fund, 240n103
Defenders of State Sovereignty and
    Individual Liberty, 247n40
Defenders of the American
    Constitution, 139
Defenders of the Christian Faith, 2
Defensive Legion of Registered
    Americans, 131
DeFries, Johnny, 178, 250n117
de la Beckwith, Byron, 164
Delaware. *See* Dagsboro, Delaware;
    Ellendale, Delaware; Gumboro,
    Delaware; Lincoln, Delaware;
    Milford, Delaware; Millsboro,
    Delaware; Newark, Delaware; Ocean
    View, Delaware; Wilmington,
    Delaware
Delaware Court of Chancery, 16, 20
Delaware State Board of Education,
    19, 21
del Valle, Pedro, 144, 147, 236n21;
    and Crommelin, 111, 129, 131,
    138–41; and the military, 135,
    138–41, 149
Department of Racial and Cultural
    Relations (National Council of
    Churches), 92
desegregation: in Clinton, Tennessee,
    39–71; and ex-military men, 134–
    50; in Milford, Delaware, 15–38;
    in Nashville, Tennessee, 72–100
    passim; segregationist attempt at
    "strategic delay" of, 4, 6; terrorist
    responses to, 153–83. *See also* civil
    rights movement
Diamond, Sara, 9
Dickey, Minnie Ann, 222n15

Dilling, Elizabeth, 88
Doar, John, 175
Douglas, Stephen A., 162
Doyle, Andrew, 80, 98, 99
Doyle, William, 146
Duke, David, 35, 132, 206, 214
Dupes, Ned, 160
Durr, Virginia, 118, 126, 127
Dykeman, Wilma, 99

East High School (Nashville,
    Tennessee), 76
Edwards v. South Carolina, 189
Eisenhower, Dwight D., 59, 136,
    142, 213; lack of proactivity of, 67,
    68; sending troops to Little Rock,
    Arkansas, 125, 149
Ellendale, Delaware, 20
Ellington, Buford, 95
Engelhardt, Sam, 62
Engel v. Vitale, 195
Ennix, Coyness, 75
Epps, Gail Ann, 222n15
Epstein, Benjamin, 198
Erwitt, Elliott, 50
evangelical churches, support for
    segregationist resistance, 5–6, 26, 87.
    See also churches
Evans, Edward C., 18

Fairfield, Alabama, 191–92
Fair Labor Standards Act of 1938, 108
Fairness Doctrine, 197, 199
Faquin, Arthur, Jr., 181
Farmer, James, 174, 175, 176
far right, 2, 8–10; far right activism, 2,
    3, 148, 154, 206, 214; other names
    for, 10. *See also* National States'
    Rights Party
fascism, 6, 10, 49, 55; and anti-
    Semitism, 7, 136; crackdown on
    after World War II, 7; European
    fascism, 139, 153, 182, 187; fascism

Hockett, Fred, 68, 70, 166
Hodges, Luther, 73
Holden, Anna, 81, 232n55
Holmes, Oliver Wendell, 199, 200
Holocaust, 2, 7, 120, 187, 193, 198, 204, 209.
Hooks, Benjamin L., 203
Hoover, J. Edgar, 51, 127, 176
Horton, David, 50
Horton, Willie, 206
Hospital Survey and Construction Act of 1946, 115
Hosse, Douglas E., 79, 90
House Un-American Activities Committee, 180
Human Relations Council, 177
Hutton, Carolyn, 58

Ice Cube (rap artist), 209
Internal Revenue Service, 33–34
Internal Security Counterintelligence Program, 179–80
Islam, Stoner's hatred of, 164–66
It Can't Happen Here (Lewis), 1–2

Jackson, Edward, 89
Jackson, Robert H., 34
Jackson, William, 79
Jacksonville, Florida, 38, 160, 163, 171
James, Earl, 120
Janowitz, Morris, 136, 137
Jarrell, Henry A., 95
Jewish Community Center (Nashville, Tennessee), 93
Jewish defense agencies, 120, 187, 197, 204; and hate speech, 122–24, 192–94. *See also* Anti-Defamation League of B'nai B'rith
Jewish War Veterans, 192
Jews: calls for repatriation of, 157, 163; as masterminds of civil rights movement, 156; as a mongrelized race, 140; seen as controlling the

NAACP, 59, 248n57; segregationists inciting fear of Jewish Communists, 7, 29, 50, 58, 60–61, 100, 103, 121, 137–40, 149, 177; Stoner desiring to expel or exterminate, 156, 157. *See also* anti-Semitism; Holocaust
Jim Crow, 6, 135, 160; defenders' need to win northern public opinion, 4, 37, 40, 61, 63, 162; efforts to justify and defend, 7, 25, 92, 118, 127, 182, 185; legal foundations for demolished, 197, 204
John Birch Society, 10, 143
Johnson, Hinton, 165
Johnson, Jim, 118
Johnson, Lyndon B., 169, 180, 199
Jones, LeRoi, 70
Jones, Robert E., 257n11
Jones Elementary School (Nashville, Tennessee), 79

Kaltenbach, Fred, 156
Kasper, Frederick John, Jr., 3, 106, 130, 160, 171, 193, 199, 231n43; and Agassiz, 52–53; and anti-Semitism, 29, 55, 58–60, 93–94, 99–100, 117, 131, 226n82; biographical data, 49–50, 99–100; calls for violence, 57–58, 105, 122, 127, 148, 167, 213, 225n78; as a candidate for U.S. president, 98, 163; in Clinton, Tennessee, 39–71, 72, 210–11, 212–13; criminal and trial record of, 40, 44–48 passim, 52, 56, 60, 62–65, 72, 80–81, 89, 95–96, 98, 226n86; and Crommelin, 111–12, 124; efforts to neutralize, 68–71; FBI investigations of, 53, 67, 88, 97–98, 100, 230n27; and freedom of speech, 45, 64, 185, 199; in Greensboro, North Carolina, 73–75; in Louisville, Kentucky, 72–73; memberships of, 10; mental health of, 49, 51, 99; mobilizing

militants. *See* paramilitary organizations; white racial militants

military officers and far-right politics, 134–50, 156; institutionalization of racism in military, 136; reasons for ex-military officers to be involved in massive resistance, 135–37; use of top-down model, 150. *See also* Bowles, Bryant, Jr.; Crommelin, John; del Valle, Pedro; Walker, Edwin A.

Miller, William (segregationist), 35

Miller, William E. (judge), 76, 81, 93

Millsboro, Delaware, 20

miscegenation, 21, 52–53, 60, 85, 92, 162, 184

Mississippi. *See* University of Mississippi

Mississippi State Sovereignty Commission, 70

Montgomery, Alabama, 111, 123

Moore, Harry T., 30

Moore, O'Neal, 174

Morgan, Juliette Hampton, 126

Morrell, Ben, 138

Mosley, Oswald, 182

Muhammad, Elijah, 164, 165, 166

Mullins, Eustace, 223–24n48

Murrow, Edward R., 41

Muse, Benjamin, 22

Muslims, Stoner's hatred of, 164–66

Mussolini, Benito, 139

Myrdal, Gunnar, 2

NAACP. *See* National Association for the Advancement of Colored People

NAAWP. *See* National Association for the Advancement of White People

Nashville, Tennessee, 5, 74–100 passim, 213

Nashville Association of Churches, 77

Nashville Community Relations Conference, 77

Nashville Jewish Community Center, 127

Nashville Jewish Community Relations Committee, 83

Nashville Ministers Association, 77

National Association for the Advancement of Colored People, 6, 36, 113, 164; accused of violent activities, 87; efforts to limit or ban, 111, 122, 194; efforts to suppress Stoner, 185–86, 187–88, 194–203, 204, 253n23; Legal Defense and Educational Fund, 191–92; in Milford, Delaware, 20–21, 31, 32, 38; misappropriation of name of, 25; New York State Conference, 37; seen as managed by Jews, 59, 248n57; segregationist claim that NAACP was Communist controlled, 148–49; spoof of NAACP membership application, 70–71; in St. Augustine, Florida, 169; suits filed by, 16, 20–21, 42

National Association for the Advancement of White People, 3; anti-Semitism, use of, 29–30, 36; attempts to resurrect organization, 35; and Bowles, 19–20, 22, 24–38 passim; chapters and affiliates, 28, 32, 36, 38; efforts to suppress, 34, 37; and Kasper, 71, 226–27n95; in Milford, Delaware, 19–20, 28, 29–30; in South Carolina, 36; in Washington, D.C., 33

National Council of Churches, 86; Department of Racial and Cultural Relations, 92

National Economic Council, 138

National Front, 182

National Institute of Mental Health, 112

National Repatriation Committee, 163

National Security Council, 142

Pomeroy, Eugene Cowles, 139
Potito, Oren, 162–63
Pound, Ezra, 140; *Blast*, 53; and
   Crommelin, 111–12; and Kasper,
   49–53, 55, 96–97, 99, 223–24n48
Presbyterian Church of the United
   States, 85
Priest, Percy, 43
Pro-Blue program, 142, 143
Project Alert, 138
Pyne, Joe, 24

quarantine strategy for handling hate
   speech, 106, 123–24, 192–93, 194,
   197, 204

Raab, Earl, 8
Race Relations Institute conferences
   (Fisk University), 75
racial terrorism, 6, 9, 30, 93, 153–83,
   213–14. *See also* terrorism;
   violence
racism, 4, 61, 112, 196–97, 198–200;
   biological racism, 114, 153; decline
   in respectability of, 6, 7, 28, 61, 166–
   67, 175–76; institutionalization of
   racism in military, 136; rural racism,
   56, 136, 160, 201, 204, 237n40;
   Soviet Union use of as propaganda,
   15–16, 61; theological racism, 85,
   86; white working class racism, 85.
   See also military officers and far-right
   politics
radio: and Nazi propaganda, 156; use
   of by segregationists, 24, 122, 145,
   148, 185, 193–94, 197, 201; use of in
   black freedom struggle, 24. *See also*
   media
Ramsay High School (Birmingham,
   Alabama), 167
Randolph, A. Philip, 64
Ray, James Earl, 181, 251n133
Ray, Jerry, 251n133

Reagan, Ronald, 206
*Red Lion Broadcasting, Inc. v. Federal
   Communications Commission*, 199
Reed, Charles, 88–89
Reform Temple (Atlanta, Georgia),
   127, 163
repatriation: of African Americans,
   157, 163, 164, 185, 206; of Asians,
   163; of Jews, 157, 163
Rhodesia as model for segregationists,
   182
Ribuffo, Leo, 9
Richmond, Virginia, 38
Rimmer, J. G., 27
Robertson, Alex, 200
Robertson Junior High School (Oak
   Ridge, Tennessee), 42
Rockwell, George Lincoln, 51, 129,
   131, 193, 194, 240n113
Rogers, Creed, 174
Roman Catholic Church,
   desegregating elementary schools in
   Nashville, Tennessee, 76
Roosevelt, Eleanor, 71, 143
Roosevelt, Franklin D., 1, 215n1
Rorty, James, 22
Rosenberg, Julius and Ethel, 50
Roth, Philip, 215n1
Roy, Ralph Lord, 22
Rucker, Elza, 179
Rudge, Olga, 97
Russell, Richard, 65
Ryan, Richard, 181

Salisbury, Harrison, 132
Sanctuary, Eugene Nelson, 156
Sanua, Marianne, 193
Sarna, Jonathan, 84
Scarritt College, 75
Schafer, Stephen, 9
Schenck v. United States, 199, 200
Schmitz, John, 198
school prayer, 195, 202

Workman, William D., Jr., 6, 24, 37, 211

World War II: Crommelin's career during, 3, 106, 113, 125–26, 135; del Valle's career during, 138; Ezra Pound's pro-fascist broadcasts, 49; impact on anti-Semitism, 7, 185, 193, 198; impact on political extremism, 2; influence on race relations, 4, 6–7, 135, 153, 185, 188; Walker's career during, 141

Worth, Cedric, 107

Young, Andrew, 169
Young, H. Albert, 19, 29, 34

Zionist conspiracy, 59, 157

Politics and Culture in the Twentieth-Century South

A Common Thread: Labor, Politics, and Capital Mobility in the Textile Industry
by Beth English

"Everybody Was Black Down There": Race and Industrial Change in the Alabama Coalfields
by Robert H. Woodrum

Race, Reason, and Massive Resistance: The Diary of David J. Mays, 1954–1959
edited by James R. Sweeney

The Unemployed People's Movement: Leftists, Liberals, and Labor in Georgia, 1929–1941
by James J. Lorence

Liberalism, Black Power, and the Making of American Politics, 1965–1980
by Devin Fergus

Guten Tag, Y'all: Globalization and the South Carolina Piedmont, 1950–2000
by Marko Maunula

The Culture of Property: Race, Class, and Housing Landscapes in Atlanta, 1880–1950
by LeeAnn Lands

Marching in Step: Masculinity, Citizenship, and The Citadel in Post–World War II America
by Alexander Macaulay

Rabble Rousers: The American Far Right in the Civil Rights Era
by Clive Webb

CPSIA information can be obtained at www.ICGtesting.com
Printed in the USA
LVOW131935231011

251654LV00001B/4/P